Old World, New World

Jeffersonian America

JAN ELLEN LEWIS, PETER S. ONUF, AND
ANDREW O'SHAUGHNESSY, EDITORS

Old World, New World

America and Europe in the Age of Jefferson

EDITED BY LEONARD J. SADOSKY,
PETER NICOLAISEN, PETER S. ONUF, AND
ANDREW J. O'SHAUGHNESSY

University of Virginia Press

CHARLOTTESVILLE AND LONDON

University of Virginia Press
© 2010 by the Rector and Visitors of the University of Virginia
All rights reserved
Printed in the United States of America on acid-free paper

First published 2010
1 3 5 7 9 8 6 4 2

Library of Congress Cataloging-in-Publication Data
Old world, new world : America and Europe in the age of Jefferson /
edited by Leonard J. Sadosky ... [et al.].
p. cm. — (Jeffersonian America)
"This volume contains a selection of contributions from a conference
entitled 'The Old World and the New: Exchanges Between America and Europe
in the Age of Jefferson,' held at the Salzburg Seminar in Salzburg, Austria,
on October 12–16, 2005" — Pref.
Includes bibliographical references and index.
ISBN 978-0-8139-2847-0 (cloth : alk. paper) — ISBN 978-0-8139-2848-7 (pbk. :
alk. paper) — ISBN 978-0-8139-2852-4 (e-book)
1. United States—Relations—Europe—Congresses. 2. Europe—
Relations—United States—Congresses. 3. United States—Civilization—
1783–1865—Congresses. 4. Europe—Civilization—18th century—Congresses.
5. Americans—Europe—History—18th century—Congresses. 6. Jefferson,
Thomas, 1743–1826—Congresses. 7. Adams, John, 1735–1826—Congresses.
8. Bonaparte, Elizabeth Patterson, 1785–1879—Congresses. I. Sadosky, Leonard J.
D34.U5O43 2010
303.48'2730409033—dc22
2009026473

To the staffs of the Salzburg Seminar and of the Robert H. Smith
International Center for Jefferson Studies, with gratitude
for their excellent work in fostering a spirit of peaceful cooperation
and understanding between Europe and America

Contents

Contents

Preface

This volume contains a selection of contributions from a conference entitled "The Old World and the New: Exchanges Between America and Europe in the Age of Jefferson," held at the Salzburg Seminar in Salzburg, Austria, on October 12–16, 2005. The setting for this conference was very symbolic, since the Salzburg Seminar was established by an idealistic group of Harvard graduate students in the immediate aftermath of the Second World War to teach short courses on American civilization. The founders were keen to distance themselves from the political imperatives of the Cold War, but the Seminar essentially became a place of Atlantic exchange, with a particular mission to explain the United States to Europe. The Seminar was also the impetus, and for many years the host, of the European Association for American Studies. In the 1960s the focus of the Seminar changed, as it began to present courses with a broader global content, and the former emphasis on the United States had all but disappeared by 1979. Readers interested in learning more about the early years of the Salzburg Seminar are directed to a volume written by Thomas H. Eliot and Lois J. Eliot entitled *The Salzburg Seminar: The First Forty Years* (Ipswich, MA, 1987).

The theme of the conference on which this volume is based reflects the original concerns of the Seminar and the subject of a book by its former assistant director, Robert O. Mead, entitled *Atlantic Legacy: Essays in American-European Cultural History* (New York, 1969). The conference was one of a regular series of international conferences sponsored by the Robert H. Smith International Center for Jefferson Studies under the direction of Andrew Jackson O'Shaughnessy. There were twenty-one participants from Europe and the United States, including Frank Cogliano, Julie Flavell, Eliga Gould, Frank Kelleter, Charlene Lewis, James Lewis, Jeanie Grant Moore, Peter Nicolaisen, Peter Onuf, Andrew O'Shaughnessy, Sarah Pearsall, Sandra Rebok, Martha Rojas, Leonard Sadosky, Richard Ryerson, James Sofka, Lucia Stanton, Gaye Wilson, and Philipp Ziesche. John McCusker delivered the keynote speech, and Gordon Wood gave the farewell address. The sessions were held in the splendid conference facilities of the Salzburg Seminar at the Schloss Leopoldskron, which dates, appropriately, from the eighteenth century, having been built for Archbishop Leopold Firmian in 1736.

In addition to thanking all the conference attendees for their participation, the editors wish to thank the staffs of the Salzburg Seminar and the Robert H. Smith International Center for Jefferson Studies, whose efforts allowed the conference to move forward for the enrichment and enjoyment of all involved. In particular, special thanks go the Salzburg Seminar's American Studies Alumni Association Leader, Marty Gecek; to Program Director Susanna Seidl-Fox; and to Conference and Banqueting Manager Markus Hiljuk. At the Robert H. Smith International Center for Jefferson Studies, special thanks go to Assistant to the Saunders Director, Sanders Goodrich, who coordinated the October 2005 conference; and to her successor, Joan Hairfield, who coordinated a May 2006 meeting of the editors at the Jefferson Library on the International Center's campus. For the use of the library, special thanks go to Thomas Jefferson Foundation Librarian Jack Robertson and Library Services Coordinator Eric Johnson. A final note of thanks goes to the University of Virginia Press and to editor Richard Holway for taking on this project and seeing it through to production.

ANDREW J. O'SHAUGHNESSY

Abbreviations

AFC   *Adams Family Correspondence,* ed. Lyman H. Butterfield and
Marc Friedlaender. 6 vols. to date. Cambridge, MA, 1973–.

AHP   *The Papers of Alexander Hamilton,* ed. Harold C. Syrett and
Jacob E. Cooke. 27 vols. New York, 1961–87.

AJL   *The Adams-Jefferson Letters: The Complete Correspondence between
Thomas Jefferson and Abigail and John Adams,* ed. Lester J.
Cappon. Chapel Hill, NC, 1959.

Ford   *The Writings of Thomas Jefferson,* ed. Paul Leicester Ford. 10 vols.
New York, 1892–99.

JA   John Adams

JAH   *Journal of American History*

JER   *Journal of the Early Republic*

JMP   *The Papers of James Madison,* ed. Robert Rutland et al. 17 vols.
Vols. 1–10, Chicago, 1962–77; vols. 11–17, Charlottesville, VA,
1978–91.

JSH   *Journal of Southern History*

L&B   *The Writings of Thomas Jefferson,* ed. Andrew A. Lipscomb and
Albert Ellery Bergh. 20 vols. Washington, DC, 1903–4.

LC   Library of Congress, Washington, DC.

Notes   Thomas Jefferson, *Notes on the State of Virginia,* ed. William
Peden. Chapel Hill, NC, 1954.

PJA   *The Papers of John Adams,* ed. Robert J. Taylor, Gregg L. Lint,
Richard A. Ryerson, and James C. Taylor. 13 vols. to date.
Cambridge, MA, 1977–.

Smith   *The Republic of Letters: The Correspondence between Thomas
Jefferson and James Madison, 1776–1826,* ed. James Morton Smith.
3 vols. New York, 1995.

TJ   Thomas Jefferson

TJP   *The Papers of Thomas Jefferson,* ed. Julian Boyd et al. 32 vols. to date. Princeton, NJ, 1950–.

TJW   *Thomas Jefferson Writings,* ed. Merrill D. Peterson. New York, 1984.

WMQ   *William and Mary Quarterly,* 3rd ser.

Old World, New World

Introduction

PETER S. ONUF

Throughout his career Thomas Jefferson imagined an impassable boundary between Europe and America, Old World and New. To avoid the "broils of the European nations," he wrote to Elbridge Gerry in 1797, he wished "there were an ocean of fire between us and the old world."[1] As the new nation teetered on the brink of war with Britain in 1812, he again hoped to insulate it from European entanglements: "The meridian of the mid-Atlantic should be the line of demarkation between war and peace."[2]

Jefferson understood that the two "worlds" could never be separated, and his imaginary boundaries implicitly acknowledged the weakness and vulnerability of the new United States within the system of European states. Because there was no recognized place for neutrals—no safe harbor for non-belligerents—European wars inevitably threatened American independence. Victory in the Revolution demonstrated the new nation's dependence on foreign alliances. Jefferson's isolationist fantasies testify to his "realistic" assessment of America's insecurity in a war-prone world. There would be no United States without war, but war jeopardized its continuing existence.

American independence was the unintended consequence of Patriot agitation for constitutional reform *within* the British empire. On the eve of the Revolution, American provincial societies were more self-consciously British than they ever had been. Burgeoning transatlantic commercial connections promoted a cultural "Anglicization," and growing wealth enabled increasing numbers of Americans to return to the metropolis.[3] The deepening political crisis that destroyed the empire was spurred by the frustrated aspirations of provincial elites who exulted in their English rights and British identity. Patriot resistance leaders were understandably reluctant to kill their king and so dissolve "the political bands which have connected them" to their former fellow subjects in Britain.

Escaping British despotism meant embracing the European balance of power, gaining recognition and more tangible support from the "other powers of the earth," which would enable the new nation "to assume . . . the separate & equal station to which the laws of nature and of nature's God entitle them."[4] More direct trading connections with Europe would benefit Europeans as well as Americans. The free trade envisioned by Thomas Paine in *Common Sense* and by John Adams in the Model Treaty promised a more integrated, prosperous, and progressive trading world, freed from the shackles of British mercantilism. In their cosmopolitan vision the invidious distinctions that defined Old World and New would dissolve as the distance between them diminished.[5]

American revolutionaries insisted that the happy "mediocrity" of fortunes and the absence of an aristocratic ruling class provided the most durable foundation for the progress of civilization. Situated on the edge of the empire, Americans could see its defects clearly. Provincial Patriots were driven to resistance by their conviction that the rights of Englishmen remained in full force throughout the empire and rejected the prevailing metropolitan assumption that "rights" necessarily diminished on the imperial periphery. Appropriating and elaborating a republican critique of the British constitution, revolutionaries believed their "political science" would constitute a critical contribution to mankind's future happiness.

The great powers of Europe undeniably had achieved a higher level of civility than the new societies across the Atlantic, but the prevalence of corruption, luxury, and privilege—their radically imperfect constitutions—jeopardized their future progress. Jefferson and his fellow revolutionaries could thus depict the British metropolis as degenerate, recasting provincial defects as virtues and so overcoming, or at least assuaging, their sense of cultural inferiority. Perhaps, as Bishop George Berkeley had famously predicted in 1725, "the Course of Empire" would indeed move "Westward."[6]

John Adams acknowledged the new nation's continuing cultural deficit in a famous letter to his wife, Abigail: "I must study Politicks and War that my sons may have liberty to study Mathematicks and Philosophy. My sons ought to study Mathematicks and Philosophy, Geography, natural History, Naval Architecture, navigation, Commerce and Agriculture, in order to give their Children a right to study Painting, Poetry, Musick, Architecture, Statuary, Tapestry and Porcelaine."[7] Many revolutionaries had sacrificed their lives, and others their ambitions, so that subsequent generations might achieve ever-higher levels of civility. Americans would not simply recapitulate the progress of European civilization, however, for Adams's children and grandchildren would be building on a solid and durable republican foundation. As civilization reached its highest stage of development in the New World, the Revolution would be redeemed.

The essays in this volume explore the implications of the Americans' nation-making project for the Atlantic world in Jefferson's time. American independence did *not* initiate an era of isolation and "free security" as the new nation turned westward, away from Europe. To the contrary, commercial, cultural, and political connections multiplied and intensified, and independent Americans were increasingly drawn into an interdependent Atlantic system.

Independence exacerbated provincial Americans' anxieties about their place in the world. From the metropolitan perspective, overseas colonies were degenerate, uncivilized places where settlers mixed promiscuously with darker-skinned natives. The Europeans' brutal competition for New World riches and the "savage injustices" they committed against native peoples evoked images of their own barbarous ancestors in a not-so-distant past.[8] The conventional distinction between Old World and New was an invidious one, pivoting on the lawlessness and incivility of distant colonial settlements.[9] Movement across the Atlantic could thus be understood as a regressive movement, backward in time, that deprived settlers of the benefits of civil society and plunged them into barbarism.[10] Anxious to vindicate their own civility, Jefferson and his fellow Patriots offered a counter-narrative that linked movement across space with progress through history: their Revolution would inaugurate a "new order for the ages."[11]

Jefferson sought to correct metropolitan misperceptions in his famous exchange with the comte de Buffon. As Gordon Wood shows, the data Jefferson assembled in his *Notes on Virginia* on the relative size of New World animals, the natural endowments of Indians, and the incidence of "geniuses" in the American population were designed to demonstrate the new nation's potential. Though at a great disadvantage compared with European countries, "where genius is most cultivated, where are the most excellent models for art, and scaffoldings for the attainment of science," the United States, the examples of Washington, Franklin, and Rittenhouse suggested, would "produce her full quota of genius." It was equally clear to Jefferson that Britain, despite its present cultural superiority, was not producing its fair share of geniuses. "The sun of her glory is fast descending to the horizon," he concluded: "her philosophy has crossed the Channel, her freedom the Atlantic, and herself seems passing to that awful dissolution, whose issue is not given human foresight to scan." The British metropolis that had once dominated the American provincial imagination was little more than an empty shell. Instead of promoting the progress of "science or of civilization," the mother country now "wages war" against her former children with a savage "spirit."[12]

Jefferson's vindication of American nature, and of the natural genius of Americans, challenged the theory of creole degeneracy advocated by Buffon and other European natural historians and thus offered a more hopeful prospect for the New World. As long as "liberty shall have votaries," wrote Jefferson, Washington would be remembered "among the most celebrated worthies of the world, when that wretched philosophy shall be forgotten which would have arranged him among the degeneracies of nature."[13] But Jefferson nonetheless accepted the conventional distinction between the two worlds and acknowledged the Americans' civilizational deficit. His very presence in Paris reflected France's essential role both in winning the Revolutionary War and in creating a new diplomatic and commercial order that would secure America's independence and prosperity. Paris was also the great metropolis of modern civilization, the home of its leading philosophers—Voltaire, Raynal, Buffon himself—and therefore the new nation's vital ally in its progress toward higher levels of civility.

Jefferson celebrated the New World's boundless potential—his *Notes* include exhaustive inventories of Virginia's natural resources—*not* its present stage of development, notwithstanding the precocious achievements of a few geniuses. "Civilization" itself constituted a common, "universal" framework that linked New World and Old. When American revolutionaries boldly asserted that their republican experiment had initiated a new epoch in the history of "mankind," they insisted on their "equal station" in the European family of nations and claimed a leading role in the progress of its civilization.

New World and Old World were defined against each other, for better (the westward course of empire) or for worse (creole degeneracy). In declaring themselves independent, Anglo-Americans sought to transcend the political and cultural distance that separated them from the metropolis, but they could not banish the idea of the metropolis itself. They could substitute dependency on the European balance of power for the problematic protection—and perceived despotism—of British imperial rule; with Jefferson, they could turn to Paris rather than London as an alternative center of science and civilization. But the "independence" that was secured by victory in the war and recognized by the other powers did not immediately or completely transform the Americans' world. To the contrary, it only underscored Americans' weakness and vulnerability, their continuing dependence on European—and to a distressing extent British—commerce and credit, and the hollowness of their cultural pretensions.

The Revolution promised much more than it could possibly deliver: only in the narrowest political sense had provincial Patriots escaped metropolitan domination. And Jefferson's continuing anxieties about assaults on American independence—from "aristocrats" and "monocrats" within the country and their foreign counter-revolutionary allies abroad—testify to the Union's fragility. American revolutionaries could only hope to revolutionize the diplomatic world if their nation-making project succeeded. But how could they overcome powerful centrifugal tendencies that retarded national development and sustained their dependent, provincial character?

Jefferson's characteristic penchant for invoking binary oppositions—his Manichean tendency to juxtapose good and evil, republican and monarchical, New World and Old—illuminates the complex and ambiguous experience of living in a revolutionary age. He needed to draw sharp boundaries in a world where lines were constantly shifting and difficult to discern; he conflated categories, globalizing and moralizing distinctions between true friends of republican enlightenment and its inveterate foes. Who would be more conscious of the need for such boundaries than a formerly loyal British subject who recognized the need for decisive action and declared himself and his countrymen independent? July 4, 1776, the day "Americans" both recognized themselves as a people and sought the recognition of other peoples, was the pivotal moment in Jefferson's career, the temporal boundary between old and new, British and American. All of Jefferson's binary oppositions grew out of the fundamental nation-making, self-constitutive act of declaring independence. Independence defined a new people and inscribed new boundaries, simultaneously clarifying the limits of loyalty and multiplying the dangers of promiscuous border crossing. The revolutionaries' anxieties about forging the new nation's republican character reflected an underlying concern with the volatile and contingent loyalties of would-be citizens, with their own conceptions of history and geography.

It took a leap of faith to imagine that thirteen former British colonies might constitute a single new nation. Half of Britain's colonies in the Western Hemisphere—another thirteen—resisted rebel entreaties and never took the leap. To do so meant to rupture a colonial connection that had shaped their history, defined their identity, and sustained their prosperity. Beyond local and regional ties with their neighbors, the colonies had relatively little contact with one another before the imperial crisis. Historically, the strongest bond of union was common allegiance to the British crown. Common grievances against George III's "despotic" policies forced colonists to turn to one another and improvise the first trans-provincial, continental institutions.

When Anglo-Americans finally abjured their allegiance and "killed" the king, they broke their ties with London, the capital city of the empire and their great metropolis. London was the center of the world for Julie Flavell's "decadent" colonists, the place where they could fulfill their social aspirations and display their wealth and cosmopolitan sophistication. Some colonial visitors to the metropolis claimed to be appalled by its luxury, corruption, and vice, and their testimony played a crucial role in fostering the provincial myth of American virtue and moral superiority. But others, in equally characteristic provincial fashion, embraced metropolitan fashion with an exuberant, ostentatious enthusiasm that appalled respectable Londoners. In fact, for most colonists in London (or at home), the distinction between metropolitan vice and provincial virtue was hardly self-evident. In any case, Britain remained the standard, defining the best and the worst in their world. The critique of British decadence—and of provincial "decadents"—was itself generated in Britain and exported to the colonies. Contingency was as important as principled conviction in resolving questions of loyalty and identity for provincial Anglo-Americans. When revolutionaries sought to draw new national boundaries, the accident of residence was the first and most important contingency. The Atlantic world was the creation of people—and peoples—who circulated through its proliferating trade networks. The normal flow of immigrants, voluntary and coerced, was disrupted by the American Revolution, but the war entailed the transportation of troops and the military and political displacement of peoples on a massive scale.

In theory, individuals across the continent made the same decision about their own political future that Jefferson and his fellow congressmen made in Philadelphia: citizenship in the new republics was "volitional," a matter of choice.[14] But the determinants of loyalty and the specific circumstances in which Anglo-Americans made, or were forced to make, decisions about the war were complicated and ambiguous, particularly for those with strong transatlantic connections. Patriots may have pursued a provincial agenda, seeking closer engagement with the metropolis, equal rights as overseas Britons, and broader opportunity within a British-dominated Atlantic trading system, but the provincial Anglo-Americans who had benefited most from commercial and official ties in the empire were often among the revolution's foremost victims. The Loyalist families Sarah Pearsall describes were separated from their "country" and from one another; their correspondence sustained sentimental attachments across great spaces. The empire was redefined in these fractured families as they adjusted to the disruptive logic of nation-making.

The Loyalist diaspora reveals the ongoing significance of transatlantic connections that now transcended national boundaries. Just as the Revolution made Americans who remained in London "foreigners," Loyalist refugees were also alienated from their formerly provincial homes. By redefining loyalties and identities, the Revolution made a world of difference not only for these displaced people but for Anglo-Americans generally. For Patriots, the same forces that worked to disrupt Loyalist families strengthened and transformed traditional attachments to family and province—Jefferson's "country," Virginia—by expanding the limits of patriotism to the entire continent. Displaced Loyalists might see themselves, by default, as "citizens of the world," but citizens of the new nation became part of the larger world by staying in place: national identity was the threshold of a new cosmopolitanism, establishing a place for Americans in an emerging international order.

Revolutionaries articulated new definitions of citizenship and national community, making explicit and consensual previously implicit and unquestioned political identities. By linking nation-making with liberation from "foreign" imperial rule and with the constitution of republican governments, provincial Patriots saw their revolution as a model for benighted peoples throughout the world. Grounded in "natural" attachments to particular places, the new nation was inclusive and expansive, tending toward universality. The American revolutionaries' bid for recognition was itself a claim to an equal standing among nations; having established a new standard for legitimacy based on the principle of popular sovereignty, they could imagine that the nations of the Old World were *less* than equal, constitutionally defective and therefore prone to revolution.

Revolutionary republicanism promised to obliterate distinctions—all true nations were self-created equal—even as it reinforced distinctions between nations and even between revolutionary republics. Paradoxically, the diplomatic precepts and practices of the Old Regime gained a new lease on life despite, or perhaps because of, the advent of the new republican era.[15] The myths of popular sovereignty and national self-determination lent a new urgency to the first law of nature, self-preservation, for the nation now represented not merely the narrow interests of a ruling class but the more exalted interests of the people as a whole and therefore of mankind generally. Enemies proliferated in the republican imagination, for anyone who challenged or threatened the republic in any way was by definition a "foreigner."

Republican nationalists did not have to look far for enemies. Geopolitical rivalries that antedated the revolutions in America and France persisted, and national interests remained paramount, regardless of regime change. While the American Revolution was still being fought, Leonard Sadosky writes, the British statesman William Eden recognized the emerging structure of a post-Revolutionary international system that included the United States. In some ways, nothing—beyond the addition of a new nation to the European system—seemed to change. But in other crucial ways, revolutions on both sides of the Atlantic and reactions to them changed the world beyond recognition. The "Age of the Democratic Revolution" initiated a new era of revolutionary and counter-revolutionary nationalism that gave rise to a recognizably modern international order.[16]

Thomas Jefferson and John Adams were acutely conscious of their new national, post-provincial identity when they sought to promote their country's interests at foreign courts. The more cosmopolitan Jefferson may have been much more at home in Europe than the self-consciously provincial Adams. But as Peter Nicolaisen reminds us, Jefferson remained curiously detached from European affairs, convinced of the superiority of America's republican institutions and of the superior wisdom of the common people. If the Dutch would achieve genuine liberty, "a great deal of blood" would have to flow, Jefferson observed in 1786, years before he famously contemplated a more comprehensive bloodletting in France: "Were there but an Adam & an Eve left in every country, & left free, it would be better than as it is now."[17] The Americans had shed vast quantities of blood to gain their own freedom, and Europeans could expect to pay the same price. The neurotic Adams, frustrated by his inability to forge the personal connections that facilitated diplomatic success, was less bloody-minded but even more skeptical about Europe's prospects. Richard Ryerson's essay shows how this prickly and stubborn provincial cherished his alienation, finding better company in dead authors than in living contemporaries and resolutely focusing his attention on the danger of an incipient *American* aristocracy.

Adams and Jefferson both expected that the differences between Europe and America they found so striking would diminish over time. Adams worried that the new nation would become Europeanized as homegrown "aristocrats" grasped power; Jefferson predicted bloody republican revolutions in Europe on the American model. Neither fully grasped the paradoxical logic of an emerging international order that simultaneously made nations more alike while accentuating their differences. Rising to the level of independent

nationhood, Anglo-Americans transcended their provincial subordination—and imputations of degeneracy—to become more recognizably
"European." At the same time, they were drawn more directly into conflicts
between European nations and therefore became more conscious of their
own distinctive national interests. The practices of diplomacy, including the
elaborate protocols of gift giving that Martha Rojas describes, thus became
critical sites for negotiating national identity.

Jefferson and his fellow diplomats learned to conform to court etiquette
while upholding the new republic's honor and independence. The cultural
geography of Old World and New, metropolis and province, no longer
applied. Jefferson grappled with the challenges of self-presentation—and
representing his nation—during his Paris years. Gaye Wilson depicts Jefferson as a cosmopolitan provincial who understood and exploited the nuances
of the fashions in clothing still being set in London, the fashion metropolis.
Jefferson's portraits struck a careful balance between genteel elegance, showing that he was not a provincial rustic, and an appropriate casualness and
simplicity that evoked "republican" sentiments—and his limited budget.

Jefferson's performances during his tenure in Paris from 1784 to 1789
illuminate the complexities of the apparently simple opposition between
Old World and New that was so central to his worldview. The most obvious
point to make is that these two worlds were really one and that the distinction between them reflected the broader European encounter with the world
beyond—and with itself. The Anglo-Americans of Jefferson's "new" world
were simply transplanted (in his terminology, "expatriated") Europeans, the
successors of Anglo-Saxons who had founded a new nation in Britain. Jefferson thus insisted that Americans were simply enacting the latest stage in
the dynamic, westward progress of *European* civilization.

The transatlantic spread of revolutionary republicanism epitomized
the integrative processes that Europeanized America and Americanized
Europe. At first most American observers welcomed the French Revolution,
imagining that Europe would follow the American example in establishing
enlightened new regimes. No American was more enthusiastic about the
French Revolution than Jefferson. When republicanism was on the offensive
and the counter-revolutionary "conspiracy of kings" in retreat, the distinction between New World and Old seemed less and less compelling. The
neat congruence of geography and regime type collapsed: the "sister republic" of France was in the vanguard of a new order for the civilized world as
a whole, making transatlantic distinctions meaningless.

The course of the French Revolution made such an optimistic view difficult to sustain, even for Jefferson. But even when Jefferson despaired of

Europe's renovation, predicting that the Old World would be drenched in "rivers of blood" before its peoples gained their freedom, he continued to cherish personal and scientific connections with enlightened Europeans.[18] His self-proclaimed membership in the "republic of letters," as Lucia Stanton suggests in her history of Jefferson's moldboard plow, transcended the "real" world of politics and war and sustained an imagined community of enlightenment and progress: "votaries of science" constituted "one family," regardless of conflicts between nations.[19] By distinguishing science from politics, Jefferson could thus sustain the provincial fantasy of reunion with the metropolis, even in wartime.

Jefferson's faith in the ultimate success of the French Revolution, whatever the cost in blood, never wavered. After he returned to the United States in 1789, Philipp Ziesche shows, a steady stream of American ideologues and adventurers was drawn to Paris, the new revolutionary metropolis. Thomas Paine and like-minded colleagues did not disdain or dismiss national attachments as would revolutionaries of later generations. To the contrary, the self-determining, self-constituted nation was the revolutionary negation of oppressive and despotic old regimes. Paine was a proud citizen of the United States, the first new nation, and he was equally proud to become a citizen of revolutionary France; when his native Britain finally gained its independence, he would be a British citizen as well. It soon became apparent that national identities were not so fluid or interchangeable—to Paine in particular, as he languished in a Paris prison. But Paine's confusion was understandable, for nationalism in the Jeffersonian age expressed powerful cosmopolitan impulses even as it unleashed new and unprecedentedly virulent strains of particularism. The reverse image of the revolutionary cosmopolitan—the citizen of every free nation—was the counter-revolutionary "foreigner," whose attachments were weak and loyalties suspect. Paine played both roles.[20]

In the wake of revolutions, the Atlantic world looked different. The cosmopolitanism of aristocrats who circulated through the courts of Europe or of provincial Anglo-Americans who gravitated to the British metropolis gave way to a new *international* cosmopolitanism grounded in strong ties to the "imagined communities" of emergent nation-states.[21] As Paine discovered, the boundaries between nationalism and cosmopolitanism were not always well marked, and the penalties for crossing them could be severe. The Americans' successful bid for independence may have fulfilled their yearnings for a recognized place in the world, but it also underscored their new nation's weakness and vulnerability in the European diplomatic system; their reliance on European, and to an extraordinary extent British, capital, credit, and markets; and their ongoing subservience to European fashion and culture. Well into the nineteenth century, as Charlene Boyer Lewis shows, elite Americans looked to Europe for cultural cues. Elizabeth Patterson Bonaparte was a celebrity because of her social successes in the Old World, beginning with her celebrated, brief marriage to the emperor's brother, and her audacious flaunting of conventional modes of behavior and dress in republican America. Convinced as they might be of the superiority of their new republican order, independent Americans would nonetheless long remain subject to the Old World's cultural power.

The experience of chronic diplomatic crisis and military conflict in the first four decades of its history revealed the growing importance of European ties to the new nation's survival and development. At the same time, the American Revolution transformed the European state system, preparing the way for a cataclysmic revolution in France that would demolish the Old Regime balance of power. The great, ongoing struggle between France— the new nation's revolutionary ally—and counter-revolutionary Britain shaped American politics in the turbulent 1790s and beyond. Federalists accused Republicans of being pawns of the French, and Republicans accused Federalists of being pawns of the British. Such charges reflected anxieties about the persistence of metropolitan influence and the tenuousness of national loyalties in a weak and vulnerable federal republic.

Polemical exchanges about "foreign influence" reinforced national feeling in both parties as combatants burnished their own patriotic credentials and impugned their opponents'. In fact, there was broad agreement on foreign policy issues—it was clearly in the new nation's interest to avoid "entangling alliances"—even as deepening domestic divisions threatened to rip the Union apart. Anxious about their opponents' vulnerability to foreign influence—their persistent provincialism—American partisans misconstrued each other's motives and failed to recognize their common patriotic commitments. Jefferson's conciliatory rhetoric in his first inaugural address brought these shared values to the fore: "We have called by different names brethren of the same principle. We are all federalists, we are all republicans."[22] The result of the American Revolution was not to draw Americans into the new forms of provincial subordination and dependency that were signified by the "different names" Americans called each other in the 1790s but rather to create a new nation with its own metropolis. Americans were no longer "British," nor were they "French," notwithstanding the wartime alliance that had made independence possible. But their national future depended on their ability to avoid entanglements, project power, and protect vital interests in a dangerous world.

American revolutionaries created a new nation but not a New World. Jefferson's fervent belief that the republican United States represented the virtuous antithesis of the corrupt and vicious European Old Regime expressed his own deep-seated provincialism. Fearing for the success of their sometimes desperate experiment in republican government, American Patriots protested too much. Nation-making drew them into the vortex of European diplomacy and power politics, compromising the very differences that Jefferson and other provincial nationalists celebrated. As Americans vindicated their claim to separate nationhood, they became one nation among many in the dynamic, expanding, war-prone world that modern nations made.

NOTES

1. TJ to Elbridge Gerry, 13 May 1797, *TJP,* 29:363–64.

2. TJ to Dr. John Crawford, 2 Jan. 1812, L&B, 13:119.

3. T. H. Breen, *The Marketplace of Revolution: How Consumer Politics Shaped American Independence* (New York, 2004).

4. Declaration of Independence, 4 July 1776, *TJW,* 19.

5. John E. Crowley, *The Privileges of Independence: Neomercantilism and the American Revolution* (Baltimore, 1993).

6. George Berkeley, "On the Prospect of Planting Arts and Learning in America" (1725), in John Bartlett, *Familiar Quotations,* 10th ed. (1919).

7. JA to Abigail Adams, 12 May 1780, *AFC,* 3:342.

8. Adam Smith, *An Inquiry into the Nature and Causes of the Wealth of Nations,* ed. R. H. Campbell and A. S. Skinner (Indianapolis, 1981), IV, i, §32, 448.

9. Eliga H. Gould, "Zones of Law, Zones of Violence: The Legal Geography of the British Atlantic, circa 1772," *WMQ* 60 (2003): 471–510.

10. Ronald Meek, *Social Science and the Ignoble Savage* (Cambridge, 1976); Roy Harvey Pearce, *Savagism and Civilization: A Study of the Indian and the American Mind* (Baltimore, 1965).

11. Smith, *Wealth of Nations,* IV, i, §32, 448.

12. *Notes on the State of Virginia,* query 6 (Animals), *TJW,* 190–91.

13. Ibid., 190.

14. James Kettner, *The Development of American Citizenship, 1608–1870* (Chapel Hill, NC, 1978).

15. Robert W. Tucker and David C. Hendrickson, *Empire of Liberty: The Statecraft of Thomas Jefferson* (New York, 1990).

16. Robert R. Palmer, *The Age of the Democratic Revolution: A Political History of Europe and America, 1760–1800,* 2 vols. (Princeton, NJ, 1959–64).

17. TJ to C. W. F. Dumas, 22 Sept. 1786, *TJP,* 10:397; TJ to William Short, 3 Jan. 1793, ibid., 25:14.

18. TJ to Benjamin Austin, 9 Jan. 1816, L&B, 14:389.

19. TJ to Caspar Wistar, 16 Dec. 1800, quoted in Lucia Stanton, "Better Tools for a New and Better World," in this volume. See also Douglas L. Wilson, "Jefferson and the Republic of Letters," in *Jeffersonian Legacies,* ed. Peter S. Onuf (Charlottesville, VA, 1993), 50–76.

20. Philipp Ziesche, "Cosmopolitan Patriots in the Age of Revolution, 1788–1800" (PhD diss., Yale University, 2006), introduction.

21. For the significance of creole revolutionaries in the development of modern ideas of nationhood, see Benedict Anderson, *Imagined Communities: Reflections on the Origin and Spread of Nationalism,* rev. ed. (New York, 1991).

22. TJ, first inaugural address, 4 Mar. 1801, *TJW,* 493.

Environmental Hazards, Eighteenth-Century Style

GORDON S. WOOD

We today think we have problems with our environment. Our worries seem endless. We are anxious about global warming and greenhouse gas emissions; the effect of aerosol sprays on the ozone layer; hazardous wastes in our water supplies; and toxic substances in our foods. But compared with the environmental problems faced by our nation at the very beginning of its history, our present difficulties and anxieties do not seem all that overwhelming. At least we now have the Environmental Protection Agency to look after us. Americans living in the republic at the end of the eighteenth century had no such governmental protection, and they faced a threat from their environment that we can scarcely appreciate. Americans of the early republic were told by the best scientific authorities of the Western world that the American natural environment was deleterious to all animal life. This was not a case of people's use of energy warming the atmosphere or of some industrialists polluting the water here and there. The environmental problems of the early republic were natural and not man-made, and that was what made them so frightening. They were apparently inherent in nature itself. There was in fact something terribly wrong with the climate of the New World that made it harmful to all living creatures. This was not the conclusion of a few crackpots or of some fanatic European aristocrats eager to malign American republicanism. It was the conclusion of the greatest naturalist of the Western world, the French scientist George-Louis Leclerc, comte de Buffon. In the rambling thirty-six volumes of his *Natural History*, published between 1749 and 1800, Buffon presented a profoundly pessimistic but scientifically grounded picture of the American environment. There was in the New World, Buffon wrote, "some combination of elements, and other physical causes, something that opposes the amplification of animated Nature."[1]

The American continents, said Buffon, were newer than those of the

Old World. They had remained longer under the sea. They had, it seemed, only recently emerged from the flood and had not as yet properly dried out. America's air was moister and more humid than that of the older continents. Its topography was more irregular, its weather more variable, its forests and miasmatic swamps more extensive. In short, America had an unhealthy climate in which to live.

Animals in the New World, said Buffon, were underdeveloped—smaller than those of the Old World. America did not have any lions. The American puma was scarcely a real lion; it did not even have a mane, and "it is also much smaller, weaker, and more cowardly than the real lion." The New World had no elephants; in fact, no American wildlife could be compared to an elephant in size or shape. The best that America had, Buffon wrote sarcastically, was the tapir of Brazil, but "this elephant of the New World" was not bigger than a six-month-old calf. In America there were no rhinoceroses, no hippopotamuses, no camels, no giraffes. All the American animals were "four, six, eight, and ten times" smaller than those of the older continents. Even the domestic animals introduced to America from Europe tended to shrink and dwindle under the influence of the New World's climate. Apparently only the pig was able to hold its own in comparison with Old World animals.[2]

Buffon's conclusion about the environment was stark and frightening: "Living nature," he wrote, "is thus much less active there, much less varied, and we may even say, less strong."[3] The only living things that seemed to flourish in the dank, wet American climate were reptiles—snakes, toads, frogs, and other cold-blooded creatures that, said Buffon, often grew to gigantic sizes.

It was unsettling enough to learn that the peculiar American habitat had affected animal life. But to learn that the environment of the New World was also unhealthful for humans was truly alarming. Buffon claimed that the American environment was responsible for the apparently retarded development of the native Indians, who seemed to be wandering savages frozen in the first hunting-gathering stage of social development without any structured society. The Indians, Buffon said, were like reptiles; they were cold-blooded. Their "organs of generation are small and feeble." The natives of the New World had no hair, no beards, no ardor for their females. Their social bonds were weak; they had very few children and paid little attention to those they had. In some way this strange, moist climate of the New World had devastatingly affected the physical and social character of the only humans native to it. The outlook for humans of the Old World transplanted to this forbidding environment was therefore not a happy one.[4]

It is difficult for us today to appreciate the degree of ignorance people in the eighteenth century still had about the New World. Jefferson probably had the best library in the world dealing with the geography and natural history of the American West; nevertheless, this well-read American believed that the Rockies were no larger than the Blue Ridge Mountains and that mammoths and other prehistoric creatures still roamed along the upper Missouri, where, he believed active volcanoes existed. Since the great German scientist Alexander von Humboldt had not yet traveled to the Americas and published his remarkable findings, even educated Europeans continued to hold strange ideas about the New World.

Of course, at the beginning Europeans had expected the climate of America to be similar to that of the Old World. Indeed, the first definition of *climate* in the *Oxford English Dictionary* reads, "A belt of the earth's surface between two given parallels of latitude." As late as 1796 Jedidiah Morse's *American Geography* continued to define the word that way. People naturally assumed that places that were the same distance from the poles or from the equator would have the same climate, and they were surprised to find the contrary. The latitude of London was north of Newfoundland's; that of Rome was the same as New York City's. Yet the climates of these places on the same latitude were very different. It was out of this sense of difference between the Old World and the New and the fantasies it generated that Buffon gathered his scientific evidence. His conclusions were all based on hearsay.[5]

The great naturalist's theories about the New World were taken up by others, including Corneille de Pauw, the Abbé Raynal, and the Scottish historian William Robertson, and through such writers they entered the popular thinking about America in the late eighteenth century. Many European intellectuals had a vested interest in the character of the New World. Many of the French philosophes like Voltaire were struggling to reform the *ancien régime*, and they turned the New World into a weapon in their struggle. America in their eyes came to stand for all that eighteenth-century France lacked—natural simplicity, social equality, religious freedom, and rustic enlightenment. Not that the reformers expected France to become like America. But they wanted to contrast this romantic image of the New World with the aristocratic corruption, priestly tyranny, and luxurious materialism they saw in the *ancien régime*. Idealizing all that was different from the luxury and corruption they saw around them, many of the liberal French philosophes created "a Mirage in the West," a counter-cultural image of America with which to criticize their own society.[6]

It was to contest this idealized image of America that other writers and philosophes picked up Buffon's theories about the New World and used them against the reformers and their image of the noble savage. In 1770 Raynal published a popular four-volume history of the European colonies in America, in which he expressed astonishment "that America has not yet produced a good poet, a skilled mathematician, a genius in art or any science." In 1785, perhaps in hopes of settling the issue once and for all, Raynal sponsored a competition in France for the best essay answering the question, "Has the discovery of America been beneficial or harmful to the human race?" Eight essays survive, four on each side of the question. No prize was awarded. During the last quarter of the eighteenth century America became a political football in the Old World's struggle over reform.[7]

But for the Americans learning of Buffon's findings the issue was no simple intellectual or academic matter. If Buffon's scientific claims were true, then the chances for the success of the new American republic were not good. Many eighteenth-century Englishmen and Europeans had never expected much from the people of the New World. For them the term *American* had often evoked images of unrefined if not barbarous persons, degenerate and racially debased mongrels living amidst African slaves and Indian savages thousands of miles from civilization. Hessian soldiers arriving in New York in 1776 were surprised to find that there were actually many white people in the New World.[8] Now the best scientific findings of the day seemed to reinforce these images of the degeneracy of the New World.

Of course, most Americans in the generation following the Revolution did not let these English and European charges seriously dampen their optimism and enthusiasm for the future. Instead, they reacted to these charges with indignant dismissal, exaggerated boasting, or extensive scientific comparison. Perhaps it was true, conceded Jefferson, who took these charges more seriously than most, that America had twice as much rain as Europe, but, he said, in America it fell "in half the time."[9]

Yet many Americans seemed to have an underlying fear that the European critics might be right after all. There did seem to be something peculiar about America's climate. Regions with temperatures well below zero in winter could swelter in heat close to one hundred degrees Fahrenheit in summer; and swings of forty degrees Fahrenheit in twenty-four hours were not uncommon. No place in Europe had these sorts of radical variations in temperature. The American climate did seem to have more moisture. Humidity was often high, and the heavier rainfall alternated with an unusual number of sunny cloudless skies. Some speculated that these peculiarities were due to the existence of so much uncultivated land covered by dense forests in America. Europe's climate had once been like America's, but once most of its trees had been cut down and its swamps drained, its climate had changed.

The devastating epidemics of yellow fever that erupted in American cities during this period, beginning with the catastrophe in Philadelphia in 1793, which killed 10 percent of the population, were not duplicated elsewhere in the Western world. This led some Americans, including Jefferson, to conclude that the disease was indeed "peculiar to our country." Because the sun rarely shone in the middle and northern parts of Europe, the Europeans, said Jefferson, could "safely build cities in solid blocks without generating disease."[10] But America's unusual atmosphere—the cloudless skies and the intense heat and humidity—fermented the garbage and filth in the cities, creating putrefaction that released effluvia and morbific fluids that bred disease; thus, in America, said Jefferson, "men cannot be piled on one another with impunity." He hoped that some good might come out of these epidemics of yellow fever: Americans might be inhibited from building the sorts of huge, sprawling cities that existed in Europe.[11]

Although America's cities were scarcely crowded or dirty by European standards, many Americans decided that their cities had to be designed differently from those in the Old World. Urban renewal in the early republic was born out of these concerns. Jefferson was especially worried about New Orleans, which promised to become "the greatest city the world had ever seen. There is no spot on the globe to which the produce of so great an extent of fertile country must necessarily come." But at the same time, unfortunately, "there is no spot where yellow fever is so much to be apprehended." He decided that New Orleans and other American cities had to be "thin-built." He thought they ought "to take the chequer board" for a plan, with "the white squares open and unbuilt for ever, and planted with trees."[12]

Not just Jefferson but many other leading intellectuals of the day, such as Benjamin Rush, Noah Webster, and Benjamin Latrobe, also concocted plans for cleaning and renovating America's cities. Rush was the most well known and most influential physician of his generation, and as the leading physician in Philadelphia he was intimately involved in the 1793 yellow fever epidemic.

Unfortunately, despite his courage during the epidemic, Rush tended to lose many of his patients, largely because he was an inveterate bleeder. Rush believed that all diseases could be reduced to one—fever caused by convulsive tension in the blood vessels—and thus he tended to bleed his patients regardless of the nature of their illnesses. From consumption to insanity, he treated all diseases by reducing tension through purging and bloodletting.

His problem came from overestimating the amount of blood in the human body: he thought most people had twelve quarts of blood, double the six quarts the average person has. Since he often took from his patients as many as five quarts of blood in a day and a half, it is not surprising that he lost many of them. The Federalist journalist William Cobbett termed Rush's method of bleeding "one of those great discoveries which are made from time to time for the depopulation of the earth." This was one of the statements that Rush used in his successful suit for libel against Cobbett.[13]

Rush, who had theories about everything, naturally had theories about yellow fever. While some believed that the disease came from the West Indies, Rush thought it had to have domestic origins. Why else would the disease be confined to America? His notion of local origins, however, was not very popular in Philadelphia. Dr. Charles Caldwell, of Philadelphia, was a medical colleague who agreed with Rush, at least at first. Of all the intellectuals, Caldwell drew up the most elaborate plans for urban renewal to deal with the effluvia that caused yellow fever. Caldwell was one of those characters that only early nineteenth-century America could produce. To say that he was full of himself is an understatement. Although he denied that his *Autobiography*, which he completed shortly before his death in 1853, could be compared to that of Benjamin Franklin, he thought that he and Franklin were "identical" in their "ambition and effort to excel in all, whether bodily or mental, that is either done or attempted by us." He also believed that he had something in common with illustrious scientists such as Galileo, Leibniz, Newton, Harvey, and others, not in terms of their greatness, he conceded, but in terms of the persecution they had suffered for the benefits they had brought mankind. During his career he became a great promoter of phrenology, the pseudoscience that deduced intelligence from the structure of the head. He supposedly began his lectures by stating that the United States could boast of only three great heads—Daniel Webster's, Henry Clay's, "and modesty prevents me from mentioning the third." Caldwell was most proud of his skills in lecturing. He declared that since 1798 or 1799 he had "delivered, by appointment, a greater number of public addresses, which afterward by request appeared in print, than any other man in the United States."[14]

In two of these addresses, in 1801 and 1802, Caldwell laid out his solution for the problem of yellow fever. He thought all of America's cities, which were simply "vast factories of this febrile poison," would have to be rebuilt. Because people needed to live above the miasma that was causing the disease, they needed lofty buildings at least two stories high with thick walls and small windows to keep the sun out—more or less like the buildings in Italy. The cities must also have many squares and many trees, especially Lombardy poplars, which he considered the best kind of tree for soaking up the miasma and emitting vital air.[15]

Caldwell seems to have conceded that the Europeans were correct in their judgment about America's climate. Instead of denying the Europeans' charges, he turned them around by claiming that America's climate was simply more stupendous than any other. "Nature," he said in an oration in 1802, was more "bold and gigantic in her operations" in America. "Compared to our own, how diminutive and humble are the mountains, rivers, lakes, and cataracts of the old world!" Of course, he mentioned Niagara Falls—that "manifestation of omnipotence"—as everybody did, but the rest of America's nature was equally magnificent. Look at America's forests, he exclaimed. "Are not the forests of Europe . . . swallowed up in the grandeur of those of America?"[16]

Like many other American boosters, Caldwell easily got carried away with the greatness of America. "How delightful then to reside in the bosom of such sublimity! Who does not glory in being born an American!" It stood to reason, he said, that America had bigger and more powerful diseases than other places. "Our *diseases* are not only frequent but aspire to the same scale of greatness with our other phenomena." He even tried to justify Dr. Rush's excessive bloodletting. American doctors, he said, had to take out so much more blood than European doctors because the fevers in America were so much more powerful than those in Europe. In the end, after describing all of his elaborate plans for redoing America's cities, Caldwell offered a simpler solution to the problem. "Perhaps," he suggested, "there is nothing which would contribute more materially to the prevention of diseases of our country than the general adoption of flannel under-clothes." The Europeans tended to wear more flannel than Americans, and flannel, he said, was better able "to keep up a cutaneous action, and preserve perspiration in an equable state." Like so many other Americans, Caldwell was simply trying to make the best of a bad situation.[17]

This preoccupation with the climate grew out of Americans' Enlightenment assumption that people were the products of their environment, physical as well as cultural. Human nature was malleable, shaped and formed by experience and external circumstances, including even the climate. Since, as most people believed, humans had all sprung from the same origin, as recorded in Genesis, only the effects of the environment through time could account for the obvious differences among them. Even skin color was explained in environmental terms, which makes many of our modern notions of race irrelevant for the eighteenth century. Many believed that the Negro's blackness came from the intense African sun, that somehow the African's skin had become scorched. Benjamin Rush, however, had a different theory. In a paper delivered before the American Philosophical Society in 1799 he argued that the Negro's skin color came from a disease, leprosy, caused by the excessive African heat. In the different climate of America, some Americans thought, the African Americans' skin would gradually become lighter, perhaps eventually white. The South Carolina historian David Ramsey, who believed "all mankind to be originally the same and only diversified by accidental circumstances," claimed that "in a few centuries the negroes will lose their black color. I think now they are less black in Jersey than Carolina."[18]

All this emphasis on the power of climate had ominous implications for Americans. If the climate of the New World was powerful enough to create peculiar American diseases or to affect the color of people's skin, then Buffon's charges were very serious indeed. In fact, they lay behind the only book Thomas Jefferson ever wrote.

In his *Notes on the State of Virginia* Jefferson systematically attempted to answer the famous theories of Buffon; in fact, he requested that one of the first copies of his book be delivered directly to Buffon. The parts of the book that today are often skipped over or eliminated entirely in modern abbreviated editions—the tables and statistics about animals that Jefferson compiled in query 6—are precisely those parts that Jefferson considered central to his work.[19]

Side by side, in order of size, Jefferson lists the animals of the Old World and New, giving the weights of each in pounds and ounces. In almost every case the American animal is bigger. If the European cow weighed 763 pounds, the American cow was 2,500 pounds. If the European bear weighed 153.7 pounds, the American bear weighed 410 pounds. As Jefferson describes the various American animals—the moose, the beaver, the weasel, the fox— and finds them all equaling or bettering their European counterparts, he gets carried away with excitement and even brings in the prehistoric mammoth to offset the Old World elephant. He even matches Buffon's sarcastic reference to the tapir, "the elephant of America," being but the size of a small cow. "To preserve our comparison," wrote Jefferson, "I will add that the wild boar, the elephant of Europe, is little more than half that size."[20]

Jefferson scarcely hid his anger at Buffon's charges, and he raised question after question about the sources of the great naturalist's data. Who were those European travelers who supplied the information about America's animals? Were they real scientists? Was natural history the object of their travels? Did they measure or weigh the animals they spoke of? Did they know the animals of their own countries? Did they really know anything at all about animals? Jefferson's conclusion was clear: Buffon and the other European intellectuals did not know what they were talking about.[21]

Jefferson did not like personal confrontations, but when he went to France in the 1780s as American minister he prepared himself for his first meeting with Buffon by taking with him "an uncommonly large panther skin" he had purchased in America for just that purpose. He was introduced to Buffon, who was the curator of King Louis XVI's cabinet of natural history, as someone who had combated several of Buffon's theories. Jefferson did not hesitate to press Buffon about his ignorance of American animals. The earnest American minister especially stressed the great size of the American moose and told Buffon that it was so big that a European reindeer could walk under its belly. Finally, in exasperation, the great European naturalist promised that if Jefferson could produce a single specimen of the moose with foot-long antlers, "he would give up the question."[22]

That was all Jefferson needed; he went busily to work, imploring friends in America to send all the skins, bones, and horns they could find, or better still, entire stuffed animals. In January 1786 he told his Virginia colleague Archibald Cary that the comte de Buffon was "absolutely unacquainted with our Elk and our deer. He has hitherto believed that our deer never had horns more than a foot long." Americans, Jefferson told Cary, had to set this European scientist straight. Therefore, Jefferson asked, "will you take the trouble to procure for me the largest pair of buck's horns you can, and a large skin of each colour, that is to say a red and a blue? If it were possible to take these from a buck just killed, to leave all the bones and hoof of the legs and feet in the skin, so that having only made an incision all along the belly and neck, to take the animal out at, we could by sewing up that incision and stuffing the skin, present the true size and form of the animal." "It would be," he told Cary, "a most precious present."[23]

It is hard to imagine what it must have been like when bits and pieces of America's animals began to arrive at Jefferson's Paris residence. Travel was not good for many of the specimens: the birds and animals sent whole decayed badly, and often they arrived missing hair and all sorts of parts. Governor John Sullivan, of New Hampshire, took the most trouble, for he was commissioned to get the moose that was to demolish Buffon's theories once and for all. Sullivan sent a virtual army into the northern wilderness of New Hampshire and even cut a twenty-mile road through the woods to drag it out. By the time the specimen arrived in Portsmouth to be readied for its transit across the Atlantic, it was half-rotten, and all its hair and head bones had been lost. So Sullivan sent along to Paris the horns of some other animal, blithely explaining to Jefferson that "they are not the horns of this Moose but may be fixed on at pleasure."[24]

Understandably, Jefferson was not entirely happy with the impression his bones and skins were making on Buffon. Although he asked his correspondents in America to send him the biggest specimens they could find, he continually apologized to Buffon for their smallness. In the fall of 1787, while his colleagues back home were drawing up a new national constitution, Jefferson could think of little else but demolishing Buffon's theories. On October 1, 1787, the day after Sullivan's moose arrived in Paris, Jefferson presented it to the French naturalist along with the horns and parts of various other animals, including caribou, elk, and deer. But he begged Buffon "not to consider those now sent as furnishing a specimen of their ordinary size." Indeed, he told Buffon, "I have certainly seen some of them which would have weighed five or six times as much." Apparently these specimens convinced Buffon of his errors, for according to Jefferson, the French naturalist promised to set these things right in his next volume, but he died before he could do so.[25]

Buffon died in 1788, but Jefferson continued to be interested in the size of American animals. In 1789 he urged the president of Harvard to encourage the study of America's natural history in order "to do justice to our country, it's productions, and it's genius." In the mid-1790s, on the basis of some fossil remains, probably belonging to a prehistoric sloth, he concocted the existence of a huge super-lion, three times bigger than the African lion, and presented his imagined beast to the scientific world as the Megalonyx, "the great claw."[26]

The most exciting scientific find of the period was Charles Willson Peale's 1801 exhumation near Newburgh, New York, of the bones of a mammoth. Peale displayed his mammoth in his celebrated museum, and in 1806 he painted a marvelous picture of what was perhaps the first organized scientific exhumation in American history. Peale's discovery electrified the country and put the word *mammoth* on everybody's lips, a development that Federalist intellectuals delighted in mocking. A Philadelphia baker advertised the sale of "mammoth bread." In Washington a "mammoth eater" ate forty-two eggs in ten minutes. And the ladies of Cheshire, Massachusetts, sent President Jefferson a "mammoth cheese" weighing 1,230 pounds, a gift from the heart of Federalism that he welcomed as "an ebullition of the passion of republicanism in a state where it has been under heavy persecution."[27]

But it was not enough to have larger animals than the Old World. More important were human beings, something Jefferson was very sensitive about.

He delighted in telling a story passed on to him about a dinner party that took place in France in the 1780s hosted by Benjamin Franklin at which the Abbé Raynal was present. During the dinner Raynal began one of his usual tirades about the degeneration of animals and humans in the New World. Franklin, good humored as always, suggested that the matter be tested empirically. As it happened, there were six Americans on one side of the table and six Frenchmen on the other. All the Americans were tall and well built, while the Frenchmen were all unusually small, Raynal himself, according to Franklin, being "a mere shrimp."[28] A generation later the story of the dinner party in Paris was still being told in America. The irrepressible Charles Caldwell recounted a version in his *Autobiography.* But the best and most embellished account was by the British immigrant John Bristed: in his *Resources of the United States of America* (1818) Bristed told how "six stout, well-proportioned, tall, handsome" Americans put in the shade the "ludicrous" Frenchmen, who were "all little, lank, yellow, shrivelled personages, resembling Java monkeys" and who "peeped up at their opposite neighbours, and were silent."[29]

In his *Notes on the State of Virginia* Jefferson was very anxious to refute Raynal's charges that America had no geniuses. He worked out a mathematical calculation of genius and concluded that America had contributed its share: Franklin, Washington, and the Philadelphia mathematician and astronomer David Rittenhouse, three for a population of just over 3 million. Since France had 20 million people, it should have about eighteen geniuses, and, said Jefferson, it probably did. England, with 10 million people, should have nine geniuses, but it had none. "The sun of her glory is fast descending to the horizon. Her Philosophy has crossed the Channel, her freedom the Atlantic, and herself seems passing to that awful dissolution, whose issue is not given human foresight to scan."[30]

Jefferson's lifelong defense of the prowess and virtue of the Indian grew out of this same passionate desire to protect the American environment against European aspersions. Buffon was wrong, he wrote. The Indian "is neither more defective in ardor, nor more impotent with his female, than the white reduced to the same diet and exercise." The difference between the native peoples of America and Europeans was "not a difference of nature, but of circumstance." There were good reasons why Indian women bore fewer children than whites, why the Indians' hands and wrists were small, why they had less hair on their bodies; and those reasons, said Jefferson, had nothing to do with America's soil or climate.[31]

Even some American critics thought that Jefferson had gone too far in examining so minutely the various parts of the Indian's body, but for

Jefferson the stakes were high. Jefferson could readily doubt the capacities of blacks, who, after all, came from Africa, but he could never admit any inferiority in the red men, who were products of the very soil and climate that would mold the people of the United States. For Jefferson the Indian had to be "in body and mind the equal of the white man."[32]

Others agreed. The Reverend James Madison, president of the College of William and Mary and a second cousin of the famous Founder, had much more hope for the Indian's assimilation into white society than he did for the African's. He told Jefferson of reports of an Indian near Albany who had gradually whitened in the past two years. But contrary to Dr. Rush's theories, he knew of no African's changing color. "It seems as if Nature had absolutely denied to him the Possibility of ever acquiring the Complexion of the White."[33] (Of course, Jefferson might have reminded the Reverend Madison that many slave children were in fact becoming whiter. Jefferson knew only too well that they were the consequences of what he called "the perpetual exercise of the most boisterous [meaning coarse or savage] passions" between the white planters and their female African slaves.)[34]

Jefferson was scarcely the only American worried about the environment of the New World. Indeed, it seemed at times as if the entire American intellectual community was involved in examining the soil and climate of America. Nearly every issue of every magazine, from the *American Museum* and the *American Register* to the *Medical Repository* and *Nile's Weekly Register,* seemed to mention America's climate. Calls went out everywhere for information about the American habitat. Was America's climate in fact less healthy than the Old World's? Was it really wetter in America than in Europe, and if so, could anything be done about it? Clergymen in such obscure places as Mason, New Hampshire, faithfully compiled meteorological and demographic records, and otherwise exclusively literary journals such as the *Columbia Magazine* and the *North American Review* published periodic weather charts sent from distant correspondents in Brunswick, Maine, and Albany, New York. Indeed, temperature-taking became everyone's way of participating in the fact-gathering of enlightened science. Between 1763 and 1795 Ezra Stiles, president of Yale, filled six volumes with his daily temperature and weather readings. Madison's father included so many weather readings in his journal that Madison called it his "father's meteorological diaries."[35] Every intellectual felt the need to present a paper to some philosophical society on the subject of America's climate. The *Transactions of the American Philosophical Society* for the year 1799 contained no fewer than six articles on America's climate.

All these writings and all this temperature-taking showed that Americans were actually changing their climate. By cutting down forests and filling in swamps, they were moderating the extreme temperatures that had existed decades earlier. If Americans could change the weather, then they could change anything. It was left to Samuel Williams, Hollis Professor of Natural and Experimental Philosophy at Harvard, to present empirical evidence on how this manipulation of the weather might be done. Williams set out to measure just how much moisture American trees gave off. He first figured out that two leaves exuded sixteen grains of water in six hours. The next step, counting the number of leaves on a tree of ordinary size, was clearly the hardest; 21,192 was the figure he arrived at. From then on it was easy to calculate how much moisture was expelled by a tree in twelve hours, and then how much was expelled by an acre of trees. In the end he concluded that 3,875 gallons of water were given off by an acre of forest every twelve hours.[36] So cutting down all America's immense forests would, it seemed, actually dry up the climate and make it more like that of the Old World. Americans had always enjoyed their carefree destruction of trees, much to the astonishment of travelers from Europe, where forests were scarce and precious. Now their indiscriminate tree-cutting had a scientific rationale.

All this interest in cutting down forests and measuring the size of animals suggested an underlying anxiety that the European critics of America, like the Abbé Raynal, might be right after all. By about 1800 there were numerous Phi Beta Kappa addresses worrying about America's lack of intellectual achievement. No one was sure why America was not producing great works of literature, but the nature of the climate was a possibility. Charles Brockden Brown abandoned his career as a novelist in part to devote his energies to examining America's environment. In 1804 he translated the comte de Volney's disparaging *Tableau du climat et du sol des États-Unis d'Amérique* (*A View of the Soil and Climate of the United States of America*), even though a London English edition was already available, mainly because he wanted to argue with Volney in his notes.[37]

In 1800 the American Philosophical Society formally petitioned Congress to transform the decennial census into a detailed mortality and occupational survey "to determine the effect of the soil and climate of the U.S. on the inhabitants thereof," promising even before the data were in that "truths will result very satisfactory to our citizens; that under the joint influence of soil, climate and occupation the duration of human life in their position of the earth, will be found to be at least equal to what it is in any other; and that its population increases with a rapidity unequaled in all others."[38]

Newspapers and journals became fascinated with the longevity of people and sought to report the numbers of all those who lived beyond eighty, ninety, or a hundred.

From this desire to defend the American environment came all the excited exaggerations of America's magnificent rivers, expansive forests, and sublime cataracts. Jeremy Belknap, a Federalist clergyman and historian, devoted much of his three-volume *History of New-Hampshire* (1784–92) to refuting Old World critics who had "represented America as a grave to Europeans." He offered detailed longevity charts and overblown descriptions of New Hampshire's weather that no modern travel brochure could better. The air of New Hampshire's forests, he wrote, was "remarkably pure.... A profusion of effluvia from the resinous trees impart to the air a balsamic quality, which is extremely favorable to health, and the numerous streams of limpid water ... cause currents of fresh air which is in the highest degree salubrious."[39]

Of course, Jefferson, the perennial Pollyanna, remained optimistic. "I prefer much the climate of the United States to that of Europe," he told the comte de Volney in 1805. "I think it a more cheerful one." England's climate was especially gloomy, which had led to many English suicides. Fortunately, he said, "our cloudless sky ... has eradicated from our constitutions all disposition to hang ourselves, which we might otherwise have inherited from our English ancestors."[40]

In time, of course, Buffon's charges and the problem of America's climate were largely forgotten. America's bumptious political and cultural environment, especially with the growth of a market economy, tended to overwhelm the geographical environment. The busyness of Americans, their search for the almighty dollar, seemed to dominate everything, making the physical climate appear inconsequential by contrast. Dr. Rush and others now began to worry that all this busyness might affect Americans' mental health, even to the point of causing insanity, and they began planning asylums for all those driven insane by the chaos of the commercial culture.

But traces of these European accusations about America's physical environment tended to linger on through the nineteenth century; and they help explain why Americans had the notorious habit of boasting of the bigness of nature in their country. "Saw ye ever such a land as this?" Herman Melville has his countrymen say to foreigners in his 1849 novel *Mardi*. "Is it not a great and extensive republic? Pray, observe how tall we are; just feel of our thighs; are we not a glorious people? Here, feel of our beards. Look round; look round; be not afraid; behold those palms; swear now, that this land surpasses all others."[41]

By the mid-nineteenth century perhaps many of Melville's readers had lost the historical context in which this obsession with America's size and health had arisen. There was a time, however, at the very beginning of America's national history when such extravagant boasting was both understandable and justifiable. So the next time any of us drives through an American town or county that brags about having the largest sunflowers or the biggest pigs in the world, we might just recall where it all began.

NOTES

A condensed version of this essay appears in *Empire of Liberty: A History of the Early Republic,* published by Oxford University Press (2009), and is used by permission of Oxford University Press, Inc.

1. George-Louis Leclerc, comte de Buffon, *Natural History, General and Particular,* quoted in *Was America a Mistake? An Eighteenth Century Controversy,* ed. Henry Steele Commager and Elmo Giordanetti (New York, 1967), 60. On this well-worked subject, see Gilbert Chinard, "Eighteenth-Century Theories on America as a Human Habitat," *Proceedings of the American Philosophical Society* 91 (1947): 25–57; Philippe Roger, *The American Enemy: A Story of French Anti-Americanism* (Chicago, 2005), 1–29; and esp. Antonello Gerbi, *The Dispute of the New World: The History of a Polemic, 1750–1900* (Pittsburgh, 1973), to which this essay is much indebted.

2. Buffon, quoted in Gerbi, *Dispute of the New World,* 4; Buffon, *Natural History,* quoted in Commager and Giordanetti, *Was America a Mistake?* 53, 60.

3. Buffon, quoted in Gerbi, *Dispute of the New World,* 4.

4. Buffon, *Natural History,* quoted in Commager and Giordanetti, *Was America a Mistake?* 60, 61.

5. Karen Ordahl Kupperman, "The Puzzle of the American Climate in the Early Colonial Period," *American Historical Review* 87 (1982): 1262–89.

6. Durand Echeverria, *Mirage in the West: A History of the French Image of American Society to 1815* (Princeton, NJ, 1957).

7. Ibid., 173–74.

8. Stanley Weintraub, *Iron Tears: America's Battle for Freedom, Britain's Quagmire: 1775–1783* (New York, 2005), 65; Stacy Schiff, *A Great Improvisation: Franklin, France, and the Birth of America* (New York, 2005), 169; T. H. Breen, "Ideology and Nationalism on the Eve of the American Revolution: Revisions Once More in Need of Revising," *JAH* 84 (1997): 29–32; Stephen Conway, "From Fellow-Nationals to Foreigners: British Perceptions of the Americans, circa 1739–1783," *WMQ* 59 (2002): 65–100.

9. TJ to comte de Volney, 8 Feb. 1805, *TJW,* 1155.

10. TJ to Gov. William Henry Harrison, 27 Feb. 1803, L&B, 10:368; TJ to Gov. William C. C. Claiborne, 7 July 1804, quoted in *The Portable Jefferson,* ed. Merrill Peterson (New York, 1975), 499–500.

11. TJ to Benjamin Rush, 12 Sept. 1799, *TJP,* 31:183–84. See also Edwin T. Martin, *Thomas Jefferson: Scientist* (New York, 1952), 131–47.

12. TJ to Claiborne, 7 July 1804, *Portable Jefferson*, 499–500; TJ to Benjamin Rush, 12 Sept. 1799, *TJP*, 31: 183–84.

13. Carl Binger, *Revolutionary Doctor: Benjamin Rush, 1746–1813* (New York, 1966), 229; Richard Harrison Shryock, *Medicine and Society in America: 1660–1860* (New York, 1960), 70.

14. Charles Caldwell, *Autobiography of Charles Caldwell, M.D.*, ed. Harriot W. Warner (New York, 1968), xxiv–xxv, 419.

15. Charles Caldwell, *An Oration on the Causes of the Difference, in Point of Frequency and Force, between the Endemic Diseases of the United States of America, and those of the Countries of Europe* (Philadelphia, 1802), 14; idem, *Medical and Physical Memoirs: Containing, Among Other Subjects, A Particular Enquiry into the Origin and Nature of the Late Pestilential Epidemics of the United States* (Philadelphia, 1801), 21–22, 46–47, 51, 55, 117.

16. Caldwell, *Oration*, 5, 6, 7.

17. Ibid., 7, 8–9, 13, 16, 18, 32, 34.

18. David Ramsey to TJ, 3 May 1786, *TJP*, 9:441.

19. Jefferson's *Notes on the State of Virginia* was first published in a French edition in 1785. The first American edition appeared in 1787, followed by two editions in 1800 and five in 1801.

20. TJ, *Notes*, 43–58, quotation at 55.

21. Ibid., 54.

22. Gerbi, *Dispute of the New World*, 264.

23. TJ to Archibald Cary, 7 Jan. 1786, *TJP*, 9:158. Even Jefferson's friend James Madison joined in the task of refuting Buffon. In a long, thoughtful letter on demography and political economy, he included an incredibly detailed description of an American weasel, comparing it with some of Buffon's European quadrupeds. Madison to TJ, 19 June 1786, *JMP*, 9:76–81.

24. John Sullivan to TJ, 16 Apr. 1787, *TJP*, 11:296.

25. TJ to Buffon, 1 Oct. 1787, ibid., 12:194; Martin, *Jefferson: Scientist*, 187.

26. TJ to Joseph Willard, 24 Mar. 1789, *TJP*, 14:699; TJ to Bishop James Madison, 1 Apr. 1798, ibid., 30:236; Palisot de Beauvois to TJ, 25 Apr. 1798, ibid., 30:293–97; *Transactions of the American Philosophical Society* 4 (1799): 246–60.

27. Charles Coleman Sellers, *Mr. Peale's Museum: Charles Willson Peale and the First Popular Museum of Natural Science and Art* (New York, 1980), 123–58.

28. Martin, *Jefferson: Scientist*, 191; Echeverria, *Mirage in the West*, 65. William Carmichael, who was present, told Jefferson about the dinner party. Carmichael to TJ, 15 Oct. 1787, *TJP*, 12:240–41.

29. Martin, *Jefferson: Scientist*, 210.

30. TJ, *Notes*, 65.

31. Ibid., 58–62.

32. TJ to Chastellux, 7 June 1785, *TJP*, 8:184–86.

33. Rev. James Madison to TJ, 28 Dec. 1786, ibid., 10:643.

34. TJ, *Notes*, 162.

35. *JMP*, 9:17.

36. Samuel Williams, *Natural and Civil History of Vermont,* 2nd ed., 2 vols. (Burlington, 1809), 1:90–91.

37. Constantin-François Volney, *A View of the Soil and Climate of the United States of America, translated, with Occasional Remarks by C. B. Brown* (Philadelphia, 1804).

38. American Philosophical Society Memorial to U.S. Congress, 7–10 Jan. 1800, *TJP,* 31:294.

39. Jeremy Belknap, *The History of New Hampshire,* 3 vols. (1784–91; Dover, 1812), 3:171–72.

40. TJ to Volney, 8 Feb. 1805, *TJW,* 1155.

41. Melville, *Mardi* (1849; New York, 1982), 1171.

Decadents Abroad

Reconstructing the Typical Colonial American in London in the Late Colonial Period

JULIE FLAVELL

The figure of the alienated American colonist in London on the eve of independence has become a historian's stereotype. Whether the subject is political radicals immersed in the unreal hothouse of City politics, southern planters who felt socially discounted, or pretty much any colonist scandalized by the swirling cauldron of political and cultural corruption that was the empire's capital, the analytical framework of "alienated provincial" is a well-established one. Even Benjamin Franklin, whose love of London is well known, admittedly remained at the margins of its society, unable to gain acceptance in its best circles.

From our vantage point, it is natural that such a stereotype should emerge. Since we know that national independence was right around the corner for Americans, it makes sense to characterize colonists visiting their ancestral capital as having a shared reaction to the place, albeit a rather negative one. Casting them all in the role of alienated provincial is, in effect, a simple matter of rolling back the "innocents abroad" motif of the nineteenth century to the late colonial period, and it lends historical continuity to an image of Americans abroad that is familiar to us today.

The stereotype is also a necessary corollary to a large body of scholarship that depicts the mainland American colonies in the eighteenth century as sharing a love-hate mentality toward their mother country that was the seedbed of American national identity. Drawing on core-periphery theory to model the relationship between Britain and her Atlantic provinces and pointing to the century-long cultural process of Anglicization that made the colonies both more like one another and more alike in their view of England, scholars have shown that the colonists were deeply conflicted over their desire to aspire to metropolitan standards versus their desire to conserve local norms. This conflicted reaction toward the metropolis was an important catalyst to the growing rift with Britain in the late colonial period. Where the cultural hegemony of the metropolis gave rise to a colonial sense of inferiority, compensatory images emerged of the colonies as refuges of traditional English virtue and simplicity, with the metropolis cast in the role of the corrupt and decadent Old Country.[1]

The adaptive responses of colonists who visited the metropolis ought to be a significant test case for the thesis. But although provincial Americans venturing to London are presumed to have been culturally or socially alienated in many scholarly works, with alienation usually expressed through an extreme sensitivity to corrupt metropolitan lifestyles, no in-depth study of their acculturative encounters there has ever been undertaken.[2]

In this essay I offer a preliminary revision of the stereotype of the alienated provincial in London. It starts by considering the characteristics of the total American presence in London in the 1760s and 1770s and then focuses on one type of colonial visitor in particular, wealthy planters and merchants, whose numbers there were on the rise in the period just before the American Revolution. These colonial visitors, mainly from the colonies south of New England, were the forerunners of the elite American tourists of the nineteenth and early twentieth centuries. Together with their retinue of enslaved black Americans, they were an important presence in London during the late colonial period, and an important corrective to the impression of social alienation. They were part of a growing trend of wealthy provincials moving around the English Atlantic, an integrative trend that was merely interrupted, not stopped, by the American War of Independence.

In the eyes of their English contemporaries, these wealthy visitors came closest to embodying the "typical American" in London, far closer, indeed, than Franklin and his better-remembered circle. In fact, if colonial Americans who ventured to London had been summed up by eighteenth-century Londoners themselves—if contemporary Londoners had generated their own stereotype of visiting colonists—the unflattering soubriquet to emerge would probably have been something like "decadents abroad." This is because American colonists in London on the eve of independence were associated with the decadent lifestyles of Britain's exploitation settlements in America. Benjamin Franklin may have been the most famous colonist to walk London's streets in the late colonial period, but with his white, Yankee persona he was not the most typical.

There is a bias toward a white northern experience in our knowledge of colonials in London on the eve of American independence. This is in part because of the understandable scholarly preoccupation with the politics of the Revolution at the center of empire. Benjamin Franklin is of course the indisputable leading figure here, followed by the American Wilkites, with their close connections to the Boston Sons of Liberty.[3] But the northern bias also reflects the limitations of the historical sources. No figures or records were ever kept on the colonists who came and went in London. Since they were British subjects whose presence in the metropolis was unproblematical, there would have been no reason to do so. Colonial American visitors to London thus remain somewhat elusive, making chance appearances in sources such as diaries, letters, and incidental lists. For this reason, it is easier to reconstruct the London experiences of colonists who had an institutional affiliation or were involved in an organized activity or connection. Many of these were northerners, for example, individuals connected with the English Dissenters in London and the Club of Honest Whigs (for whom, writes Colin Bonwick, "America was New England writ large").[4] Of two groups for which we do have lists—the colonial candidates for Anglican ordination and colonial itinerant Quakers traveling to the mother country—most were from the northern or middle colonies.[5] Then there is the roster of talented Pennsylvanians, who for their own reasons have remained in the historical limelight: Benjamin West, the "father of American art," and his American school of artists; Pennsylvania medical students abroad who were intent on founding the first American medical school; scions of Provost William Smith's Philadelphia literary circle, visiting London as the center of British culture and anxious to prove that the colonies could produce their own literature.

That other well-known group, the students at the Inns of Court, might serve as a corrective, with its distinctly southern bias. Out of more than one hundred colonial students attending the Inns from 1755 to 1775, almost three-quarters were from the colonies of Maryland and southward. But it is much more difficult to generalize about planters in London than to reconstruct the experiences of the American Wilkites or the circle of Americans who were associated with Benjamin Franklin and who emerge so vividly from his voluminous correspondence.

Perhaps by default, then, the experiences of northerners in London have become the defining ones for colonists as a whole. No comprehensive study has ever been published of the colonial American presence in London in the late colonial period.[6] Important works that have established the stereotype of colonial residents in London as increasingly alienated in social, political, and cultural terms in the years before the Revolution—notably Pauline Maier's *From Resistance to Revolution,* Michael Kammen's book *A Rope of Sand,* and seminal articles by Paul Langford on the start of the Revolution as seen from London—have focused on politics and political activists. With the important exception of the Virginians Arthur and William

Lee, who were closely connected with the Massachusetts Assembly and the Boston Sons of Liberty, it is colonists from the North whose names figure in these works.[7] Southern colonists in London are seen through the lens of these better-known visitors, even though the numbers would suggest that it should be the other way around. (The southern students at the Inns of Court alone outnumber all the colony agents, Wilkites, and culturally ambitious Philadelphians put together.) Colin Bonwick's assertion in his study of radical English Whigs and their American associates that "the most distinguished families of Virginia, Maryland, and the Carolinas," like the northern colonists who appear in his book, were "indelibly middle class in England" has gone unchallenged.[8]

Recent scholarship has enabled us to fit the medley of colonial types in London into a larger context. A list of colonial Americans in London who can be identified from surviving sources reveals that more than half were from the colonies south of Pennsylvania.[9] The same data reveal that while the northerners in this list went to London for a variety of reasons, southerners went chiefly as leisure travelers, part of the trend of elite tourism that was emerging throughout the English-speaking Atlantic during the eighteenth century. Of course, lists of this kind leave out a great deal. A recent estimate of the colonial American population in London based on a statistical method that compensates for incomplete or missing data indicates that in the early 1770s alone there were at least five hundred white mainland American men in London, more than twice the number appearing in the lists that formed the basis of the calculation.[10] The estimate excludes not only white women and children but also American-born common seamen and black Americans accompanying their white masters to London. These last two groups were a significant presence, but they remain the most elusive in extant sources.

The reasons that colonial Americans went to London were legion. It was the center of the English-speaking world for trade, finance, and banking, the empire's administrative center and biggest port, the fountain of art and literature, the center of scientific endeavor, the chief nursery of music and theater, the leader in journalism and print culture, the model of fashion and good taste, and the home of the Court of St. James. It was also the biggest shopping center in the British Atlantic empire, with shops whose numbers and goods outrivaled even those of Paris. Colony agents, land speculators, printer's and merchant apprentices, aspiring authors, actors, and artists, applicants for holy orders, fund-raisers for the new colleges in the colonies, amateur and commercial botanists, milliners keeping up with the latest fashions—all of these ventured to London in the years before independence.

But only two categories of colonial visitors, those connected with transatlantic trade, whether businessmen or common sailors, and wealthy leisure travelers and their families and servants, numbered in the hundreds. Although the precise numbers of colonists crossing on merchant business or as merchant sailors are uncertain, what is certain is that they grew in proportion to the steady growth of transatlantic trade during the century. What we do know grew much faster, however, was the number of colonists traveling for leisure and tourism. After the Seven Years' War, wealthy colonists began to travel to Britain in unprecedented numbers.[11] This was in part the result of a consumer revolution in America that resulted in the emergence of something like "organized tourism" within the mainland colonies. Wealthy colonists were traveling more as a strictly leisure pursuit, and more were traveling overseas. The packet service from mainland America, which had been initiated after 1755 and had become much safer after the Peace of Paris in 1763 drove French privateers from the sea, facilitated the business.[12]

Thus, the late colonial period marked the emergence of a type of American overseas visitor to Europe whose numbers were destined to far outstrip those of the businessman over the next fifty years. It was the beginning of a trend that has never stopped. Leisure travelers accounted for most of the rise in the number of Americans going to Europe in the nineteenth century. As the packet services improved at the end of the Napoleonic Wars, five thousand Americans on average ventured to Europe annually. The advent of steam travel after 1850 brought the number nearer to thirty thousand. There was a big market in wealthy tourists eager to experience Old World culture, and within the limits of technology the shipping lines were responding to it.[13]

At the start of this trend, in the period between the end of the Seven Years' War and the beginning of the American Revolution, there were probably as many as four hundred of these wealthy Americans in London at any one time.[14] The figure is closer to a thousand if one includes the West Indian absentees, who were still reckoned "Americans" before the War of Independence.[15] This was an impressive showing in the days when an English tourist boom in Paris, just across the English Channel, was numbered in the thousands rather than the tens of thousands.[16]

This was the same set of colonial tourists who increasingly after mid-century made seasonal pilgrimages to mainland American resorts. During the hottest summer months, wealthy colonists from Antigua and Jamaica, South Carolina, Virginia, Maryland, Philadelphia, and New York escaped the terrible climates of the swamp-infested tropics and the dirt of the city and journeyed to spas and summer resorts at places such as Newport, Rhode

Island, Berkeley Warm Springs, Virginia, and Bristol Spring, Pennsylvania. Newport, which was becoming "the Bath of America" in the decade before the Revolution, attracted almost a hundred genteel visitors from the Carolinas, Philadelphia, and the West Indies in 1772. Even Charleston, South Carolina, was apparently a breath of fresh air to the West Indians. Crèvecoeur noted that they flocked there, their health exhausted by "the debilitating nature of their sun, air, and modes of living," hoping for a "revolution of health."[17]

The origins of the mainland elite tourists reflected the chief regional divide of colonial continental America, which was, as John Murrin put it, New England versus everyone else.[18] They were rich genteel merchants and planters from New York, Philadelphia, the Chesapeake, the Carolinas, and Georgia. This was a type that contemporaries recognized was thin on the ground in New England. The exception was Boston, where one could find, in the words of the British merchant Richard Oswald, "Gentlemen, of good Education & manners."[19]

In taking to the sea these colonial elites were doing what they had always done, namely, copying their gentrified English counterparts. The received view in the polite English-speaking world of the eighteenth century was that the only way to acquire gentlemanly polish was to leave home. For the English gentry this meant frequent trips to London and educating their sons (and to a lesser extent their daughters) at boarding schools, university, and, ideally, through Continental travel. The grand tour as the completion of a gentleman's son's education was de rigueur.[20] Indeed, the grand tour could be called an English invention, since it was the English who had the wealth and the personal liberty to wander throughout Europe almost at will.[21] After 1763 more and more well-to-do mainland colonials followed in the footsteps of the English gentry, crossing the Atlantic to experience London society, make the grand tour, and send their children to Eton, Winchester, Oxford, Cambridge, and the Inns of Court.

This is not to say that these trips were purely status-seeking exercises. The business advantages afforded to a planter or merchant who enjoyed an extended stay in the empire's biggest port were of course considerable. And the children of the wealthy often underwent apprenticeships at English merchant houses to launch their business careers. Well-known examples include Henry Laurens, Henry Cruger, and John Hancock. But a sojourn in the mother country offered another, more intangible but very real advantage, especially for the young: the acquisition of the manners and air of an English gentleman. Good manners and gentlemanlike sociability had a very practical advantage in Britain's eighteenth-century empire. A man without a pedigree or an estate could gain an entrée into many English social and business circles if he displayed the manners of a gentleman.[22] The affability and courtesy acquired from a polite education constituted, in effect, the established character of a man of business in eighteenth-century Britain and her American colonies.[23] Those who did not travel tended not to have it, as John Adams admitted when he bemoaned the difference between his fellow New Englanders and the other delegates at the Continental Congress.[24]

These late colonial tourists, then, were not distancing themselves from their native societies. They were becoming more involved in an Atlantic world to which all the colonial communities belonged.[25] And when they reached the metropolis, they quickly became willing participants in another, more short-term trend, London's housing boom of the 1760s.

Staying in Georgian London was very expensive, and this ensured that those who lacked the means would have to travel there without family, keep their visits as short as possible, and, typically, stay in lodgings—the most comfortable arrangement for those who could not afford to set up house for themselves. Benjamin Franklin was in lodgings in Craven Street throughout his seventeen-year sojourn in London. The story of his relationship with his landlady, Margaret Stevenson, and her daughter Polly is well known (the Stevensons became a surrogate family, and one that he seemed to prefer to the Franklins back in Philadelphia). Given the solicitude of his landlady, Franklin was probably at least as comfortable as he would have been in a household of his own. But lodgings of this sort—just a room or two, or at most (as in Franklin's case) a storey of the house to oneself—would never do for the wealthy colonial families who crossed over for an extensive stay. With children and servants in tow, often a coach to keep, and space required for entertaining, wealthier visitors wanted a house.

In 1754 Eliza Lucas Pinckney, of South Carolina, in London with her husband, Charles, took an entire house, fully furnished, in Craven Street. The Pinckneys had wanted an unfurnished house so that they could arrange it to suit their own taste, but as Eliza wrote to a friend, "Would you think it—have not been able to get a tolerable unfurnished house from Temple Barr to Charing Cross so that we are obliged to take a furnished one. 'Tis however a very handsome one and gentilely [*sic*] furnished in a very good street and in the Center of every thing."[26] True, Craven Street was a central location for colony agents like Benjamin Franklin, Charles Pinckney, and Henry Marchant, of Rhode Island, who lodged there in 1771. It was within walking distance of the government offices in Whitehall. And it was techni-cally located in the elegant West End, rather than the City.

But Eliza Pinckney was probably putting a brave face on things. Craven Street was right near busy workaday Charing Cross, where proclamations were read and the pillories stood.[27] Not far away was the Strand, notorious for its prostitutes. In tone at least, it was closer to the world of tradesmen and merchants in the City than to the spacious, elegant residential squares of the West End.

The Peace of Paris a few years later ushered in a new phase of prosperity and optimism, not only for the British empire in general but for London developers in particular. The rich of London were richer and more numerous than ever, and they needed more living space. At mid-century, Oxford Street was still the northern boundary of the West End, with the villages of Marylebone and Paddington standing among farms and fields. It was inevitable that the city would leap this boundary, and the New Road was designed to the north, replacing Oxford Street as London's northern frontier and resulting in the engulfment of these villages. (It was naively contended that the New Road—part of it is known today as Euston Road, with its busy railway stations—would mark the end of London's advance on the countryside.)[28] The elegant urban housing that rapidly sprang up in the area was a few years too late for Eliza Pinckney, but it was there that many of her fellow South Carolinians would purchase houses in the period after 1763.

Berners Street, a short thoroughfare leading directly onto Oxford Street whose existence dates from this time, provides a vital example of a popular residential choice for South Carolinians. Several of its houses were designed by the notable Georgian architect William Chambers, who lived at Number 53.[29] The South Carolina merchant Benjamin Stead lived there with his family. Sir James Wright, South Carolina attorney general and governor of Georgia, lived there with his son, who attended Eton, Cambridge, and the Inns of Court. The wealthy planter Ralph Izard, who had also had a thoroughly English education, settled in Berners Street in the 1770s with his New York wife, Anne Delancey, and their growing family. Izard would later serve the American cause as a Revolutionary diplomat in France and Tuscany, but when he bought his new house in Marylebone he had by all appearances determined to make London his home for life. On this street, whose classical regularity allowed its residents to see every neighbor's comings and goings, lived also the Beresfords, who were relations of the Izards. The Beresfords, of South Carolina, were intermarried with the Delanceys. The widowed Beresford was in London to oversee her son's education at the Inns of Court, and her two grown daughters took the opportunity to see the capital. Manigaults, Applebys, and Austins came and went as well, visiting fellow Carolinians.[30]

South Carolinians were not the only Americans to choose Berners Street. Stephen Sayre, of New York, whose bank on Oxford Street was thriving in the early 1770s, lived there with his mistress, Mrs. Pearson.[31] Just around the corner, in Newman Street, lived the families of the artist Benjamin West, by now history painter to the king, and Lloyd Dulany, the wealthy Maryland planter.

The Brailsfords complete the known South Carolinian contingent in Berners Street. Samuel Brailsford went to London with his family but prudently shipped his son and daughter off to nearby boarding schools.[32] Brailsford was a wealthy transatlantic merchant with extensive business connections in Bristol. His house in Berners Street, a considerable walk from the coffeehouses and business district of the old City, marks him— along with Benjamin Stead—as one of the new breed of London merchants who no longer wished to live above their own countinghouses. This was a recent trend, starting roughly at the accession of George III. Rich business-men who wished to insulate their families from the social pollution of the City were purchasing homes in the West End. Many City merchants held out against this practice until well into the nineteenth century, and its obvi-ous pretensions to gentility aroused derision among City dwellers. Perhaps the derision was deserved, for the issue was not simply one of money. The wealthy West Indian Beeston Long was content to live above his offices in Bishopsgate, in the heart of the City.[33] The Virginian William Lee and Joshua Johnson, of Maryland, both tobacco merchants, also followed the old practice, keeping their homes and their countinghouses at a single address on Tower Hill.

But numerous colonial Americans proved that they were not on the side of social democracy with respect to this issue. The Allens of Pennsylvania, in London while James and Andrew studied at the Inns of Court, were obliged upon their arrival to stay at David Barclay's house in Cheapside, in the heart of the business district. But a City merchant's house was hardly a fashion-able address. Andrew and his brother quickly arranged something for their father, Chief Justice William Allen, and their two sisters in "a rather more agreeable Part of the Town," Golden Square in Westminster.[34] The Barclay house had been used by three successive monarchs to view the Lord Mayor's Parade. George III and his new wife Charlotte had watched the parade from the Barclay's balcony in 1761, just a few years previous to the Allens' visit. But even this apparently was not enough to redeem the address in the eyes of the visiting Pennsylvanians.[35]

When James Boswell saw the new developments in Marylebone in 1772, he remarked on their remoteness from the rest of the town, commenting that now "people live at such a distance from each other that it is very inconvenient for them to meet."[36] Georgian London was a place where one could walk from one end to another in a couple of hours. The urban sprawl was beginning to change that, and as Boswell noted, it had a social impact. Boswell was exaggerating a little; Marylebone is not all that far from the rest of the old City, but its relative exclusivity probably added to its attractions for the new wealth that was anxious to distance itself from trade and the City.

Marylebone is best known as the home of those other erstwhile Americans, the West Indians. West Indian sugar planters had always come to London in greater numbers than their mainland American counterparts, but despite the longer history of absenteeism, they were still considered nouveau riche by Londoners.[37] They had the money to live in the metropolis—they have been called the equivalent of today's oil barons—and their island homes lacked the necessary educational institutions for their children. As a result, they, more than mainland Americans, often came to regard England as their home. The rate of absenteeism from the British West Indies was frequently deplored by contemporaries as detrimental to the development of the colonies (though the actual figures were largely guesswork). But West Indian absentees were no different from mainland colonists in one respect: their numbers in London increased after the Peace of Paris.[38]

It was because they availed themselves of so many of the new houses that sprang up north of Oxford Street that the district came to be associated with them. In Berners Street lived Mrs. Susanna Vaughan, a lady whose family had a fortune founded in slave labor in the West Indies.[39] Far grander was Portman Square, less than a mile away, where the wealthy Jamaican Lady Home lived. Her superb residence, designed by Robert Adam and deceptively described as a terraced house, had one of the finest interiors in Georgian London.[40] In the years before the American Revolution, other great families whose wealth was founded on sugar lived in Portman Square, and Home House was something of a gathering place for West Indian absentees.[41] Scions of the Beckford family of Jamaica were to be found in Soho Square, which was much closer to Berners and Newman streets. There stood the house of William Beckford, Georgian London's most famous West Indian, who was twice lord mayor of London.[42] His brother Richard bought the house next door when he was elected MP for Bristol.

The neighborhoods of Marylebone and Soho brought together the same wealthy colonial elites who met at mainland American resorts during the summer season. The same names that were announced in the newspapers of Newport, Rhode Island—Wright, Izard, and many others from mainland

America and the island colonies—were found on the doorplates of these London suburbs.[43] The cross-colony sociability that took place in the resorts of America continued in the metropolis. In effect, a preexisting social circle was in place for colonists of this rank who ventured to London. A look at the families and friends of a few well-known figures will serve to illustrate.

The South Carolina planter and merchant Henry Laurens hardly needs an introduction. In 1771 the future president of the Continental Congress crossed the Atlantic with his three sons, John, Harry, and Jemmy, who were to undergo an English education. Like most wealthy Carolinians, Laurens had relatives in England. He was related by marriage to the Moultries, who followed the practice of educating their children in England. One young Moultrie attended school with Harry Laurens at Islington, near London. Another was studying at the Inns of Court.[44] The Charlestonian John Moultrie was heir to the Shropshire estate of George Austin, Laurens's English business partner. As a friend of the Izards and the Steads, Laurens was also a constant visitor in Berners Street. Not far away, in Broad Street in Soho, was the house of another close friend and business associate, William Manning. Manning was a West Indian merchant whose family had long been established in St. Kitts.[45]

At the Manning house, South Carolinians and West Indians mixed promiscuously. Here Steadman Rawlins's sons, from the island of St. Kitts, played with young Harry Laurens during school holidays.[46] Laurens's eldest son, John, eventually married one of the Manning girls, and so did Benjamin Vaughan, of Jamaica, whose father was a London merchant.[47] Richard Oliver, of Antigua, and John Baker, of St. Kitts, were also part of the Laurens-Manning circle.[48]

Laurens's American associates in London were preponderantly from South Carolina and the West Indies, but he knew many other Americans. He knew many wealthy Pennsylvanians, among them the Biddles, the Fishers, and the Whartons. Nicholas Biddle was in London while Laurens was there, looking into a career in the Royal Navy. The merchant William Fisher, Laurens's Philadelphia business partner, sent his son Billy to school in England under Laurens's protection in 1771. Another Philadelphia acquaintance was Joseph Wharton Jr., son of the Quaker Joseph Wharton (dubbed the "merchant prince" by Carl Bridenbaugh), who was in London by the end of the Laurens's stay.[49] In addition, Laurens knew Arthur Lee, of Virginia, and the Delanceys of New York. And his American connections ensured that his English associates were on an equivalent social level. While on a jaunt to Bath, for example, he mixed with Lord Charles Greville Montagu, who had just completed his term as governor of South Carolina, and Sir William Draper, who was by then married to one of the ubiquitous Delanceys.[50]

Ralph Izard's London social network was still more formidable. In addition to his friends and relations in Berners Street, his uncles Edward Fenwick and William Middleton lived in England. Their sons, like Ralph, were receiving an English education. The Middletons owned property in Carolina, England, Barbados, and Jamaica.[51] These wealthy planters had aristocratic connections. William Middleton the younger eventually became a Member of Parliament and a baronet. John Izard Wright Jr., a distant cousin of Ralph's, also inherited a baronetcy.[52] Ralph's cousin Sarah Izard married Lord William Campbell, the youngest son of the fourth Duke of Argyll, who would be the last royal governor of South Carolina.[53] Through her, he knew the Duke of Richmond.[54] And Izard was connected through marriage to General Thomas Gage, the second son of Viscount Gage, who is better known as the British commander in chief at the start of the Revolutionary War. Gage was married to a cousin of the Delanceys'. Among the military upper crust, Izard also knew Admiral Sir Peter Warren, the hero of Louisbourg, who had married yet another Delancey.[55] The Izards and the Delanceys knew Horace Walpole, of Strawberry Hill.[56] Despite the well-known connection between many Carolina elites—including Izard—and the Rockingham party, Ralph's contacts were sufficiently high ranking to allow him personal access to cabinet ministers during the mounting crisis in 1775, when he and others sought to avert all-out war between Britain and her colonies.[57]

It was not only South Carolinians who profited from a preexisting social circle when they arrived in England. The New Yorker Henry Cruger went to Bristol, England, to undertake a merchant apprenticeship as a young man. He served his merchant apprenticeship with a kinsman; the Cruger family business had branches in England, America, and the West Indies. Cruger married the daughter of Samuel Peach, of Bristol. He eventually moved to London to act as MP for Bristol, where his father-in-law's cousin, another Samuel Peach, lived. Cousin Samuel was a London merchant and an MP. He was married to Christina Cox, of Virginia.[58] As the son of a well-to-do New York family, Cruger also knew the Delanceys, whom one seemed to find everywhere in England.[59]

When the Lee brothers Arthur, Francis Lightfoot, Richard Henry, Thomas, and William, of Virginia, went to England for their schooling, they were looked after by their maternal cousins the Ludwells, who lived in London. William later married Hannah Ludwell. Their sister Alice Lee, also in England for her education, married the Pennsylvanian William Shippen, who was in London studying medicine.[60] The Shippen connection must have opened more doors in London for the Lees; when Peggy Shippen and her husband, Benedict Arnold, went to London after the war, she already had English relatives there.[61] Hannah Ludwell's sister Lucy married John Paradise, a distinguished English philologist. The two lived an elegant lifestyle in London that was financed by what one scholar called their "spectacular improvidence."[62] And the Lees had a very well-connected cousin in London in the person of Edmund Jenings, of Maryland, who owned property not only in Maryland but also in Yorkshire and Virginia. Jenings, who had a leisurely and largely unnecessary legal practice, had been educated at Eton, Cambridge, and the Middle Temple and was a friend of William Eden, who headed the British secret service during the War of Independence.[63]

Delancey, Vaughan, Laurens, Lee, Izard, Cruger, Moultrie, Rawlins, Wright, Beresford, Jenings, Middleton, Fenwick—all of these names and many others appeared on the rolls of the Inns of Court in the late colonial and Revolutionary period, marking each family as among the wealthy elites of Britain's American empire. These elite colonial types, with trade and social networks that crisscrossed the English Atlantic, lived in an arc that stretched from Boston and New York to the Caribbean. The number of those who traveled to the mother country for education and pleasure increased as their native provinces descended toward the tropics. The Caribbean colonies probably sent as many again as the total from America's mainland, perhaps more. The cultural reality of New England's image as the deviant region in the Anglo-American Atlantic world is reflected in the fact that only three from that region enrolled at the Inns of Court between 1755 and 1775.

Benjamin West's painting *The Cricketers* is an attractive illustration of the cross-colony sociability to be found in London during the heyday of Britain's American empire. Painted for Ralph Izard in 1764, when he was just a young man, it shows him leaning on his cricket bat—he was reputed to be an excellent sportsman—and next to him on his left is young Andrew Allen, of Pennsylvania (the same Allen who took a house in Golden Square for his wealthy merchant father and sisters when they went to London). Seated next to Andrew are the Carolinian Ralph Wormeley and Andrew's brother James Allen. To Izard's right is a young member of the large Beckford clan of Jamaica.[64] These young men were in England for their education. The Allens were studying law at the Inns of Court when they joined Ralph Izard and his circle.

In light of the patterns of intercolonial sociability illustrated here, it is no surprise that young William Franklin, of Pennsylvania, met and married a West Indian heiress while he was in London. William's marriage to the wealthy Elizabeth Downes, of Barbados, has always been the subject of curiosity, partly because of Benjamin Franklin's apparent disapproval of the match. Why did William marry her? Was it for money? Was it for social position? And who exactly was she?[65] Whatever mystery may surround young Franklin's personal motives, there is nothing surprising in the circumstance of a Pennsylvania student at the Inns of Court making the acquaintance of a West Indian woman and marrying her. Shippens married Lees, Allens married Delanceys, Hallowells married Vaughans, so why should Franklins not marry Downeses?

We have been looking at these Atlantic elites, who enjoyed the advantage of a social circle that was already in place upon their arrival in London. Of course, as remarked at the start of this essay, there were many types of colonial visitors in London, and their visits varied in business, social, and cultural terms. There were merchants on business who made (by eighteenth-century standards) "flying visits," staying only a few weeks and taking only a superficial impression of the empire's capital. There were sailors who disembarked at the London docks and simply roved the streets, taking in the curiosities. Some people arrived literally burdened with letters of introduction.[66] Some arrived with none at all, as did Benjamin Franklin on his first voyage to London, tricked into making the journey by Governor Keith. Some looked up rich relatives, who, once found, accepted them as long-lost cousins.[67] Others discovered long-lost English relations who were too poor to take them in.[68] Some had business at Whitehall and St. James that ended in heartbreaking failure. Others were dazzled by their own success. Some found they could not get so much as an invitation to dinner from a London merchant. Others were literally besieged by guests as soon as they set foot on English soil.[69] There were colonists from the North and the South, the backwoods and the coast, socially isolated or not, of different religions, ethnicities, and races.

Can we make generalizations about the acculturative stress felt by all these American colonial types when they ventured to London, for example, by describing them as alienated? The attempt poses a significant challenge. Viewed from the perspective of London, different colonies and colonial types clearly experienced different levels of social and cultural integration with the mother country. They did not come from one province, but from a string of very different ones that were ranged around the English Atlantic. And the reality of sectionalism, which was to be the bane of the new republic, is apparent in the histories of the various types who ventured there.

In addition, these visitors were not yet foreigners. They were British provincials, and as such their adjustments to migration within what was still a shared national culture must be subtler and more difficult to uncover.[70]

In the quest for a common American response to the center of empire on the eve of American independence, much has been made of comments on the corruption and luxury of London life found in letters of colonial visitors.[71] But English provincials also passed such strictures on life in the Great City. That colonists spoke in deprecating terms of London corruption meant little in an age when such comments were fashionable clichés. Jane Austen, on a jaunt to London in the 1790s, wrote jokingly to her sister, "Here I am once more in this Scene of Dissipation & vice, and I begin already to find my Morals corrupted." This was the sort of remark that was expected of visitors to London in the eighteenth century, whether American colonists or what Franklin referred to as the "honest rough British gentry" of the countryside.[72]

If the wealthy colonial visitors to London after 1763 chimed in with the provincial cliché about metropolitan corruption and even indulged in a degree of self-congratulation on the notion that the colonies had escaped it, this does not necessarily mean that they embodied a stereotype of provincial alienation. Their levels of social integration, as we have seen, make this unlikely. London was the epitome of modern living in the eighteenth-century Atlantic world, and it was bound to provoke strong responses, from Dr. Johnson's eulogies to Dr. Price's strictures on "the Great Wen." Henry Laurens made a joke of the contradictory views he encountered:

> In a morning's Conversation with one intelligent sensible Friend, one too who is near the Helm often observing Movements and Pointings of the State Compass, [he] had lamented to me, Alas, Sir! This Country is undone. We shall soon be crush'd by our own Weight. We are sinking under Corruption & shall become a Province of some neighbouring State, or be reduced to a State of Dependance upon our own Colonies. And in the Evening another who is equally versant in Affairs of Government, and as well acquainted with the general State of Europe, had exulted in the Thought that England was the happiest Kingdom upon Earth. See, Sir, said he, as we were riding around the Skirts of the City, and pointing at innumerable new Buildings, large and elegant, which are rising in a hundred different Places, See the Marks of our Poverty & Distress. Great Britain is yet but in her Infancy, and even this Great City very far from it's Zenith.[73]

Laurens and his wealthy, traveled friends had a sophisticated understanding of London's commanding—and ambiguous—position as a cultural modernizer in the English-speaking world of the eighteenth century.[74]

Large as the group of wealthy mainland colonists in London was, we have seen that it did not comprise all, or even the majority, of the Americans to be found walking London's streets. But there is evidence that colonists of this type alone, together with their African American servants, were numerous enough to attract public attention in the metropolis. In 1765 Dr. John Fothergill wrote angrily, "How many people are there, and those too of no small Figure, who know no Difference between the Inhabitants of North America, and those of the West-India Islands?" Fothergill wrote this in a pamphlet opposing the Stamp Act. Like others in his Club of Honest Whigs, he was embarrassed by the fact that white colonists, while appealing for their liberties, owned slaves. He assured Londoners that the "Northern North Americans," those north of Maryland, lived lives of "Diligence and Frugality" on small farms. And he blamed the confusion on colonists from the mainland's "Southern District." These wealthy colonists in the streets of London, admitted Fothergill, did seem like the West Indians, with their "Shew and Extravagance" and their retinue of "dark Attendants."[75]

Dr. Fothergill's remark touched upon another very important colonial presence in London, and one integral to that of the wealthy white colonists, namely, the African Americans. White mainland and West Indian planters' practice of taking black servants to London was common. Their numbers can only be guessed at, but like the white colonial population, they were growing. The black population of Georgian London as a whole grew steadily throughout the eighteenth century. By the eve of the American Revolution it was large enough to attract the notice of public figures such as Sir John Fielding, who saw London's blacks as an addition to the City's already numerous poor. Contemporary estimates suggested that there were fourteen thousand blacks living in England, most of them in London. These were not all Americans. Some were first-generation Africans who were spin-offs of the slave trade. Some were native-born Londoners. Of the Americans, many were servants, but others would have been black merchant seamen.[76]

Nevertheless, collectively they can only have added to the impression—so deplored by Dr. Fothergill—of America as a string of plantation colonies, and of the typical American as a wealthy planter. Londoners had good reason to be much more conscious of Britain's plantation colonies than they were of the colonies to the north. The products of these colonies had transformed Britain's economy and way of life in the past 150 years. Evidence of their existence greeted one everywhere in London's streets. They were eaten, smoked, snorted, and drunk daily in the empire's capital. Tobacco, sugar, and rum were everywhere, advertised in the newspapers, sold in shops, puffed and consumed in taverns, coffeehouses, and drawing rooms. Snuff-taking was at an all-time high. Most of the tobacco came from the Chesapeake. Most of the rum came from the West Indies. The goods from these tropical and semi-tropical colonies were continuously being unloaded at London's busy wharves.[77] Along with the products came the slaves who worked the plantations. London had been a slaving port since the seventeenth century. For sheer visibility in the streets of London, nothing from the northern colonies could compete with all this.

As Dr. Fothergill hinted, all this was not good for America's image. The eighteenth-century stereotype of the plantation colonies as seedbeds of decadence, cruelty, and depravity was widespread. Fothergill himself bought into it wholeheartedly. Still raging at the mistaken idea that most mainland Americans were wealthy planters, he took a swipe at the lifestyles of the West Indians:

> Bred for the most Part at the Breast of a Negro Slave; surrounded in their Infancy with a numerous Retinue of these dark Attendants, they are habituated by Precept and Example, to Sensuality, Selfishness, and Despotism. Of those sent over to this Country for their Education, few totally emerge from their first Habitudes; view them as Sons, Husbands, Fathers; as Friends, Citizens, and Men, what Examples! Splendor, Dress, Shew, Equipage, every thing that can create an Opinion of their Importance, is exerted to the utmost of their Credit. They are thought rich, and they are so indeed, at the Expence of the poor Negroes.

The challenge for Dr. Fothergill was to persuade his English readers that mainland Americans were substantially different. If the British people were to become better informed about the mainland colonies, he wrote defensively, it would prevent them "from inferring, that because an opulent West Indian vies in Glare with a Nobleman of the first Distinction, therefore a poor American Farmer is able to bear the same heavy Load of Taxes, or ought to be placed in the same scale of Ability."[78]

Dr. Fothergill was not likely to succeed in diverting Londoners' attention from the mainland exploitation colonies. Not only did Londoners see more and more wealthy planters and black servants in the streets but they saw a new form of oppression and violence seep into their everyday life that was firmly connected with both the West Indies and North America: the practice of slave-keeping. This exotic import, together with its effect on English society, was attracting public attention in the late colonial period.

Slavery had no clear legal status in England, but slave owners imported the practice with impunity. Slaves were openly bought and sold through the newspapers. A "Negro Girl, aged about fifteen years" was advertised for sale in the *Public Ledger* in 1767. A "well made, good-tempered Black Boy" who had "lately had the smallpox" was advertised for sale to "any Gentleman" in a London paper of 1769. In 1763 the *Gentleman's Magazine* described the sale of a black boy by auction on English soil as "perhaps the first instance of the kind in a free country."[79]

The determination of London's slave owners to keep hold of their forbidden property was obvious. Slaves from wealthy London households wore copper padlocked collars engraved with the names of their masters. Runaway slaves were advertised in the London papers. In 1768 a member of the large Beckford clan, living in Pall Mall, published an ad for a slave boy who had disappeared. A slave girl ran away from her mistress in Hatton Garden, and a reward was offered for her return. A "Negro Man" absconded from his master near Temple Bar and was promised "all the good Usage he has hitherto experienced" if he returned.[80]

Slaves who would not return willingly to the colonies were sometimes forcibly removed from the kingdom, causing public scenes. Slaves were bound, gagged, and dragged away when their masters deemed it necessary. A particularly sordid account got into the London newspapers in the early 1770s: A runaway slave was overpowered and forced on board a ship in the Thames, bound for the West Indies. Before anyone could stop him, he shot himself in the head. This episode provided the inspiration for Thomas Day's popular poem appearing in 1773, "The Dying Negro." The whole issue of forced removal came to a head in 1772 with the much-publicized Somerset case, in which a Virginia slave successfully challenged his master's right to return him to America.

John Fothergill might protest, but there was no reason for Londoners to make nice distinctions between mainland and Caribbean colonies with respect to slaveholding. After all, slavery was found throughout the colonies, and seen from the distance of Britain, the colonies all looked much the same. The celebrated Somerset was from Boston, not the notorious West Indies. The London newspapers, which reported details of slave atrocities and slave uprisings, made no distinction between the mainland plantation colonies and the colonies to the north. In 1763, for example, the London papers ran a story of a young white lady in Massachusetts who was knocked down with a hot flat-iron by a black servant, then brutally axed to death. Phillis Wheatley, who traveled to London in 1773 as the first slave to become a published poet, was from Massachusetts. The newspapers were quick to remark upon her Boston origins. "The people of Boston boast themselves chiefly on their principles of liberty," argued one. "One such act as the purchase of [Phillis's] freedom, would, in our opinion, have done them more honour than hanging a thousand trees with ribbons and emblems." Although one contemporary argument in defense of slavery was that white people were unfitted to labor in tropical climates, it was observed that in the northern colonies, "tho' the climate in general is so wholesome and temperate, the pernicious practice of slave-holding is become almost general."[81]

Yet despite widespread metropolitan awareness of this uniquely colonial institution, there was no need for colonists to mount a public defense of colonial slaveholding in London, and only rarely did they do so. Despite the odd jibe in the press, the British public was still largely indifferent to the practice. The anti-slavery movement would not become widespread in Britain until after American independence. In fact, at the same time that the Somerset case was under review, Richard Cumberland's play *The West-Indian* was a hit on the London stage. Cumberland, who was one of the first playwrights to depict the provincial types of Britain's empire, struck a chord with both British and colonial audiences.[82] Londoners took to heart his main character, Belcour, a loveable West Indian youth who had to travel to London to learn that he must not beat his inferiors with a rattan cane.[83] Belcour, the planter and slave owner, was accepted as an English hero with a twist by London audiences. It was not until later in the century that West Indian planters would become confirmed villains in the metropolis. And the play was a favorite with Americans visiting Britain. It was performed at Edinburgh University, in Scotland, in 1772, "at the desire of the West Indian and American students."[84]

But the conflation of the West Indies and the mainland colonies in metropolitan minds did bear a strange fruit that aroused much resentment among colonists. Visiting Americans frequently reported that English people thought that most of the colonists were of African descent. There is plenty of evidence that this was a common impression in England, no doubt the result of the fact that most ordinary Englishmen, when they thought of the settled parts of America, thought of plantations and slave gangs. The Marylander Daniel Dulany Jr., in England in the 1750s, commented sarcastically, "Perhaps in less than a century, the ministers may know that we inhabit part of a vast continent, and the rural gentry hear that we are not all black."[85]

James Otis, writing from the distance of Boston, complained that "the common people of England" pictured the colonists as "a compound mongrel mixture of English, Indian, and Negro." And in an echo of Dr. Fothergill, he fumed that New England, New York, and Virginia were commonly taken in Britain to be West Indian islands.[86] He spluttered to his English audience, "You think most if not all the Colonists are Negroes and Mulattoes—You are wretchedly mistaken—Ninety nine in a hundred in the northern Colonies are white, and there is as good blood flowing in their veins, save the royal blood, as any in the three kingdoms."[87] Visiting England in 1775, the Bostonian Josiah Quincy was told by a British army officer that two-thirds of the people of Britain "thought the Americans were all Negroes!" English crowds who gathered to gape at American prisoners of war at the beginning of the American Revolution were astonished to find them all white. "Why," cried one, "they look like our people.[88]

Daniel Dulany's wish that a century might see the end of such misconceptions was barely granted. George Catlin, touring London with an American Indian exhibit in the 1840s, joked that he was repeatedly obliged to tell the English public, "The Americans are white, the same colour exactly as the English, and speak the same language, only they speak it a good deal better." In 1862 a New Yorker commented on certain "eccentricities of opinion" of "our dear cousins over here: First, that we Americans are black, certainly not white."[89] English knowledge of the provincial societies, geography, and racial distribution in America was undoubtedly faulty. But the English were correct in their perception of Americans as a multi-racial people, a perception that many white Americans obviously resented. Yet for as long as the notion of Britain's first Atlantic empire survived, of New England as America's deviant region and the colonies to the south as the generic "Americans," that perception would persist.

This essay began with the assertion that if eighteenth-century Londoners were to generate their own stereotype of the typical colonial visitor to London, the unflattering soubriquet that would emerge would probably be "decadents abroad." We have seen that rich white planters and their slaves were the most conspicuous group of colonists in London on the eve of independence. As a final note on the figure these colonists cut in London, some of the rare generalizations made about Americans in London in the late colonial period concerned the sons of these wealthy families. The comments on these youths, who were sent to the metropolis for their education, were not positive. Henry Laurens wrote frankly of "the general censure which the people here pass upon American youth." Laurens would have known: he was charged with overseeing several young Carolinians who were suspected of gadding about in the City's coffeehouses (and worse). James Allen, studying at the Inns of Court, commented that "Americans are particularly remarkable for being wild & Extravagant."[90] William Lee had an unpleasant experience with a young relation sent to school under his care, whom he described as possessing "the full American Idea of extravagance & dissipation." Dr. Fothergill himself privately referred to a Pennsylvania youth sent to him as "a wild, unsubdued, unstable American" who would be better off in England than under the influence of "the warm spirits of America" back home—this after the doctor's public protests about the virtuous colonies north of Maryland.[91]

Each of these remarks reveals that a general impression of colonial Americans in London did exist in the minds of the London circles they frequented, one that embraced a stereotype of a plantation society. And if visiting Americans sometimes thought the metropolis seemed corrupt and decadent, the metropolis apparently thought the same of America. All of this qualifies Linda Colley's remark that white Americans had no recognizable identity in the metropolis during the late colonial period. In fact, they tended to be associated with exploitation settlements, to be seen as rather like West Indians.[92]

This colonial type—what Frank Thistlethwaite calls "America's Atlantic connection"—outlived American independence. For the first half of the nineteenth century, before the developing U.S. economy caused Americans to turn inward, these wealthy Atlantic American types with their preexisting English connections continued to venture to the center of the English-speaking world. The South Carolinians, who are said to have "adhered to British cultural precedents" long after the Revolution, carried on their commitment to education abroad and the grand tour, crossing to London and also to many parts of Europe. After only a brief letup, and despite Jefferson's strictures on the dangers of corruption, American youths continued to seek out a European education, even going abroad to study what was by then technically foreign, English law at the Inns of Court. One of Ralph Izard's sons entered the Middle Temple in the 1790s.[93]

The best-known American authors to travel to England and publish their impressions during the early years of the republic, Washington Irving and James Fenimore Cooper, both had English connections. (Cooper was married to another Delancey and knew the Izards; Irving's family had a business with branches in England and America.) John Quincy Adams, who was married to the only "foreign" First Lady ever to grace the White House, was in fact married to a daughter of Joshua Johnson, of Tower Hill, whom he met while in London in the 1790s. The term *foreign*, which was applied to Louisa Johnson during the U.S. presidential campaign in 2004 (when there was the possibility that John Kerry's wife, Teresa, might be another foreign-born First Lady), would have meant little to Adams's contemporaries. And in an echo of the old, colonial sectionalism, antebellum cosmopolitan planters and wealthy Philadelphians continued the sociability they had enjoyed during the eighteenth century, ignoring the emerging new sectionalism grounded in diverging labor systems.[94] In the 1850s, William Makepeace Thackeray could still recall this type of colonial American visitor in London when he wrote his historical novel *The Virginians,* in which his hero, the tobacco planter Harry Esmond, arrives in London with his black servant, condescends to his City attorney, and looks forward to visiting his aristocratic English relations, who were assuredly not "indelibly middle class."

This wealthy colonial type, whose numbers grew, and continued to grow, even after national independence, provides an alternative model to the historian's colonial stereotype of the "alienated provincial" that anticipates Mark Twain's "innocents abroad" of the nineteenth century. What is indicated is the need for a more sensitive model that allows for variations based on region, race, and social origin in reconstructing the responses of visiting colonists to the metropolis. Perhaps continental America was not, as John Adams claimed, foreordained to become one nation with an inherently exceptionalist and isolationist mentality. The wealthy colonists who integrated metropolitan society so successfully on the eve of American independence suggest another possibility; to ignore their presence is to impose a teleological meaning on the acculturative encounters of Americans with their mother country at the end of the colonial period.

NOTES

The author wishes to thank Richard Dunn, Peter Onuf, Andrew O'Shaughnessy, and Steven Sarson for their comments, encouragement, and advice on various drafts of this essay.

1. For examples of leading scholarship that has employed the core-periphery model or depicted the colonists as in an identity crisis that inhered in a sense of cultural inferiority with respect to the mother country, see John Clive and Bernard Bailyn, "England's Cultural Provinces: Scotland and America," *WMQ* 11 (1954): 200–213; John M. Murrin, "A Roof without Walls: The Dilemma of American National Identity," in *Beyond Confederation: Origins of the Constitution and American National Identity,* ed. Richard Beeman, Stephen Botein, and Edward C. Carter III (Chapel Hill, NC, 1987), 333–48; Richard B. Sher, "Scottish-American Cultural Studies, Past and Present," in *Scotland and America in the Age of Enlightenment,* ed. Sher and Jeffrey R.

Smitten (Edinburgh, 1990), 1–27; Jack P. Greene, "Search for Identity: An Interpretation of the Meaning of Selected Patterns of Social Response in Eighteenth-Century America," in *Imperatives, Behaviors, and Identities: Essays in Early American Cultural History*, ed. Greene (Charlottesville, VA, 1992), 143–73; idem, *The Intellectual Construction of America: Exceptionalism and Identity from 1492 to 1800* (Chapel Hill, NC, 1993), 162–99; and T. H. Breen, "Ideology and Nationalism on the Eve of the American Revolution: Revisions *Once More* in Need of Revising," *JAH* 84 (1997–98): 13–39. For my comments on the limitations of core-periphery theory as a model for uncovering acculturative responses of visiting colonists to the metropolis, see Julie M. Flavell, "The 'School for Modesty and Humility': Colonial American Youth in London and their Parents, 1755–1775," *Historical Journal* 42 (1999): 377–403.

2. For important examples of works that describe colonial visitors' preoccupation with metropolitan corruption, see Bernard Bailyn, *The Ideological Origins of the American Revolution* (Cambridge, MA, 1967), 89–92; and Greene, "Search for Identity," 168. Seminal works in establishing the stereotype of the alienated provincial in Britain by Pauline Maier, Paul Langford, and Michael Kammen are discussed in the text below. Recent works that put forward this view of the colonial experience of the metropolis include Gordon Wood, *The Americanization of Benjamin Franklin* (New York, 2004), 95–97, 113–15 (although Wood follows the view that Franklin himself was an exception to the norm of the threatened provincial in London); see also Trevor Burnard, "The Founding Fathers in Early American Historiography: A View from Abroad," *WMQ* 62 (2005): 754–57, for a very perceptive discussion of recent works that have stressed the importance of a conflicted bipolar provincial mentality in the rise of an embryonic American nationalism.

3. I am not going to list the many biographies of Franklin here. The best-known works on the agents and political activists in London are Michael Kammen, *A Rope of Sand: The Colonial Agents, British Politics, and the American Revolution* (1968; New York, 1974); Jack Sosin, *Agents and Merchants: British Colonial Policy and the Origins of the American Revolution, 1763–1775* (Lincoln, NE, 1965); John Sainsbury, *Disaffected Patriots: London Supporters of Revolutionary America* (Montreal, 1987); and Pauline Maier, *From Resistance to Revolution: Colonial Radicals and the Development of American Opposition to Britain, 1765–1776* (1972; New York, 1974).

4. Colin Bonwick, *English Radicals and the American Revolution* (Chapel Hill, NC, 1977), 44–45.

5. James B. Bell, "Anglican Clergy in Colonial America Ordained by Bishops of London," *Proceedings of the American Antiquarian Society* 83 (1973): 103–60; Susan Lindsey Lively, "Going Home: Americans in Britain, 1740–1776" (PhD diss., Harvard University, 1996), 53.

6. For a descriptive survey of colonial Americans in Britain during the entire colonial period, see William L. Sachse, *The Colonial American in Britain* (Madison, WI, 1956).

7. By Paul Langford, see "British Correspondence in the Colonial Press, 1763–1775: A Study in Anglo-American Misunderstanding before the American Revolution," in *The Press and the American Revolution*, ed. Bernard Bailyn and John B. Hench

(Worcester, MA, 1980). See also idem, "London and the American Revolution," in *London in the Age of Reform,* ed. John Stevenson (Oxford, 1977).

8. Bonwick, *English Radicals and the American Revolution,* 35.

9. The regional origins of Americans in London from 1770 to 1775 were as follows: New England (MA, NH, CT, RI), 17.1%; Middle Colonies (PA, NJ, DE, NY), 25.5%; Upper South (VA, MD, NC),13.2%; and Lower South (SC, GA), 45.1%. The figures corroborate William Sachse's impressionistic assertion of fifty years ago, based on his trawl through archives on the East Coast for his monograph *The Colonial American in Britain,* that most colonists in Britain were from the South. See also *The Papers of Benjamin Franklin,* ed. L. W. Labaree et al., 37 vols. (New Haven, CT, 1959–2003); *The Papers of Henry Laurens,* ed. George C. Rogers Jr. et al., 16 vols. (Columbia, SC., 1974–2003); E. A. Jones, *American Members of the Inns of Court* (London, 1924); and Register of Emigrants, Treasury Papers (PRO), 1773–1775.

10. Julie M. Flavell and Gordon Hay, "Using Capture-Recapture Methods to Reconstruct the American Population in London," *Journal of Interdisciplinary History* 32 (2001): 47–49.

11. Ibid., 38; Sachse, *Colonial American in Britain,* 18, 32, 123, 150; Michael Kraus, *The Atlantic Civilization: Eighteenth Century Origins* (Ithaca, NY, 1949), ch. 2. Two lists of American visitors to London corroborate the long-standing impression of increased colonial travel to the metropolis after 1760: Susan Lively's list of Americans in Britain from 1740 to 1776 ("Going Home," 35); and my own unpublished database of mainland Americans and West Indians in Britain from 1755 to 1775.

12. Barbara G. Carson, "Early American Tourists and the Commercialization of Leisure," in *Of Consuming Interests: The Style of Life in the Eighteenth Century,* ed. Cary Carson, Ronald Hoffman, and Peter J. Albert (Charlottesville, VA, 1994), 374; Ian K. Steele, *The English Atlantic, 1675–1740: An Exploration of Communication and Community* (New York, 1986), 10.

13. Foster Rhea Dulles, *Americans Abroad: Two Centuries of European Travel* (Ann Arbor, MI, 1964), 27, 44.

14. The figure is based on the assumption that at least half of the estimated population of 500 white adult males cited above were well-to-do colonists from New York, Pennsylvania, and the southern colonies. But wealthy colonists of this type were able to afford to travel to London as families and commonly did so. For example, there were at least fifty South Carolinian families living in London in the late colonial period. See Jack P. Greene, "Colonial South Carolina and the Caribbean Connection," in Greene, *Imperatives, Behaviors, and Identities,* 84. There are many examples of wealthy colonial families in London from the other mainland colonies, but they have never been quantified. It is apparent that their numbers increased as their colony of origin moved southward. Since the estimate of 250 wealthy Americans in London does not include women or minors, I am factoring them in to reach a suggested total of about 400.

15. Trevor Burnard, "Passengers Only: The Extent and Significance of Absenteeism in Eighteenth Century Jamaica," *Atlantic Studies* 1 (2004): 189.

16. Lynne Withey, *Grand Tours and Cook's Tours: A History of Leisure Travel 1750 to 1915* (London, 1998), 6.

17. Carl Bridenbaugh, "Baths and Watering Places of Colonial America," *WMQ* 3 (1946): 151–81; idem, "Colonial Newport as a Summer Resort," *Collections of the Rhode Island Historical Society* 26 (1933): 10, 23; J. Hector St. John de Crèvecoeur, *Letters from an American Farmer and Sketches of Eighteenth Century America*, ed. Albert E. Stone (London, 1968), 167.

18. Murrin, "Roof without Walls," 343.

19. Richard Oswald, "Sketch of an Examination at the Bar of the House," enclosure in a letter from Oswald to Lord Dartmouth, 27 Feb. 1775, Staffordshire Record Office, Dartmouth MSS, D(W)1778/II/1165.

20. Peter Roebuck, *Yorkshire Baronets, 1640–1760: Families, Estates and Fortunes* (Oxford, 1980), 53.

21. Withey, *Grand Tours and Cook's Tours*, 7.

22. Trevor Burnard, *Creole Gentlemen: The Maryland Elite, 1691–1776* (New York, 2002), 231.

23. John Brewer, "Commercialization and Politics," in *The Birth of a Consumer Society: The Commercialization of Eighteenth-Century England*, ed. Neil Mckendrick, John Brewer, and J. H. Plumb (London, 1982), 214.

24. JA to Abigail Adams, 3 Aug. 1776, in *Letters of Delegates to Congress, 1774–1789*, ed. Paul H. Smith et al., 25 vols. (Washington, DC, 1976–2000), 4:611.

25. Steele, *English Atlantic*, 277–78.

26. Eliza Lucas Pinckney, *The Letterbook of Eliza Lucas Pinckney, 1739–1762*, ed. Elise Pinckney (Columbia, SC, 1997), 80.

27. Ben Weinreb and Christopher Hibbert, eds., *The London Encyclopedia* (London, 1983), 142.

28. John Summerson, *Georgian London* (1945; Cambridge, MA, 1978), 165; Peter Thorold, *The London Rich: The Creation of a Great City from 1666 to the Present* (1999; London, 2001), 133, 146, 151.

29. Weinreb and Hibbert, *London Encyclopedia*, 61.

30. *Papers of Henry Laurens*, 8:107n, 9:xiii, 647n; Jones, *American Members of the Inns of Court*, 16, 229.

31. John Alden, *Stephen Sayre: American Revolutionary Adventurer* (Baton Rouge, LA, 1983), 46.

32. *Papers of Henry Laurens*, 8:148, 307, 326.

33. Summerson, *Georgian London*, 64; Thorold, *London Rich*, 19, 142.

34. Andrew Allen to Benjamin Chew, 2 July 1763, Chew Papers, Historical Society of Pennsylvania, Philadelphia.

35. Christopher Hibbert, *George III: A Personal History* (1998; London, 1999), 51.

36. James Boswell, quoted in Thorold, *London Rich*, 138.

37. James Raven, *Judging New Wealth: Popular Publishing and Responses to Commerce in England, 1750–1800* (Oxford, 1992), 221–22, 228, 245–56.

38. Thorold, *London Rich*, 131, 142; Burnard, "Passengers Only," 179–80.

39. *Papers of Henry Laurens,* 8:329n. I am grateful to Peter D. G. Thomas for information regarding the Vaughan family of Goldengrove.

40. Weinreb and Hibbert, *London Encyclopedia,* 402–3. Home House, still standing, is now used by the Courtauld Institute of Art.

41. Thorold, *London Rich,* 142–44.

42. Weinreb and Hibbert, *London Encyclopedia,* 816.

43. Bridenbaugh, "Colonial Newport as a Summer Resort," 6.

44. *Papers of Henry Laurens,* 7:544–45; Gregory D. Massey, *John Laurens and the American Revolution* (Columbia, SC, 2000), 9; Jones, *American Members of the Inns of Court,* 161.

45. Massey, *John Laurens and the American Revolution,* 41.

46. *The Diary of John Baker, Barrister of the Middle Temple, Solicitor-General of the Leeward Islands,* ed. Philip C. Yorke (London, 1931), 16, 195, 428, 455. Like so many other rich Atlantic merchants—the Carolinian James Crokatt, for example—Manning also had a country house in the London area.

47. Vaughan lived in Mincing Lane, close to Manning's countinghouse in St. Mary Axe—all near Cornhill and the business district. On Vaughan's address, see *Papers of Henry Laurens,* 8:327n. On Manning's addresses, see *Diary of John Baker,* 16.

48. *Papers of Henry Laurens,* 8:121n.

49. Ibid., 7:567, 558–59; *Papers of Benjamin Franklin,* 18:84; Carl Bridenbaugh and Jessica Bridenbaugh, *Rebels and Gentlemen: Philadelphia in the Age of Franklin* (1942; Westport, CT, 1978), 232.

50. *Papers of Henry Laurens,* 9:224–26.

51. Andrew O'Shaughnessy, *An Empire Divided: The American Revolution and the British Caribbean* (Philadelphia, 2000), 17; Sachse, *Colonial American in Britain,* 189.

52. *Papers of Benjamin Franklin,* 21:158; Jones, *American Members of the Inns of Court,* 224.

53. *Diary of John Baker,* 308, 429; *Correspondence of Mr. Ralph Izard of South Carolina,* ed. Anne Izard Deas (New York, 1844), 193; Maurie D. McInnis, *In Pursuit of Refinement: Charlestonians Abroad, 1740–1860* (Columbia, SC, 1999), 108.

54. See *The Yale Edition of Horace Walpole's Correspondence,* ed. Wilmarth S. Lewis, 39 vols. (New Haven, CT, 1937–), 6:63.

55. Julian Gwyn, *An Admiral for America: Sir Peter Warren, Vice Admiral of the Red, 1703–1752* (Gainesville, FL, 2004), 22–23; *Papers of Henry Laurens,* 9:394.

56. See *Yale Edition of Horace Walpole's Correspondence,* 6:63; 32:68, 98; 33:104.

57. Rebecca Starr, *A School for Politics: Commercial Lobbying and Political Culture in Early South Carolina* (Baltimore, 1998), 61; Julie M. Flavell, "American Patriots in London and the Quest for Talks, 1774–1775," *Journal of Imperial and Commonwealth History* 20 (1992): 335–69.

58. Julie Flavell, "Cruger, Henry (1739–1827)," in *Oxford Dictionary of National Biography,* ed. H. C. G. Matthew and Brian Harrison, 60 vols. (Oxford, 2004), 14:516–17; John Brooke, "Cruger, Henry (1739–1827, of Bristol," in *The History of Parliament: The House of Commons, 1754–1790,* ed. Lewis Namier and John Brooke,

3 vols. (London, 1964), 2:280–82. See also J. A. Cannon, "Peach, Samuel, MP," in ibid., 3:254–55.

59. Henry Cruger to Horatio Gates, 16 Nov. 1770, Horatio Gates Papers, New-York Historical Society.

60. James McLachlan, *Princetonians, 1748–1768: A Biographical Dictionary* (Princeton, NJ, 1976), 120.

61. See William Sterne Randall, *Benedict Arnold: Patriot and Traitor* (New York, 1990), 593.

62. Louis W. Potts, *Arthur Lee, A Virtuous Revolutionary* (Baton Rouge, LA, 1981), 20; William Howard Adams, *The Paris Years of Thomas Jefferson* (New Haven, CT, 1997), 201.

63. James H. Hutson, "Letters from a Distinguished American: The American Revolution in Foreign Newspapers," *Library of Congress Quarterly Journals* 34 (1977): 294, 304.

64. McInnis, *In Pursuit of Refinement*, 100.

65. Sheila L. Skemp, *William Franklin, Son of a Patriot, Servant of a King* (New York, 1990), 38–39; Vernon O. Stumpf, "Who Was Elizabeth Downes Franklin?" *Pennsylvania Magazine of History and Biography* 97 (1970): 533–34; R. C. Simmons, "Colonial Patronage: Two Letters from William Franklin to the Earl of Bute, 1762," *WMQ* 59 (2002): 124–25.

66. This could go too far. A friend of the Laurenses requested that his Carolina friends refrain from even mentioning his visit to anyone, as he wished to avoid the endless round of socializing that would result. See *Papers of Henry Laurens*, 7:128.

67. For example, George Boyd, of New Hampshire, who proved to be related to the Earl of Erroll. See *Papers of Benjamin Franklin*, 21:272.

68. This happened to Franklin's friend James Ralph when he reached London as a penniless young man. See Benjamin Franklin, *Autobiography and Other Writings*, ed. Ormond Seavey (Oxford, 1993), 43.

69. Lively, "Going Home," 239; Flavell, "School for Modesty and Humility," 396.

70. Charlotte Erickson, *Invisible Migrants: The Adaptation of English and Scottish Immigrants in Nineteenth Century America* (1972; Ithaca, NY, 1990), 2–3.

71. Since Bailyn's *Ideological Origins of the American Revolution*, the letters of young colonial students in London have been used frequently by historians commenting on American reactions to the metropolis. For problems with this type of testimony, see Flavell, "School for Modesty and Humility."

72. Paul Langford, "Manners and Character in Anglo-American Perceptions, 1750–1850," in *Anglo-American Attitudes: From Revolution to Partnership*, ed. Fred M. Leventhal and Roland Quinault (Aldershot, Hants., 2000), 80–81; Claire Tomalin, *Jane Austen: A Life* (1997; London, 2000), 135; H. W. Brands, *The First American: The Life and Times of Benjamin Franklin* (2000; New York, 2002), 216.

73. *Papers of Henry Laurens*, 8:323.

74. Peter Borsay, "The London Connection: Cultural Diffusion and the Eighteenth-Century Provincial Town," *London Journal* 19 (1994): 21–35.

75. Dr. John Fothergill, *Considerations Relative to the North American Colonies* (London, 1765), 36, 42–43; Bonwick, *English Radicals and the American Revolution,* 47.

76. Gretchen Holbrook Gerzina, *Black London: Life before Emancipation* (New Brunswick, NJ, 1995), 5, 136; M. Dorothy George, *London Life in the Eighteenth Century* (1925; London, 1987), 140; W. Jeffrey Bolster, *Black Jacks: African American Seamen in the Age of Sail* (Cambridge, MA, 1997).

77. Wallace Brown, "The British Press and the American Colonies," *History Today* 24 (1974): 331; Bernard Bailyn, *Voyagers to the West: A Passage in the Peopling of America on the Eve of the Revolution* (New York, 1987), 3, 55, 114, 229.

78. Fothergill, *Considerations Relative to the North American Colonies,* 41–42.

79. Granville Sharp, *A Representation of the Injustice and Dangerous Tendency of Tolerating Slavery; or of Admitting the Least Claim of Private Property in the Persons of Men, in England* (London, 1769), 88; Gerzina, *Black London,* 7.

80. Gerzina, *Black London,* 11, 104, 115; Sharp, *Representation of the Injustice and Dangerous Tendency of Tolerating Slavery,* 88; *The St. James's Chronicle, or The British Evening-Post,* no. 160 (18–20 March 1762).

81. Brown, "British Press and the American Colonies," 329; *Phillis Wheatley: Complete Writings,* ed. Vincent Carretta (London, 2001), xxii; Sharp, *Representation of the Injustice and Dangerous Tendency of Tolerating Slavery,* 81.

82. Kenneth Silverman, *A Cultural History of the American Revolution: Painting, Music, Literature, and the Theatre in the Colonies and the United States from the Treaty of Paris to the Inauguration of George Washington, 1763–1789* (1976; New York, 1987), 237.

83. Richard Cumberland, *The West Indian: A Comedy As it is performed at the Theatre Royal, in Drury-Lane* (London, 1771).

84. Alvin R. Riggs, "The Colonial American Medical Student at Edinburgh," *University of Edinburgh Journal* 20 (1961–62): 148.

85. Daniel Dulany Jr., quoted in Burnard, *Creole Gentlemen,* 222.

86. James Otis, *The Rights of the British Colonies Asserted and Proved* (Boston, 1764), in *Pamphlets of the American Revolution, 1750–1776,* vol. 1, *1750–1765,* ed. Bernard Bailyn (Cambridge, MA, 1965), 435–36.

87. James Otis, quoted in Breen, "Ideology and Nationalism on the Eve of the American Revolution," 32.

88. Josiah Quincy, *Memoir of the Life of Josiah Quincy, Junior* (Boston, 1874), 244–45; Francis D. Cogliano, *American Maritime Prisoners in the Revolutionary War: The Captivity of William Russell* (Annapolis, MD, 2001), 42–43.

89. Richard D. Altick, *The Shows of London* (Cambridge, MA, 1978), 276; Henry Steele Commager, ed., *Britain through American Eyes* (New York, 1974), 381.

90. *Papers of Henry Laurens,* 7:490; James Allen to Chew, 12 Dec. 1764, Chew Papers.

91. Sachse, *Colonial American in Britain,* 54; *Chain of Friendship: Selected Letters of Dr John Fothergill of London, 1735–1780,* ed. Betsy C. Booth and Christopher C. Booth (Cambridge, MA, 1971), 305, 278.

92. Linda Colley, *Britons: Forging the Nation, 1707–1837* (New Haven, CT, 1992; New York, 1996), 141.

93. Frank Thistlethwaite, *America and the Atlantic Community: Anglo-American Aspects, 1790–1850* (New York, 1963), 174–76; McInnis, *In Pursuit of Refinement,* 14–18; Dulles, *Americans Abroad,* 29; C. E. A. Bedwell, "American Middle Templars," *American Historical Review* 25 (1920): 689.

94. Daniel Kilbride, "The Cosmopolitan South: Privileged Southerners, Philadelphia, and the Fashionable Tour in the Antebellum Era," *Journal of Urban History* 26 (2000): 563–65.

"Citizens of the World"

Men, Women, and Country
in the Age of Revolution

SARAH M. S. PEARSALL

A man unconnected is at home every where; unless
he may be said to be at home no where.

—SAMUEL JOHNSON, 1759

"From *experience*," declaimed Betsey Galloway with all the world-weariness
of youth in a 1779 letter to her mother, "I have formed such an opinion of
Mankind that I wish for little society. Where ever I could get the most to
live on with you, there I would go whether at Nova Zembla or Otaheite. . . .
I shall never feel myself *at home* without you."[1] Invoking two places meant to
convey the farthest ends of the earth, the arctic island of Nova Zembla and
the Tahitian islands recently reached by the British in the Pacific, Betsey,
living in London with her exiled Loyalist father, Joseph, sought to reassure
her mother, Grace, left behind in America, of the continued strength of
their affectionate ties.[2] Facing the grim distance of an unfriendly Atlantic,
as well as the economic realities of their situation, Betsey used her letter to
convey her own sensible love for her mother, as well as the ways in which
"home" depended on people as much as on places. Not having a home of
her own, living in London in temporary accommodations, she informed
her mother that London could never truly be "home" as long as her mother
was not there. Betsey further declared: "I trust in God that our miseries will
soon have an end, for my own part I am a citizen of the world and with you
could be happy any place."[3] A self-termed "citizen of the world," Betsy was
happy nowhere and so could be unhappy everywhere.

What did it mean for a woman without a country or even a permanent
home to declare herself a "citizen of the world"? Such a claim to cosmopolitanism is not exactly what might be expected of a woman who, as a
generation of women's historians have shown, was not even rightly to be

considered a full citizen of any country.[4] On the whole, focusing on the political changes of the Revolution, historians have used print sources and legal decisions to ascertain an individual's relationship to the state. Historians now know much more about how early republican American newspapers discussed the rights of man and woman, how British periodicals developed understandings of British-ness, and how legal decisions, such as those in the case of *Martin v. Massachusetts,* both reflected and shaped ideas of citizenship and belonging.[5] Yet too much remains unclear about how ordinary and largely obscure individuals, especially but not exclusively women, understood their own loyalties in an era of considerable change.

Women trying to make sense of their place in the world in the aftermath of a life-altering Revolution did not necessarily make use of the categories that historians have often used: patriot, loyalist, even British or American. Instead, they often recast notions of "country" on the basis of "friends." Attending to this move in the letters of individuals, especially women, allows for a more general comprehension of the dynamics of an Atlantic world and the central virtues of familiarity and sensibility that emerged from it in the course of the eighteenth century. Understanding both personal circumstances and general concepts requires attention both to the individual stories and to the larger context. As many letter writers of the eighteenth century knew, global understandings could best be explained with reference to the personal. Like them, we need to turn our attention from country to friends even to understand the force of national change. Affectionate attachments, especially those nurtured by letters, helped to make sense of worlds turned upside down.

The argument of this essay is that many individuals, especially women, did not define themselves in the political categories historians have deployed, but they did seek to nurture familiar and sensible attachments in situations of change. Many in this era, especially but not exclusively women, understood their ties in terms of familiarity and sensibility, and they used these concepts, deriving from an Atlantic world, in order to negotiate attachments in a time of displacement. Both geography (beyond American) and chronology (beyond the era of the American Revolution) require some expansion in order to make sense of such changes. With their country lost to them, the individuals under consideration here focused more strongly on friends and family as many disavowed "disinterested patriotism." Such a move allowed them to exclude to some degree the horrors at their doorstep and to maintain a tenuous grasp on continuity in a time of shocking transformation.

Writing about feeling and friendship in letters became an important way of insisting upon connections in an age of manifest disconnections. Sensibility and familiarity received particular attention as key virtues in a world in which they seemed all too elusive. The culture was a transatlantic one that continued well into the 1780s.[6] In part, such notions thrived because there had already been so much distance, war, and trauma. But there were also new ways of coping with dislocation, as print culture became more widespread and novels like Samuel Richardson's *Pamela* became popular with larger audiences. Letters with claims of sensibility and familiarity were an important tool for those privileged enough to have access to them in ameliorating the agonies of living through the displacement of an Atlantic boom time.

All kinds of individuals in the eighteenth-century Atlantic world had cause to ponder their attachments and to make claims about the continued strength of at least some of them. To that end, I concentrate on the stories and letters of a few individuals from the mid-Atlantic and southern colonies, plucked from a much larger set of Atlantic examples.[7] All of them faced disruptions that profoundly altered their lives. Focusing in this manner allows for close attention to the words that such individuals themselves used, as well as the ideals that animated them. While Revolutionary letters reveal less than we might like about the Revolution itself, they do reveal much about the underlying beliefs that allowed individuals to make sense of difficult, demanding change. These letters come from elite families, those with the time, leisure, literacy, and resources to send and receive letters. They thus provide the greatest information about a limited stratum. Because of the accidents of survival, they provide only a portion, and not necessarily an especially representative one, of letters of this era. Letters are not diaries; they always play to particular audiences.[8] Constant reassurances of continued affection, then, may have been less what individuals wanted to write than what they thought recipients expected them to write. Still, making sense of writers' expectations of their readers elucidates broader ideals.[9] Such letters, written from different individuals in different locales in different years, also form patterns, ones that illuminate central preoccupations of the age.

Concepts of familiarity, sensibility, and attachment had long shored up families facing disruption as a result of all sorts of Atlantic movements and motions. It is helpful, therefore, briefly to define these terms. In 1755 Samuel Johnson defined *familiar* both as "domestick; relating to a family" and as "affable; not formal . . . unceremonious; free; . . . unconstrained."[10] This concatenation, being both domestic and also free, is a vital one. Achieving familiarity was a critical goal of these letter writers, and letters themselves defined relationships not only as "domestick" but also as affable, informal, and free. I follow Johnson's definition of *familiarity* to imply a relation that allowed for a lack of ceremony and for freedoms of affections. I define *sensibility* as the ability to possess and display a feeling heart. Notions of sensibility could overlap with sympathy, in that both could refer to feelings (for instance, of suffering). Both were also about physical reactions to objects and bodies in particular. Nonetheless, sensibility was a quality within the possessor. Familiarity and sensibility allowed literate and elite family members to announce their feelings for one another, as well as to remain attached even when physically separated. Many in this era believed that both qualities originated in the domestic setting. Both familiarity and sensibility were ways of maintaining connections, or relations that united two individuals in ties that implied certain personal, political, and financial obligations.

In the devastation wrought by the American Revolutionary War, these concepts provided ballast for individuals set adrift in uncertain vessels, helping them to ponder their situation, assess the behavior of others, and remain attached to loved ones. The American Revolution put all kinds of pressures on individuals, not only those who were committed to the Revolution and its principles but also those who cared little for them. Many people, especially women, responded to these pressures by forming their own notions of what it meant to be a friend, a citizen, a citizen of the world. By so doing, they were able to find some agency in a situation in which loss had removed much of their power. To understand what Betsey Galloway may have meant by calling herself a "citizen of the world," it is necessary to consider the major dislocations of her era (if briefly) and to place her in the context of others of her ilk who articulated similar concerns.[11] After all, connections would not have received so much anxious attention had they not seemed to be in jeopardy.[12]

Given the enduring importance of the household as a foundation for social order, eighteenth-century Atlantic displacement was a source of profound concern. The effects of wartime separations, in both specific individual terms and general demographic ones, were suffered both by those who left and those who were left. Part of the calamity of war, declared one British magazine during the American Revolutionary War, was in its domestic effects: "What mournful scenes in private families have these flames already occasioned! How many more such scenes may justly be apprehended!"[13] This magazine, like other contemporary texts, linked the domestic and the distant, pointing out the household disorder bound to attend war. The American Revolution caused the kinds of domestic divisions that arise from a civil war,[14] but it also caused domestic divisions within individual households.[15]

Mournful scenes of families separated by war and the Atlantic were common in the Anglophone Atlantic world in the eighteenth century. Migration, economic imperatives and desires, trade, colonization, slavery, war, revolution—all of these conspired to separate individuals from families in the eighteenth-century Atlantic world.[16] In an era of revolution, in particular, they also served to sever the connections between friends and country. National allegiances, like family allegiances, were thought to be "natural," stemming from sensible ties. For many social and political commentators of the day, the concatenation of "friends" (by which many meant family) and "country" (by which many meant what we might today term *nation*, though they might also have meant region or locality) was so commonplace as to seem to them entirely natural. In his *Essay on the Nature and Conduct of the Passions and Affections*, for example, Francis Hutcheson traced out an ever-widening circle of benevolent sympathy, from the family to the community and country to all humanity. Repeatedly, Hutcheson linked love of family with love of country. Thus he contended that most individuals would willingly risk death to save their friends and country: "A Fly or Maggot in its proper haunts, is as happy as Hero, or Patriot, or Friend, who has newly delivered his Country or Friend, and is surrounded by their grateful Praises."[17] Hutcheson also presumed such affections to be natural, citing "Natural Affection, Friendship, Love of a Country, or Community, which many find very strong in their Breasts."[18] Moreover, he posited that most people's lives were "employed in Offices of natural Affection, Friendship, innocent Self-Love, or Love of a Country."[19] For Hutcheson and others, including Adam Smith (himself a neo-Stoic of sorts), these were all limited attachments, which needed ultimately to give way to general benevolence for all of humanity and God.

Like Hutcheson, many letter writers, regardless of political affiliation, identified a link between the personal ties of friends, family, and country.[20] John Forbes, writing to his brother Bennet from Kiel, Germany, in 1810, stated that he wished he could visit the United States for the purpose of "seeing my Country & friends there."[21] Mary Ricketts, unwillingly sojourning with her husband in Jamaica in 1757, imagined her delight at returning to England: "I want Nothing to make my happiness Compleat But to be restored to my friends & Country." Later, she "ardently Wish[ed] for that Joyful Period which is to Restore me to valued Friends, Health, Happiness, & England."[22] Margaret Cowper, living in Scotland as the daughter of an exiled Loyalist, offered advice to her cousin Eliza Mackay, who was trying to decide whether to settle with her family in her native Georgia or in England: "Country is not everything & yet it is a great deal. to part from dear, natural, long tried, friends is a cruel thought."[23] Margaret's use of the word *natural* signals an understanding similar to that evinced by Francis

Hutcheson. But her sense of country had nothing to do with politics or republics and everything to do with friends.

For many, if not most, individuals, friends and country were connections that reenforced each other, building on each other over time. For individuals living through the regime change of the American Revolution, this mutually reenforcing system of attachments was disrupted. Some chose to shift allegiances, or rather found that their long-standing allegiances (for example, to the British government) were shifted for them (as those termed *Loyalists* experienced). Others suffered when their head of household chose other allegiances; this was especially true for women forced into an identity as Loyalists even when their own loyalties were hardly so clear. Deprived of country and sometimes friends, these individuals, adrift in the Atlantic world, often offered far more explicit consideration of their own connections than did most. In so doing, they tended to privilege familiar connections of family and friends over that of country.

Much of the social theory of the eighteenth century focused on developing limited attachments (to family, friends, and country) into general ones of benevolence toward all humanity and God as a means of achieving full moral virtue. For people such as Betsey Galloway, citizen of no country, the claim to be a "citizen of the world" was not an assertion of general benevolence but rather a reassurance to a mother far away of the strength of family ties.[24] A claim to a "cosmopolitan" identity was a way of reasserting the most intimate of familiar ties. The concept "citizen of the world" was an old one, first appearing in ancient Greek Stoicism and used repeatedly in the eighteenth century in a variety of printed literature to indicate someone who was a disinterested inhabitant, more concerned with general benevolence than with limited attachments to city, county, or country. The *Oxford English Dictionary* defines the citizen of the world as "one who is at home, and claims his rights, everywhere; a cosmopolitan."[25] This is certainly how it was used in Oliver Goldsmith's *Citizen of the World,* a classic eighteenth-century text about distance and dislocation, a fictional set of letters from an imagined Chinese protagonist in London, Lien Chi Altangi, satirizing London society to his friends back home.[26] But Betsey did not use the phrase as Goldsmith and other authors did. Instead, she used it to imply that she did not care what country she was in as long as she was with her mother. This was not general over limited attachment. Rather, it was a claim that family was more important to her than country, despite the costly loyalism of her father. In altering the meaning of this phrase to fit her circumstances, she not only shifted the cultural precept but also reassured herself and her mother of the importance of the virtues of sensibility and familiarity.

Like Lien Chi Altangi and numerous other protagonists, both fictional and factual, Betsey used letters to maintain connections and to emphasize these virtues.[27] In the eighteenth century, there were many models for using familiar letters to remain connected with family left behind. Indeed, much of the literature of the era, from well-known novels such as *Pamela, Evelina,* and *The Man of Feeling* to magazine and newspaper stories of all kinds, also dealt with the consequences of familial separations, as generations of heroes and heroines, separated from their families of birth, wandered the wide world, trying, sometimes vainly, to avoid evil seducers, bad associations, and a host of other perils. In that great age of the epistolary novel they generally used letters. "Dear Father and Mother, I Have great Trouble," begins *Pamela,* both book and heroine.[28] Such an opening communicates both her distance from her family of birth and also the trouble and chaos ensuing from this separation. It also signals a desire to maintain attachments despite distance and "Trouble." Many magazine stories also trumpeted the disorder that attended family divisions.[29] In a sense, the kind of disconnections endured by Pamela reflected a central concern of the age: not so much the "American revolution against patriarchal authority," though this aspect was certainly present, but instead how to navigate and make sense of distance and disconnection and to reestablish trustworthy, stable, and enduring connections.[30] As deployed by all of these fictional characters, letters were a chief means of maintaining attachments in an uncertain world.

The ways in which the individuals considered here, such as Betsey Galloway, made sense of their situations and navigated the confusions and dangers of their own worlds allied them with the fictional heroes and heroines of the age, such as Altangi. So too did their use of letters. Letters were a lifeline for the Galloway family in the uncertain years of the Revolution. Betsy's father, Joseph, after failing to persuade the Pennsylvania assembly to accept his peace plan, had been exiled as a Loyalist, his assets seized. Grace inherited land from her father, which remained in her name and which she hoped to retain despite the confiscation of her husband's property. So when her husband fled with Betsy, first to New York and then to London, Grace stayed behind, hoping to hold on to the family assets. Joseph apparently was not eager to take his daughter with him to London, informing Grace in the autumn of 1778: "But with whom could I leave her, in a Strange Place destitute of either father or Mother. I have Sought a proper place, but none has been offerd. . . . And the thought of her returning to her Enemies & to you in your present situation was too dismal to her as well as myself."[31] Issues of familiarity appear already here, since it was unthinkable to leave their daughter in a "Strange Place," "destitute" of parents or other "connections" who could shield her from the ravages of war. Joseph too was loath to leave America, but he could see no alternative, or so he conveyed to Grace. Leaving his wife behind but taking his daughter, Joseph, along with Grace and Betsey, embarked on a painful course of reestablishing and maintaining connections in difficult circumstances.[32] One of the ways in which they did so was through brief letters, often rolled up into tiny scrolls so that they could be spirited across enemy lines.

Given these constraints, it is not surprising that Betsey's letters to her mother stress enduring affections while also highlighting her own sense of distance, one wrought by national and familial separation. Betsey wrote of her decision to leave New York and go to England, "You ask me my dear Mama if I am willing to go to England, you know I have only a choice of difficulties, could I return to you or could I be certain that you would come to me, nothing on earth would induce me to go ... [but] our seperation seems at present unavoidable." In the same letter, Betsey mourned, "I have daily wished for a mother, or even a friend to open my heart to but found none ... but do endeavour to keep up your spirits, for that we may meet no more to part in this world, is the only pleasure I now promise myself."[33] What Betsey most desired was a "friend," someone upon whom she could rely. Betsey appears to have liked London, but she went to some lengths to convey to Grace that she could find no true happiness there while separated from her mother. While she conceded that "london is the most agreable place I can have an Idea of," she claimed that "I would with Pleasure give up all the allurements of london once more to enjoy your society."[34]

Betsey described herself as a citizen of the world in part to convey that even the delights of the metropolis could not erase her sorrowful mother from her mind, but she did so while stressing her status as a woman of sensibility. When the increasingly despairing Grace apparently wrote that she was glad that her daughter was fond of England and happy there despite their separation, Betsey upbraided her:

> How my dear Mamma could you suppose I was fond of england? I believe the inhabitants of this globe are much the same in every *civilized* part of it. Those that have money are flattered and hosted by the Philadelphians, those who have not are neglected by them. I know the latter to be the case here, but have not been in a situation to prove the former. There are some good people in Philadelphia. ... No doubt there are some here but in general the People here are either too polite or feel too much for themselves to feel for others.[35]

Betsey here implied two distinctions, one between civility and incivility (she found both Philadelphia and London to be places of civility) and one between feeling and unfeeling (in this, she was a person of feeling, while many in both cities, but especially London, were not). This latter distinction was a critical one, as it was for her a means of comprehending the "globe." It was after this claim that Betsey went on to declare that she would never be "at home" without her mother.

In so privileging her family over her national identity, Betsey also succeeded in emphasizing again her status as a woman of feeling. For her sensibility and familiarity were key virtues, ones emphasized both in her affectionate claims to her mother and in the anecdotes she told, such as one in which she informed her mother that she had made some friends in London:

> Here is one lady who treats me with the most affectionate attention, she often enquires after you and expresses her wishes to relieve all the pain I feel at being absent from you. I go to her house without ceremony, last week I dined there ... as I had a Cold did not eat as much as she wished, she pressed me exceedingly, I happened to say that since I left you no one had asked me to eat a second time but herself.- - - the tear of sensibility that lightened her countenance convinced me that her professions of regard are sincere. I have another very agreable acquaintance who is a truly worthy sensible well-bred woman.

Here Betsey emphasized that her new friends in London exercised both welcome familiarity (allowing her to go to a home "without ceremony") and sensibility (both women are described with precisely that word). Concentrating on the sensibility of her London friends, Betsey went on to stress her own: "I have this gratification that I am treated with as much respect as if Papa was in the ful possession of his fortune, but what are externals to domestic happiness, when I think of your situation and my being from you, it damps every pleasing reflection and reduces my mind to that state which the horrors of our situation too justly create."[36] Such a claim—that familiarity and "respect" were offered to her even when her father had lost his fortune—showed her mother that she was not entirely friendless in London; it also demonstrated that polite circles were still open to her. Nevertheless, emphasizing her own distress and the importance of "domestic happiness," Betsey offered reassurance to herself and her mother. In so doing, and in downplaying the politics of their situation (while admitting the economics of it), she embraced her own version of being a "citizen of the world" as well as a person of feeling.

Another daughter of a Loyalist refugee adopted similar strategies as she made her way in the world. Born in Georgia in 1776, Margaret Cowper was the daughter of an American woman and a Scottish-born Loyalist. Margaret herself was educated in England along with her Georgia cousin Eliza McQueen (whose father fought on the Patriot side), with whom she kept up correspondence and visited for decades. Thanks to family exile and debts occasioned by Revolutionary losses, Margaret and her immediate family sojourned in England, Jamaica, Georgia, Spanish East Florida, Scotland, and England again, all before she turned thirty.

In the midst of her physical revolutions, Margaret reflected on her connections to previous locales, emphasizing her affectionate attachment to them. Thus, writing from Jamaica in early 1800, she went on about various mutual friends in Georgia, apologizing that "we take so much pleas[ure in?] nothing as Old times past—therefore do not think me tiresome in introducing them [so?] often— ... it is one of my chief pleasures to think of the past, to Repeat to myself all that has most interested me, & impress it if ... [illegible] possible more deeply on my memory, fearful lest it should escape." In fact, Margaret entreated Eliza to send "a large map of the United States ... we should be very glad of *that* [so that we might enjoy?] the minute Geography of Country we love so well."[37] Such love, transcending politics but incorporating friends, indicated the ways in which connections were paramount for her. In another letter, upon parting from a friend, she declared, "I have half left my heart behind me."[38] And in another, she began, "My Heart has played Truant my Dear Girls ever since you left us, it followed you to Town ... & keep it quietly & peacably I cannot."[39] All of these images, borrowed from a culture of sensibility, served to focus attention on her status as a woman of feeling.[40] They also allowed her to cope with the dislocations she faced.

As images of hearts divided from bodies indicate, Margaret also emphasized the fracturing that came from her sense of exile and dislocation. Writing several years later from Scotland to Eliza, in England, she began:

we Received the welcome long lookd for letters from our beloved friends in England—in England? how far distant than are we?—oh that we were nearer. what strange fatality ever involves us in anxiety & regrets. some opposition that will not let us be at peace. one friend here another there inclination on one side necessity on the other.[41]

As this letter makes clear, even Margaret's grammar was fractured, just as her friends and self were (divided, in this case, between inclination and necessity).

Attachments were paramount for a woman whose metaphors indicated her sense of their possible loss. She repeatedly referred to herself as a vagabond. Sometimes she did so humorously, as when, in 1796, she remarked of her sister and herself "how we laugh without reason my dear when we compare ourselves sometimes to the [roaming?] Arabs! unsettled, wandering! we know not whither."[42] At other times her tone was more serious. She informed Eliza that "never till lately did I consider myself so much a pilgrim & so dependent, as I find all Creatures are, (I do not mean on their Supreme Governour—I was alway's sensible of that) on one another."[43] Margaret's sense of herself as a wandering pilgrim dependent on others indicates her own sense of need. In her view, her dislocation was intimately related to separation from loved ones and her own travels. She was equally explicit about the ways in which a lack of stability left her with an enduring sense of disorientation. In 1806, after years of being tossed on the currents of the Atlantic and the currents of a life of expatriation, she admitted wearily to Eliza that "I do almost envy those people who live in the place which gave them birth, where they have [grown?], & strengthen'd every tie [in?] habit their friends form'd by degrees & every dear association of childhood, youth, experience. not rudely torn asunder or weaken'd & shook so that doubts & discontent may arise without Supplying better things."[44]

Margaret was painfully aware of the ways in which her ties were limited by her peregrinations. Her own wistful emphasis on "dear association[s]" demonstrates both her sense of loss of them and the way in which community, locality, and friendship should all work together to form the individual. Usually, ties of friends and country would have contributed to her sense of self and her place in the world, but for her, torn from her native land and her usual connections by her father's political choices, only "doubts & discontent" remained.

Equally concerned to demonstrate her sensibility was yet another "poor refugee" and "Loyalist" daughter, Anna Shoemaker Rawle. Like Betsey Galloway, Anna was writing to her mother, Rebecca, the wife of a Quaker and suspected Loyalist In 1780, in language reminiscent of Grace Galloway, Anna fretted that she had not heard recently from her family: "A hard lesson this is to submit to. Seen at a distance our lot would have appeared forlorn and gloomy, such as the human heart must have sunk under—happily it was hid from us—and now we have only to call sweet hope and calm reflection to our aid, and to strip misfortune of her terrors."[45] That same summer, her mother mourned that "I find it a Severe trial thus to take Leave on one fr[ien]d. after another."[46] A year later, Rebecca lamented that "we are but poor refugees."[47] Like the Galloways, these individuals also claimed that they could find happiness only in each other. Anna informed her mother in September 1780 that

> the strange misfortunes of the family are such as to make retrospec-
> tion very painful; we must then anticipate those comforts that now
> are denied, and look forward to a reward for the present. Yet it is
> too natural to dwell upon uncommon events, and to regret the past
> happy days. . . . Strange that I then could complain of any thing, but
> if ever Providence shou'd destine us to meet again, I shall be the most
> contented of human creatures.[48]

Looking back to remembered happiness and forward to imagined bliss, just as Margaret Cowper had looked to the happy remembered past, Anna thus sought in her letters to find some pleasing connection with her mother.

Like Betsey Galloway, Anna Rawle emphasized the strength of sus-taining sensibility and familiarity in the face of political and other hor-rors. Anna, still living in Pennsylvania, was in much closer proximity to Patriots, which did not make her feel any more warmly toward them. In fact, while disavowing politics, she criticized them for their lack of sensibility, a standard complaint lodged by other such women. Anna condemned those Americans who under the guise of "disinterested patriotism" in fact had little sympathy for the trials of Loyalists: "There is a meaness and depravity of mind in extracting pleasure from the grievous afflictions of others which nothing can excuse."[49] For Anna Rawle, even political dissonance could not excuse a failure of sympathy for the suffering other. It was a vision that in some respects excluded the very war being fought on her doorstep. It was also a statement about sensibility with clear political overtones: not only did patriots lack sensibility but they in fact took sadistic pleasure in "the grieveous afflictions of others."

In contrast to Betsey, Anna disavowed the status of a citizen of the world even as she embraced that of a woman of feeling. Whereas similar pressures made Betsey term herself a citizen of the world, meaning by this that family overrode country, Anna determined upon a complete rejection of the term:

> Nothing is more common than to be attached to one's native place. I
> have read of people who called themselves citizens of the world, and

affected to esteem all countrys alike, but I shall ever believe that those who pretend to such universal love, and to possess an equal fondness for every climate, are in reality destitute of sensibility, and have taken up this mask to conceal their indifference for friends, country, kindred and all the soft ties of Nature.[50]

For Anna, the citizen of the world, like the "disinterested patriot," was in danger of ceasing to be a person of feeling. Rather than upholding the ideal of the citizen of the world in which personal attachments gave way to general ones, she castigated those who could ignore personal affections, "the soft ties of Nature." Anna used the term *citizen of the world* differently than Betsey Galloway, but with much the same import: personal loyalties were more important than some kind of general benevolence or broader patriotic affiliation. As with Betsey, such claims could offer reassurance to a mother far from her daughter.

In fact, in spite of rejecting the status of a citizen of the world, Anna Rawle embraced a family-based cosmopolitanism just as Betsey had. In a letter from late 1780 she noted that she was willing to live even in a despicable independent America (if not Nova Zembla!) if it meant that her family would be reunited: "Some people are positive of a peace in the spring. How delightful is that prospect; even the once odious independency will cease to be disagreable, if it will be a means of restoring you all in health and safety to your friends and to us."[51] When peace still had not prevailed by March 1781, Anna was even more explicit in her statement of allegiance. She worried that her mother had had to flee to England, and she regretted "the thought of being at a greater distance." She maintained that she did not care whether the family ended up in America or Britain, declaring, much as Betsey had, that "could we be together, all country's would be alike to me."[52] Familial allegiances were to subsume political ones.

In the stories of all three women, then, it is possible to witness not necessarily strong allegiances to either the Loyalist or the Patriot side (despite Anna's rejection of "odious independency") but instead emphasis on broader, transatlantic ideals of sensibility and familiarity. It is thus impossible to comprehend the ideals that motivated them with reference solely to the American side, or to the Revolution itself. These women did not lament their relegation to a "private sphere." Instead, they comprehended the entire "globe" through the prism of domestic affections. While feeling was always nurtured, the strong emphasis on sensibility and familiarity was a hallmark of the era, in all kinds of personal and political discourse, throughout the

Anglophone Atlantic. This supports the idea that the concepts that held most purchase for many individuals, especially women, were those based in a transatlantic literary culture, concepts having little to do with "disinterested patriotism."

It might be argued at this point that this was a gender-specific reaction, that men would not have privileged these virtues over patriotism or loyalism. While it is certainly true that women, left out of many vital political decisions, may have privileged other concepts more often than men, men sometimes did the same. Nevertheless, gender is not absent from this story. Men's letters tended to sound the loudest claims to familiar affections when the recipients of their letters were women. Consider briefly, for instance, the self-consciously thoughtful letters of Thomas Coombe, an Anglican minister in training in London just before the American Revolution who returned to Pennsylvania only to become a Loyalist and end up back in Britain. Despite greatly admiring Dr. Benjamin Franklin, with whom he came into contact in London society in the 1770s, he at one point disavowed Franklin's version of patriotism. After he demurred from describing the wonders of London to his sister in a 1770 letter, Thomas went on:

> England I have often told you has many Charms, but Pennsylvania has more. Dr. Franklin's Motto is—"Where there is Liberty, that is my native Country." However, tho' I do not think the Doctor's Definition a just one, yet I am fully of Opinion, that there is as much true Liberty in America as in any Part of the World. I would therefore rather say—"Where my Family & Friends are, that is my native Country," whether it be the Island of Britain, or the Continent of America.[53]

Thomas thus altered Franklin's definition of what constituted "native Country" in ways that better suited him and that assured his family, and his sister in particular, of his love for them and for his native home. He continued in a meditation that might have done a philosopher proud:

> We may fancy, till we have made the Experiment, that we have reasoned ourselves out of our tender Affections, but rest assured that all Philosophy is absurd which is contrary to Nature. Those Affections were implanted in us by the Creator for wise & good Purposes. Impossible therefore must be all Efforts to eradicate them. For myself, I sincerely pity the Man who has in any Degree deadened their Influence.

Like Anna Rawle, Thomas condemned individuals who would put aside the natural ties of affection for patriotism. He continued, "Patriotism is a Vice, when it so far attaches us to our own Country, as to make us disregardless of the Interest of another."[54]

The eighteenth century offered many opportunities for patriotism, but it also offered opportunities for skepticism about it. Samuel Johnson, after all, declared patriotism to be "the last refuge of a scoundrel."[55] In an age when "connexions" (between nerves, between individuals, between countries) were paramount, a nationalism that privileged country at the expense of friends was to be regarded with some caution. Thus, even while Thomas signaled his belief that he was a citizen of the world, he sought to emphasize his continued attachment to his land and his family. In March 1770 he again conceded that he loved certain aspects of life in England: "I bear a warm Heart for old England. Patriotism ceases to be a Virtue, when it makes us blind to the Good which is to be found in other Countries." Still, later in the letter he carefully reassured his sister that "I now begin to look forward with anxiety to the Period of my Return. Feelingly awake to the Endearments of Family & Friendship, I would not even wish to love but for the Pleasures which these afford. And therefore tho' I must always entertain a high Affection for my English Friends, yet compared with those in America, they are but Friends of yesterday."[56] In June 1769 Thomas expressed delight at the cool blue skies of an English summer, in contrast to the "intolerable Heat" of Philadelphia. Nonetheless, he sought to convince his sister that he would still be happy to leave England: "Don't imagine however that I shall regret the Change, for what is the Pleasure which we derive from clear Skies & pleasant weather when put in Competition with the Happiness of domestic life—of Friendship & of Benevolence!"[57] Here the limited attachment of friendship was conflated with a more general benevolence, both of which were located in the "Happiness of domestic life," a claim with which he felt his sister would agree.

Another individual caught in the Revolution, this one a Patriot, writing to a war-torn Boston, inquired of a family member whose husband was sympathetic to the British:

> I am extremely anxious to know what change the Alteration of the state of Boston has produced in your Family and those Connections which Blood Intimacy have nearly allied to both of us. Such are the Miseries of Civil dissentions, they sever the most intimate relations. . . . Whatever may be your or my political Opinions, Our friendship has had an origin & has been cemented by offices of

kindness which the capriciousness of human fortune cannot shock or alter. No, let the Wreck of time produce what it will, I shall ever treasure you among my first, best & dearest of friends. Blast the man that would sully the Connection.[58]

Even in the face of mounting political dissonance, claims of enduring affection from both of these men went to the women they knew and cherished. Both privileged connections of friendship, even while admitting the force of politics, in letters specifically to women.

There is a gender-specific element to the tendency to privilege connections in these ways, but it was not only women who did so. Indeed, sometimes men used this language with each other, as when one American wrote to a Loyalist exile in London in 1783, "The Political Storm that has so long afflicted this once happy Country I hope will now be succeeded by a serene Sky and that I may soon again have the pleasure of taking you by the hand and of renewing our former friendship."[59] Nevertheless, women often influenced the ways men wrote about these topics and addressed them, an indication of women's agency in shaping transatlantic cultures of sensibility and familiarity. This agency was limited: Thomas Coombe may have informed his sister that his country was where family and friends were, but he willingly left that family when he felt that he could not support the Revolution, returning to England as a Loyalist exile. Women often had little such choice, and so understandably they tended to cling more resolutely to claims of the enduring importance of affectionate ties. Still, what is interesting is not that this made them provincial or bound by the domestic but that they were able to cope with different national identities because familiar ones remained paramount. An earlier generation of historians searched to find female Patriots and Loyalists, eager to place women in the development of national identities and politics. Some women do fit neatly into such categories, and their stories are important. However, many of them, and some men too, do not fit as neatly. Thus it is necessary to search out the broader contours of their experience and to understand better other ideals that motivated them.[60]

Many of the ideals that animated personal correspondence in this era arose from transatlantic cultures of politeness, sensibility, and familiarity. These together formed a kind of social glue when the Atlantic, and all kinds of wars, revolution, and chaos, pushed people apart. Using familiar letters, just as so many literary heroes and heroines did in the later eighteenth century, gave such individuals one way to remedy the "great Trouble" that could arise from household dislocation and the attendant breaking apart of the natural ties of friends and country. Women in particular, excluded from formal political participation, recast understandings of country in ways that accommodated a much more personal, and familiar, sense of their place in the world.

This is an Atlantic story, but aspects of it are particular to the American Revolutionary context. First, the Revolution exacerbated the need for some of those caught on its front lines to find new friends.. Second, the need to forge and maintain connections took on particular political resonance in the creation of a new nation, one in which the ties that bound individuals remained yet to be entirely determined. Finding ways to connect individuals who may have lacked the "natural" ties of friendship became a central preoccupation for Revolutionary leaders, as Gordon Wood has posited.[61] Some individuals rejected "disinterested patriotism" in favor of personal connections; others did the reverse. Either way, they contributed to a sense of these "natural ties" as separate and even sometimes in conflict. What faced many Americans after the Revolution and its political ruptures, in an era of considerable geographical and social mobility, was a need to replace "the soft ties of Nature" with something altogether more man-made.

Still, the lessons learned in the eighteenth-century Atlantic crucible remained critical, as new generations made their way in uncertain worlds. This partly explains why the conservative Gouverneur Morris could disparagingly refer to Thomas Paine as "a mere adventurer from England, without fortune, without family or connexions."[62] At home everywhere and nowhere, such individuals, in part created by an Atlantic world, increasingly inspired concern, as ideals of cosmopolitan slowly receded in some circles on both sides of the Atlantic.[63] The weakening of "traditional forms of social organization" because of geographical mobility was an aspect of early republican America, as Wood has pointed out, but this weakening, and the worries that accompanied such a breakdown, had been occurring, and in many more places, well before the American Revolution.[64] This, then, is a small story that points to larger issues of both Atlantic continuity and American change. As the fictional Lien Chi Altangi mused at the end of his story in *The Citizen of the World*, "I shall therefore spend the remainder of my life in examining the manners of different countries. . . . *They must often change, says Confucius, who would be constant in happiness or wisdom*."[65]

NOTES

I would like to thank the participants at the "The Old World and the New: Exchanges between America and Europe in the Age of Jefferson" Conference in Salzburg, Austria, in October 2005 for insightful comments on an earlier version of this essay. Warm thanks, too, to Professor Andrew O'Shaughnessy and the Robert H. Smith International Center for Jefferson Studies at Monticello for the opportunity to present this work at such a memorable venue. For advice on various incarnations of this work, I am grateful to the editors of this volume, especially Leonard Sadosky, as well as Laurel Thatcher Ulrich, Jan Lewis, Toby Ditz, Peter Kail, and especially Susan Pearson, although I alone am responsible for any errors. A portion of the material is this essay appears in chapter 1, "Fractured Families: The Perils and Possibilities of Atlantic Distance," of my monograph, *Atlantic Families: Lives and Letters in the Later Eighteenth Century,* published by Oxford University Press (2008), and is used by permission.

1. Elizabeth Galloway to Grace Galloway, 17 July 1779, Joseph Galloway Papers, Manuscript Division, LC (hereafter Galloway Papers, LC). The Galloway story is detailed in, among other sources, John E. Ferling, *The Loyalist Mind: Joseph Galloway and the American Revolution* (University Park, PA, 1977); and Grace Growden Galloway, "Diary of Grace Growden Galloway, 1778–1779," *Pennsylvania Magazine of History and Biography* 55 (1931): 35–94, 58 (1934): 152–89.

2. For instance, Nova Zembla was used in these ways in a divorce case from a slightly later period. See the *Times* (London), 23 Feb. 1797, 3.

3. Elizabeth Galloway to Grace Galloway, n.d., Betsey Galloway file, Galloway Papers, LC.

4. Indeed, the Patriot doctor Benjamin Rush observed disparagingly (questioning women's larger benevolence), "How seldom do we meet with a female citizen of the world," even though at least one woman with whom he corresponded, Robina Miller, declared herself as such. For a brief, intelligent discussion of this encounter, see Sarah Knott, "Benjamin Rush's Ferment: Enlightenment Medicine and Female Citizenship in Revolutionary America," in *Women, Gender and Enlightenment,* ed. Knott and Barbara Taylor (Basingstoke, 2005), 649–66, quotation on 660. Works that have considerably advanced our understandings of women and citizenship in this period include Linda K. Kerber, *Women of the Republic: Intellect and Ideology in Revolutionary America* (New York, 1980); idem, *Toward an Intellectual History of Women* (Chapel Hill, NC, 1997); Mary Beth Norton, *Liberty's Daughters: The Revolutionary Experience of American Women, 1750–1800* (Boston, 1980); Joan R. Gundersen, "Independence, Citizenship, and the American Revolution," *Signs* 13 (1987): 59–77; idem, *To Be Useful to the World: Women in Revolutionary America, 1740–1790,* rev. ed. (Chapel Hill, NC, 2006); Linda K. Kerber, Nancy F. Cott, Robert Gross, Carroll Smith-Rosenberg, and Christine Stansell, "Beyond Roles, Beyond Spheres: Thinking about Gender in the Early Republic," *WMQ* 46 (1989): 565–85; and Jan Lewis, "'Of Every Age Sex & Condition': The Representation of Women in the Constitution," *JER* 15 (1995): 359–87.

5. See, among others, Rosemarie Zagarri, "The Rights of Man and Woman in Post-Revolutionary America," *WMQ* 55 (1998): 203–30; idem, *Revolutionary Backlash: Women and Politics in the Early American Republic* (Philadelphia, 2007); Linda Colley, *Britons: Forging the Nation, 1707–1837* (New Haven, CT, 1992); Kathleen Wilson, *The Island Race: Englishness, Empire and Gender in the Eighteenth Century* (London, 2003); Dror Wahrman, *The Making of the Modern Self: Identity and Culture in Eighteenth-Century England* (New Haven, CT, 2004); and Linda K. Kerber, "The Paradox of

Women's Citizenship in the Early Republic: The Case of *Martin vs. Massachusetts*, 1805," in *Toward an Intellectual History of Women*, 261–302.

6. Sarah Knott has claimed that this culture was in decline in Britain at the time of the American Revolution: "Critics agree that in Britain the culture of sensibility was facing unprecedented criticism, even entering crisis later that same decade [the 1780s]. . . . What a contrast to the uses of sensibility on the other side of the Atlantic." "Sensibility and the American War for Independence," *American Historical Review* 109 (2004): 19–40, quotation on 34. I am less convinced. While there were countercurrents, appeals to sensibility occurred in numerous British political contexts, including those to win compensation for Loyalists and those surrounding the abolition of the slave trade, throughout the 1780s and even into the 1790s. They also occurred in more domestic settings.

7. When discussing members of the same family, I refer to individuals by their first names to avoid confusion.

8. For further discussion of letters as sources, see Sarah M. S. Pearsall, *Atlantic Families: Lives and Letters in the Later Eighteenth Century* (Oxford, 2008), introduction.

9. Jan Lewis pointed this out in the introduction to *Pursuit of Happiness: Family and Values in Jefferson's Virginia* (Cambridge, 1983).

10. Samuel Johnson, *A Dictionary of the English Language*, 2 vols. (London, 1755), vol. 1.

11. There have been numerous studies of loyalism. For a recent helpful overview, see Maya Jasanoff, "The Other Side of Revolution: Loyalists in the British Empire," *WMQ* 65 (2008): 205–32.

12. My focus is on the Anglophone North Atlantic. Studies deploying an Atlantic approach are increasingly too numerous to mention. Useful recent theorizing about the "Atlantic turn" includes Bernard Bailyn, *Atlantic History: Concept and Contours* (Cambridge, MA, 2005); David Armitage, "Three Concepts of Atlantic History," in *The British Atlantic World, 1500–1800*, ed. David Armitage and Michael J. Braddick, rev. ed. (Basingstoke, 2009), 11–27; Alison Games, "Atlantic History: Definitions, Challenges, Opportunities," *American Historical Review* 111 (2006): 741–57; and Alison Games, Peter A. Coclanis, Paul W. Mapp, and Philip J. Stern, "Forum: Beyond the Atlantic," *WMQ* 63 (2006): 675–742.

13. "The Fatal Separation: A Moral Tale," *Town and Country Magazine*, 1779, 133–35, quotation on 133.

14. Helpful discussions of the complicated issues of identity involved in this civil war occur in Dror Wahrman's work. See Dror Wahrman, "The English Problem of Identity in the American Revolution," *American Historical Review* 106 (2001): 1236–62, as well as his *Making of the Modern Self*.

15. On domestic divisions, see Stephen Conway, *The British Isles and the War of American Independence* (Oxford, 2000), ch. 3.

16. As I argue in the first chapter of *Atlantic Families*.

17. Francis Hutcheson, *An Essay on the Nature and Conduct of the Passions and Affections with Illustrations on the Moral Sense* (1742; Gainesville, FL, 1969), 129.

18. Ibid., 14.

19. Ibid., 109.

20. For a fruitful exploration of the confluence of family and friend, see Naomi Tadmor, "The Concept of the Household-Family in Eighteenth-Century England," *Past & Present* 151, no. 1 (1996): 111–40; and idem *Family and Friends in Eighteenth-Century England: Household, Kinship, and Patronage* (Cambridge, 2001).

21. John M. Forbes to Ralph Bennet, 15 Sept. 1810, Forbes Family Papers, Massachusetts Historical Society, Boston.

22. Mary Ricketts to her sister, 1 Dec. 1757, 23 June 175[8], Ricketts Family Correspondence and Papers, Add. 300001, Manuscripts Division, British Library.

23. Margaret Cowper to Eliza McQueen Mackay, 2 Feb. 1807, Mackay-Stiles Papers, Southern Historical Collection, University of North Carolina, Chapel Hill (hereafter Mackay-Stiles Papers, SHC).

24. Elizabeth Galloway to Grace Galloway, n.d., Galloway Papers, LC.

25. See *Oxford English Dictionary*, s.v. "citizen," http://www.oed.com.

26. Oliver Goldsmith, *The Citizen of the World, or Letters from a Chinese Philosopher residing in London to his friends in the East* (1760–61; London, 1969).

27. Examples in family letter collections from the period are too numerous to mention. One Loyalist exile in London declared to his brother in Virginia: "Never was Mortal more completely set afloat, and where I shall land again, Heaven only knows." Isaac Low to Nicholas Low, 2 Mar. 1785, Nicholas Low Papers, box 1, Manuscript Division, LC (hereafter Low Papers, LC). Published collections that deal with transatlantic family connections in the Age of Revolution include *The Letters of Don Juan McQueen to His Family Written from Spanish East Florida, 1791–1807* (Columbia, SC, 1943) and *The Letters of Robert Mackay to His Wife, Written from Ports in America and England, 1795–1816* (Athens, GA, 1949), both edited by Walter Charlton Hartridge; Anne Hulton, *Letters of a Loyalist Lady, being the Letters of Anne Hulton, Sister of Henry Hulton, Commissioner of Customs at Boston, 1767–1776* (Cambridge, MA, 1927); Vere Langford, "Dwarris of Jamaica," *Caribbeana* 5 (1919): 19–32: Geraldine Mozley, ed., *Letters to Jane from Jamaica, 1788–1796* (London, 1938); J. Hall Pleasants, "Letters of Molly and Hetty Tilghman," *Maryland Historical Magazine* 21, nos. 1–3 (1926): 20–39, 123–49, 219–42; *Letters of James Murray, Loyalist*, ed. Nina Moore Tiffany (Boston, 1972); Harrison Tilghman, "Letters between the English and American Branches of the Tilghman Family," *Maryland Historical Magazine* 33 (1938): 148–75; and A. F. Wedd, ed., *The Fate of the Fenwicks: Letters to Mary Hays (1798–1828)* (London, 1927). There are also many unpublished collections of transatlantic family letters that highlight the epistolary uses of familiarity and sensibility. Some of those upon which my work relies include those mentioned here, as well as, for instance, the Carlyle Family Papers, the Severn Eyre Letterbook, the Jenings Family Papers, and the Stevens Family Papers, all at the Virginia Historical Society, Richmond; the John and Eliza Ambler Papers, Duke University Rare Books and Manuscript Library, Durham, NC; the Brownrigg Family Papers, University of Chapel Hill, North Carolina Manuscript Library; the Letters of Loyalist Ladies, Historical Society of Pennsylvania, Philadelphia; the Dudley Family Papers and the Malbone/Brinley Papers, Newport Historical Society, Rhode Island; the Robertson Family Papers, Chicago Historical Society; the Thomas Ruston Papers, the Pinckney Family Papers, the John Martin

Papers, the John Leeds Bozman Papers, and the Hannah Hobart Papers, all at the Library of Congress; the John Brown Family Papers and the Dr. Daniel Robert Letters, New-York Historical Society; the Barrell Family Papers, Manuscripts Collection, Columbia University Library, New York; the Chandler Letters, American Loyalists Box, New York Public Library; the Parker Family Papers, Liverpool Library Record Office and National Library of Scotland; the Tharp Family Papers, Cambridgeshire County Record Office; and the Pierce Butler Letterbooks, Manuscripts Division, British Library.

28. Samuel Richardson, *Pamela, or, Virtue Rewarded,* 2 vols. (London, 1741), 1:1.

29. See, e.g., "The Fatal Separation."

30. Jay Fliegelman, *Prodigals and Pilgrims: The American Revolution against Patriarchal Authority, 1750–1800* (Cambridge, 1982).

31. Joseph Galloway to Grace Galloway, n.d., Galloway Papers, LC.

32. The Galloway story did not end happily. At one point, separated from her family and reduced to a two-room apartment, Grace lamented that "cou'd short-sighted Mortals see into future events, perhaps they may Avert some evils, & procure themselves some Alleviation of their Misery, by takeing contrary Measure. Then shou'd I never have trusted all My soul holds dear, to this cruel seperation." The "cruel separation" never ended, as Grace died in May 1782, before she was reunited with her husband and daughter. Grace Galloway to Elizabeth Galloway, 27 Nov. 1778, Galloway Papers, LC.

33. Elizabeth Galloway to Grace Galloway, n.d., ibid.

34. Ibid.

35. Elizabeth Galloway to Grace Galloway, 17 July 1779.

36. Elizabeth Galloway to Grace Galloway, 2 Feb. 1780, ibid.

37. Margaret Cowper to Eliza McQueen Mackay, 15 Jan. 1800, Mackay-Stiles Papers, SHC.

38. Margaret Cowper to Eliza McQueen Mackay, 26 Sept. 1809, ibid.

39. Margaret Cowper to Eliza McQueen Mackay and Mary Ann Cowper, Friday Night [1796], ibid.

40. The trope of the disembodied but feeling heart was ubiquitous in this era. It appears repeatedly in Fanny Burney, *Evelina, or the History of a Young Lady's Entrance into the World,* 3 vols. (London, 1778), as well as in *Letters of the Late Rev. Mr. Laurence Sterne, to His Most Intimate Friends,* 3 vols. (London, 1775); *Letters of the Late Ignatius Sancho, An African,* 2 vols. (London, 1782); and many anonymous letter-writing manuals.

41. Margaret Cowper to Eliza McQueen Mackay, 8 Nov. 1806, Mackay-Stiles Papers, SHC.

42. Margaret Cowper to Eliza McQueen Mackay, 1796, ibid.

43. Margaret Cowper to Eliza McQueen Mackay, 14 July 1796, ibid.

44. Margaret Cowper to Eliza McQueen Mackay, 4 Dec. 1806, ibid.

45. Anna (Shoemaker) Rawle to Rebecca Shoemaker, 29 July 1780, Shoemaker Family Papers, Historical Society of Pennsylvania (hereafter Shoemaker Papers, HSP).

46. Rebecca Shoemaker to Peggy and Anna Rawle, [June 1780], ibid.

47. Rebecca Shoemaker to Peggy and Anna Rawle, 20 June 1781, ibid.

48. Anna Rawle to Rebecca Shoemaker, 20 Sept. 1780, ibid.

49. Anna Rawle to Rebecca Shoemaker, 27 Mar. 1781, Shoemaker Papers, HSP.

50. Anna Rawle to Rebecca Shoemaker, 8 May 1781, ibid.

51. Anna Rawle to Rebecca Shoemaker, 11 Nov. 1780, ibid.

52. Anna Rawle to Rebecca Shoemaker, 7 Mar. 1781, ibid.

53. Thomas Coombe to Sally Coombe, 23 Apr. 1770, Thomas Coombe Papers, Historical Society of Pennsylvania (hereafter Coombe Papers, HSP).

54. Ibid.

55. Samuel Johnson, quoted in James Boswell, *The Life of Samuel Johnson*, 3 vol. (Dublin, 1792), 2:211 (entry of 7 Apr. 1775). Boswell noted of this pronouncement, "at which many will start": "let it be considered, that he did not mean a real and generous love of our country, but that pretended patriotism which so many, in all ages and countries, have made a cloak for self-interest."

56. Thomas Coombe to Sally Coombe, 7 Mar. 1770, Coombe Papers, HSP.

57. Thomas Coombe to Sally Coombe, 19 June 1769, ibid.

58. William Hooper to Dorothy Forbes, 2 Apr. 1776, in *Letters of James Murray, Loyalist*, ed. Nina Moore Tiffany (Boston, 1972), 239.

59. Samuel Verplank to Isaac Low, 27 Apr. 1783, Low Papers, LC.

60. This Atlantic context parallels some of the claims about the transatlantic origins of what has been termed *Republican motherhood* made by Rosemarie Zagarri, among others. See Rosemarie Zagarri, "Morals, Manners, and the Republican Mother," *American Quarterly* 44 (1992): 192–215.

61. "How to attach people to one another and to the state? That was one of the central obsessions of the age. Lacking our modern appreciation of the force of nationalism, eighteenth-century thinkers had difficulty conceiving of what Bishop Butler called 'the distinct cements of society' in anything other than personal terms, in terms of the individual's relationship to some other individual." Gordon Wood, *The Radicalism of the American Revolution* (New York, 1991), 215.

62. Morris made this comment when the Continental Congress was considering making Paine secretary of foreign affairs during the war. Quoted in *The Complete Writing of Thomas Paine*, ed. Philip S. Foner, 2 vols. (New York, 1945), 1:xviii.

63. On the United States, see David Waldstreicher, *In the Midst of Perpetual Fetes: The Making of American Nationalism, 1776–1820* (Chapel Hill, NC, 1997). On Great Britain, see Colley, *Britons*.

64. Gordon Wood has argued that "this spectacular growth and movement of people further weakened traditional forms of social organization and intensified people's feelings of equality." Wood, *Radicalism of the American Revolution*, 226.

65. Goldsmith, *Citizen of the World*, 350, emphasis in original.

Reimagining the British Empire and America in an Age of Revolution

The Case of William Eden

LEONARD J. SADOSKY

The early weeks of September 1778 found Frederick Howard, Earl of Carlisle, safely within the City of New York—one of the few North American cities that still professed loyalty to his king and country—contemplating the causes and implications of months of failed diplomacy. The head of a commission sanctioned by King George III, Carlisle, along with his fellow commissioners William Eden and George Johnstone, had spent the summer of 1778 traveling through the colonies of the mid-Atlantic seaboard seeking to engage the Continental Congress in negotiations that they hoped would end the now three-year-old American Revolutionary War. Although the commissioners were empowered to offer the Americans the most generous terms for reconciliation that had yet been offered during the course of the war, they were spectacularly unsuccessful. The commissioners had made a number of attempts to engage congressional delegates and ordinary Americans in some kind of dialogue, but all had come to naught. The Continental Congress had refused to even officially read their correspondence, let alone consider their terms for negotiation.[1]

Now, on September 9, 1778, Carlisle penned a private letter to Eden assessing both the reasons for their failure and the current prospects for Britain, America, and the wider world. Carlisle believed that Eden was the most obvious person to direct these concerns, as the commission that Carlisle led had largely been a product of Eden's design. The Durham-born lawyer Eden had been a close adviser of Lord North's since his elevation from undersecretary of state to the Board of Trade in March 1776. As an adviser of North's, Eden directed elements of the secret service and provided North with intelligence about American affairs generally and American agents in Europe in particular. Eden's own agents had convinced him that American support for the Revolutionary cause was not widespread, an assumption that influenced his design for the peace commission that would come to bear the name of his friend Carlisle. Eden had proposed rewiring the circuitry of the British Empire in order to accommodate, at least in part, the Americans' more federalized vision of the imperial constitution. Now, both Eden and Carlisle were forced to imagine the British Empire preserving itself in a new political world in which the customary bounds of diplomacy and warfare had seemingly been cast aside.[2]

In his letter of September 9 Carlisle offered Eden a chilling vision of the future that was almost apocalyptic in tone. He quite rightly perceived that the Treaty of Alliance between the United States and the Kingdom of France had changed the dynamics of the geopolitical system within which Britain and its empire had existed and within which British political leaders had made their calculations regarding political, diplomatic, and commercial policy. "The French interference gives a new colour to every thing that relates to the American contest," Carlisle began bluntly. He made it clear that the stakes of the American War were far higher than they had been the previous year. "The Question is no longer which shall get the better, Gt. Britain or America, but whether Gt. Britain shall or shall not by every means in her power endeavour to hinder her colonies from becoming an accession of strength to her natural enemies, and destroy a connection that is contrived for our ruin and might possibly effect it, unless prevented by the most vigorous exertions on our part."[3] The alliance between France and the United States had thus not only expanded the operational scale of the war in America, it had transformed its political scope. Calculations that British policymakers such as Carlisle and Eden, as well as their superiors, Lord North and King George III, had made in the context of an imperial crisis would now have to be made in the context of a general inter-imperial war, a war that would be contested in what was now, given the manifest autonomy of the American states, a transformed geopolitical landscape.

The accommodation of American autonomy in the wake of the Franco-American Alliance provoked more than a rethinking of the North ministry's strategy in the waging of the American War, although it certainly did provoke that.[4] More than a simple change in military strategy, the American states' entry into the world of European diplomacy called for a reconceptualization of the boundaries and structures of the eighteenth-century transatlantic system of states. Through an examination of the writings of William Eden in the aftermath of the failure of the Carlisle Commission, I shall demonstrate that Eden was one of several British political leaders at the forefront of a rethinking of the position of Britain within the Atlantic world. During the war with America, British political leaders and commentators began an intellectual struggle to reconcile the mercantilist political economy of empire of the seventeenth and eighteenth centuries with emerging notions of a liberal, free-market political economy put forward by Enlightenment writers. They did this amidst a period of intense inter-imperial conflict, when the prospects that the British Empire might diminish or expand in size were both equally plausible outcomes. The reconciliation of all these tensions—the emergence of a British Empire that was in relative stasis in the Americas (following the loss of the thirteen colonies), growing in Asia, Africa, and the Pacific, and guided by a political economy that was a hybrid of mercantilism and liberalism (usually labeled *neomercantilism*)—is usually identified with the various responses within the British government and public sphere following the Treaty of Paris (1782–83).

Eden's writings give evidence that the direction British policy and political discourse took in the postwar period had its origins during the American War itself. Eden's subsequent negotiation of a commercial reciprocity treaty with France in 1786 (as a minister extraordinary and plenipotentiary during Pitt's ministry) points to an evolution in his thinking on the issues of imperial organization and political economy and illuminates the existence, more generally, of nuances in British political economic and geopolitical thought during the period between the close of the American Revolution and the beginning of the French Revolution. I argue for a more expanded and nuanced view of a story, already acknowledged by historians, of the development of British-American relations in light of the emergence of the Second British Empire.[5]

In addition to contributing a more detailed understanding of Eden's writings and speeches to our conception of British imperial thought, I argue for a reconfiguration of the terms historians often use to understand the political-intellectual revolution wrought by American independence. The independence of the United States prompted changes in the public discourse about political economy, diplomacy, and imperial organization, not to mention more theoretical discussions within the transatlantic public sphere about the efficacy of republican government, the nature of revolution, and the progress of history. All three of these more concrete realms of thought and action—political economy, diplomacy, and the organization of the empire—had a strong spatial, or geographical, component. The independence of the United States effected a geographical revolution, as new, independent states were demarcated and acknowledged in 1783 where none had been in 1774. I also incorporate the study of geopolitics in order to provide a category of analysis within which to consider the interconnectedness of normally disaggregated fields of study, an interconnectedness that Eden and his contemporaries grasped intuitively. Changes in British thinking about political economy, about the proper course of diplomacy, and about the constitution and structure of the British Empire were all parts of a larger whole—a changed geopolitical order. Even before the American Revolution ended, Britons were coming to terms with the reality that their former colonists had, in some way, changed the shape of the world. However, the degree to which the world had changed and what exactly this new shape was and would be remained open questions.

While George III, the North ministry, and the majority of the British political nation were most certainly unwilling to concede American independence in the autumn of 1778, the defeat of John Burgoyne's forces in New York, the formalization of the Franco-American Alliance, and the failure of the Carlisle Commission forced the British leadership and the British public to acknowledge that they were involved in a far different war than they had been during the two and a half years between the battles of Lexington and Saratoga.[6] The reality of the new autonomy of the American colonies had altered the shape of the Atlantic states system.[7] Strategic decisions would have to be rethought, or at least recalibrated, accordingly. While Carlisle, Eden, and Johnstone remained in America, their thoughts turned away from the contemplation of the reconciliation of Britain and America and toward the necessity of a vigorous prosecution of war against the Americans.

The commissioners saw America as technically autonomous—the American colonies had pulled out of the British Empire—but not truly independent. In allying themselves with France, the Americans had committed themselves to supporting the interests of Britain's mortal enemy. And if America was to be an adjunct of French power in the Atlantic system, then America had to be weakened as much as possible. Carlisle invoked the metaphor of naval warfare to explain the new ethos to Eden: "We must do what every individual would do in a similar case, burn the ship, rather than suffer it to fall into the hands of the enemy who would immediately turn her guns against you."[8] When Eden and Carlisle joined together to write an official dispatch to American Secretary Lord George Germain, they had completely accepted the notion that the allegedly independent United States were merely adjuncts of France. "It may be doubted even whether peace can be attained if Great Britain should be so far sunk as to yield to the ungrateful claim of independency, for it would be absurd not to suppose that many of the rebel leaders are under the influence, if not the immediate pay, of France." Furthermore, the authors noted, "it would be equally absurd to imagine that France will ever permit them to make a peace separate from her."[9]

As the Carlisle Commission accepted failure and its members made preparations to return to Great Britain, they issued a farewell message to the former British Americans labeled "Manifesto and Proclamation." The document was addressed not just to the members of the Continental Congress but to the governments of the individual states (although it was careful to refer to them as "Colonies, Plantations, and Provinces" rather than states) and to all "free Inhabitants" of the said colonies ("free inhabitants of this once happy Empire") as well. The Manifesto and Proclamation was a final plea for reconciliation, offering amnesty and pardon to any American who chose to reaffirm loyalty to King George III and the British Empire. For those who refused reconciliation and chose to continue to pursue independence, the Manifesto and Proclamation made it clear that, owing to the alliance with France (or, more properly, "the pretended alliance with France"), there would be a transformation in "the whole nature and future conduct of this war." Great Britain would now be forced to unleash "the extremes of war." For America "now professes the unnatural design not only of estranging herself from us but of mortgaging herself and her resources to our enemies"; America was committed to "the aggrandizement of France." "Under such circumstances the laws of self-preservation must direct the conduct of Great-Britain, and if the British Colonies are to become an accession to France, will direct her to render that accession of as little avail as possible to her enemy." The Manifesto and Proclamation was a final offer of reconciliation and simultaneously a warning that Great Britain would be prepared to unleash the methods of destructive, total war on Americans who refused to reconcile.[10]

The extreme language of the Manifesto and Proclamation provoked derision both in Britain and in America. In the United States, the Continental Congress took one look at the its rhetoric and fired back in kind. In early 1779 Congress published a lengthy pamphlet entitled *Observations on the American Revolution*. The pamphlet, written anonymously by the delegate Gouverneur Morris, recounted the causes that had driven the American colonists to revolution and promised that "if war is prosecuted in a manner not conformable to the law of nations, the conduct of her enemies shall be retaliated."[11] Extremism would be met with extremism.

The opposition to the North ministry took the publication of the Manifesto and Proclamation and the failure of the Carlisle Commission as an opportunity to pounce. On December 7, 1778, the opposition leader, Charles Watson-Wentworth, Marquess of Rockingham, attacked the Manifesto and Proclamation on the floor of the House of Commons. Rockingham (and others) denounced the extreme language that promised the meting out of the "severities" of war upon the Americans as inhumane, un-Christian, and contrary to the laws of nations. At the same time, Rockingham perceptively questioned whether this proclamation, issued in the wake of the Carlisle Commission's failure, had not changed British policy. "But now, says the Manifesto, a new era in politics has arisen, the nature of the contest has changed," Rockingham observed. "America is relinquished, and all the advantages of being connected with her totally abandoned." If America was to be treated as an enemy nation, was it sound policy to continue a war to subdue her? Rockingham wondered. While the North ministry's allies in the Commons were unwilling to give Rockingham and the opposition any ground during the debates on the Manifesto and Proclamation, Rockingham had perceived the fundamental insight that had driven Eden and Carlisle when they drafted the proclamation.[12] American autonomy and the American alliance with France changed the geopolitical dynamic of the eighteenth-century Atlantic. Where Britons had generally seen the American colonies as disorderly domains to be pacified, they would now increasingly see the American states as autonomous, or at least semi-autonomous, agents of the enemy.[13]

Upon their return to Great Britain in the winter of 1778–79, Carlisle and Eden did not take the failure of their commission lying down. Eden spent the early days after his return to Britain attempting to ascertain exactly who had sabotaged the work of the commission that he had been responsible for designing. He quickly turned his mind from the narrow concern about political payback and focused on the larger, looming questions of the effects the change in the Atlantic geopolitical order would have on Great Britain and the British Empire.[14] He thus spent the early part of 1779 drafting a series of essays assessing the progress of the American War and the state of the British Empire as a whole. The essays took the form of epistles to Carlisle. *Four Letters to the Earl of Carlisle from William Eden, Esq.* was first published in London in 1779, and *A Fifth Letter to the Earl of Carlisle from William Eden, Esq.* appeared in 1780. The essays discuss a variety of topics—the progress of the American War, British commerce with Ireland, the public debt and public credit, the state of Britain's population, and the nature of commercial regulation within the British Empire as a whole. Eden was responding to the changed geopolitical situation: by 1779 Britain found itself at war not only with its American colonies but also with the kingdoms of France and Spain.

The *Fifth Letter,* entitled "On Population; on Certain Revenue Laws and Regulations Connected with the Interests of Commerce; and on Public

Oeconomy," was a pointed rejoinder to the arguments made by Richard Price in *Observations on the Populousness of England and Wales,* namely, that the ongoing war effort was leading to a transformation of English economy and society that was not in the nation's best interests, and that therefore the American War needed to be abandoned. While Price's program would become grist for the neomercantilists, such as Lord Sheffield, after the American War, Eden's critiques prefigured theirs. Beyond the dispute with Price, Eden's essays of 1779–80 contain a coherent and interlocking vision of British political economy, British military and diplomatic strategy, and the constitution and proper regulation of the British Empire. Taken together, they constitute a clear and cogent vision of how Britain could and should accommodate itself to the changed geopolitical order wrought by the actions of the former American colonists.

The notion of geopolitical order requires some explanation. The term *geopolitics* has been used by scholars for more than a century to describe the spatial conception and deployment of political power.[15] In recent years, however, geographers and political scientists have undertaken a modification and expansion of the notions of what geopolitics is and how it can be studied; it has come to embrace, in the words of one theorist, the "examination of geographical assumptions, designations, and understandings that enter into the making of world politics."[16] Conceptions of politics, the structure and operation of the international states system, and the proper ordering of economic production, commerce, and consumption—the "international political economy"—all have a geographical component.[17] A geopolitical order implicitly or explicitly bounds most modern political and economic thought. Geopolitical orders in turn constrain or at least order modes of thinking, conceptualizing, and discussing issues and problems relating to the international states system and the international political economy. Geopolitical orders beget geopolitical discourse. Both of these categories are historically contingent; that is, they change over time. Geopolitical orders and geopolitical discourses are "dialectically interwoven"; they change alongside and in relation to each other. In other words, as the relationships between states change, the mutual understandings that govern those relationships— constitutions, diplomacy, political economy—undergo changes to accommodate the new realities. Changed understandings of what is constitutional, what is diplomatically possible, or what constitutes a proper ordering of political economy in turn permit new realities to develop on the ground.[18]

In his essays of 1779 and 1780 William Eden put forward a twofold argument on the state of the British Empire during the American War. In doing so, he came to terms with an Atlantic geopolitical order in a state of transformation and thus began to initiate a new geopolitical discourse. The first major point he argued was that Great Britain was now in a very different war from the one that had begun in 1775. France's recognition of American independence and the entry of France and, subsequently, Spain into a state of open hostility with Britain transformed what had been an internal dispute within the British Empire into a war between European states. American independence was changing the calculations made by the various European powers and thus subtly changed the established geopolitical order. Eden's second major argument was that although many developments gave a surface appearance of British weakness and decline, the exact opposite was true: Britain was poised to survive and thrive in the emerging order. Because of the nature of modern warfare, Britain actually held a stronger position than did its rivals. Much of this strength was rooted in Britain's financial and commercial system, and it was here especially that Eden's vision prefigured that of the postwar neomercantilists. All told, Eden's observations of the changing nature of the transatlantic order and the strengths of the British Empire, as well as his policy prescriptions, anticipated policies he and others put forward and adopted after the close of the American Revolutionary War.

Eden acknowledged that the entry of France and Spain into the war appeared on the surface as the normal acts of sovereign states within the established transatlantic geopolitical order. He began by noting that the actions of France and Spain, in joining with the colonial rebels, were understandable in the context of the "great game" of eighteenth-century, balance-of-power diplomacy. "It was indeed consistent with all the workings of human nature, that the reputation and memory of our former victories over France and Spain, instead of quieting forever the restless spirit of the Family Compact [the implicit alliance between the two Bourbon monarchies], should make those powers more alert than ever to injure us, and at the same time more cautious." Therefore, France and Spain had "accordingly conceived that they had an interest in making the rebellion of our Colonies tedious and expensive to us."[19] Eden cautioned his readers against judging the actions of Spain and France too harshly, as the "morality of States certainly takes, and is perhaps intitled to, a much greater latitude than is allowed to the morality of individuals." Invoking the established metaphor of the world of diplomacy and statecraft as a theater, Eden could confidently assert that "the truth is, the contentions of empires, and the transactions of extensive wars, exhibit, only on a larger theatre, all the reverses, disappointments, and uncertainties, which are seen among individuals at a gaming-table."[20]

Statesmen, like gamblers, often made decisions in the heat of the moment that they might come to regret later. "But these matters ought not to excite the passionate feelings of any man who possesses a moderate knowledge of the history and nature of the species," Eden noted, apparently attempting to comfort the minds of his readers, for "such a man will know that similar events have happened in every period of the world."[21] The rebellion of the colonies had become a European war like any other, at least on the surface. "We are engaged in a war against France and Spain," Eden noted flatly. Indeed, the second of the *Four Letters to the Earl of Carlisle* was entitled "On the Present Circumstances of the War between Great Britain and the Combined Powers of France and Spain." The words *United States of America* and *Continental Congress* appear nowhere in Eden's text. The man who in early 1778 was prepared to grant the American colonies almost everything they asked for, short of their independence, was unwilling to treat the Americans with even a modicum of respect in 1779 and 1780. The entry of France and Spain into the war, the American alliance with France, and the continued unfolding of the campaigns on land and sea made the initial causes of the American Revolution now seem almost irrelevant. "The cause of our present war with [France and Spain] will soon be as much out of the question as the original principle of the American revolt," Eden asserted in his 1779 essay.

While Eden still hoped for the return of the American colonies to the fold of the British Empire, that was only one of Britain's many goals. "In the course of a war, it sometimes happens that the original object becomes a purpose of the second or third magnitude," he noted. "The original great object of this war is the recovery of our Colonies (and we should never lose sight of that object); but our first purpose at present is to establish our superiority at sea against France and Spain."[22] In this regard, the American War of Independence seemed like another European war. It had begun with the contest over how the colonies should and could be governed, which was unique, but as the war widened, with France and Spain on one side (with the Americans) and Britain on the other, it now took on the character of a conventional eighteenth-century European war. During this period in the aftermath of the Franco-American Alliance, there was a good deal of uncertainty in the direction of the British war effort, and other commentators besides Eden came to endorse the view that the European components of the war should be emphasized over operations in the North American theater.[23] Yet this was only part of the story. As Eden further elaborated the nature of the conflict in which Britain was involved—what was at stake and what kind of effort would be needed to win—he began to argue that in many ways the American War had become a different kind of war.

That France and Spain had decided to deal Britain a political setback was not in and of itself revolutionary; the break from the established geopolitical order was found in the kind of political setback France and Spain would cause Britain if they successfully detached the American colonies from the British Empire. The Bourbon monarchies sought not simply to reset the European balance of power but to fatally undermine a key source of Britain's commercial, military, and naval strength. The metaphors Eden employed are revealing: "The house of Bourbon seized the hour of our embarrassments, and came upon us like an armed man in the night, *in hope of crushing us forever*, they came with all the greatness of collected strength, with the confidence of certain victory, with the foretaste of an early triumph."[24] And now France and Spain held great advantages over Great Britain. "The plain result of our situation (for we must not cover any part of it from our own eyes) is this—We are engaged in a war against France and Spain, under many new and considerable disadvantages."[25] Britain had no allies. Worse, "the united fleets of our enemies exceed in number, and in the aggregate of their apparent strength, any naval force that we are yet able to produce."[26] Furthermore, when the war began, taxes in Britain were already high, and the national debt enormous. Compounding all of this was the situation on the ground in the realm that was the first cause of the war itself. "North America, once the strength of our loins, is now become our weakness; and not negatively so; she is actually and extensively employed in the hands of our enemies to weigh us down."[27]

What Eden perceived was the totality of the crisis that confronted Britain in the American War, a totality that rendered the American War different from any previous European conflict. The British system of commerce and finance, Britain's military and naval strength, and the state of the European diplomatic system—all were being unraveled by the American declaration of independence, French recognition of it, and the concomitant spatial reorganization of the British Atlantic. As the war wore on into 1780, Eden saw that the "balance of power (hitherto the *perpetuum mobile* of politics) still remains suspended."[28] Things were not returning to normal. Britain's situation only promised to get worse, not better. The removal of the North American colonies from the British Empire, and France's complicity in this process, had changed everything.

> The stakes, involuntary indeed deposited on our part, are our Colonies, our Islands, all our commercial establishments and distant possessions, our navy, our foreign garrisons, the free entrance and use of the different seas, and all the various parts of that complicated

machine of trade, credit and taxation, which forms our position among the states of the world.[29]

The loss of the American colonies had the potential to undermine the multifaceted and interlinked foundations of empire—commercial, financial, military, and naval—that sustained British power and security. In assisting the rebellious American colonists to pull apart the British Empire, France and Spain were, in effect, threatening the destruction of the British state and nation. Eden laid out the stakes in dramatic fashion.

> The only question between us and our enemies is, whether we are to subsist as a nation, possessing its own liberties, pursuing its own commerce, and observing the rules of justice to all the world? Or whether we shall be deprived of our dependencies, be stript of our maritime power, become total and immediate bankrupts to all the world, and hold a crippled trade and commerce hereafter at the good will and compassion of the House of Bourbon?[30]

This was obviously not just another European war. France and Spain (along with the American colonies) had undertaken a course of action that fundamentally upset the established geopolitical order.

At the same time that William Eden perceived that Spanish and French intervention in the American War held out the potential for a geopolitical transformation that could fundamentally weaken Great Britain, he also saw that Britain had the means to succeed within the emerging geopolitical order. Part and parcel of the new order emerging during the American Revolutionary War was an increased recognition of the reality that that war was being fought on a greater scale than any other war in recent memory. "The system of modern war," Eden noted, which "spins out contests through several campaigns," placed many demands on the eighteenth-century state. It called for

> the levying and preparation of armies for the field; the recruiting of those armies, which, in the civilization of present times, can only be effected by drawing individuals from manufacture, agriculture, and other lucrative employments; the pay and subsistence of armies so formed; their transport from place to place; their clothing, arms, camp equipage, ammunition and artillery, articles of great cost (to which, in the instance of maritime states, must be added, the immense and complicated charge of naval force).

The demands this placed on the state were as enormous as they were unprecedented, at least in Eden's argument. "All these considerations united, have made the modern science of war a business of expence unknown to former times."[31] The only saving grace was that the necessity of these expenses was felt equally by all the powers involved. "The nature and necessity of great military force in modern states, form too obvious and too trite a subject to be insisted on," Eden asserted. "That necessity, as well as the expence attending it, both increase with the progress, advancement and riches of each particular society." The states that realized the interconnection between the maintenance of commerce, financial stability, the logistical support for military endeavors, and ultimately, success in the field would achieve victory. Thus Eden claimed that "a war carried on by this country must be a war of enterprize, and not of defence; the advantages of the former are peculiar to Great Britain." Eden's "war of enterprise" recognized the connections between success in commerce and success in warfare. "If by our naval exertions we can effectually protect our commerce, and preserve our carrying trade; our riches, the life of war, are as safe as our springs or rivers; and floods of treasure will flow into the kingdom with every tide."[32]

Eden's holistic geopolitical vision, which saw commerce, finance, and military policy as a seamless whole, anticipated the economic nationalism of neomercantilists of the 1780s. Likewise, Eden's policy prescriptions echoed the neomercantilists' peculiar economic liberalism, as both were informed by a reading of Adam Smith and other Scottish Enlightenment political scientists, and both called for unfettered commerce within, and only within, the bounds of the British Empire.

Eden's third essay of the *Four Letters* was entitled "On the Public Debts, on the Public Credit, and on the Means of Raising Supplies." Here Eden noted that the "spirit of trade, which has been so fortunate for this country in its operations and effects, has not always been kindly disposed towards the true and liberal principles either of commerce or taxation." Furthermore, "the present system of our trade and revenue-laws" were far from liberal and were in many places "a very motley mixture of political oeconomy and popular prejudice."[33] Eden called for paying down the national debt and lessening the nation's tax burden, taxing luxuries over necessities. He invoked Adam Smith's writings, calling for an "equality of taxation," which would "oblig[e] every individual to contribute in proportion to what he enjoys within the state," and he went on to delineate what the proper spheres and objects of taxation were.[34]

Eden's political economy was ordered by the new geopolitical reality. The British Empire needed to liberalize its economy within the empire's borders so that it could run as efficiently as possible to supply and maintain the British army and navy in the increasingly expensive task of waging modern war. During the course of the year following the publication of the *Fifth Letter to the Earl of Carlisle,* British defeats at sea and then on land revealed that calls for reform had come a little too late. After the battles of the Virginia Capes and Yorktown it was clear that in some way or another Great Britain would be forced to accept American independence.

The American Revolution had changed the shape of the world. On this there was much agreement. But as to how exactly, and to what end, there were many divergent opinions, of which Eden and the other British neo-mercantilists' was only one. When discussions about declaring independence began in the Continental Congress, the leaders of the American Revolutionary movement understood that they were calling for change within the established geopolitical order. The delegate Richard Henry Lee's resolution of June 7, 1776, urging Congress to take up discussion of a declaration of independence simultaneously called for Congress to draft a plan of confederation among the states and "to take the most effectual measures for forming foreign Alliances."[35] The Declaration of Independence was aimed not only at British and American audiences.[36] Later in 1776, John Adams led Congress in the drafting of a "Plan of Treaties," which was designed to serve as a blueprint for the United States' diplomacy with the various European powers; the Americans would seek commercial treaties opening up markets on both sides of the Atlantic, while eschewing treaties of political alliance. Almost simultaneously, the American diplomat Silas Deane, attempting to open negotiations with France, wrote a series of essays in which he outlined a vision of a new Atlantic world in which France would have access to the American raw materials, agricultural produce, and markets for finished goods that Great Britain had enjoyed for more than a century. Attempting to alleviate any potential anxieties among the diplomats of Continental Europe, both Adams and Deane offered visions of a new geopolitical order conceptualized within established geopolitical discourse.[37] It was only after the achievement of American independence and the Treaty of Paris's ratification of the new geopolitical order that a new geopolitical discourse began to emerge in both America and France. The American Revolution was seen by many as the midwife to a truly new world order, whether in the form of Ezra Stiles's Christian millennialism or the marquis de Condorcet's revolutionary enthusiasm.[38]

In Great Britain, American independence was greeted with much less fervor than on the European continent. In the wake of Lord Cornwallis's

1781 defeat at Yorktown, the majority of politically active Britons conceded the futility of trying to retain the thirteen colonies within the British Empire, and Lord North's ministry fell, finally, in March 1782. The initial peace negotiations between the American and British ministers thus opened in 1782 under the aegis of the new ministry of longtime opposition leader Rockingham. Power for negotiating an end to the American War was split between the two leading figures of Rockingham's coalition government— William Petty Fitzmaurice, Earl of Shelburne, who held the office of secretary for home, colonial, and Irish affairs, and Charles James Fox, who was secretary of foreign affairs.[39] Since Great Britain had not recognized the independence of the United States in the spring of 1782, negotiations with the Americans fell to Shelburne, and negotiating an end to the war with France, Spain, and the Netherlands became Fox's responsibility. Fox favored a quick recognition of American independence in order to use that as leverage for negotiating a more favorable settlement with the Continental powers. Shelburne, who actually was more sympathetic to the American cause than Fox, hoped to preserve some form of union with the American states and thus wanted to take time with the American peace settlement in order to guarantee a future harmonious relationship. This difference in vision, combined with differences in personality, put Shelburne and Fox at odds with each other. This became a greater problem when Rockingham died on July 1, 1782, just three months after taking office. Control of the ministry devolved to Shelburne, and Fox resigned his office. While Shelburne reorganized the cabinet (bringing in, among others, William Pitt the Younger), he did not have many allies in the House of Commons, and politicians loyal to both Fox and Lord North began to plot his downfall. With the proverbial clock ticking, Shelburne now favored a quick reconciliation with the Americans, and his chief negotiator, the Scots merchant Richard Oswald, was given fairly wide latitude to offer the Americans generous peace terms.[40]

The resulting Preliminary Articles of Peace, concluded on November 30, 1782, infuriated most politically aware Britons and mortally weakened support for Shelburne's ministry, which collapsed early in 1783, shortly after the treaty was presented to Parliament. The Preliminary Articles granted the Americans very favorable terms. The boundaries of the United States were set at the Mississippi River in the west, the northern boundary of the Floridas in the south, and from the coast of Maine and New Brunswick to the Lake of the Woods in the north, roughly the present-day northern boundary. Exclusive rights to treat with dozens of American Indian nations, nearly all British allies, were given over to the United States. The Mississippi

River would be open to American trade. American fishermen were granted permission to fish the Grand Banks and the Gulf of St. Lawrence and to dry their catch on the Canadian coast. The Americans promised to see that pre-Revolutionary debts to British creditors were paid, and despite British desires to ensure compensation for property confiscated from Loyalists, the Americans only promised that Congress would "recommend" a program of restitution to the individual state governments. Commercial arrangements would be decided by subsequent negotiation and legislation.[41]

Commerce was the linchpin around which the British-American relationship would evolve. Shelburne's vision for the future of the relationship between Great Britain and the United States had been influenced by British political economists who, during the middle decades of the eighteenth century, had begun to argue cogently and increasingly for Britain and other European nations to adopt policies of free trade. Writers such as Josiah Tucker and Adam Smith saw the mercantilist system codified by the Navigation Acts as inefficient, unjust, and ultimately untenable, as the North American colonies promised to continue to grow in population and wealth. Before too long the center of the British Empire's population and economic energy would be in North America rather than in the British Isles. Independence for the United States was thus only natural. In order to profit from America's inevitable rise, Shelburne wanted to return British-American trade to its (relatively unfettered) pre-Revolutionary state. Since Britain's industrial sector was still growing, and America would remain overwhelmingly agricultural into the foreseeable future, British manufacturing, commercial, and financial interests could grow wealthy selling to American farmers. This was the logic behind Shelburne's American Intercourse Bill, brought forward in the Commons by Pitt in March 1783.

The American Intercourse Bill, had it become law, would have returned British-American commerce to the same footing it had been on before the American Revolution began. The now-independent Americans would have full access to British markets both in the home islands and throughout the empire. The American Intercourse Bill was the keystone of Shelburne's plans for an Anglo-American rapprochement that would guarantee Britain's future prosperity. Unfortunately, by the time William Pitt the Younger, serving as Chancellor of the Exchequer, presented the bill to the House of Commons on March 5, 1783, Shelburne had resigned from the ministry and the jockeying to succeed him had begun. The last gasp from a dying ministry, the American Intercourse Bill would fail, but not before leading members of the Commons would take their shots at it and, by extension, at Shelburne's vision of a free-trade Atlantic. Economic nationalism would rule the day. And the loudest voice against the American Intercourse Bill in the House of Commons was none other than William Eden.[42]

Eden's objections to the American Intercourse Bill were rooted in the same geopolitical vision that he had laid out in his essays of 1779–80. Eden believed the stakes of such legislation to be enormous. "This Bill would introduce a total revolution in our commercial system, which [Eden] was afraid would shake it to its very basis, and endanger the whole pile." Eden worried that the American Intercourse Bill would be a de facto repeal of the Navigation Act, leaving Ireland suddenly unbound or unprotected (depending on the context) by the mercantile system. Since the United States were closer to the West Indies than to Ireland, they would likely usurp Ireland's share of the West India provision trade. With no restrictions on the types of goods that could be carried in American bottoms, American merchant ships would then begin to carry British manufactures to North America as well. These developments would promote an increase in the American carrying trade and a decrease in the British merchant marine, leading to a decrease in the supply of merchant seamen available to Great Britain in a time of war. Seeing commercial regulation, the carrying trade, the mercantile sector, and the preservation of British sea power as interconnected realms, Eden portrayed the American Intercourse Bill as a source of multiple potential dangers to the British Empire and the British nation. The United States of America was a foreign power and had to be treated as such.[43]

Attacking the American Intercourse Bill in March 1783, Eden was one of a growing chorus of economic nationalists who set policy for the new coalition ministry of Charles James Fox and Lord North. Rather than the American Intercourse Bill, the signature measure of the Fox-North ministry was the Orders in Council of July 2, 1783. While the new regulations allowed Americans to trade with the British Isles, the July Orders in Council closed the British West Indies to American shipping. The United States was to be treated as a foreign country in matters of commercial policy. This was the program advocated most famously by John Holroyd, Lord Sheffield, in his widely read pamphlet *Observations on the Commerce of the American States*. Sheffield, along with Charles Jenkinson (later Lord Hawkesbury) and George Chalmers, constituted the core of the neomercantilist movement. Like Shelburne, the neomercantilists were influenced by the economic theories of the writers of the Scottish Enlightenment, especially Adam Smith. Yet, whereas Shelburne had wished to apply Smithian economic liberalism to the entire international political economy, the neomercantilists were more limited in their application of the principles of free trade. They called for free and unfettered trade within the British Empire but were protective nationalists when it came to dealing with trade outside of the empire. Economic liberalism would make the empire more efficient, but the prerogatives of national self-protection would not be sacrificed. Now on the outside of the empire, America, like any other foreign power, would have to fend for itself. Hence the July 2, 1783, Orders in Council. The verdict of Sheffield in 1783 was that of Eden in 1779. The Americans, in having the West Indian trade denied to them, were getting exactly what they had asked for; in inscribing the names of the United States as independent entities on the map of the world, they had chosen their fate.[44]

Neomercantilism's triumph was never complete, however. By the beginning of 1784 the Fox-North coalition would be succeeded by a ministry led by William Pitt the Younger. Pitt would continue to head the ministry until 1801. Under Pitt, the spirit of neomercantilism would persist, but during the years before the French Revolutionary Wars elements of Shelburne's economic policies would find their way into the ministry's commercial and diplomatic program. While not committed to absolute free trade, Pitt turned to the policy of commercial reciprocity, especially in negotiations with other European countries. Pitt and his foreign minister during this period, Lord Carmarthen, sought to reintegrate Britain into the European balance of power and also find markets for British industrial manufactures on the Continent. The key to achieving both ends would be commercial treaties premised on the principle of reciprocity: each party would open a proportionate share of its markets to the other. Between the beginning of Pitt's ministry and 1792, Great Britain entered into commercial negotiations with eight different European sovereigns, including those of Spain, Russia, Prussia, the Netherlands, and France.[45] The 1786 commercial treaty between France and Great Britain was negotiated by none other than William Eden, testimony not only to his political instincts (in accommodating himself to service to the Pitt ministry) but also to the inherent flexibility and fluidity in the geopolitical vision of British policymakers after the settlement of the American War. Such flexibility of vision would serve Britain well in the years to come, in the wake of the transformation of geopolitical order and discourse that would occur as a result of the French Revolution and the resulting Revolutionary and Napoleonic wars.

NOTES

I wish to thank all of the participants in the October 2005 conference at the Salzburg Seminar for their stimulating discussion and helpful suggestions about how to improve this essay. Additional thanks go to Sara Gregg, David Hollander, Johann Neem, Peter Nicolaisen, Peter Onuf, and Andrew O'Shaughnessy for helping me to improve this essay after the conference.

1. For an account of the events of the Carlisle Commission, see Charles R. Ritcheson, *British Politics and the American Revolution* (Norman, OK, 1954), 255–84; Weldon A. Brown, *Empire or Independence: A Study in the Failure of Reconciliation, 1774–1783* (Baton Rouge, LA, 1941; Port Washington, NY, 1966), 205–92; and Eric Robson, *The American Revolution in Its Political and Military Aspects* (New York, 1966), 200–219. For the Carlisle Commission considered in the context of transatlantic diplomacy, see Leonard J. Sadosky, "Revolutionary Negotiations: An Intellectual and Cultural History of American Diplomacy with Europe and American Indians in the Age of Jefferson" (PhD diss., University of Virginia, 2003).

2. For a sketch of the career of William Eden, see Stephen M. Lee, "Eden, William, first Baron Auckland (1744–1814)," in *Oxford Dictionary of National Biography*, ed. H. C. G. Matthew and Brian Harrison, 60 vols. (Oxford, 2004), 17:690–93. My understanding of the notion of an "imperial constitution" and use of the term is informed by Jack P. Greene, *Peripheries and Center: Constitutional Development in the Extended Polities of the British Empire and the United States, 1607–1788* (Athens, GA, 1986).

3. Frederick Howard, Earl of Carlisle, to William Eden, 9 Sept. [1778], BL, Add. MSS 34416:33–34. Add. MSS 34412–17, microfilmed as *Materials Related to the American Revolution from the Auckland Papers in the British Museum*, in *British Records Relating to America in Microform*, ed. W. E. Minchton (East Ardsley, Wakefield, Yorkshire, n.d.).

4. In late 1778, at the urging of Lord George Germain, Sir Henry Clinton invaded Georgia, inaugurating the ministry's "Southern Strategy"; over the next three years the bulk of British military attention was devoted to attempts at securing a foothold in the southern states, which were perceived to be more Loyalist. For the formulation of Germain's strategy and the role of his undersecretary, William Knox, in the process, see Lelland J. Bellot, *William Knox: The Life and Thought of an Eighteenth-Century Imperialist* (Austin, TX, 1977), esp. 140–84. For details of the southern campaigns, see Don Higginbotham, *The War of American Independence: Military Attitudes, Policies, and Practice, 1763–1789* (New York, 1971), 352–88; and Sylvia R. Frey, *Water from the Rock: Black Resistance in a Revolutionary Age* (Princeton, NJ, 1991).

5. To be sure, there were commentators and policymakers in Britain who conceptualized (and even welcomed) the prospect of American independence before and during the War of the American Revolution, including Richard Price and Adam Smith. See Vincent T. Harlow, *The Founding of the Second British Empire, 1763–1793*, vol. 1, *Discovery and Revolution* (1952; London 1964), 198–222; and Eliga H. Gould, *The Persistence of Empire: British Political Culture in the Age of the American Revolution* (Chapel Hill, NC, 2000), 148–80. For the emergence of "neomercantilism"—the combination of economic liberalism and economic nationalism that drove British commercial policy in the years following American independence (normally associated with the writings of John Holroyd, Lord Sheffield)—see Vincent T. Harlow, *The*

Founding of the Second British Empire, 1763–1793, vol. 2, *New Continents and Changing Values* (London, 1964), 254–328; and John E. Crowley, *The Privileges of Independence: Neomercantilism and the American Revolution* (Baltimore, 1993), esp. 67–93. For a general account of the creation of the "Second British Empire," see Harlow, *Founding of the Second British Empire,* vols. 1 and 2; and C. A. Bayly, *Imperial Meridian: The British Empire and the World, 1780–1830* (London, 1989). For the evolution of the British-American relationship after the American Revolution, see Charles R. Ritcheson, *Aftermath of Revolution: British Policy towards the United States, 1783–1795* (Dallas, 1969); and Bradford Perkins, *The First Rapprochement: England and the United States, 1795–1805* (Berkeley, CA, 1967).

6. Some Britons had seen the American War in a European context years before the events of 1778. See Eliga H. Gould, "American Independence and Britain's Counter-Revolution," *Past & Present,* no. 154 (Feb. 1997): 107–141, esp. 112–13.

7. I use the word *autonomy* to denote the status of the United States in British eyes carefully. In 1778 Great Britain obviously was not willing to recognize American independence and sovereignty, which had been declared in July 1776 and which France had recognized in February 1778. Yet, the Treaty of Alliance forced Britons to recognize that the American colonies were playing a role in the international states system, albeit one that, in British eyes, served the interests of another power. *Autonomy* conveys the freedom of choice and agency that Americans had taken upon themselves and that Britons were grudgingly forced to acknowledge.

8. Carlisle to Eden, 9 Sept. [1778].

9. See Carlisle, Eden, and Henry Clinton to Germain, 21 Sept. 1778, in *Documents of the American Revolution, 1770–1783,* ed. K. G. Davies, 21 vols. (Dublin, 1972–81), 15:204.

10. Carlisle, Eden, and Clinton, "Manifesto and Proclamation," 3 Oct. 1778, Add. MSS 34416:38.

11. [Gouverneur Morris], *Observations on the American Revolution* (Philadelphia, 1779), 121–22.

12. Marques of Rockingham, speech in House of Commons, 7 Dec. 1778, in *Parliamentary History of England, from the Earliest Period to the Year 1803,* 36 vols. (London, 1814), 20:1–8. The debates on the Manifesto and Proclamation can be found in ibid., 20:1–46.

13. Although the discussions leading up to the Carlisle Commission saw Eden and others considering the American states as de facto independent entities, at this point in time they were never seen, de jure, as anything but parts of the British Empire. Tellingly, the Carlisle Commission's members were officially charged with "quieting the Disorders now subsisting in certain of our Colonies, Plantations, and Provinces in North America." See George III, "Orders and Instructions to the Earl of Carlisle, Lord Viscount Howe, Sir William Howe, William Eden, and George Johnstone, Commissioners," 12 Apr. 1778, in *Facsimiles of Manuscripts in European Archives Relating to America, 1773–1783,* ed. 20 vols. (London, 1889–95, Wilmington, DE, 1970), vol. 4, no. 440.

14. On 21 March 1778 Lord George Germain issued orders calling for the

evacuation of Philadelphia and a redeployment of British forces to the Caribbean and Canada. See Ritcheson, *British Politics and the American Revolution*, 254–56. The Carlisle Commission's arrival in the middle of the Philadelphia evacuation severely handicapped its work. Eden and Carlisle realized this immediately. See William Eden, "Minute," 29 July 1778, in Stevens, *Facsimiles*, vol. 5, no. 508; Earl of Carlisle, "Reply to the Minute of William Eden," 29 July 1778, ibid., no. 509; Alexander Wedderburn to Eden, [Aug. 1778], ibid., no. 514; and Eden to Wedderburn, 23 Oct. 1778, ibid., no. 539. Carlisle and Eden formally complained to Lord North upon their return to England. See Eden to North, 10 Feb. 1779, ibid., no. 555.

15. Although the term *geopolitics* was originated by the Swedish political scientist Rudolf Kjellén, responsibility for its popularization is normally assigned to the nineteenth-century British geographer Halford Mackinder. After Mackinder's 1904 lecture "The Geographical Pivot of History" to the Royal Geographical Society, *geopolitics* soon gained widespread acceptance in the academies and popular press of early twentieth-century Europe, America, and Japan. The origins of *geopolitics*, the somewhat checkered career of the discipline in the middle decades of the twentieth century (including its appropriation by the Third Reich), and its revival in the 1990s are all discussed in the essays contained in *Geopolitical Traditions: A Century of Geopolitical Thought*, ed. Klauss Dodds and David Atkinson (London, 2000). For Kjellén and Mackinder in particular, see Michael Heffernan, "*Fin de Siècle, Fin du Monde?* On the Origins of European Geopolitics, 1890–1920," in ibid., 27–51.

16. John Agnew, *Geopolitics: Re-visioning World Politics* (London, 1998), 2.

17. My conceptualization and discussion of geopolitical order and geopolitical discourse is informed by John Agnew and Stuart Corbridge, *Mastering Space: Hegemony, Territory, and International Political Economy* (London, 1995); see 13–76 for the major theoretical definitions. Agnew and Corbridge define the geopolitical order as "the routinized rules, institutions, activities, and strategies through which the international political economy operates in different historical periods," each of which has a "geographical element" that "is intrinsic to it." They define *international political economy* as the understandings of the (internal and external) construction and deployment of state power and the use of state power to order economic activity. I go a little beyond Agnew and Corbridge in enfolding into the notion of international political economy the cultural work done by international markets through the processes of commerce and consumption.

18. Ibid., 46–48.

19. Eden, *Four Letters*, 42.

20. Eden, *Fifth Letter*, 7.

21. Eden, *Four Letters*, 43.

22. Ibid., 57.

23. The defeat at Saratoga, the advent of the Franco-American Alliance, and the ultimate failure of the Carlisle Commission fueled a debate within the cabinet about the proper conduct and direction of the war. See Robson, *American Revolution in Its Political and Military Aspects*, 175–99. For George III's role in holding the cabinet together, see Andrew Jackson O'Shaughnessy, "'If Others Will Not Be Active, I Must

Drive': George III and the American Revolution," *Early American Studies* 2 (Spring 2004): 1–46, esp. 25–33.

24. Eden, *Fifth Letter,* 7, emphasis added.

25. Eden, *Four Letters,* 44.

26. Ibid., 45. Eden's observation was an astute one. With the addition of Spain to the French war effort, allied naval power was on its way to outstripping that of the Royal Navy. See Jonathan R. Dull, *The French Navy and American Independence: A Study of Arms and Diplomacy, 1774–1787* (Princeton, NJ, 1975); and idem, *A Diplomatic History of the American Revolution* (New Haven, CT, 1985), 107–13.

27. Eden, *Four Letters,* 44.

28. Eden, *Fifth Letter,* 8.

29. Eden, *Four Letters,* 48–49.

30. Ibid., 48.

31. Ibid., 51. Eden astutely (again) perceived the emergence of what John Brewer has labeled the "fiscal-military state." See Brewer, *The Sinews of Power: War, Money, and the English State, 1688–1783* (Cambridge, MA, 1988).

32. Eden, *Four Letters,* 57–58.

33. Ibid., 66.

34. Ibid., 87–94, quotation on 88.

35. "Resolution of Independence," 7 June 1776, in *TJP,* 1:298.

36. See David Armitage, "The Declaration of Independence and International Law," *WMQ* 59 (2002): 39–64. More expansive discussions of the international dimensions of the American Revolutionary project can be found in Frederick W. Marks, *Independence on Trial: Foreign Affairs and the Making of the Constitution* (Baton Rouge, LA, 1973); Peter Onuf and Nicholas Onuf, *Federal Union, Modern World: The Law of Nations in an Age of Revolutions, 1776–1814* (Madison, 1993); and David C. Hendrickson, *Peace Pact: The Lost World of the American Founding* (Lawrence, KS, 2003).

37. For an overview of these developments, see Dull, *Diplomatic History of the American Revolution.* More detailed descriptions of American diplomacy in France during the American Revolution can be found in William C. Stinchcombe, *The American Revolution and the French Alliance* (Syracuse, NY, 1969); Ronald Hoffman and Peter J. Albert, eds., *Diplomacy and Revolution: The Franco-American Alliance of 1778* (Charlottesville, VA, 1981); and Brian N. Morton and Donald C. Spinelli, *Beaumarchais and the American Revolution* (Lanham, MD, 2003). For the negotiation of the Treaty of Paris, see Dull, *Diplomatic History of the American Revolution,* 137–51; and Richard B. Morris, *The Peacemakers: The Great Powers and American Independence* (New York, 1965), 246–410. For John Adams, see James H. Hutson, *John Adams and the Diplomacy of the American Revolution* (Lexington, KY, 1980). For a reading of Silas Deane's essay-based diplomacy in France, see Sadosky, "Revolutionary Negotiations," ch. 3.

38. See Ezra Stiles, *The United States Elevated to Glory and Honor: A Sermon Preached Before His Excellency Jonathan Trumbull . . .* (Worcester, MA, 1785); and Marie Jen Antoine Nicolas Cartiat, marquis de Condorcet, "The Influence of the American Revolution on Europe" (1786), trans. and ed. Durand Echeverria, in *WMQ*

25 (1968): 85–108. For millennial elements in Revolutionary-era political thought, see Michael Lienesch, *New Order of the Ages: Time, the Constitution, and Making of Modern American Political Thought* (Princeton, NJ, 1988).

39. Both of these offices were new ones, having been created by reorganizing the offices of secretary of state (Northern Department), secretary of state (Southern Department), and American secretary.

40. Harlow, *Founding of the Second British Empire*, 1:223–29; John Ehrman, *The Younger Pitt: The Years of Acclaim* (New York, 1969), 77–89. For further background on Shelburne, see Charles R. Ritcheson, "The Earl of Shelburne and Peace with America, 1782–1782: Vision and Reality," *International History Review* 5 (1983): 322–45.

41. Harlow, *Founding of the Second British Empire*, 1:223–97.

42. Ibid.

43. William Eden, "Debate in Commons on the American Intercourse Bill," 7 Mar. 1783, in *Parliamentary History of England*, 23:602–8.

44. For the Fox-North coalition government, see John Cannon, *The Fox-North Coalition: Crisis of the Constitution, 1782–4* (Cambridge, 1969). On neomercantilism, see Crowley, *Privileges of Independence*, 67–93; and [John Lord Sheffield], *Observations on the Commerce of the American States, with an Appendix* (London, 1783). For additional background on the formulation of British policy toward America after the Treaty of Paris, see Ritcheson, *Aftermath of Revolution*, esp. 3–45.

45. See Ehrman, *The Younger Pitt*, 467–515; and John Ehrman, *The British Government and Commercial Negotiations with Europe, 1783–1793* (Cambridge, 1962).

John Adams, Thomas Jefferson, and the Dutch Patriots

PETER NICOLAISEN

In September 1787 King Frederick William II of Prussia ordered twenty thousand troops to march upon the Netherlands. He justified the invasion as an attempt to avenge an insult allegedly committed against his sister, Princess Wilhelmina, wife of Prince William V of the House of Orange. William V was stadtholder of the Netherlands, a hereditary office that traditionally established its occupant as the executive authority in the country.

In the spring and summer of 1787 the long-standing dispute over the issue of sovereignty in the republic and, more specifically, the stadtholder's constitutional powers had reached such intensity that the Netherlands were on the verge of a full-blown civil war. On the one side were the so-called Patriots, a loosely organized movement of both aristocratic regents and democratically minded middle-class citizens unified by their opposition against the stadtholder. On the other side were the Orangists, followers of the stadtholder of all ranks, including the lower classes, who wanted to restore the old order, a complex hierarchy at the top of which stood the prince. The conflict had set the European great powers at odds with one another. France supported the Patriots and, with the Patriot Party in the ascendancy, in 1785 had entered into an alliance with the Netherlands, while England all along backed the Orangists. Things came to a boil in June 1787, when members of a Patriot free corps stopped Princess Wilhelmina on her way from Nijmegen to The Hague. For the preceding six months she and her husband had been more or less exiled in Nijmegen; the purpose of her trip to The Hague, the regular seat of the court, was to rally support for the Orangist cause.

Outraged by what she felt was a personal affront by the Patriots, Wilhelmina appealed to her brother Frederick William II for help. After a series of unsuccessful attempts to obtain the apology he insisted upon, the king ordered his troops in motion. Once they had crossed the border into the Netherlands, the troops met with surprisingly little resistance from the Patriot militia and free corps. The rebellion against the Orangist regime subsided within weeks, and the old order was quickly restored. Many of the Patriot leaders were persecuted and found refuge in France, the Austrian Netherlands, the German principalities, and the United States.[1]

For a number of reasons the events in the Netherlands were of interest to the United States. The second country to acknowledge American independence and form a treaty of amity and commerce with the United States, the Netherlands had secretly helped the Americans during the War of Independence, mainly through contraband trade; in addition, Dutch bankers were the new nation's foremost source of money.[2] But Americans looked to the Netherlands for other reasons as well. For more than two centuries the country had been a republic; since the Union of Utrecht in 1579 it had consisted of seven provinces loosely held together by the assembly of the States General and the office of the stadtholder, the hereditary Prince of Orange. Many Americans wondered whether the Dutch constitutional makeup could possibly serve as a model for the United States.[3] The internal strife in the Netherlands reached its peak at almost exactly the time when the Constitutional Convention was meeting in Philadelphia. It is no wonder, then, that the civil disturbances in the Low Countries were anxiously observed by Americans who were on the scene in Europe.

Officially, the United States was represented in the Netherlands by John Adams, whom Congress had appointed minister plenipotentiary late in 1780, a few months after he had set out from Paris to Amsterdam to negotiate a loan with Dutch bankers. The historian Jan Willem Schulte Nordholt has vividly told the story of Adams's fierce struggle to achieve recognition of his status and, with that, of American independence. Adams finally met with success on April 19, 1782, a year after presenting his credentials to Their High Mightinesses, the deputies of the States General at The Hague.[4] As one of the negotiators of the Treaty of Paris, Adams was often absent from The Hague even before his appointment as minister plenipotentiary at the Court of St. James in 1785. Since he was not replaced in the Netherlands, in terms of diplomatic protocol his service there did not end until his recall in 1788. Whatever diplomatic business turned up was left in the hands of Charles W. Dumas, a German-born man of letters and enthusiast for the American cause. Dumas, an ardent Patriot who regularly supplied Congress with information about the state of affairs in the Netherlands, was remunerated for his services, but his status as chargé d'affaires was never officially confirmed. Beginning in 1785, he sent most of his reports through Thomas Jefferson in Paris.[5] Jefferson did not visit the Netherlands until 1788, and then only briefly, but his interest in the political affairs of the country eventually seems to have equaled, if not surpassed, that of John Adams.

In this essay I am concerned with the way in which the two leading American diplomats in Europe responded to a complex international situation. The chain of events that in its early stages promised to introduce in the Netherlands a political system akin to the one they had helped to establish in America under diplomatic and military pressure from neighboring countries quickly led to a debacle. More than in Adams's and Jefferson's success or failure as diplomats, I am interested in their attitudes toward the events they witnessed and toward the people involved. My contention is that even in these early years of American nationhood Adams and Jefferson showed a sense of separation from, and superiority to, European affairs that provided an underpinning for the policy of neutrality and non-entanglement they advocated. Adams in particular believed that if, in contrast to the Dutch, the Americans had succeeded in their revolution, it was because Americans somehow were better people than Europeans. Jefferson differed from Adams mainly in emphasis. The downfall of the Patriots confirmed his conviction that monarchy was the root of all evil in Europe. He saw the Dutch people as victims of the "monarchical" and "aristocratical" forces competing against each other, with "the single head" eventually winning out, and he praised the United States for having established its own, superior system of government. Some of his comments foreshadow his response to the revolution in France, but in general he remained remarkably detached from the civil strife threatening to tear the Netherlands apart. As both American diplomats were close to the scene of the conflict in the Netherlands, the episode provides an opportunity to compare and contrast their reactions to the events they witnessed and to assess their attitudes as a crisis involving the major European powers unfolded under their eyes.[6]

Notoriously given to blunt and outspoken comments, John Adams never tried to conceal the strong dislike he took to the country and its people soon after he arrived in the Netherlands in the summer of 1780. True, in a letter to his wife, Abigail, in the early weeks of his stay he showed himself "very much pleased with Holland" and praised "the Frugality, Industry, [and] Cleanliness" he found here. These virtues, he believed, "deserve the Imitation of my Countrymen"; they had led to "immense Wealth, and great Prosperity." The next sentence contains a curious reservation: the people, he observed, "are not Ambitious, and therefore happy."[7] Their lack of ambition soon rankled him. "The Love of Fame, the Desire for Glory, the Love of Country, the Regard for Posterity, in short, all the brilliant and sublime Passions are lost, and succeeded by nothing but the Love of ease and money," he complained. He found the republic "unanimated by a Love of military Glory, or any aspiring Spirit"; instead he considered it "sunk in Ease [and] devoted to the Pursuits of Gain."[8] "Fear is ever the Second Passion in minds governed by Avarice," he thundered, and he spoke contemptuously of "the Nation . . . trembling for their Commerce, their Money in the British Funds, their East and W. India Possessions."[9] His strictures of the country's lack of republican virtues were echoed in his private correspondence. In a note to Abigail he deplored "a general Littleness arising from the incessant Contemplation of Stivers and Doits" typical of the Dutch; this "littleness," he believed, "pervades the whole People."[10]

In Adams's eyes the Dutch lack of ambition and the fact that they "have no public Spirit in them" had made them defenseless.[11] In December 1780, on the eve of the Fourth Anglo-Dutch War (which England declared to prevent the accession of the Netherlands to the League of Armed Neutrality), he observed that "war is to a Dutchman the greatest of Evils." Once war had broken out, he noted that the Dutch were "furious" for peace. "Multitudes are for Peace with England at any Rate—even at the Expense and Risque of joining them in the War against France, Spain, America, and all the rest. They are in a Torpor a Stupor, such as I never saw any People in ever before."[12] While on occasion he may have been willing to concede that "the Dutch have an undoubted right to judge for themselves whether it is for their interest to connect themselves with us or not," what he really held against them was their unwillingness to take risks in favor of the United States, for the widespread fear he complained of had immediate consequences for the purposes he was pursuing: "No Man dares engage for me— very few dare see me," he lamented, irritated by the people's "apprehensions" that kept them from offering him the loan he was seeking. As it was, he sourly noted that "there is as yet no Possibility of borrowing any Money" from the Dutch.[13] In brief, he felt that the country owed him both recognition and money. But the Dutch were not to be trusted. "This Republic is a Jilt," he told Abigail. "When you think you have her Affections, all at once you find you have been deceiv'd." After a while, it seems, he gave up: "The Dutch have an Understanding Peculiar to themselves. They dont think like other Men upon any Thing."[14] Then, disarmingly, he breathed a sigh that generations of Americans have breathed after him: "What can be the Ground of the Malice, of so many, against America?"[15]

Adams's letters suggest that he was painfully conscious of the tension resulting from his firm belief in the future strength of the nation he represented and his simultaneous awareness of its current weakness. A few months before setting out for the Netherlands he had sent his "Transla-tion" of Thomas Pownall's "Memorial . . . On the Present State of Affairs Between the Old World and New World" to the president of Congress, a text emphasizing the superiority of the spirit of the American people over the spirit of the people of Europe. According to Pownall, with the Ameri-cans "all is Enterprize and Experiment," not least because of the "perfect Liberty" they enjoy "of using any mode of Life they choose." Pownall pre-dicted that America would therefore soon "become the arbitress of the com-mercial . . . and of the political business of the World." Adams agreed. "Gov. Pownall Speaks like an oracle," he wrote, amazed "that our country, so young as it is, so humble as it is, thinking but lately so mean of itself, should . . . so completely accomplish a revolution in the system of Europe and in the sentiments of every nation in it, is what no human wisdom, perhaps, could foresee."[16] To Benjamin Franklin he complained that "America is treated unfairly and ungenerously by Europe," and he fumed that "America . . . has been too long Silent in Europe. Her Cause is that of all Nations and all Men: and it needs nothing but to be explained to be approved."[17] When his negotiations about a loan were stalled, he burst out:

> Let them go on, lending their Money and hiring their Ships to En-gland to enable her to murder People of whom neither the Lender nor the Borrower are worthy. Time will Shew them, how much Wis-dom there is in their unfeeling Sacrifice of every Sentiment and every Principle upon the Altar of Mammon. The Less America has to do with such People the better it will be for her.[18]

On the same day he wrote to a friend:

> Indeed America will never derive any good from Europe of any Kind. I wish We were wise enough to depend upon ourselves for every Thing, and upon them for nothing. Ours is the richest and most in-dependent Country under Heaven, and We are continually looking up to Europe for Help! Our Riches and Independence grow annually out of the Ground.[19]

Adams knew, of course, that this was an illusion, at least for the time being, and that circumstances forced him to continue seeking a loan.

Aggravated by the pervasive avarice of the people of the Netherlands (his irritation was increased by "the mass of pestilential exhalations from the stagnant waters," the "poisonous Steams," and the "putrid lakes" of the country; at one point he said, "I shall carry Holland in my veins to my grave"), Adams also found little to praise in the political constitution of the republic.[20] After a year and a half in Amsterdam, he wrote in one of his regular letters to the president of Congress that "the Constitution of Government [here] is so complicated and whimsical a thing, and the Temper of the Nation so peculiar, that this is considered everywhere as the most difficult Embassy in Europe."[21]

The "Constitution of Government," of course, had always been a matter of serious interest to him. The peculiar variety he encountered in the Netherlands baffled him. When, assisted by Dumas, he presented his "Memorial" about the future relations between the United States and the United Provinces to the States General, he learned that the sovereignty of the republic was not only divided among the stadtholder and Their High Mightinesses, the deputies of the States General, but also resided in the states of the individual provinces; additionally, the towns and cities, each of them "considered an independent republic," as he said, wielded power through their regents, whose decisions, in the case of Amsterdam for instance, often had more weight than those of the provincial states, if not those of the States General.[22] The stadtholder, the Prince of Orange, as Adams learned, was captain general of the army and admiral general of the navy; his real source of power, however, lay in his right to appoint the deputies and regents in the majority of the cities and most of the provinces.[23]

To Adams this system seemed to border on the absurd, as did the endless deliberations among those who were involved in the decision-making process. "The Councils of this People are the most inscrutable, of any I ever Saw," he wrote in April 1781; half a year later he found that "it is still as problematical as ever what is the political system of this republic, and, indeed, whether it has any system at all. They talk much and deliberate long, but execute nothing."[24]

As late as October 1782 Adams was still wondering about the powers the various agencies of government wielded.[25] Dumas, "indefatigable in his Way," helped him to find out.[26] He also informed Adams about the burgomasters, the pensionaries and grand pensionaries, and the presidents and secretaries of the States General and the states of the provinces, all of whom had to be consulted because they had political weight and their opinions mattered. When asked by Robert Livingston why he had taken the unusual step of printing his "Memorial," Adams could rightfully argue that in order to reach the people involved in the process of deciding about his recognition as minister of the United States, four thousand or even five thousand copies barely sufficed.[27]

While Adams did not establish an immediate connection between the "most singular constitution of government" and the internal strife agitating the country, the civil dissension in the Netherlands was a frequent subject of his letters. As he wrote to the president of Congress,

> The Nation has indeed been in a violent fermentation and Crisis. It is divided in Sentiments. There are Stadthouderians and Republicans: there are Proprietors in English Funds, and Persons immediately engaged in Commerce. There are Enthusiasts for Peace and Alliance with England, and there are Advocates for an Alliance with France, Spain and America, and there are a third Sort who are for adhering in all things to Russia, Sweeden [*sic*], and Denmark. Some are for acknowledging American Independence and entering into Treaties of Commerce and Alliance with her: others start at the Idea with Horror, as an everlasting Impediment to a Return to the Friendship and Alliance with England. Some will not augment the Navy without increasing the Army: others will let the Navy be neglected rather than augment the Army.

What was to be dreaded in "this perfect Chaos of Sentiments and Systems, Principles and Interests," he went on to say, was not just the "Languor, ... Weakness and Irresolution" everywhere to be found, but the danger of "popular Tumults" and of "Seditions and Commotions among the people."[28]

Although he claimed that he had never "taken any share" in the factions dividing the republic, there is no doubt that if he felt any sympathies for any of the people at all, these lay with the movement identifying itself as *Patriotten*. When he told Livingston that "although I cultivate the friendship of the patriots, I shall not give offence to the court," he was less than candid. Not only was he actively taking sides when he employed an outspoken Patriot like Dumas as a semi-official agent of the United States (upon Adams's recommendation, Dumas moved into the "Hôtel des Etats Unis" in The Hague, a house Adams had bought even before he was officially recognized), but he also counted such leading Patriots as Jean de Luzac, editor of the *Leyden Gazette,* and Joan Derk Van der Capellen, author of the pamphlet *Aan het Volk Van Nederland* (To the People of the Netherlands), generally judged to be the most revolutionary text written by a Patriot, among his personal friends.[29] Consisting "of a great variety of powers and characters opposed in principle and interest," the Patriots, in Adams's view, were held together by their "design ... to clip what they think are the unconstitutional exuberances of the prince's power." As he saw it, most of them belonged to "the middle rank of citizens," while their opponents were "of the higher and lower classes."[30] They appealed to him not only because of their republican tendencies but also because of their pronounced anti-British sentiments. The "Republican Party," he reported, "have ever leaned towards an Alliance with France, because she has ever favoured the Republican Form of Government in this Nation," while "Family Alliances . . . have attached the Executive Power of this Government in such a manner to England, that nothing but Necessity could cause a separation."[31] But he was quick to caution against premature expectations: "The people of the seven United Provinces appear to me of such a character that they would make wild steerage at the first admission to any share in government; and whether any intimation of a desire of change at this time will not divide and weaken the nation is a problem."[32]

When the States General finally recognized him—as James Hutson has argued, they may have been persuaded by the French ambassador de Vauguyon rather than by the strength of Adams's "Memorial"—business interests and political sympathies for once seemed to converge.[33] Soon after his arrival in the Netherlands, Adams had written to the president of Congress that "those Persons who are both able and willing to lend Us Money, are the Patriots, who are willing to risk British and Stadtholderian Resentment for the Sake of extending the Commerce, Strengthening the political Interests, and preserving the Liberties of their Country."[34] The owners of one of the three banking houses that now came forward with a loan, Nicholas and Jacob van Staphorst, were indeed staunch supporters of the Patriots.[35] By this time the caveat Adams had expressed earlier—that the Patriots would refuse to lend money to the United States "without forming a political Connection with Us"[36]—seems no longer to have worried him. What bothered him now was not the politics of the moneylenders but their avarice. To Livingston he wrote, "I can represent my situation in this affair of a loan by no other figure than that of a man in the midst of the ocean negotiating for his life among a school of sharks."[37]

Once he had achieved his goals—the acknowledgement of American independence, a treaty of amity and commerce with the United Provinces, and, not least, a loan of 3 million florins, later raised to 5 million florins— Adams's interest in the Netherlands lost much of its earlier urgency.[38] But he kept informed about the political affairs of the country. On his return from Paris to The Hague for a short visit in the summer of 1783, he noted that the Patriot leaders were complaining "in the most pathetic terms, of the cruel situation of the friends of America and France in this Republic. They . . . say that they are looking round every way like drowning men for support. . . .

With Great Britain enraged against them, with a formidable party in the Republic furious against them, with the King of Prussia threatening them, and abandoned by France, their prospects are, they say, as disagreeable as can be conceived."[39]

In Paris he had spoken with David Hartley, the British commissioner, urging the British government to respect the balance between the "Partisans of the Statholder vs. the Republicans" so that the liberties of the Netherlands would not be jeopardized. His argument, as we learn from his diary, was surprisingly non-ideological: "Human Life, in that Country, struggling against the Sea, and in danger from so many quarters, would be too painfull and discouraging without Liberty." He also recorded that he had asked Hartley to suggest to the British minister that he "seek the Acquaintance and Friendship of the Principal Patriots in all the Provinces and give them Assurances of his Court that nothing should be attempted against their Constitution."[40] At The Hague Adams made an effort to talk with both sides, but his overall sympathies continued to be with the Patriots.[41] In September 1786—by which time Abigail had joined him and they were in the Netherlands for a brief visit from England—he paid what was perhaps his most gallant tribute to the Patriots, who had recently achieved a significant political success, replacing the ancient, appointed regents in Utrecht with elected candidates. In a letter to Thomas Jefferson, whom he had seen in England earlier in the year, Adams wrote: "We were present at Utrecht at the August Ceremony of Swearing in their new Magistrates. In no instance of ancient or modern History have the People ever asserted more unequivocally their own inherent and unalienable Sovereignty."[42]

The rest of the story as it relates to Adams is quickly told. In 1787, a few weeks before the incident involving Princess Wilhelmina took place, he was in Amsterdam to negotiate another loan. Despite the riots he witnessed in the city, he felt certain that "if no foreign Power interferes," the Patriots would prevail.[43] By September he feared that "the Republick of Holland is in the Utmost danger of being extinct: and if the old Forms are hereafter preserved, the Prince will be so much Master, in Reality, that the Friends of liberty must be very unhappy, and live in continual disgrace and danger." He was almost certain that war would break out because of the Prussian invasion, a move he contemptuously referred to as a "Romantick quarrel to revenge an Irreverence to a Princess, as Silly a Tale as the Trojan Wars on Account of Helen."[44] Condemning the invasion as a violation of the law of nations and "a most outragious Insult, in the face of the whole World," he emphasized the necessity for "the United States [to] take the coolest Precautions, while they fulfil their Engagements with Honor, to maintain their Neutrality inviolate." In his view it was of utmost importance that the United States "act the part, in Holland, of perfect independence and honest impartiality between the different Courts and nations who are now struggling for their friendship."[45]

At the same time, he feared for the "Friends of Liberty" in the Netherlands and hoped that "our friends the Dutch may be able to escape the evils of war in a manner consistent with their true interest and honor." But all in all, he was not overly worried that anything would happen to them: "You will not hear of those rigorous prosecutions and cruel punishments of the patriots in Holland, which are held out in terror; neutrality, eternal neutrality, will still be the passions and politics in the United Provinces, both of Stadtholderians and patriots. There are no warlike characters among them."[46] Contrary to his expectations, he soon had to concede that "there are many worthy characters, now exiles from Holland, and refugees in Germany, the Austrian Netherlands, and France, for whom I have many years entertained an esteem and an affection, whose situation is truly deplorable." To Jefferson he confessed, "I tremble and agonize for the suffering Patriots in Holland," and again, "My worthy old Friends the Patriots are extreamly to be pittied." He was willing even to include "their deluded Persecutors" in his sympathy and summed up the state of affairs in a single sentence: "That Country I fear is to be ruined, past all Remedy." In a way, the nation as a whole was at fault: "No rational Plan of a Reformation of their Government has been concerted by the People or their Leaders. It is a repetition of the Catastrophy of all ill constituted Republicks, and is a living Warning to our United States."[47] Nor did his friends Dumas or the Van Staphorsts escape his censure. They should have acted more circumspectly, he wrote to John Jay, and not taken "so decided a part in favor of France and against the Stadtholder."[48] His final verdict, in the spring of 1788, was harsh: "The Patriots in this country were little read in History, less in Government: knew little of the human heart and still less of the World. They have therefore been the Dupes of Foreign Politicks, and their own undigested systems."[49]

Jefferson was aware of the civil disturbances in the Netherlands even before his arrival in Europe in the late summer of 1784. While still in Annapolis, he wrote to James Madison that "the United Netherlands are in high fermentation. The people now marshall themselves in arms and exercise regularly under the banners of their towns. Their object is to reduce the powers of the Stadtholder."[50] It is likely that his acquaintance with Gijsbert Karel van Hogendorp, a young Dutch aristocrat who introduced himself to Jefferson in Annapolis, increased his interest in the country—he recommended Hogendorp to George Washington "as the best informed man of his age I have ever seen" and entered into a lively, if short-lived correspondence with him.[51] Hogendorp, an outspoken and energetic supporter of the Prince of Orange, warned Jefferson (who had meanwhile assumed his duties as American envoy in Paris) against the "dangerous struggle of parties in our Government." He blamed the Patriots for their lack of moderation and deplored the fact that the nation as a whole, instead of "resting satisfied with her success in reassuming such rights as must be her's in order to entertain an equipoise to the Stadholder's influence," had been "imposed upon by some daring men who should wish to lay the foundation of their own greatness on the ruin of the Stadholder's constitutional authority."[52]

When, a year later, Hogendorp told his "respectable friend" that he ought to know that "though a friend to liberty, my principles do not agree with many who call themselves by the same denomination," Jefferson answered right away, generously supplied information about the fiscal system of the United States for which Hogendorp had asked, and concluded diplomatically, "I feel a sincere interest in the fate of your country, and am disposed to wish well to either party only as I can see in their measures a tendency to bring on an amelioration of the condition of the people, an increase in the mass of human happiness. But this is a subject for conversation."[53] That conversation, alas, did not take place, for Hogendorp apparently never responded to Jefferson's letter. He belonged to the inner circle of Princess Wilhelmina and was among those who persuaded her to make her fateful trip to The Hague. His later rise to fame in the Netherlands was such that Jefferson certainly would have heard about him, but it seems that the two men had no further contact.

Instead, Charles Dumas became one of Jefferson's main sources of information about the events in the United Provinces. Unlike Adams, who relied on Dumas in many ways, Jefferson never warmed to "that ancient and worthy servant of our country," as Benjamin Franklin called him.[54] Throughout their correspondence, which lasted almost until Dumas's death in 1796, Jefferson remained courteous but reserved and usually forwarded the often long-winded messages the self-styled chargé d'affaires addressed to Congress without any comments.[55] Nonetheless, in his remarks to Dumas we occasionally do get an idea of his attitude toward the problems facing the Netherlands even before the crisis of 1787. Foreshadowing a more famous letter that he would write a few years later, Jefferson told Dumas in the fall of 1786:

The affairs of your Republic seem at present under a cloud which threatens great events. If the powers of the Stadtholder should be thereby reduced to such only as are salutary and the happiness of the people placed more within the command of their own will, it will be worth a great deal of blood. These struggles are a great sacrifice to the present race of men but valuable to their posterity. I sincerely wish the issue of this contest may give to the mass of people that increase of happiness which alone can justify it being attempted.[56]

One may wonder about the sincerity of sentiments expressed in such elegant, almost sinuous language, but this is a problem we often have with Jefferson. A week before Princess Wilhelmina started out on her trip to The Hague—Jefferson had just returned from his long journey through the south of France—he once again assured Dumas of his sympathy: "I wish nothing may be gathering in the horizon to obscure the prospects of the patriotic party. My prayers for their prosperity are warm."[57] After the defeat of the Patriots, when Dumas was harassed by the reestablished Orangist authorities, Jefferson tried to console him. "I sincerely sympathize with you in your sufferings," he wrote, adding apologetically, "I am forbidden by my character to meddle in the internal affairs of an allied state." The neutrality he thought he had to observe did not keep him from doing what he could to protect Dumas and his family against angry attacks by the mobs of the street.[58]

While he tried to keep informed about Dutch affairs, Jefferson was reluctant to take sides. As early as 1785 he mentioned the "danger of internal revolution" in the Netherlands; a year later he found "the republican party ... to be quite triumphant."[59] But he generally withheld judgment. To John Jay he reported in 1786 "that the parties in the United Netherlands have come to an open rupture. How far it will proceed cannot now be foreseen." In June 1787 he considered "the cause of the Patriots ... a little clouded at present"; then, with a civil war imminent, he told Edward Rutledge, somewhat superciliously, "The distractions of Holland thicken apace. They begin to cut one another's throats heartily," a phrase he seems to have liked so well that he repeated it a few weeks later in a letter to Edmund Randolph. His attitude of almost studied indifference gave way to a sense of agitation only when he considered the threat of foreign interventions:

May [the British and the French] not propose to have a force on the spot to establish some neutral form of a constitution which these powers will cook up among themselves?, without consulting the parties for whom it is intended? . . . Wretched indeed is the nation in whose affairs foreign powers are once permitted to intermeddle!

At this point he was convinced that England and France, because of "their insuperable poverty," would not go to war over the Netherlands. Instead, "they will compel a suspension of hostilities, and either arrange and force a settlement on the Dutch, or if they cannot agree themselves on this, they will try to protract things by negociation." Should the disputes lead to an armed struggle, "the law of self-preservation . . . must oblige France to abandon the Dutch or to patch up by negociation the best terms she can for them."[60]

Watching the clouds gather over the Netherlands from his position in Paris, Jefferson seems never to have given the Patriots much of a chance to succeed in their efforts to introduce even "a temperate mixture of Democracy" in their country. As he summed up the state of affairs in a letter to the president of Congress of August 6, 1787, he mentioned "the fatal coalition" behind the Prince of Orange, which, "if it's progress be not stopped by a little moderation in the Democrats, . . . will turn the scale decidedly in favor of the Stadhoulder." By aiming too high—"they talked of establishing Tribunes of the people, of annual accounts, of depriving the magistrates at the will of the people &c., of enforcing all this with the arms in the hands of the corps francs"—the Patriots were driving even the "moderate Aristocrats" back into the fold of the stadtholder and thus brought about "a schism" in their movement.[61]

Jefferson's tone changed dramatically when he turned to the threat of a military intervention by King Frederick William II of Prussia, who had succeeded his uncle Frederick the Great upon the latter's death in 1786. Outraged by the unexpected move of the Prussian king, Jefferson expressed his moral indignation in strong terms. France and England, he asserted,

> were labouring jointly to stop the course of hostilities in Holland, to endeavor to effect an accommodation . . . when all of a sudden, an inflammatory letter written by the Princess of Orange to the K. of Prussia induces him, without consulting England, without consulting even his own council, to issue orders by himself to his Generals to march 20,000 men to revenge the insult supposed to be offered his sister. With a pride and egotism planted in the heart of every king, he considers [his sister] being stopped in the road as a sufficient cause to sacrifice a hundred or two thousand of his own subjects and as many of his enemies, and to spread fire, sword and desolation over the half of Europe.[62]

Jefferson's anger did not abate in the following weeks. He wrote to John Rutledge of the "blessed effect of kingly government, where a pretended insult to the sister of a king is to produce the wanton sacrifice of a hundred or two thousand of the people who have entrusted themselves to his government"; to George Washington he spoke of "the bad passions of kings and those who would be kings." His irritation rose to an even higher pitch as he dashed off more letters on the subject: "The stoppage of the sister of a king is sufficient cause to sacrifice the lives of hundreds of thousands of better people and to lay the most fertile parts of Europe to ashes."[63]

In the person of the king of Prussia, it seems, Jefferson found a culprit who confirmed all his suspicions about the evils of monarchy and on whom, at least temporarily, he could lay the blame for the debacle to which the movement of the Patriots had led. He feared that war would break out; only the poor financial state of both France and England would prevent it. For a while he entertained hopes that, on the basis of a French alliance with the Russian and Austrian empires, "the Patriotic party in Holland will be peaceably placed at the head of their government." When the invasion actually took place and Patriot resistance in the Netherlands quickly crumbled, he was relieved to hear from the Dutch ambassador in Paris that the American "depot of money" was safe and that "the people of Amsterdam would be surely so wise as to submit, when they should see that they could not oppose the Stadholder."[64] A few days later he asked John Adams, "Are we to suppose the game already up, and that the Stadtholder is to be reestablished, perhaps erected into a monarch, without this country [France] lifting a finger in opposition to it?"[65]

As it dawned on him that the French court had not only "been completely deceived" in its interpretation of the new diplomatic situation but sorely misled the Patriots, he could barely contain his disappointment about the shameful role the foremost ally of the Americans had assumed:

> The King of France ... declares he has no intention to intermeddle with force in the affairs of Holland, and that he will entertain hostile views in no quarter for what has been done there. He disavows having ever had any intention to interpose with force in the affairs of that republic. This disavowal ... includes no apology to soothe the feelings which may be excited in the breasts of the patriots of Holland at hearing the king declare he never did intend to aid them with force, when promises to do this were the basis of those very attempts to better their constitution, which have ended in it's ruin as well as their own.[66]

In a private letter accompanying his official report to John Jay he laid the blame for France's surrender on the new French premier, the archbishop of Toulouse, who in Jefferson's eyes was "solely chargeable with the loss of Holland." France should have decided to fight, he exclaimed, convinced "that in a war for the liberties of Holland, all the treasures of that country would have been at their service. They have now lost the cow which furnishes the milk of war."[67] Perhaps he was thinking of his earlier predictions that France would support the Patriots in Holland "even at the expense of war"; it appears that he too had been misled in his expectations.[68]

Given the relief the French decision not to go to war afforded Britain, Jefferson was afraid that Britain might now turn against the United States: "They may think the moment favourable for executing any purposes they may have in our quarter. We are therefore never safe till our magazines are filled with arms."[69] As for the diplomatic consequences that might arise from the new situation in Europe, he was hedging his bets. "Perhaps the spring may unfold to us the final arrangement which will take place among the powers of this continent," he wrote in December.[70] Then, on his journey in the spring of 1788 to Amsterdam, where he joined John Adams in his negotiations with the Dutch bankers, Jefferson learned of the reestablishment of the stadtholder at first hand. Public pressure was such that on his arrival in Amsterdam he felt obliged, as did everybody else, to don the colors of the Prince of Orange. On the evening of the Prince's birthday, he told William Short, "the illuminations were the most splendid I had ever seen and the roar of joy the most universal I had ever heard." His report to John Jay reads like a summary of the events: "The court of Versailles seems to pursue immoveably it's pacific system: and from every appearance in the country from which I write we must conclude it's tragedy is wound up. The triumph appears complete and tranquillity perfectly established. The numbers who have emigrated are differently estimated from 20. to 40. thousand."[71]

Surprisingly, the "tragedy" of the country to which the fall of the Patriots had led is hardly mentioned at all in the notes Jefferson took during his brief stay in Holland in the spring of 1788.[72] But the Dutch conflict kept agitating him. In 1795, when he learned of the victory of the French army against the stadtholder's troops, he was elated. "The French in Amsterdam and Van Staphorst President of the revolutionary committee! Bravo!" he exclaimed, overjoyed by what he felt were "the great prosperities of our first two allies, the French and the Dutch."[73]

The most explicit testimony to the impact the events of 1787 had on Jefferson, however, is to be found in his 1821 *Autobiography*. By that time all his earlier enthusiasm had disappeared. As he now saw it, the failure of the

Patriots' attempt "to establish a representative and republican government" in the United Provinces was due primarily to the ignominious role of the stadtholder, "a stupid man . . . in arms against the legitimate authority of the country" and guilty of "treasonable perfidy" against his people. The villain of the piece at this point was no longer Frederick William II of Prussia, who in the *Autobiography* appears as no more than a man of "little understanding, much caprice, & very inconsiderate." Together with the other foreign powers involved in the conflict, he created "a mere scene of bullying & demonstration," neither France, England, nor Prussia "having ever meant to encounter actual war for the interest of the Prince of Orange." The real culprit was the stadtholder. Jefferson summed up his overall sense of the affair in a scathing indictment of the Prince: "Thus fell Holland, by the treachery of her chief, from her honorable independence to become a province of England, and so also her Stadtholder from the high station of the first citizen of a free republic, to be the servile Viceroy of a foreign sovereign."[74] When he wrote these lines, the Netherlands, not least through the efforts of his erstwhile friend G. K. van Hogendorp, had long since become a constitutional monarchy. The changes the intervening years had brought about evidently had not helped to cool Jefferson's anger at the "treachery" of 1787.

The response of the two American diplomats to the crisis in the Netherlands in many respects corroborates what we know about early American foreign relations. While both Adams and Jefferson personally favored the Patriots' cause, the policy they advised Congress to pursue was in accordance with the principles of neutrality and non-entanglement the young nation had adopted early on. As Adams said, "The business of America with Europe [is] commerce, not politics or war"; beyond that, "it ought to be our rule, not to meddle, and that of all the powers of Europe not to desire us or perhaps even permit us to interfere, if they can help it."[75] The Netherlands may have been a republic and in many respects akin to the United States— in his "Memorial" of 1781 Adams had made much of the similarities between the two nations—but its recent fate illustrated all too well "the labyrinth of European politics" from which, in Madison's words, "we ought religiously to keep ourselves as free as possible."[76] Jefferson agreed. Like Adams, he advocated neutrality and kept warning against an American involvement in European affairs: "Peace should be our plan, and the paiment of our debts, improvement of our constitutions and extension of agriculture our principal objects."[77]

Although, as Adams wrote, "the real or imaginary balances of power" in Europe ought not to concern Americans, both diplomats were worried about the shift in the scale of power the demise of the Patriots and the re-establishment of the Stadtholder meant.[78] They knew that the Patriots' loss was England's gain. In fact, Jefferson blamed the Prussian king precisely for upsetting "the balance of Europe" and disturbing its peace.[79] The realignment of the balance of power had immediate consequences for America's safety; in the view of the two Americans, a weakened France and a strengthened England meant an increased threat to the United States. Their frequent reminders to Congress not to neglect the country's defense indicate how concerned they were with questions of its security.[80]

Both American statesmen insisted that the nation they represented differed significantly from the European countries involved in the conflict. In their emphasis on the contrast between European feudalism on the one hand and American republicanism on the other they pointed the way to an American self-conception that was to dominate American and, to a lesser extent, European views about the United States for years to come.[81] Adams's self-characterization as a diplomat is a case in point. With the moral fervor and self-righteousness he so frequently displayed, he claimed from the "Hôtel des Etats Unis" in The Hague that he possessed "the severity of a true republican, his high idea of virtue giving him a rigidness, which makes it difficult for him to accommodate himself to those intrigues which European politics have introduced into negociation."[82] Conversely, the Comte de Vergennes, the French foreign minister, in Adams's view demonstrated what was wrong with European politics. Vergennes, Adams wrote, "has no conception of the right way of negotiating with any free people or with any assembly, aristocratical or democratical. He can not enter into the motives which govern them; he never penetrates their real system, and never appears to comprehend their constitution."[83] His many grievances about Vergennes are here summarized in a single point: the Frenchman did not understand the idea of liberty. Again, Jefferson, who personally liked Vergennes, agreed. Vergennes, he told Madison, "is a great Minister in European affairs but has very imperfect ideas of ours [and] no confidence in them."[84]

The contrast between the two worlds included the "common people" as well. Would "American Liberty" ever have triumphed, Adams asked, "if there had not been more Faith, Honour, and Justice in the Minds of their common Citizens, than are found in the common people in Europe? Do we see in the Austrian Netherlands, in the United Netherlands, or even in the Parliament in France, that Confidence in one another, and in the Common People, which enabled the People of the United States to go through a Revolution?" The answer, of course, was no. The difference between Americans and Europeans, Adams maintained, was a basic "Want of Honesty" among Europeans. And it was because of their moral deficiency that "the common people in any part of Europe" had failed to achieve revolutionary change. "Oh Fortunate Americans," he exclaimed, "if you did but know your own Felicity!"[85]

In his darker moods Adams, like many of his compatriots, was assailed by fears that Americans might be just as given to "present Passions, Prejudice, Imagination, Enthusiasm or Caprice" as any other nation; they too might be tempted to "call in foreign nations to settle domestic differences" as soon as a serious crisis broke out among them.[86] But such doubts, it seems, did not affect his certainty that the American people, with their enterprising "spirit," would soon triumph over the Europeans, of whom the Dutch, with their "deep despondency" and "the solemn gloom ... and the universal uncertainty and timidity that had seized their minds," were but an example.[87]

Jefferson was no less convinced of the difference between Americans and Europeans, and like his compatriot he felt that the nation he represented was superior to those of the Old World. More so than Adams he focused his thoughts on the one institution that he held responsible for the evils he encountered in Europe—monarchy. For Jefferson, more acutely than for Adams, the events in the Netherlands exemplified European feudalism at its worst. In the context of the Prussian invasion of 1787 he penned some of his most extreme comments on the "blessed effects of kingly government." With Frederick William II in mind, he spoke of the "class of human lions, tygers and mammouts called kings"; in reference to the Prussian government, he famously concluded that governments in Europe are "governments of kites over pidgeons." To compare American and European governments therefore appeared to him "like a comparison of heaven and hell."[88] The contrast he saw is epitomized in a letter he wrote to Dumas just before the Prussian invasion took place. With the Philadelphia Convention still in session, he mused: "Happy for us that when we find our constitutions defective and insufficient to secure the happiness of our people, we can assemble with all the coolness of philosophers and set it to rights, while every other nation on earth must have recourse to arms to amend or to restore their constitutions."[89] Clearly, America was the better world.

Arguably, their aversion to European feudalism and their belief in the superiority of the republican institutions they saw emerging in their own country shaped Adams's and Jefferson's perceptions of the events they observed and explain why on occasion their views radically differed from those of their European colleagues. While the Americans shrugged off the "stoppage" of Princess Wilhelmina by the Patriots as an incident barely deserving serious attention, many European diplomats registered the episode with signs of shock and immediately anticipated the reaction that followed.[90] At times the sense of difference marking the response of the American diplomats manifested itself as an element of irritation at, or impatience with, a given situation; on other occasions they voiced their belief in the superiority of the American model outright. Not surprisingly, perhaps, their preoccupation with the advantages of their own country occasionally led them to see things that were not there and to miss clues European diplomats would have noted.[91] But what matters is not whether their version of the events of 1787 was right or not—few historians have ever seen the Dutch affairs quite in the same way as they did—but the sense of difference, if not division, from Europe characteristic of their response. Its republican flavor and its peculiar self-assertiveness are qualities that, as time has shown, have often determined American attitudes to European affairs. It is true that only two years later, when his republican principles were challenged by the revolution in France, Jefferson responded with a very different kind of commitment than the one he had shown in the Netherlands. The general tendencies I have noted here obviously left room for a variety of reactions. In the long run, the attitude they constituted proved rather durable.

NOTES

Most of the research for this essay was done during a fellowship at the Robert H. Smith International Center for Jefferson Studies. I would like to thank Andrew O'Shaughnessy and everyone at the ICJS for their generous help. My special thanks go to Cinder Stanton and Leonard Sadosky for their encouragement and advice.

1. For a good account of the Patriot movement, see Simon Schama, *Patriots and Liberators: Revolution in the Netherlands, 1780–1813* (New York, 1977), 65–135. See also I. Leonard Leeb, *The Ideological Origins of the Batavian Revolution: History and Politics in the Dutch Republic, 1747–1800* (The Hague, 1973), esp. 175–219. For a brief overview, see Jonathan Israel, *The Dutch Republic: Its Rise, Greatness, and Fall, 1477–1806* (Oxford, 1998), 1098–1112; and Herbert H. Rowen, *The Princes of Orange: The Stadholders in the Dutch Republic* (Cambridge, 1988), 205–29. H. T. Colenbrander, *De patriottentijd, hoofdzakelijk naar buitenlandsche bescheiden* [The Times of the Patriots, Mainly According to Foreign Documents], 3 vols. (The Hague, 1897–99), and C. H. E. de Wit, *De Nederlandse revolutie van de achttiende eeuw, 1780–1787: Oligarchie en Proletaraat* [The Dutch Revolution of the Eighteenth Century, 1780–1787: Oligarchy and Proletariat] (Oirsbeek, 1974), remain indispensable. For more recent views on the Patriot revolution, see the essays in *1787: De Nederlandse revolutie?* [1787: The Dutch Revolution?], ed. Th. S. M. van der Zee, P. G. B. Thissen, and J. G. M. Rosendaal (Amsterdam, 1988); *De Droom van de revolutie: Nieuwe benadering van het Patriotism,* ed. H. Bots and W. W. Mijnhaardt (Amsterdam, 1988); and *The Dutch Republic in*

the Eighteenth Century: Decline, Enlightenment, and Revolution, ed. M. C. Jacob and W. W. Mijnhardt (Ithaca, NY, 1992), as well as Maarten Prak, "Citizen Radicalism and Democracy in the Dutch Republic: The Patriot Movement of the 1780s," *Theory and Society* 20 (1991): 73–102; and Herbert H. Rowen, "The Dutch Republic and the Idea of Freedom," in *Republicanism, Liberty, and Commercial Society, 1649–1776,* ed. David Wootton (Stanford, CA, 1994), 310–39, 466–73, esp. 331–33. A good account of the incident involving Princess Wilhelmina is Nico Bootsma, "Das Ereignis von Goejanverwellesluis," in *Onder den Oranje Boom: Textband,* ed. Horst Lademacher (Munich, 1999), 89–102, 435. On the refugees, see Joost Rosendaal, *Bataven! Nederlandse vluchtelinge in Frankrijk, 1787–1795* [Batavians! Dutch Refugees in France, 1787–1795] (Nijmegen, 2003).

2. On the Dutch loans, see Pieter J. Van Winter, *American Finance and Dutch Investment, 1780–1805, with an Epilogue to 1840,* trans. James C. Riley, 2 vols. (New York, 1977); and James C. Riley, "Foreign Credit and Fiscal Stability: Dutch Investment in the United States, 1781–1794," *JAH* 65 (1978): 654–78.

3. On the Netherlands as a possible model for the United States, see William H. Riker, "Dutch and American Federalism," *Journal of the History of Ideas* 18 (1957): 495–521. For James Madison's extensive notes on the "Belgic Confederacy," see *JMP* 9:11–18. David C. Hendrickson, *Peace Pact: The Lost World of the American Founding* (Lawrence, KS, 2003), 47–48, 321–22, briefly discusses the Netherlands as a possible model for the United States.

4. Jan Willem Schulte Nordholt, *The Dutch Republic and American Independence,* trans. Herbert H. Rowen (Chapel Hill, NC, 1982). See also the much less favourable account of Adams's diplomatic activities in the Netherlands in James H. Hutson, *John Adams and the Diplomacy of the American Revolution* (Lexington, KY, 1980), chs. 4 and 5; and idem, "John Adams and the Birth of Dutch-American Friendship, 1780–1782," in *A Bilateral Centennial: A History of Dutch-American Relations, 1782–1982,* ed. J. W. Schulte Nordholt and Robert P. Swierenga (Amsterdam, 1982), 19–32. An earlier account is L. H. Butterfield, *John Adams and the Beginnings of Netherlands-American Friendship, 1780–1788* (Boston, 1959). Friedrich Edler, *The Dutch Republic and the American Revolution* (Baltimore, 1911), remains invaluable.

5. See Charles W. Dumas to TJ, 28 Sept. 1785, *TJP,* 7:561. Dumas had earlier sent his letters to Congress through Benjamin Franklin. Most of Dumas's correspondence with Congress is available in *The Revolutionary Diplomatic Correspondence of the United States,* ed. Francis Wharton, 6 vols. (Washington, DC, 1889) (hereafter *Rev. Corr.*); and *The Diplomatic Correspondence of the United States of America from the Signing of the Definitive Treaty of Peace . . . to the Adoption of the Constitution . . . ,* 7 vols. (Washington, DC, 1833–34) 3:459–658 (hereafter *Dipl. Corr.*). On Dumas's uncertain status, see Boyd's notes in *TJP,* 9:231n and 12:200n. For a thorough and sympathetic account of Dumas's character and activities, see Schulte Nordholt, *Dutch Republic and American Independence,* esp. 230–33.

6. Earlier accounts of Adams's and Jefferson's approaches to the Dutch crisis include Lawrence S. Kaplan, "The Founding Fathers and the Two Confederations: The United States of America and the United Provinces of the Netherlands, 1783–1789," in *Entangling Alliances with None: American Foreign Policy in the Age of Jefferson* (Kent,

OH, 1987), 35–47, 202–4; and Jonathan R. Dull, "Two Republics in a Hostile World: The United States and the Netherlands in the 1780s," in *The American Revolution: Its Character and Limits,* ed. Jack P. Greene (New York, 1987), 149–63. On Adams and the Patriots, see also Edward Handler, *America and Europe in the Political Thought of John Adams* (Cambridge, MA, 1964), 108–16; and Hutson, *John Adams and the Diplomacy of the American Revolution,* chs. 4 and 5. For the Jefferson quotations, see TJ to St. John de Crèvecoeur, 9 Aug. 1788, *TJP,* 13:485.

7. JA to Abigail Adams (hereafter AA), 4 Sept. 1780, *AFC,* 3:410. In a letter written a few months later, Adams noted the same qualities but found that "here, these are only private Virtues and begin and end in Self." The Dutch had no "public Spirit in them." JA to William Temple Franklin, 7 Dec. 1780, *PJA,* 10:398. On Adams's attitude toward the Netherlands and the Dutch, see also Schulte Nordholt, *Dutch Republic and American Independence,* esp. 109–12.

8. JA to president of Congress, 27 and 16 May 1781, *PJA,* 11:340, 318.

9. JA to president of Congress, 25 Nov. 1780, ibid., 10:371–72. See also JA to James Warren, 9 Dec. 1780, ibid., 395: "No Resentment of Injuries, or Insults—No Regard to National Honour or Dignity, will turn them out of their pacific Course. . . . Such a Nation of Idolators at the Shrine of Mammon never existed I believe before."

10. JA to AA, 18 Dec. 1780, *AFC,* 4:35. As Schulte Nordholt notes, Adams here echoed widespread prejudices about the Dutch national character. *Dutch Republic and American Independence,* 5.

11. JA to William Temple Franklin, 7 Dec. 1780, *PJA,* 10:398.

12. JA to president of Congress, 18 Dec. 1780, ibid., 419; JA to Francis Dana, 12 Mar. 1781, ibid., 11:196. See also Edler, *Dutch Republic and the American Revolution,* 176n, which states that Adams "misunderstood the situation."

13. JA to Robert Livingston, 14 Feb. 1782, *Rev. Corr.,* 5:162; JA to president of Congress, 18 Dec. 1780 and 14 Jan. 1781, *PJA,* 10:420, 11:45.

14. JA to AA, 4 Jan. 1782, *AFC,* 4:273; JA to Edmund Jenings, 31 Dec. 1780, *PJA,* 10:464.

15. *Diary and Autobiography of John Adams,* ed. L. H. Butterfield, 4 vols. (Cambridge, MA, 1961), 2:456 (28 Feb. 1781) (hereafter *DA*).

16. *PJA,* 9:178, 172, 180, 166; on the importance of Pownall's "Memorial" for Adams's thinking, see the editorial note beginning on 9:157–64. JA to president of Congress, 28 Apr. 1780, *Rev. Corr.,* 3:639.

17. JA to Benjamin Franklin, 16 Apr. 1781, *PJA,* 11:261; JA to Dana, 18 Apr. 1781, ibid., 269.

18. JA to Joan Derk van der Capellen tot den Pol, 9 Dec. 1780, ibid., 10:403.

19. JA to Cotton Tufts, 9 Dec. 1780, *AFC,* 4:29.

20. JA to Franklin, 4 Oct. 1781, *Rev. Corr.,* 4:767; JA to AA, 18 May 1783, *AFC,* 5:162; JA to Livingston, 16 June 1783, *Rev. Corr.,* 6:490.

21. JA to president of Congress, 14 Jan. 1782, *Rev. Corr.,* 5:100.

22. Ibid., 99.

23. See JA to president of Congress, 25 Nov. 1780, *PJA,* 10:373.

24. JA to president of Congress, 6 Apr. 1781, ibid., 11:248, and 1 Nov. 1781, *Rev. Corr.,* 4:813–14.

25. See the following entry in Adams's diary: "What are the Powers of the Council of State?—how many Members? Who appoints them? Are they for Life, or Years, or at Will? When do they sit? What objects of Administration have they? Is their Power Legislative, Executive or Judiciary?" *DA,* 3:13.

26. Ibid., 15.

27. JA to Livingston, 19 Feb. 1782, *Rev. Corr.,* 5:187. The complexity of the Dutch constitution is borne out by the description Dumas sent to the president of Congress in his letter of 1 Dec. 1783, *Dipl. Corr.,* 3:461–69. See also standard texts such as Schama, *Patriots and Liberators,* esp. 45–58, and the extensive discussion of the "Call for Constitutional Restoration" in Leeb, *Ideological Origins of the Batavian Revolution,* 175–97. In view of his earlier criticisms, the short paragraph Adams devoted to the Dutch constitution in his 1787 *Defence of the Constitutions . . . of the United States* is surprisingly positive. He praises its "sagacity" and "wisdom," speaks of its "consideration of the people," and, curiously, claims that the Dutch "have never had any exclusive preferences of families or nobles." Written as they were with "the critical situation" of the country in mind, his remarks probably are not to be taken too seriously. See John Adams, *A Defence of the Constitutions of Government of the United States of America,* 3 vols. (Philadelphia, 1787), 1:69.

28. JA to president of Congress, 19 Mar. 1781, *PJA,* 11:214.

29. JA to Livingston, 14 Feb. and 4 Sept. 1782, *Rev. Corr.,* 5:162, 688. Adams considered Capellen's pamphlet a fine example of the impact the American Revolution had on "the assuming pride of the people" and the growth of "democratical principles" in Europe. JA to president of Congress, 25 Oct. 1781, ibid., 4:812. On Adams's relations with individual Patriots, see also Schulte Nordholt, *Dutch Republic and American Independence,* esp. chs. 7 and 8.

30. JA to Arthur Lee, 4 Sept. 1785, in Richard Henry Lee, *Life of Arthur Lee,* 2 vols. (Boston, 1829), 2:256.

31. JA to president of Congress, 25 Sept. 1780, *PJA,* 10:177.

32. JA to president of Congress, 25 Oct. 1781, *Rev. Corr.,* 4:812.

33. Hutson, *John Adams and the Diplomacy of the American Revolution,* 75–116.

34. JA to president of Congress, 25 Sept. 1780, *PJA,* 10:178. Capellen warned Adams "not to expect [the bankers] to lend on principle. Such generosity would surpass the limits of virtue in most men. Nevertheless, I can assure you that a vast plurality of my nation, certainly more than 4/5 parts, likes the Americans and hopes for their complete success. . . . The only people who will never be won over are those attached to the court." Capellen to JA, 24 Dec. 1780, ibid., 432.

35. On Adams's negotiations, see the fascinating account in Van Winter, *American Finance and Dutch Investment,* ch. 3. According to Riley, "Foreign Credit and Financial Stability," Adams, instead of addressing the "most substantial firms," which were Orangist, "had to turn to firms that were more congenial politically, if less imposing as bankers." (657–58).

36. JA to president of Congress, 25 Sept. 1780, *PJA,* 10:178.

37. JA to Livingston, 16 May 1782, *Rev. Corr.,* 5:420. See also Adams's later letter to John Jay, "There is a despotism in this country in the government of loans, as absolute as that of the grand signior; five or six people have all the money under

their command, and they are as avaricious as any Jew in Jews' Quarter. This country revenges itself in this way, upon the powers of Europe, for the insults it receives from them in wars and negotiations." JA to Jay, 13 Feb. 1784, in *The Works of John Adams*, ed. Charles Francis Adams, 10 vols. (Boston, 1850–56), 8:180–81 (hereafter *WJA*). George Shackelford's contention that the Willinks were Jews is unsubstantiated; according to Van Winter, the Willinks were "an old Mennonite family." See Shackelford, *Jefferson's Adoptive Son: The Life of William Short, 1759–1848* (Lexington, KY, 1993), 72; and Van Winter, *American Finance and Dutch Investment*, 86.

38. On the figures, see Riley, "Foreign Credit and Fiscal Stability," 657; see also *DA*, 3:9n.

39. JA to Livingston, 3 Aug. 1783, *Rev. Corr.*, 6:632. See also JA to Livingston, 25 July 1783, ibid., 596–97, where Adams related the Patriot Party's claim that France had "betrayed and deserted them" in the peace negotiations.

40. Entry of 20 May 1783, *DA*, 3:121–22; JA to Livingston, 16 June 1783, *Rev. Corr.*, 6:490; JA to AA, 18 May 1783, *AFC*, 5:162.

41. See JA to Livingston, 23 and 25 July 1783, *Rev. Corr.*, 6:591–95, 596–97.

42. JA to TJ, 11 Sept. 1786, *TJP*, 10:348.

43. JA to Jay, 16 June 1787, in *The Emerging Nation: A Documentary History of the Foreign Relations of the United States under the Articles of Confederation, 1780–1789*, ed. Mary A. Giunta et al., 3 vols. (Washington, DC, 1996), 3:532 (hereafter *Emerging Nation*).

44. JA to Jay, 23 Sept. 1787, ibid., 592–93, and *Dipl. Corr.*, 2:807; JA to Jay, 22 Sept. 1787, *Emerging Nation*, 3:588, and *Dipl. Corr.*, 2:804–5.

45. JA to Jay, 30 Nov. 1787, *Emerging Nation*, 3:664; 22 Sept. 1787, ibid., 588; 15 Nov. 1787, *WJA*, 8:461.

46. JA to Jay, 15 Nov. 1787, *WJA*, 8:460.

47. JA to Jay, 30 Nov. 1787, ibid., 462; JA to TJ, 28 Oct. 1787, *TJP*, 12:292; JA to TJ, 10 Nov. 1787, ibid., 335; JA to John Jay, 9 Oct. 1787, *Emerging Nation*, 3:620–21.

48. JA to Jay, 15 Nov. 1787, *WJA*, 8:461.

49. JA to AA, Mar. 1788, quoted in Schulte Nordholt, *Dutch Republic and American Independence*, 276.

50. TJ to Madison, 1 Jan. 1784, *TJP*, 6:438.

51. TJ to George Washington, 6 Apr. 1784, ibid., 7:84. On Hogendorp, see H. van der Hoeven, *Gijsbert Karel van Hogendorp: Conservatief of liberal?* (Groningen, 1976); see also Gijsbert Karel van Hogendorp, *The College at Princetown, May 1784*, ed. Howard C. Rice (Princeton, 1949), iii–xii. Schulte Nordholt comments briefly on Hogendorp's negative views of America, *Dutch Republic and American Independence*, 259–62.

52. Hogendorp to TJ, 20 Jan. 1785, *TJP*, 7:610.

53. Hogendorp to TJ, 2 Aug. 1786, ibid., 10:190; TJ to Hogendorp, 25 Aug. 1786, ibid., 299.

54. Franklin to Livingston, 25 June 1782, *Rev. Corr.*, 5:513.

55. Jefferson met Dumas when he passed through The Hague in March 1788, but he made no effort to see him again. The tone of his letters suggests that he was not particularly fond of him. See TJ to Jay, 27 Jan. 1786, *TJP*, 9:235–36; TJ to James Monroe,

27 Jan. 1786, ibid., 237; TJ to Monroe, 10 May 1786, ibid., 503; and TJ to Madison, 20 June 1787, ibid., 11:482.

56. TJ to Dumas, 22 Sept. 1786, ibid., 10:397.

57. TJ to Dumas, 14 June 1787, ibid., 11:471.

58. TJ to Dumas, 14 Nov. 1787, ibid., 12:359–60. As Jefferson told Dumas in a letter of 3 Oct. 1787, he had asked the ambassadors of both the United Provinces and Prussia "to have an efficacious protection extended to your person, your family, and your effects." Ibid., 199–200. On Dumas's precarious situation after the reestablishment of the stadtholder, see his various letters in *Dipl. Corr.*, 3:582–658; JA to TJ, 28 Oct. 1787, *TJP,* 12:292; Boyd's extensive note, ibid., 200–202; Hendrick Fagel to JA, 18 Oct. 1787, *Emerging Nation,* 3:632–33; and Schulte Nordholt, *Dutch Republic and American Independence,* 293–99.

59. TJ to Madison, 18 Mar. 1785, *TJP,* 8:39; TJ to Louis Guillaume Otto, 7 May 1786, ibid., 9:470.

60. TJ to Jay, 26 Sept. 1786, ibid., 10:406; TJ to Jay, 21 June 1787, ibid., 11:490; TJ to Edward Rutledge, 14 July 1787, ibid., 589; TJ to Edmund Randolph, 3 Aug. 1787, ibid., 672; TJ to Benjamin Vaughan, 2 July 1787, ibid., 533; TJ to Edward Carrington, 4 Aug. 1787, ibid., 679–80.

61. TJ to Jay, 6 Aug. 1787, ibid., 11:696. R. R. Palmer used this passage as evidence for his argument in his article "The Dubious Democrat: Thomas Jefferson in Bourbon France," *Political Science Quarterly* 72 (Sept. 1957): 388–404, 396. See also Schulte Nordholt, *Dutch Republic and American Independence,* 275.

62. TJ to Jay, 6 Aug. 1787, *TJP,* 11:697.

63. TJ to John Rutledge, 6 Aug. 1787, ibid., 701; TJ to Washington, 14 Aug. 1787, ibid., 12:38; TJ to David Humphreys, 14 Aug. 1787, ibid., 32.

64. TJ to Jay, 24 Sept. 1787, ibid., 12:171. Although Jefferson had left all negotiations about the American foreign loans in Adams's hands, he was in touch with the American bankers in Amsterdam and had frequently tried to push the project of transferring the debt Congress had incurred in France to Dutch bankers in order to ease the pressure on France. See his letters to Jay, 26 Sept. 1786, ibid., 10:405–6; to Madison, 20 June 1787, ibid., 11:481–82; to JA, 1 July 1787, ibid., 517; to Madison, 2 Aug. 1787, ibid., 664; and to Benjamin Hawkins, 4 Aug. 1787, ibid., 684. Pieter Van Winter, in *American Finance and Dutch Investment,* 248–56, discusses Jefferson's proposal in detail. See also Riley, "Foreign Credit and Fiscal Stability," 662–63. On the effect of the political upheaval in the Netherlands on the issue of American loans, see ibid., 673; and Van Winter, *American Finance and Dutch Investment,* 289–90.

65. TJ to JA, 28 Sept. 1787, *TJP,* 12:189–90.

66. TJ to Jay, 3 Nov. 1787, ibid., 309–12.

67. TJ to Jay, 3 Nov. 1787, ibid., 315.

68. As the attitudes of England and Prussia became more rigid, Jefferson seems to have been less sure of France's resolution. See TJ to John Banister Jr., 19 June 1787, ibid., 11:476; and TJ to Jay, 21 June 1787, ibid., 490–91.

69. TJ to Jay, 3 Nov. 1787, ibid., 12:312.

70. TJ to Carrington, 21 Dec. 1787, ibid., 446.

71. See *Jefferson's Memorandum Books,* ed. James A. Bear and Lucia C. Stanton,

2 vols. (Princeton, NJ, 1997), 1:697; TJ to William Short, 10 Mar. 1788, *TJP,* 12:659; and TJ to Jay, 16 Mar. 1788, ibid., 673.

72. In his "Notes of a Tour through Holland and the Rhine Valley" Jefferson identified the political affiliation of some of the people he met—"Hodson the best house. Stadhouderian.... Vollenhoven, An excellent old house, connected with no party"—but did not go beyond this. See ibid., 13:8–33, 10.

73. TJ to John Taylor, 15 Apr. 1795, *TJP,* 28:328; TJ to William Branch Giles, 27 Apr. 1795, ibid., 337.

74. *TJW,* 67–70. In a letter of 1810 Jefferson was even more dismissive of Frederick William II, writing him off as "a mere hog in body as well as in mind." TJ to John Langdon, 5 Mar. 1810, ibid., 1218. Few historians have shared Jefferson's assessment of William V, who is mostly blamed for his indecisiveness and weakness of character. See, among others, Rowen, *Princes of Orange,* 205–29.

75. JA to Livingston, 5 Feb. 1783, *Rev. Corr.,* 6:243; JA, "Journal of the Peace Negotiations," 18 Nov. 1782, ibid., 11.

76. Madison to Monroe, 21 June 1786, *JMP,* 9:83. Adams also spoke of the "labyrinth" of European politics. JA to Livingston, 16 July 1783, *Rev. Corr.,* 6:554.

77. TJ to David Rittenhouse, 18 Sept. 1787, *TJP,* 12:145. To William Carmichael TJ wrote, "Neutrality should be our plan." 25 Sept. 1787, ibid., 174. For the moral principles underlying Jefferson's line of reasoning, see esp. TJ to Washington, 14 Aug. 1787, ibid., 37–38.

78. JA, "Journal of the Peace Negotiations," 18 Nov. 1782, *Rev. Corr.,* 6:11.

79. "He has shewn decidedly that he will support [England] even to the destruction of the balance of Europe, and the disturbance of its peace." TJ to Jay, 6 Aug. 1787, *TJP,* 11:696.

80. See JA to Jay, 9 Oct. 1787: "It is my duty, therefore, to advise that the best Preparations, for our own defence and Security be made, that are in our Power." *Emerging Nation,* 3:620. See also JA to Jay, 30 Nov. 1787, ibid., 665. For Jefferson's views, see n. 68 above.

81. For the general context, see Jack P. Greene, *The Intellectual Construction of America: Exceptionalism and Identity from 1492 to 1800* (Chapel Hill, NC, 1993), esp. chs. 5 and 6.

82. [JA], *Collection of State Papers relative to the first acknowledgement of the Sovereignty of the United States* (London, 1782), 4.

83. JA to Livingston, 31 July 1783, *Rev. Corr.,* 6:624.

84. TJ to Madison, 30 Jan. 1787, *TJP,* 11:95–96.

85. JA to Jay, 22 Sept. 1787, *Dipl. Corr.,* 2:806, and 23 Sept. 1787, *Emerging Nation,* 3:593.

86. JA to TJ, 9 Oct. 1787, *TJP,* 12:220–21.

87. Adams recalled the "gloom" of the Dutch even when he published his correspondence of his years in the Netherlands more than twenty years later. See *The Correspondence of the late President Adams. Originally Published in the 'Boston Patriot' in a Series of Letters* (Boston, 1809), 430.

88. TJ to Humphreys, 14 Aug. 1787, *TJP,* 12:32; TJ to John Rutledge, 6 Aug. 1787, ibid., 11:701.

89. TJ to Dumas, 10 Sept. 1787, ibid., 12:113.

90. See, e.g., the response of the Prussian minister Count Hertzberg, who in a letter to the princess spoke of "the terrible insult to the King himself" and "the atrocity" it implied, quoted in Colenbrander, *De patriottentijd*, 3:167, my translation; or Lord Carmarthen's message to Joseph Ewart, the British envoy in Berlin, which mentions the "indignity offered to the Princess of Orange," adding that the British king "did not conceive that the Province of Holland could have been so mad as not to have instantly complied with His Prussian Majesty's very first demand of reparation and punishment," ibid., 171, also my translation. Even such a seasoned (and cynical) ambassador as Sir James Harris, of Great Britain, was upset by the events. See *Diaries and Correspondence of James Harris, First Earl of Malmesbury*, 4 vols. (London, 1844), 2:326–30. Coming from the pro-Orangist side, these are biased reactions, of course, but they suggest the kind of feelings generally entertained among European officials at the time. On learning of the princess's detention, Hogendorp, Jefferson's former friend, wrote in his diary, "Mon affliction ne se décrit pas." *Journal de G. K. Van Hogendorp pendant la révolution de Hollande (Avril–Octobre 1787)*, ed. Henry de Peyster (Utrecht, 1905), 66.

91. Jefferson's representation of the Prussian invasion as the result of a sudden decision of the king, when in fact weeks of negotiations elapsed before the troops were set in motion, is a case in point. On the king's many attempts to reign in Princess Wilhelmina and the Prussian-British negotiations preceding the invasion, see *Historische und politische Denkwürdigkeiten des königlich-preussischen Staatsministers Johann Grafen Eustach von Görtz*, 2 vols. (Stuttgart, 1827–28), 2:1–201. See also Friedrich Karl Wittichen, *Preussen und England in der europäischen Politik 1785–1788* (Heidelberg, 1902), 159–69, 78–95, and passim; Friedrich Luckwaldt, "Die englisch-preußische Allianz von 1788," *Forschungen zur Brandenburgischen und Preussischen Geschichte* 15 (1902): 33–116; *Diaries and Correspondence of James Harris*, vol. 2; Alfred Cobban, *Ambassadors and Secret Agents: The Diplomacy of the First Earl of Malmesbury at the Hague* (London, 1954), and Henry de Peyster, *Les troubles de Hollande à la veille de la Révolution Française, 1780–1795* (Paris: Picard, 1905). Hutson, *John Adams and the Diplomacy of the American Revolution*, esp. 108–16, makes much of Adams's ignorance of the diplomatic activities going on around him while he was in Holland.

John Adams in Europe
A Provincial Cosmopolitan Confronts the Metropolitan World, 1778–1788

RICHARD A. RYERSON

> To take a Walk in the Gardens of the Palace of the Tuilleries, and
> describe the Statues there, . . . would be a very pleasant Amusement, and
> instructive Entertainment, improving in History, Mythology, Poetry. . . .
> But I could not do this without neglecting my duty.—The Science of
> Government it is my Duty to study, more than all other Sciences: the
> Art of Legislation and Administration and Negotiation, ought to take
> [the] Place, indeed to exclude in a manner all other Arts.—I must study
> Politicks and War that my sons may have liberty to study Mathematicks
> and Philosophy. My sons ought to study Mathematicks and Philosophy,
> Geography, natural History, Naval Architecture, navigation, Commerce
> and Agriculture, in order to give their Children a right to study Painting,
> Poetry, Musick, Architecture, Statuary, Tapestry and Porcelaine.

> —JOHN ADAMS TO ABIGAIL ADAMS, AFTER MAY 12, 1780

For John Adams scholars, as well as many historians of American culture,
the passage quoted above is among the most celebrated of all Adams's dec-
lamations. One of its most striking features is its highly accurate prediction
of the history of the Adams family, and to a lesser extent of America as a
whole, over the next century and beyond. But in its immediate context the
words project a different image: Adams's determination, under the cover of
a sincere appeal to the demands of his current diplomatic obligations, to
deny himself an intimate acquaintance with the Europe in which he had
already spent the better part of two years and in which he knew he would
probably spend several more.

Adams's reluctance to embrace European culture and society is evident
from his first arrival in France, in April 1778, to his final departure from

England just ten years later. His heavy workload partly explains this, as does his embarrassment at his rudimentary conversational French. And despite his diffidence, Adams did make several new friends in France, Holland, and England; in London he even attended the theater. Yet Adams never sought to engage the Europe that was right in front of him, and he never felt that he needed to, for at least three reasons.

First, Adams, a fifth-generation New Englander whose family had never moved more than ten miles from their initial settlement, retained enough of the moral rectitude of his small-town Puritan forebears to be more than a little uncomfortable with the social and sensuous aspects of European culture: Paris salons and the theater, the ostentatious display of the wealthy, and "Musick, Statuary, Tapestry, and Porcelaine." He did not flatly reject this metropolitan world—indeed he sincerely professed an admiration for the fine arts—but he kept it at more than arm's length. This refined elegance would be appropriate for his grandsons—not his sons, who would be too busy studying mathematics and naval architecture—but it was not for him.

A related motive for Adams's deliberate avoidance of a full exposure to European high society was his conviction, common to many Americans of his day, including some envoys and merchants raised as far south as Virginia, that the aristocratic culture of France and England was morally inferior to the simplicity of American life and potentially destructive of American values. There is a fine irony in this conviction: beginning in the 1790s and continuing well into the twentieth century, several of Adams's countrymen charged him, especially as a political thinker, with having been corrupted by European aristocracy.[1]

Yet Adams had a more personal reason for standing back from the Europe of his own day. Of all America's early diplomats, indeed of all the Founding Fathers,[2] Adams had the most profound knowledge of the Europe of the mind and of the ages. When he first sailed for France, his mastery of European history, political science, and the law from the sixteenth through the eighteenth century was unparalleled in America, and it only became deeper and broader during his stay in Europe, especially after his diplomatic burdens lightened in France and then England after 1783. However Europeans or Americans may have judged the effectiveness of Adams's mission in Europe, he was convinced that he already knew everything about contemporary Europe that he needed to know, and far more than any other American. What happened to Adams in his European decade is the story of a man with a distinctly provincial personality but a powerful, cosmopolitan mind who suddenly encountered a sophisticated metropolitan world.

Most studies of John Adams in Europe have either attempted to determine what kind of diplomacy he pursued and how successful he was as an American envoy[3] or sought to understand how his encounter with Europe shaped his political thought.[4] Here I pursue the second goal. I focus on certain experiences that affected Adams's thought in his European decade and then consider their relationship to his political theory. First, however, it will be necessary to identify the features of Adams's political thought that have made him the subject of interest to historians and political scientists alike.

Virtually all scholars of the Revolutionary era, like many of John Adams's well-informed contemporaries, have seen him as a distinctive political thinker. In a career that spanned three decades as a public figure and more than five decades as a published writer, he developed certain ideas that, in their emphasis and sometimes in their essence, were well outside the mainstream of American political thought. Central to all his published political writings after 1776 are two convictions: the importance of a strong executive to a well-balanced republic and the danger aristocratic power posed to the survival of any republic.

Several historians have concluded that both convictions grew out of Adams's decade in Europe.[5] But his view of the role of the executive, which gradually took the form of an extended, impassioned argument for a kind of "republican monarchy," began as early as 1775, three years before his first departure from America, although he continued to develop this idea in England in the 1780s.[6] Adams's concern with the threat of aristocracy to republican government, however, did not appear in his public or private writings before his return from his first European mission in 1779. And he developed this initial concern into a fully articulated theory of republican pathology over the next eight years, while serving his country in France, Holland, and England. A major goal of this essay is to advance an explanation for the relationship of this development to his experience in Europe.

Adams's first foreign service was on America's three-man commission in France (April 1778–February 1779), where he tried to mediate between the feuding Benjamin Franklin and Arthur Lee and labored mightily to bring order to the commission's chaotic paperwork and casual attitude toward daily business. His labors ended suddenly when Congress replaced the commission with a sole minister, Benjamin Franklin. Adams thought this was a good idea, but he soon became dismayed when Congress failed either to thank him for his services or to tell him what he should do next—go on a mission to Vienna or to Holland or return home. To congressional friends he put up a brave front, but to Abigail he confessed, "The Scaffold is cutt away, and I am left kicking and sprawling in the Mire, I think. It is hardly a state of Disgrace that I am in but rather of total Neglect and Contempt. . . . if I had committed any Crime which deserved to hang me up in a Gibet in the Face of all Europe, I think I ought to have been told what it was."[7]

In his campaign to secure support for America in Holland (July 1780–October 1782), as in his years in France, Adams was often deeply frustrated. For more than a year he found it difficult to make any impression on the phlegmatic Dutch burgers, and his private letters expressed mounting irritation at their caution, timidity, and devotion to money and material comfort.[8] As in France, however, Adams found himself most thoroughly confounded by his own countrymen. As long as he stayed in Holland, he got along well with Franklin, who cheerfully cooperated with Adams on their joint diplomatic responsibilities but otherwise left him alone.[9] Congress was not so accommodating. In June 1781 it revoked Adams's appointment as its sole peace commissioner and placed him at the head of a five-man commission that included Franklin, John Jay, Henry Laurens, and Thomas Jefferson. Upon learning of the commission in August, Adams claimed to have no objection to it, but Congress's instructions to the new commission would be another matter. Under pressure from the chevalier de la Luzerne, French foreign minister comte de Vergennes's envoy in Philadelphia, Congress instructed the new commission to consult with America's French allies in all its negotiations with Britain and "to undertake nothing in the negotiations for peace or truce without their knowledge and concurrence and ultimately to govern yourselves by their advice and opinion."[10]

Robert R. Livingston, Congress's new secretary for foreign affairs, quickly set to scrutinizing Adams's diplomatic behavior in Holland and then in France.[11] From Livingston's first letters to Adams, which reached Holland in February 1782, until shortly before the conclusion of peace with Britain in the summer of 1783, Adams found himself, for the first time in his life, patronized and lectured to by a countryman who knew little about Europe and cared nothing for Adams's superior knowledge and experience. On November 20, 1781, Livingston wrote to Adams that he was astonished to hear that Adams had presented his credentials to the Dutch government in the memorial of April 19 but had "not written on so important a subject and developed the principles that induced you to declare your public character, before the States [General] were disposed to acknowledge it."[12]

In his reply to Livingston of February 19, 1782, Adams began a spirited defense of his diplomacy that extended into the summer of 1783 and often brought him to the boiling point. The combination of Livingston's sharp criticisms of Adams's and Jay's wariness of consulting the French and Adams's own growing conviction of French opposition to America's securing as much territory and power as possible in the peace treaty could drive Adams into the kind of frenzy that inspired Franklin to remark, in a separate letter to Livingston, that Adams "is always an honest Man, often a Wise One, but sometimes and in some things absolutely out of his Senses."[13]

In a decade of service in Paris, Amsterdam, The Hague, and London, Adams gradually learned something about face-to-face diplomacy, grew more at ease talking to Dutchmen, Britons, and even Frenchmen, and even became more comfortable speaking in French. Yet none of his diplomatic successes depended on his developing a "diplomatic" personal style; in this respect Benjamin Franklin would always outshine him.

For Adams, however, diplomacy was never about being "diplomatic." From the outset he expected his skills and talents to be honored by Europeans, and he was surprised and frustrated when they were not. He felt that he had even better reasons to expect that his own countrymen would understand and honor his approach to diplomacy and was astonished and deeply hurt whenever Americans, especially in Congress, failed to see the virtues of his behavior. To understand Adams as a diplomat, and especially as a political thinker, we must consider the knowledge and experience that he valued.

Congress had posted Adams to Europe because of his keen intelligence and broad learning, his legal skills, his accomplished pen, and his robust appetite for business. These strengths never failed him, and he put them all to good use, especially in Holland. In Amsterdam and The Hague, Adams played the role of lobbyist and also, with valuable preparation in Paris in 1780, of propagandist. At the peace negotiations in Paris in the fall of 1782 he played the role of a seasoned, tough litigator. In each of these roles he drew on nearly two decades of legal experience.

Many members of the Continental Congress practiced law, and a few of them served as diplomats, notably Adams, Jay, and Jefferson. Yet most Revolutionary leaders whom we call lawyers were in fact lawyers and planters, or lawyers and wealthy gentlemen. By contrast, Adams's life before the Revolution was focused almost exclusively on the law. For nearly two decades, practicing law had been his sole occupation, and reading widely in law was his favorite avocation. Nearly all of his personal heroes, from his young manhood to full maturity, were lawyers or judges, beginning with Cicero, his favorite historical figure, and ending with his older contemporaries, both Tories and Patriots, who dominated the Massachusetts bench and bar on the eve of the Revolution.[14]

Adams also had a second vocation, one closely allied to, yet distinct from, his first: he was a committed and prolific published writer. Adams never wrote for hire or earned a substantial share of his income from writing (in Revolutionary America probably only Thomas Paine ever achieved that distinction), but he was a serious author who counted on his pen to achieve his immediate goals as a Massachusetts lawyer and citizen, as a congressman, and as a diplomat. And from 1786 to 1791 he wrote to achieve a broader political agenda, probably in Holland, certainly in America, and possibly even in France. Thereafter he wrote for publication only occasionally but at some length, mostly to defend his earlier diplomatic and political career or his earlier writings. As a legal and political reader, thinker, and writer Adams developed in a manner that set him apart from all his contemporaries. To begin with, his reading was heavily legal and remained so at least into the mid-1770s; only in the 1780s did he engage deeply in non-legal political philosophy and history.

Both Adams and Jefferson read more voraciously and bought more books than did virtually all of their countrymen, yet in almost opposite ways. Jefferson read widely across several fields, including literature, the arts, and the natural sciences, and was particularly attuned to contemporary European authors, some of whom he befriended in Paris. Adams read both more deeply and more narrowly. While he was tempted to explore non-legal, non-political knowledge and aesthetics, he declared that he could not do so while his nation first needed to master politics and diplomacy. For most of his adult life he paid relatively little attention to literature and the sciences and largely ignored the arts. Instead, he determined quite early to master all of European law (as well as all of English law) and then to read widely in history, philosophy, and what we would call political science. He did not exclude authors from any time or place, from ancient Athens to eighteenth-century western Europe, but he showed a preference for the most venerable learning in each area: Continental law that centered on Justinian's *Institutes* (sixth century); English law developed over some six centuries, as expounded not just by Blackstone (eighteenth century) but also by Littleton, Coke, and others (sixteenth and seventeenth centuries); and political thought from Plato and Aristotle to Machiavelli (early sixteenth century) and James Harrington (mid-seventeenth century). John Locke, who was at his most productive in the 1680s, and the Baron Montesquieu, whose great work dated from the 1730s, were for Adams fairly recent, revered authors. He did not ignore current writers—he bought, read, and referred respectfully to Hume, Rousseau, Beccaria, and other authors of the 1750s, 1760s and 1770s—but they were never central to his thought. And as he became more familiar with political thinkers of the French Enlightenment during the 1780s, he began to quarrel vigorously with them, both in the margins of their published works and then in print.[15]

The character of John Adams's reading and thinking as exemplified in his conversation and his writing provides a key to understanding his varied successes and failures and his mixed reputation as both a diplomat and a writer. Until he departed for France in 1778, his legal and political career had been an uninterrupted series of triumphs. He was too blunt to be liked by all his colleagues, but he was widely respected by Patriot leaders, especially in Congress. When he arrived in Europe, however, his mind was made up. He knew what he thought about the French Alliance, whatever Franklin or the French thought. He knew which members of Congress he most respected, whether they were riding high or low. He knew how the Dutch should feel about American independence and how the English should feel about free trade, whatever they might claim to feel. Most of what Adams knew about Europe had been learned from books read in America and written by authors long deceased. With the partial exception of the Dutch, he made it clear that he intended not to learn more from living Europeans but rather to teach them what he already knew.[16]

Adams's varied experience in Europe can be described as the engagement of a middle-class, provincial, small-town professional—and cosmopolitan intellectual—with three different kinds of societies. He encountered the first in France and Britain, two large, wealthy nations dominated by aristocrats and wealthy merchants, each centered on a sophisticated major city and having a large and powerful royal court. The Netherlands, a small nation whose political authority was divided among several local republics, both urban and rural, and whose powerful merchants were already alienated from its aristocracy and its weak, modest court, presented a very different social order. And finally there was the large, young, rapidly developing nation that lacked a traditional aristocracy and any court whatsoever, was not yet thoroughly dominated by major planters and merchants, and was not centered on any one city: the United States of America. Adams's social discomfort and lack of success in France and England was as unsurprising as his relatively greater emotional comfort and striking professional success in Holland. His most interesting and conflicted engagement, however, was with the nation from which he had been posted.

At least since the appearance of his *Defence of the Constitutions of the United States* in 1787–88, whatever Adams achieved as a diplomat has been of less interest for most Americans than what he came to believe about republican government in his European decade. Scholars have sought to understand whether the character of Adams's political thought changed fundamentally between 1778 and 1788 and, if so, what his European experiences had to do with that change. Did his growing interest in the role of aristocracy in republican societies arise out of his engagement with Europe?

Most careful readers agree that Adams's political thought changed during this European decade. In November 1779, in a letter to his close political friend Elbridge Gerry, Adams's view of the prospects for republican government first took on a dark tone that it had previously lacked.[17] For several years thereafter he refrained from expressing somber thoughts about the future of republicanism in America both in his correspondence and in his published writings, enthusiastically positive works designed to persuade the English and Dutch of America's bright future. But beginning in 1787, immediately following his first cautions against the deterioration of unbalanced republics in the first volume of his *Defence of the Constitutions of the United States*, a political pessimism reappeared in his letters.[18] Some of his contemporaries sensed his altered spirit as early as 1787, and this perception had become more widespread by 1790, even among his strongest political supporters.[19]

It appears likely that his European experience was one of the causes of this new political outlook. Adams first expressed dark fears about the future of republican government in America, not while he was abroad, but during his brief stay in Massachusetts (August to November 1779) following his first sojourn in Europe (April 1778–June 1779). In the letter in which he expressed this concern he made no mention of Europe. Yet Adams's political experience since returning to Massachusetts seems to have been largely positive. Upon his arrival in Braintree his townsmen promptly elected him to Massachusetts's constitutional convention, which then appointed him to its committee to draft the document. That large committee named him to a drafting subcommittee of three, whose other members, Samuel Adams and James Bowdoin, asked him to prepare the first draft of the entire constitution.[20] He tackled this assignment with great determination and completed it in October 1779, shortly after learning of his appointment by Congress, in late September, as America's sole peace commissioner.

To this point in his public career, however, Adams's most frustrating and ultimately humiliating experiences had all occurred in the preceding fifteen months, in France. And after his departure from Boston in November 1779, he served in Europe for eight unbroken years (February 1780–April 1788), while suffering repeated difficulties and setbacks in France, then Holland, then France again, and finally England. It was toward the end of this long decade, in 1786 and 1787, that he wrote his *Defence of the Constitutions of the United States,* which included some his sternest warnings of the dangers faced by all republican governments. It seems clear that Adams's experience in Europe shook his confidence in the future of republican society in America.

A consideration of the third question, whether his European experience shaped Adams's dark view of the role of aristocracy in a republic, again calls for an affirmative answer. In the very letter to Gerry in which he first expressed his concern about the future of American republicanism, he tied this apparently new fear to the power of men of great ambition and fortune in a republic. Adams's later writings make clear that he was revealing a deep anxiety about aristocracy. His November 1779 letter was the first occasion in all his writings in which he expressed this anxiety, but in the next seven years, all spent in Europe, Adams became fixated on the threat that aristocratic power posed to American public life. Several of Adams's critics in America, some of them former friends and supporters, eventually noticed this fixation and concluded that Europe's aristocratic courts had filled his head with a thoroughly un-American appreciation of aristocracy and destroyed his faith in republicanism.[21]

This charge seems a strange, even perverse response to the language in which Adams characterized aristocracy. Adams made clear, again and again, in public writings and in private letters, that aggressive aristocrats, with their constantly forming factions, were the greatest of all threats to the stability of republican government. And then there is the matter of Adams's quite limited association with European aristocrats and his highly critical attitude toward their role in government.

In France, with the exception of the eccentric Count Sarsfield, who particularly enjoyed Americans, and the marquis de Lafayette, Adams's only French friends appear to have been a third-level official in the French foreign office, a well-known author, and a naval officer he met when he crossed the Atlantic.[22] He befriended no other man of title or fortune and seldom went to court, even in 1778–79, when he was nominally getting along with Vergennes. Holland hardly had a court to turn Adams's head, and in any event although Prince William V, his least favorite Dutchman, received him there, he did not receive him warmly. With the exception of one titled supporter of republican government, his friends were Dutch burgers, including city officials and lawyers in Amsterdam and an academic at the University of Leyden.[23] And during his last diplomatic assignment, in London, he went to the Court of St. James, where he did not feel welcome, only when he felt he must. He and his family generally associated with dissenting preachers and writers and with several Americans from Massachusetts (including a few Loyalist refugees), Pennsylvania, and Virginia.[24]

A closer look at what Adams was saying about aristocracy in the 1780s, however, and at what his critics later said about him, shows not simple error or misinformation on either side but a fundamental misunderstanding between a solitary American thinker who was beginning to appraise the basic elements of republican government in his own country in a new way and fellow Americans who were redefining republicanism in starkly different terms.

In the 1780s and 1790s Adams was not particularly interested in the political role of a titled aristocracy, because he had come to regard as aristocrats any men who could influence and command other men (specifically voters) through their possession of almost any widely admired asset: membership in an illustrious family, a grand fortune (no matter how recently made), persuasive oratory, or even exceptional physical stature or handsome features. What made some men threatening aristocrats, however, was not their possession of these advantages but their determination to use them for their personal gain, whether to acquire or to maintain wealth or power. Adams believed that republics would have greater problems with aggressive aristocracies than any other form of government because republics, with their frequent elections and established legislative chambers, gave aristocrats the greatest opportunity to exercise their persuasive powers. America, he was convinced, had, and would always have, its own powerful aristocracies.[25]

By going to Europe Adams had discovered a threatening aristocracy—in America. His November 4, 1779, letter to Elbridge Gerry makes both the local identity and the economic and behavioral character of this aristocracy clear, although he does not yet use the label. Adams addresses this issue to explain why he had given the executive great defensive powers, especially an absolute veto, in his just-completed draft of the Massachusetts constitution:

> In such a State as this ... We never shall have any Stability, Dignity, Decision, or Liberty, without [strong executive power]. We have so many Men of Wealth, of ambitious Spirits, of Intrigue, of Luxury and Corruption, that incessant Factions will disturb our Peace, without it. And indeed there is too much to fear with it. The Executive, which ought to be the Reservoir of Wisdom, as the Legislature is

of Liberty, without this Weapon of Defence will be run down like a Hare before the Hunters.[26]

But if his European service had darkened Adams's political views, what were the characteristics of his European environment that allowed or encouraged him to see Americans differently than he had while living, working, thinking, and writing among them, in short, to see many of them for the first time as aristocrats? One answer is that in Europe he could see the avarice and corruption of Americans abroad, such as Silas Deane and Edward Bancroft, close at hand. He also witnessed the foolishness of others, such as Ralph Izard, and what he regarded as the self-indulgence of still others, notably Benjamin Franklin. None of these men, except perhaps the South Carolina slave lord Ralph Izard, would have qualified as aristocrats in Europe, but in Adams's eyes they were all aristocrats, men of wealth or great abilities who loved money, power, or fame. Yet these men were not America's most dangerous aristocrats for the simple reason that they were all in Europe.

From his European vantage point, however, Adams could clearly see aristocratic power at work in groups of wealthy, aggressive men in America, and especially in Congress. He may have first taken this view of Congress, or at least of several of its members working as a powerful faction, as early as the difficult end of his first mission in France, and his later experience in Europe only confirmed this view. While Adams had his triumphs in Holland and at the peace table, he was still left with some bitter memories. In February 1779 Congress terminated his first commission without expressing any gratitude for his labors. In 1781 it sharply reduced his power and independence of action as a peace commissioner and set a new, hectoring secretary for foreign affairs over him. And in 1783 that secretary, Robert R. Livingston, chastised America's envoys for ignoring French advice in their negotiations with Britain. On each occasion Adams felt the lash of powerful men and combinations of men whose own selfish agendas kept them, in his view, from treating their own diplomats with respect or from taking the trouble to understand the intricate demands of European diplomacy. He was left in little doubt of their lack of interest in his efforts when they quite ignored the scores of letters that he wrote to the president of Congress to enlighten them.[27]

What set Adams apart from virtually all other Americans was not his hostility to aristocracy but rather his assumption that aristocratic impulses in the new American republics would have to be institutionally contained because they could not be suppressed. Beginning no later than the early 1780s in Maryland's debate over the purpose of a senate in a republic and spreading quickly to every state, as Gordon Wood has explained, writers in the rapidly evolving American political mainstream began to deny that America had sociopolitical classes in any traditional sense. What America had, they argued, were competing interests, most typically of an urban versus rural, or mercantile versus agricultural, character. America's two-house legislatures could, according to this new political science, easily accommodate these interests and need not be viewed as upper and lower houses in an economic or social sense, as they had been before the Revolution.[28] So persuasive did this view become that it convinced men whom even Europeans would have viewed as aristocrats—including Thomas Jefferson, James Madison, and Robert R. Livingston—that they were simply good republicans and that America, in fact, had no aristocrats.

Adams strongly dissented from this view, not only in the 1780s but during the remaining four decades of his life. First, as befitted a thinker who venerated the accumulated political wisdom of the Western tradition from Plato to Montesquieu, he believed that contrasting, economic-based political and social classes had always existed, and always would exist, in every nation and climate, fused into every religion and culture, and underlying every form of effective government that man could devise. In contrast to the theorists of America's new political science, such as James Madison, who in *Federalist* Number 10 had an artful way of explaining the origins of class differences without openly referring to class and who was determined to defend the position of America's privileged orders, Adams was not afraid to connect America's most prominent citizens with aristocracies of the past.[29] Informing Adams's *Defence of the Constitutions of the United States* and virtually all his other political writings, public and private, from 1786 on, was his conviction that social class was not a social construct but an inherent, immutable, eternal property of human nature.

Second, because Americans could no more ignore human nature than could any other people, it was essential that they squarely address the problem of aristocratic power. This was particularly important in a republic that had rejected a titled aristocracy, thereby making active political power in the operation of the republic itself the principal outlet, if not the only one, for the social aspirations of wealthy and talented men. Adams never favored any attempt to erect or maintain a European-style aristocracy of hereditary titles, although he did argue that a republic could gain greater control over men with aristocratic ambitions by providing them with honorific distinctions.[30] He had no quarrel with the decision of the Philadelphia Convention to prohibit the new federal government from granting titles of nobility, and like Franklin and Jefferson, he firmly opposed America's one hereditary association of honor, the Society of the Cincinnati.

Yet he fervently believed that the new American nation and each of its several new states must control their aristocrats. For Adams the solution was obvious: place society's most aggressive, talented men in one highly visible body where the public could easily see them and which they would be proud to join. America could most effectively do this, Adams believed, by continuing to treat its upper legislative houses as "upper" houses. The predominant American title for these chambers, *senate*, was just right, conveying venerable Roman concepts of honor, distinction, and seniority. Their effectiveness as chambers of distinction was already substantial because they were, in every state, smaller than the lower houses, and their members were elected from larger districts.

But Adams went further by advocating, as he had in his 1779 draft of the Massachusetts constitution, a greater fortune as a requirement for election to the senate than for election to the lower legislative house. At the same time, however, he favored reducing the senators' power to influence the executive by denying them an advisory and consenting role for executive appointments. He first advanced this proposal in Massachusetts in 1779 and repeated it privately in 1787 as his only substantive criticism of the federal constitution.[31] But this simultaneous elevation, isolation, and limitation of both state and federal senators struck most Americans in 1787 as both unnecessary and wrong, unnecessary because they were convinced that their new nation had no aristocrats and wrong because it attempted to set one legislative house apart from the people and then curtailed the powers it could usefully employ for the public good.

But Adams had something even more shocking in store for his countrymen. The limitations that he would set upon senators (a republic's aristocrats) would not be sufficient, he believed, to curb their power over time; they would eventually break these bonds, overwhelm the executive, reduce the lower house to impotence, and thereby replace a balanced republic with a powerful oligarchy. To prevent this, Adams still had one strong card up his sleeve: a powerful executive. In his 1779 draft of the Massachusetts constitution, Adams advocated a governor with a potent arsenal of distinctions and powers, including the highest property requirements for any elected official, an almost unfettered right of appointment, and an absolute veto over legislative action. And he regarded the last power, the veto, as more than a mechanism. In any properly constituted republic, he argued, the executive was a fully equal component of a legislature comprising three parts: executive, upper house, and lower house. Thus the governor's veto was simply the exercise of his proper legislative voice.[32]

After 1776 this was political heresy for any American with solid Revolutionary credentials, which Adams undoubtedly had, and sound republican convictions, which after 1787 his contemporaries began to doubt that he possessed. Because Adams's new ideas ostensibly appeared out of the blue after he first returned from Europe, it was natural for his critics to conclude that he had developed an admiration for monarchy, and later aristocracy, while he was in Europe. This conclusion, however, was mistaken. Adams had begun to redefine republicanism itself almost three years before crossing the Atlantic. In March 1775, near the midpoint of his "Letters of Novanglus," his spirited defense of the First Continental Congress and American autonomy within the British Empire, Adams declared that if a republic were defined as "*a government of laws, and not of men*," then "the British constitution is nothing more nor less than a republic, in which the king is first magistrate. This office being hereditary, and being possessed of such ample and splendid prerogatives, is no objection to the government's being a republic, as long as it is bound by fixed laws, which the people have a voice in making, and a right to defend."[33]

In 1775 the readers of "Novanglus" little noticed Adams's redefinition of a republic amidst his long defense of America's resistance movement. And in 1779, when he proposed that Massachusetts's governor should be regarded as a third element of the legislature in his draft of the Massachusetts constitution, his fellow committeemen removed this language, without, apparently, recording any reactions to it; they did, however, keep the absolute veto for the governor. The only trace of Adams's original intention is his complaint about the committee's action in two letters, to Elbridge Gerry, quoted above, and more briefly to Benjamin Rush, both on November 4, 1779.[34]

When Adams published the first volume of his *Defence of the Constitutions of the United States* in London in January 1787, however, it became more difficult for Americans to ignore what he was up to. In that volume he rigorously applied his 1775 definition of a republic to all medieval and early modern European governments that, in his view, deserved the title, which he divided into three categories: democratic republics, aristocratic republics, and monarchical republics. His last and most controversial category included only four nations. Two were small and insignificant, but the other two were Poland and England. Adams believed that any of his three types of republics could survive and provide orderly government and justice, but he showed in detail how every example in each category was flawed to a greater or lesser degree. He argued that every European republic either must reform to long endure and prosper or had already succumbed to tyranny, oligarchy, or anarchy because it had not developed a proper republican balance between its executive (monarchical), aristocratic, and popular branches.[35]

Moreover, in the *Defence* Adams presented England as one of Europe's best republics, arguing that just a few electoral reforms to its House of Commons would make the whole a perfect republican monarchy.[36] Given the title of his work, he also made the curious decision, in this and in his two succeeding volumes, to omit any extended defense of, or even brief reference to, specific American republics, which he in fact believed were more perfect in form than any European republic, even that of England. His ever-perceptive wife, Abigail, warned Adams that Americans, on reading his *Defence*, would believe that he was "for sitting [setting] up a King."[37] John, convinced that he, and perhaps he alone, understood the proper role and powers for a republican executive, which every American government would benefit from adopting, defended his boldness.

But Abigail's prediction was sound. Several of John Adams's friends in America, upon receiving the work in April 1787, praised it and said that it would strengthen stout republicans everywhere, including those attending the Philadelphia Convention, which was just about to sit.[38] But others became alarmed at the new tone of one of America's leading republican voices. James Madison was fairly dismissive, writing to Jefferson that he found in the *Defence* nothing new and much error.[39]

In his assessment of the originality of Adams's argument Madison was both right and wrong. The *Defence* was built upon old, even ancient political wisdom and the histories of some very old republics. In a fitting tribute, John Pocock called Adams's *Defence* the last major work of political science written in the classical republican tradition that had begun in northern Italy more than three centuries earlier.[40] But Madison missed the novelty of John Adams's argument. In the context of American Revolutionary thought Adams's republican vision, however repugnant or obscure to most of his countrymen, was indeed new. It appears in no other American's writings, and Adams consistently used his old learning in the service of building up a new republican vision to defend a Revolutionary Congress in 1775, to introduce strictly balanced republican government in Massachusetts in 1779, and to urge the reform of defective republics wherever they might be found, whether in Europe or America, in 1787 and 1788.

Yet there remains a certain puzzle about Adams's motivation for writing the *Defence*. He began this work too early to be responding to the political unrest in Massachusetts that became Shays' Rebellion or to give instruction to the French just as they were beginning the major reform of their government that became the French Revolution. Bradley Thompson has argued that Adams was inspired to begin his work by his August–September 1786 visit to Holland, where he and Abigail witnessed the installation of a new republican government at Utrecht, a harbinger, he hoped, of a general Patriot Party triumph in the Netherlands.[41] And indeed, the timing of Adams's visit fits perfectly with his writing of the *Defence,* which he began in early October 1786.

Peter Nicolaisen, however, has pointed out that Adams seems to have gradually lost much of his interest in the progress of the Patriot Party after leaving Holland in the fall of 1782 and became rather pessimistic about the Patriots' chances for success over the next few years. He further argues that Adams appears not to have had a good understanding of Dutch republican history.[42] In the first volume of the *Defence* Adams deliberately refrains from saying anything about Holland because, "considering the critical situation of [the country], prudence dictates to pass it over."[43] Perhaps the curious detachment of Adams's argument from all contemporary political controversies, whether from the struggle in Holland in his first volume or from those in France and America in his second and third volumes, suggests that while two recent events—Dr. Richard Price's 1784 publication of Baron Turgot's 1778 letter criticizing America's balanced state constitutions (the stated motivation of the writing of the *Defence*) and Adams's 1786 visit to Holland—started him writing, the sheer love of his subject and the fascination of the historical and philosophical materials that he was reading, rereading, and copying wholesale into his text kept him at his desk, not through just one volume written over three months but through three volumes written over nearly fifteen months.

A certain indirectness in Adams's writings about aristocracy before his return to America in 1788—the paucity of personal letters in which he expresses his feelings about the issue and his deliberate avoidance of the subject in the *Defence* in any current context, whether in Holland, France, or America in the 1780s—must make any connection between his growing concern with aristocracy and his experience in Europe somewhat speculative.[44] But his relationships with both Europeans and Americans while abroad are suggestive, and it is these relationships that must now shape the conclusions of our argument.

Would John Adams have developed his fear of aristocracy and his proposals for controlling its threat to republican government if he had never gone to Europe? If he had, would he have been as keen to express them in print as he was in 1787–88 in his *Defence of the Constitutions* and in 1790–91 in his incomplete serial publication *Discourses on Davila*? And if his stay in Europe was crucial to the distinctive development of his political thought, did his service abroad act more as a source or a catalyst? Although these questions cannot be settled definitively, enough is known about the development of Adams's thought and his European experience to allow some tentative answers.

Because Adams's fear of aristocracy did not appear before his first stay in Europe, one can imagine that he would not have developed this theme had he remained in America. Yet the aristocracy that he feared from 1779 until his death was American, and his great reverence for his middle-class father and his semi-rural town, which shaped many of his convictions, suggests that he would have developed this anxiety to some degree in any event. As for his hope to enhance executive authority in America and make every state governor a third branch of the legislature—to create, in effect, a "republican monarchy"—this idea appears in nascent form in both his *Letters of Novanglus* in 1775 and *Thoughts on Government* in 1776. His first fully developed statement of this concept in 1779, therefore, was probably not directly dependent upon his European experience, although his fear of American aristocracy, developed in Europe, made the need for executive power more apparent to him.

On balance, it seems unlikely that Adams would have developed so deep and so well articulated a fear of American aristocracy had he never crossed the Atlantic. He certainly would not have written his *Defence* had he stayed in America, for the simple reason that he would have lacked the scholarly resources, in the form of French and Italian histories, to produce that curious work. But Adams's experiences abroad suggest a way in which his European service could have shaped his distinctive political convictions that is quite different from the mechanism proposed by contemporary critics and subsequent historians.

John Adams was, in essence, a highly sophisticated mind wrapped in a socially unsophisticated personality, a provincial cosmopolitan at ease with any book and highly persuasive in face-to-face interactions with men whom he regarded as social equals but generally ill at ease with anyone with whom he was unfamiliar. In America, whether in Massachusetts or in Congress, Adams could and did confront anyone with confidence, and he seldom failed to make his case, even with the many congressmen who enjoyed greater wealth or social standing. In the small, hardworking world of Congress Adams soon earned and enjoyed great respect.

In Europe, however, among several very different peoples, all with agendas that were often at odds with his own, and removed for several years from his family, his Massachusetts friends, and Congress, Adams lost his sense of social comfort. His critical attitude toward so much of his European experience, and toward European aristocracies, followed naturally from this disjunction between the man and the world around him. But there is no evidence that his relationship with Europeans made him pessimistic about the future of republican government in America or wary of aristocracy in his native land. For that to happen, Adams had to become estranged from America's first national aristocracy, the Congress that had once been his home.

In 1778 John Adams, long an honored member of Congress, suddenly became one of its servants, and he quickly discovered what a demotion that was. Humiliated by neglect in February 1779, ignored for much of 1780 and 1781, and then patronized and berated by Congress's secretary for foreign affairs in 1782 and 1783, Adams, like his colleague Benjamin Franklin, whom Congress treated only a little better, continued to perform his diplomatic duties admirably. But lacking Franklin's social comfort in Europe, Adams, even after his family joined him in France and England, began to retreat into his books, into the Europe of the mind, where he could explore the historical pathology of republican government at leisure. Here he could develop his fear of malignant political and social forces, which he may have conceived as early as his youth and which he stated so forcefully to Elbridge Gerry in 1779, into his extended argument in his *Defence* on the necessity of defending republican government from perennial assaults by aristocrats.

Behind Adams's immediate motivations for writing the *Defence*, behind his perceptions of aristocrats in Europe and America, of course, there is a deeper question: did Adams regard himself as an aristocrat? Under his own conception of the term, although not according to that of most Europeans, he would certainly have qualified. Although he was short and not physically prepossessing, was of modest fortune, and had only a respectable family lineage, not a splendid one, his education, intelligence, legal accomplishments, and oratorical power all placed him among those men who could sway others, one mark of an American aristocrat. And because Adams saw the negative potential of aristocrats so clearly, he would have had to admit that he had the power to do what he feared many an American aristocrat would do: dominate the body politic for his own selfish ends.

For Adams that was the final ingredient of aristocracy, the will to dominate for personal gain. Here he had to admit one failing, his intense desire for fame. If fame were regarded, as personal wealth or political power were, as a private good whose satisfaction threatened to undermine the public good, Adams could not avoid the aristocratic label. He had, of course, one defense, a defense to which any aristocrat of the new American nation could appeal. He could say that he was seeking political fame, and power, to serve the public and, specifically, to defend the people against other, less scrupulous men.

Whether one judges John Adams to have merited this exemption from the label "aristocrat" depends in part on how one views the forces that shaped him as a young man. My own conclusion is that he so intensely admired his thoroughly provincial middle-class father, Deacon John Adams, and so loved his semi-rural, unsophisticated town of Braintree, that he entered public life to defend men like his father, and towns like Braintree, against more powerful men whom he judged to be grasping aristocrats, most notably Governor Thomas Hutchinson.[45] Adams's defense of family and town against local aristocrats gradually expanded into a defense of his province and then of his nation against the entrenched establishment of the British Empire and finally against America's own national aristocratic forces, but his principal motivation did not change. What did change was his experience, from Braintree to Boston, then to Philadelphia, and finally to Paris, Amsterdam, and London. It was the cumulative effect of these last encounters that both darkened his political vision and made it more original and profound.

NOTES

I would like to acknowledge the support I received from a grant awarded by the National Endowment for the Humanities for the research and writing of this essay.

1. Those who attacked Adams's political thought between 1787, when the first volume of his *Defence of the Constitutions of the United States* appeared, and the early nineteenth century, both in private letters and in print, were generally Republicans, beginning with James Madison (see below n. 39) and his cousin the Reverend James Madison, and Adams's initial defenders generally were or became Federalists. Over time the criticisms grew sharper and began to include the charge that European aristocracies had turned Adams's head. Notable among these were Mercy Otis Warren's *History of the Rise, Progress, and Termination of the American Revolution* (1805) and John Taylor of Caroline's *Inquiry into the Principles and Policy of the Government of the United States* (1814). For a review of these early critics, see C. Bradley Thompson, *John Adams and the Spirit of Liberty* (Lawrence, KS, 1998). For twentieth-century critics making this argument, see below, n. 4.

2. Here I employ the popular label "Founding Fathers"—which seems too firmly entrenched in American culture to be dislodged—in the broader sense in which it is now generally used. I include as a Founding Father anyone who played a prominent role in shaping the text and/or securing the adoption of either the Declaration of Independence or the U.S. Constitution.

3. For assessments of Adams's diplomacy, see Richard B. Morris, *The Peacemakers: The Great Powers and American Independence* (New York, 1965); Peter Shaw, *The Character of John Adams* (Chapel Hill, NC, 1976); James H. Hutson, *John Adams and the Diplomacy of the American Revolution* (Lexington, KY, 1980); Richard A. Ryerson, introduction to *John Adams and the Founding of the Republic,* ed. Ryerson (Boston, 2001), 11–13; and Gregg L. Lint, "John Adams and the Bolder Plan," ibid., 105–14.

4. Just four works focus on the impact of Adams's European experience, and of European ideas, on his political thought: Correa M. Walsh, *The Political Science of John Adams: A Study in the Theory of Mixed Government and the Bicameral System* (1915; New York, 1969); Zoltan Haraszti, *John Adams and the Prophets of Progress* (Cambridge, MA, 1952); Edward Handler, *America and Europe in the Political Thought of John Adams* (Cambridge, MA, 1964); and John R. Howe Jr., *The Changing Political Thought of John Adams* (Princeton, NJ, 1966). But see also Thompson, *John Adams and the Spirit of Liberty.*

5. See esp. Howe, *Changing Political Thought of John Adams,* ch. 4; and the use of this argument in Gordon S. Wood, *The Creation of the American Republic, 1776–1787* (Chapel Hill, NC, 1969), ch. 14.

6. I have set out this thesis in two essays: "'Like a Hare before the Hunters': John Adams and the Idea of Republican Monarchy," *Proceedings of the Massachusetts Historical Society* 107 (1995): 16–29; and "John Adams, Republican Monarchist: An Inquiry into the Origins of His Constitutional Thought," in *Empire and Nation: The American Revolution in the Atlantic World,* ed. Eliga H. Gould and Peter S. Onuf (Baltimore, 2005), 72–92, 330–32.

7. JA to Abigail Adams, 28 Feb. 1779, *AFC,* 3:181–82. This letter, and perhaps Adams's other angry letters written to Abigail at the end of February, may not have been sent. See *AFC,* 3:173–83.

8. Peter Nicolaisen's essay "John Adams, Thomas Jefferson, and the Dutch Patriots," in the present volume, presents a revealing selection of Adams's criticisms of Dutch caution and materialism.

9. See the generally positive, cooperative correspondence between Adams and Franklin in *PJA,* vols. 10–13; and *The Papers of Benjamin Franklin,* ed. Leonard Labaree et al., 39 vols. to date (New Haven, CT, 1959–), vols. 33–39.

10. See *PJA,* 11:368–77, for the new peace commission and instructions. Of the five commission members, Jefferson never accepted this appointment, nor did he take on any diplomatic assignment or sail for Europe until 1784, after the conclusion of peace. Laurens was still a British prisoner in the Tower of London and would be released too late, and in too poor a state of health, to play a substantial role in the negotiations. It thus fell to Adams, Franklin, and Jay to decide how or whether to follow Congress's new instructions. Adams was not immediately repelled by the passage quoted from the instructions, because he did not read it. The crucial phrases were in congressman James Lovell's cipher, and Adams's received copy of the instructions makes it clear that he did not complete his decoding of the defectively enciphered passage. See ibid., 374–77, including the illustration on 376, which shows the cipher numbers and Adams's interrupted decoding. Adams may also have been distracted from his

decoding, because immediately after he received the commission and instructions on 24 August, he fell gravely ill, and he remained so for more than six weeks. See JA to Franklin, 25 Aug. 1781, ibid., 467–71. It was not until October 1782, when he arrived in Paris to join Franklin and Jay in negotiating peace with Britain, that Adams learned the instruction's full contents. *Diary and Autobiography of John Adams*, ed. Lyman H. Butterfield, 4 vols. (Cambridge, MA, 1961),3:38, 39n5. He immediately decided that the instruction concerning cooperation with France was unacceptable if it meant deferring to the French. See JA to Livingston, 31 Oct. 1782, in *PJA*, 14:3–6. And together with the equally determined John Jay, he persuaded Benjamin Franklin to ignore the comte de Vergennes in their negotiations with British envoys. See ibid., 4n.

11. See *PJA*, 12:ix, 40, 44. Livingston was appointed on 10 August 1781 but did not accept the appointment and begin his work as secretary until October.

12. Ibid., 74–75; the full text and notes are on 73–76.

13. For the full text of Franklin's letter of 22 July 1783, see Francis Wharton, ed., *The Revolutionary Diplomatic Correspondence of the United States*, 6 vols. (Washington, DC, 1889), 6:580–88. Franklin may have intended this letter to remain private, but as it arrived in Philadelphia from an American envoy and was addressed to Congress's secretary for foreign affairs, a congressional committee assigned to handle Livingston's incoming correspondence following his resignation in June 1783 was directed to open it. Elbridge Gerry, a member of that committee and a friend of Adams's, made an extract of Franklin's critical evaluation of Adams and enclosed it in a letter of 18 September 1783 to Abigail Adams. She relayed the substance of it to her husband in December 1783. See *AFC*, 5:250–52.

14. See William Pencak, "John Adams and the Massachusetts Provincial Elite," in Ryerson, *John Adams and the Founding of the Republic*, 43–71.

15. The best guide to Adams's reading of authors of the French Enlightenment is Haraszti, *John Adams and the Prophets of Progress*. On Adams's reading more generally, see Thompson, *John Adams and the Spirit of Liberty;* see also idem, "John Adams's Machiavellian Moment," *Review of Politics* 57 (1995): 389–417.

16. Shortly after his second arrival in Europe in 1780, Adams read pamphlets by Thomas Pownall and Joseph Galloway in order to improve or refute them. Sometime later, and perhaps also earlier, he read political and economic works by Dr. Richard Price, whom he admired, and a few political works by current French authors, notably Turgot and Condorcet, with whom he strongly disagreed. Almost the only European authors he read for real instruction and inspiration after 1780, however, were Greek and Italian philosophers and historians of (often quite distant) past generations, and his only writings in Europe were designed to show the errors of current European political thought.

17. JA to Elbridge Gerry, 4 Nov. 1779, *PJA*, 8:276–77.

18. Adams's well-known letter to Thomas Jefferson of 6 December 1787 is one of the earliest in which he expresses, openly and succinctly, his fear of aristocracy. *TJP,* 12:396. But this letter followed the completion of his *Defence of the Constitutions,* in which he thoroughly explored this fear.

19. See esp. the correspondences between Adams and Roger Sherman in 1789 and

between Adams and Samuel Adams in 1790 in *The Works of John Adams*, ed. Charles Francis Adams, 10 vols. (Boston, 1850–56), 6:427–42, 415–26 (hereafter *WJA*).

20. See "The Massachusetts Constitution," c. 28–31 Oct. 1779, *PJA*, 8:228–71. Adams did experience one political disappointment between his return to America in August and his completion of the draft Massachusetts constitution in October. But this frustration, like his great humiliation of the previous February, again involved Congress and his European service. He learned, through congressional friends and congressional reports, that there was grumbling in Congress that he had been too close to Arthur Lee in Paris and a feeling on the part of some congressmen that he had not been an effective commissioner. See JA to Gerry, JA to Lovell, and JA to the president of Congress, all 10 Sept. 1781, in ibid., 131–32, 133–36, 138–39.

21. Howe, *Changing Political Thought of John Adams*, ch. 4, accepts and develops this view, which Wood further develops in his *Creation of the American Republic*, ch. 14, "The Relevance and Irrelevance of John Adams."

22. These three French friends were Edmé Jacques Genet, the Abbé Gabriel Bonnet de Mably, and Bidé de Chavagnes. During his stays in France, however, Adams was much closer to a few Americans in France, to his friend in Brussels, Edmund Jennings, and to the members of his own official family, Francis Dana, John Thaxter, and Charles Storer. See *PJA*, vols. 8–14; and *AFC*, vols. 3–6.

23. Adams's friends in Holland included the nobleman Joan Derk, Baron van der Capellen tot Den Pol, the Amsterdam banker Jean de Neufville, the Leiden academician and publisher Jean Luzac, and Adams's close associate, America's quasi-official chargé d'affaires at The Hague, Charles William Frederic Dumas. See *PJA*, vols. 10–13.

24. John and Abigail Adams's friends in England included the Englishmen Dr. Richard Price and Dr. Joseph Priestly and the Americans John Singleton Copley and his wife, as well as William Vassal, who had moved to England from Massachusetts as Loyalist exiles. John Adams also received a visit from another Loyalist exile, his old friend Jonathan Sewell. The Adamses' closest friend through correspondence during John's British mission was Thomas Jefferson, in Paris. See *AFC*, vols. 6–8.

25. Both extended discussions and succinct expressions of Adams's thoughts on aristocracy appear at several points in his *Defence of the Constitutions* (1787–88); in his correspondence with Roger Sherman (1789) and Samuel Adams (1790); in his response to a congratulatory address to President Adams from Virginia citizens during the Quasi-War with France (1798); in a few of his letters to Thomas Jefferson (1813); and in his *Letters to John Taylor, of Caroline, Virginia, in Reply to his Strictures on some Parts of the Defence of the American Constitutions* (Boston, 1814), written in response to Taylor's critique of the *Defence* in his *Inquiry into the Principles and Policy of the United States* (Fredericksburg, VA, 1814). See *WJA*, 4:328–57; 5:18; 6:415–42, 448, 451, 455–57, 470, 471, 483, 493, 507; 9:217; 10:51, 65.

26. *PJA*, 8:276.

27. Adams's frequent dispatches soon began to show the effect of his mounting frustration with Congress's lack of appreciation. From February to July 1780 he wrote ninety-six letters to Congress from Paris, and from August to December 1780 he

wrote another thirty-five from Holland. Ibid., vols. 8–10. In 1781, however, Adams stopped numbering his letters to Philadelphia and wrote far fewer of them, and in 1782 his correspondence with Congress's secretary for foreign affairs, Robert R. Livingston, became episodic and contentious. One should also note that Adams was not alone in being ignored by Congress. Even Benjamin Franklin felt that body's neglect. When Franklin returned to America in 1785, Jefferson pleaded with Congress to honor him publicly to please the French and was disappointed when the delegates made their usual non-response to their envoys' years of sacrifice. One must also consider whether Congress's setting of Robert R. Livingston over its diplomats was particularly galling for a man of Adams's modest social background. Livingston, a man of great wealth and a member of one of New York's most distinguished families, was an aristocrat by almost any measure, and he seasoned his letters to Adams with a heavy dose of aristocratic hauteur.

28. Wood, *Creation of the American Republic*, 251–54.

29. See James Madison, "Federalist No. 10," in *The Federalist*, ed. Jacob E. Cooke (Middletown, CT, 1961), 58: "The diversity in the faculties of men from which the rights of property originate, is . . . an insuperable obstacle to a uniformity of interests. The protection of these faculties is the first object of Government. From the protection of different and unequal faculties of acquiring property, the possession of different degrees and kinds of property immediately results: and from the influence of these on the sentiments and views of the respective proprietors, ensues a division of the society into different interests and parties." Note how Madison has transformed traditional (and for John Adams, eternal) categories of social class into something more fluid, rational, and abstract.

30. See Thompson, *John Adams and the Spirit of Liberty*, 222–28, on Adams's view of the importance of honors and distinctions in a republic.

31. See JA to TJ, 6 Dec. 1787, in *TJP*, 12:396: "The Nomination and Appointment to all offices I would have given to the President, assisted only by a Privy Council of his own Creation; but not a Vote or Voice would I have given to the Senate or any Senator unless he were of the privy council."

32. See Ryerson, "Like a Hare before the Hunters"; and idem, "John Adams, Republican Monarchist."

33. *Letters of Novanglus*, no. 7, 6 Mar. 1775, in *PJA*, 2:314, emphasis in original.

34. *PJA*, 8:276–77 (to Gerry), 279–80 (to Rush).

35. See *A Defence of the Constitutions of Government of the United States of America, against the Attack of M. Turgot, in his Letter to Dr. Price, dated the twenty-second of March, 1778*, vol. 1 (London, 1787), in *WJA*, 4:303–27 (democratic republics), 328–57 (aristocratic republics), and 358–78 (monarchical republics).

36. *WJA*, 4:358–60.

37. Abigail Adams to John Quincy Adams, 20 Mar. 1787, *AFC*, 8:12.

38. See Thompson, *John Adams and the Spirit of Liberty*, 252–54. Thompson's review of the reactions to the *Defence*, however, greatly downplays the opposition to the work.

39. Madison to TJ, 6 June 1787, in *JMP*, 10:29–30. Thompson, *John Adams and the*

Spirit of Liberty, 254, argues that Madison was not dismissing Adams's *Defence,* but I find this argument unpersuasive, both on the basis of this letter's full text and on the evidence of Madison's lifelong hostility to Adams.

40. J. G. A. Pocock, *The Machiavellian Moment: Florentine Political Thought and the Atlantic Republican Tradition* (Princeton, NJ, 1975), 526.

41. See C. Bradley Thompson, "John Adams and the Science of Politics," in Ryerson, *John Adams and the Founding of the Republic,* 237; and idem, *John Adams and the Spirit of Liberty,* 93–94, 96.

42. See Nicolaisen, "John Adams, Thomas Jefferson, and the Dutch Patriots," in this volume. In oral discussion of the original texts of his essay and the present essay at the Salzburg conference in October 2005, Nicolaisen further remarked that Adams's statement in the *Defence* that the Netherlands had "never had any exclusive preferences of families or nobles" (see *WJA,* 4:357) is "to be taken with more than just a grain of salt."

43. *WJA,* 4:356–57.

44. I have found only two letters, JA to Gerry, 4 Nov. 1779, and JA to TJ, 6 Dec. 1787, that deal with the subject directly before 1788. See above, nn. 17 and 18. After his return to America, however, Adams became more open in writing about aristocracy to political and personal friends, notably Roger Sherman and Samuel Adams in 1789 and 1790 and Thomas Jefferson in 1813. See above, nn. 19 and 25.

45. See Pencak, "John Adams and the Massachusetts Provincial Elite."

"Behold me at length on the vaunted scene of Europe"

Thomas Jefferson and the Creation of an American Image Abroad

GAYE WILSON

After a year in Paris Thomas Jefferson wrote to a friend in his native Virginia, "Behold me at length on the vaunted scene of Europe!" "But you are perhaps curious to know," he continued," how this new scene has struck a savage of the mountains of America." This letter of September 30, 1785, to Charles Bellini, which Jefferson listed in his epistolary journal as "My view of Europe," epitomized Jefferson's ambivalent response to the Europe he was experiencing for the first time. He began answering the question he posed with a negative reply. The "new scene" was inferior to the United States politically and socially; invoking the words of the French philosophe Voltaire, Jefferson concluded that "every man here must be either the hammer or the anvil." The masses could not claim "that degree of happiness which is enjoyed in America by every class of people." He even criticized the European family structure and asserted that it did not afford the stability of that found in America. Yet he suddenly changed tone: the savage had to admit to his awe of the "vaunted scene."[1]

Jefferson could not conceal his excitement in finally experiencing the intellectual and cultural atmosphere of Europe. As a young man he had expressed a fleeting interest in taking the grand tour of Europe. Years later he refused an initial appointment to the French court because of his wife's declining health, expressing his regrets to Benjamin Franklin about not being able to join him at a "polite court" among "the literati of the first order."[2] But when he wrote to Bellini he had taken Franklin's place as American minister plenipotentiary at Versailles and could participate in the acclaimed salons and society of Paris. His letter reveals that he was not disappointed.

Jefferson freely admitted that in science the literati of Europe led America by half a dozen years. Then there was the availability of books. Even the polite manners and the "pleasures of the table" were commendable and something to be emulated in the United States. He concluded his summary by enthusing, "Were I to proceed to tell you how much I enjoy their architecture, sculpture, painting, music, I should want words."[3]

This letter was not the first instance in which Jefferson described himself as a "savage" and then claimed a preference for the woods and wilds of America to the brilliance of Europe. Throughout his five years of diplomatic service he would tout the new nation's "honest simplicity" as something "worthy of being cherished," yet after four months at his post he admitted to James Monroe that "we are the lowest and most obscure of the whole diplomatic tribe" at Versailles.[4] Despite his republican professions, Jefferson's diplomatic success depended on his being able to function effectively at a monarchical court. The need for diplomatic leverage, combined with Jefferson's personal drive for inclusion in the scientific and cultural circles of Europe, required adherence to a long-established decorum and a rigorous attention to appearance. Jefferson might pose facetiously as a "savage" in epistolary exchanges, but his clothing, accessories, and deportment, the elements of personal self-fashioning, would have to meet European expectations if he were to realize his own ambitions and those he held for his country.

When Jefferson arrived in Paris on August 6, 1784, to join his fellow diplomats John Adams and Benjamin Franklin in negotiating commercial treaties for the United States, he entered a world that placed extraordinary emphasis upon social and physical appearance. The German sociologist Norbert Elias in his influential study of *ancien régime* France, *The Court Society,* explains that rank was asserted through social display: "A duke who does not live as a duke has to live, who can no longer properly fulfill the social duties of a duke, is hardly a duke any longer."[5] Social demands on the French nobility were also felt by the diplomatic corps. Franklin, Adams, and Jefferson all expressed concern over the costs associated with attendance on the French court during their tenure. Even Franklin, who famously created his own rustic, less formal style, could not completely escape the sartorial demands of court. "As the Article of clothes for ourselves here is necessarily much higher than if we were not in public Service," he complained to Adams, "I submit it to your Consideration whether that Article ought not to be rekoned among Expenses for the Public. I know I had clothes enough at home to have lasted me my Lifetime in a Country where I was under small Necessity of following new Fashions."[6]

This imperative to look French was noted by Adams, who grumbled,

"The first Thing to be done, in Paris, is always to send for a Taylor, Peruke maker and Shoemaker." He suspected a conspiracy on the part of the French court. "For this nation has established such a domination over the Fashion, that neither Cloaths, Wig nor Shoes made in any other Place will do in Paris." "This is one of the Ways in which France taxes all Europe, and will tax America," he quipped. "It is a great Branch of the Policy of the Court, to Preserve and increase this national Influence over the Mode, because it occasions an immense Commerce between France and all the other Parts of Europe."[7] Adams undoubtedly shared such observations with his family. In a similar vein his wife, Abigail, wrote to her sister in New England: "Fashion is the Deity everyone worships in this country and from the highest to the lowest you must submit." Their young daughter Abigail, known in the family as "Nabby," wrote in her journal, "There is no such thing here as preserving our taste in any thing; we must all sacrifice to custom and fashion." Nabby saw proof of this in her own father. Even with his "firmness and resolution," he adhered to the French fashion and was "a perfect convert to the mode in everything, at least of dress and appearance."[8]

Jefferson must have been well aware of these fashion expectations when he arrived in Paris, and he proved just as willing as Adams to be a "convert to the mode." His accounts show that on his first day in the French capital he purchased a pair of fine lace ruffles, on the following day a hat, and three days later a dress sword. Lace and sword were the marks of gentility; together with a formal hat, or *chapeau bras*, they were de rigueur at the French court. Before the end of his first month in Paris, Jefferson had paid a sizable amount for what he listed simply as "clothes," in addition to itemized expenses for having shirts made, along with ruffles in both lace and cambrick, shoes, stockings, and buckles.[9] Thus began his "sacrifice to custom and fashion" in the French style that Nabby Adams had observed in her own family.

Jefferson did not complain initially about the "cost of outfit," speaking of it as a matter of course when he urged his friends James Madison and James Monroe to visit. The transatlantic trip need not be expensive, Jefferson argued, for they could stay with him as family, and their only costs beyond passage would be for theater tickets, clothing, and incidental expenses. He advised Madison that since he would be there only during the summer season, "your out-fit of clothes need not cost you more than 50 guineas," nearly as much as the cost of transatlantic passage "backwards and forwards," which Jefferson estimated at sixty or seventy guineas.[10]

Jefferson's transition from provincial gentry to a suitably groomed and attired European cosmopolitan was recorded by two young American artists

Fig. 1. Mather Brown, *Thomas Jefferson,* 1786. (National Portrait Gallery, Smithsonian Institution; bequest of Charles Francis Adams)

studying and working in London and Paris. He sat first for Mather Brown, in London, in the spring of 1786 (Fig. 1), and late the following year his image was taken in Paris by John Trumbull as a study for what eventually became Trumbull's large history painting *The Declaration of Independence of the United States of America, July 4th, 1776.* Trumbull first used his study to produce three miniature portraits of Jefferson that were given as gifts to close friends and family (Figs. 2, 3, and 4). The Brown and Trumbull portraits are the earliest known likenesses of Jefferson, and together they contribute to an understanding of how he used clothing as well as the portrait itself to craft his image.

Jefferson sat for Mather Brown during a trip to London in March and April 1786, having been summoned by his diplomatic colleague Adams for what the latter believed to be a favorable opportunity for negotiating a commercial treaty with Great Britain as well as meeting with emissaries from Portugal and Tripoli. Recalling his presentation at the English court, Jefferson remembered with some bitterness in his autobiography that "on my presentation as usual to the King and Queen at their levées, it was impossible for anything to be more ungracious than their notice of Mr. Adams & myself." Though the diplomatic negotiations proved unsuccessful, Jefferson seized the opportunity to explore London, its shops and theaters, and to join John Adams in a brief excursion into the English countryside for a study of English country houses and their gardens. He also sat for his portrait.[11]

Fig. 2. *Thomas Jefferson*, 1788, by John Trumbull, presented by the artist to Angelica (Mrs. John B.) Church. (Image ©The Metropolitan Museum of Art)

Fig. 3. *Thomas Jefferson*, 1788, by John Trumbull, painted for Maria Cosway.
(White House Historical Association [White House Collection])

Fig. 4. *Thomas Jefferson*, 1788, by John Trumbull, painted for Martha Jefferson.
(Monticello/Thomas Jefferson Foundation)

Mather Brown was a native of Boston and was related through his mother to the prominent Mather family of Congregationalist ministers. He had arrived in London via Paris, where he had spent two months with a good friend of his grandfather's, Benjamin Franklin, who introduced him at Versailles and provided him a letter of recommendation to the acclaimed Anglo-American artist Benjamin West in London. Brown arrived in the British metropolis in April 1781 to begin his studies with West, although he was never admitted to the Royal Academy.[12] By the time the Adams family arrived, in the summer of 1785, Brown had hopes of establishing himself in the London art market: "I will let them see, if an obscure yankey Boy cannot Shine as great as any of them."[13] He solicited the patronage of the Adams family, and by the time of Jefferson's arrival he had painted John Adams, Abigail, and Nabby. It is not known who suggested that Jefferson sit for Brown, but it turned into a dual commission for the young artist: Jefferson commissioned his own portrait as well as an original of Adams, and Adams requested copies of both portraits.[14]

Jefferson made little reference to his own portrait, but his stated purpose for that of Adams was "to add it to those of other principal American characters which I have or shall have."[15] Following their war for independence, Jefferson and other leading Patriots began to take interest in the well-established European tradition of collecting iconic representations of national heroes for public or semi-public display. "Pantheons" of worthies can be traced as far back as Rome, where collections of sculpted bust portraits immortalized Roman rulers and military leaders. After a hiatus in the Middle Ages, the concept of public honor through art was revived in the fifteenth century and continued to grow in Europe during the seventeenth and eighteenth centuries, when collections also began to include men notable in science and the arts and other benefactors of the public. This was especially true of pantheons that were assembled in the United States during the Revolution and post-Revolutionary era.[16]

Jefferson began his own collection of American worthies as he was preparing to leave the United States for Europe. He hurriedly commissioned from Joseph Wright, in Philadelphia, a portrait of George Washington, which he carried unfinished to Paris, where the background and uniform were completed by John Trumbull in 1786. The idea that images of notable men contributed to national honor and the education of its citizenry was widely shared. Joseph Wright's mother, Patience Wright, was an artist herself and had gained a reputation as a noted sculptor of waxworks. Excited by what she had heard of the likeness her son Joseph had taken of George Washington, she sought Jefferson's assistance in honoring "our country, by holding up the likenesses of her eminent men, either in painting or wax-work."[17]

Jefferson showed little enthusiasm for Patience Wright's waxworks, but he continued to add to his collection more painted and sculpted likenesses of worthy republicans as well as of European Enlightenment thinkers and explorers who had shaped the history of the New World or influenced the development of American political thought. On his tour through England with Adams, he commissioned a copy of a portrait he had seen of Sir Walter Raleigh, the early colonizer of Virginia. From the Uffizi Gallery in Florence he obtained copies of portraits of Columbus, Vespucius, Cortez, and Magellan. "I considered it as even of some public concern that our country should not be without the portraits of its first discoverers." John Trumbull assisted Jefferson in obtaining copies of the portraits of Newton, Bacon, and Locke—"the three greatest men that have ever lived, without any exception"—owned by the Royal Society in London. Jefferson later expressed his goal in collecting portraits: "Like public records, I make them free to be copied. . . . I wish them to be multiplied for safe preservation, and consider them as worthy a place in every collection." His intent as a collector was didactic. These works were important not so much as art but as icons of American history.[18]

Though his was a private collection, Jefferson's position as an American minister made these portraits available to a variety of visitors. After assuming his duties as minister plenipotentiary, he moved to the Hôtel de Langeac, on the Champs Élysées, where he also conducted official business. Here he received Americans who were stranded abroad or in need of passports, as well as affluent young Americans such as William and Anne Bingham, Thomas Lee Shippen, and John Rutledge Jr. on their grand tour. Many of his Europeans visitors were aristocratic, educated, well traveled, and sophisticated enough to understand the message intended in a collection of portraits of Americans placed alongside those of notable Europeans, past and present.[19] If Jefferson intended that his own portrait be displayed among these "worthies" and available for study by a diverse audience, it made sense for him to work closely with Brown in choosing the clothing, the pose, and the props needed to create an appropriate image.

Brown depicted Jefferson as elegant, formal, and aloof, very aristocratic in clothing and grooming yet surrounded with objects that placed him within a clearly republican context, of republican ideology (see Fig. 1). Jefferson wears a dark, untrimmed coat over a light striped waistcoat and shirt with a double ruffled jabot. His coat is cut in the "frock" style, which originated in England

and then made its way to France. This garment was notable for reversing the traditional trickle-down movement of fashion from the elite to the lower classes. By the end of the century the frock coat was sartorially associated with democratic leveling tendencies in fashionable society.

The frock coat gained entry into the English gentleman's wardrobe for informal country wear, especially on sporting occasions, early in the eighteenth century. Through the years the term *frock* had been applied to a variety of men's outer garments and in its earliest usage referred to either a monk's habit or a loose tunic or coat worn by the laity. By the beginning of the eighteenth century the term generally referred to the coat worn by men of England's working classes. It could be distinguished from the gentleman's formal dress coat by the loose cut of the body, lack of trim, and the use of utilitarian fabrics. The most notable feature was the turned-down collar, which served the practical function of buttoning up over the throat in inclement weather. As the coat gained popularity and acceptability, the fit became more exact, requiring finer wool suitable for tailoring, but it retained its turned-down collar. By the 1780s the collar had increased in height to match that of the formal coat, but it still had the turned-down shape, and the sleeves followed the fashionable trend of a slimmer cut with narrow cuffs or a vertical opening.[20]

The frock came to represent the English way of life, even encompassing social and political thought. An English traveler wrote in 1752 that while visiting Paris and dressed in the formal French style, "I frequently sighed for my little loose Frock, which I look upon as an Emblem of our happy Constitution; for it lays a Man under no uneasy Restraint, but leaves it in his Power to do as he pleases."[21] However, with the loss of the American colonies and with revolution against the monarchy in France, some British aristocrats viewed the growing informality in dress represented by the frock with skepticism. Lord Glenbervie wrote in his journal in 1794 that "for these last three or four years, if a man has been to Court he cannot go . . . to dine out or to an assembly without putting on a frock." He went on to speculate how this had removed barriers, leading to "leveling and equalising notions."[22]

The frock was introduced into France by fashion-conscious young men and reflected a more general vogue for things English, from the constitution to the customs of country life. The interest in English-style men's clothing was sparked by France's own changing political and social atmosphere in the last quarter of the century. Looking back from 1816, the comte de Ségur reflected in his *Memoirs* that "the laws of England were studied and envied by men of a mature age; English horses and jockeys, boots and coats after the English fashion, could alone suit the fancy of young men." Before leaving France, Nabby Adams noted that "the beaux in this country aim very much at the English dress."[23]

Jefferson was conscious of this change in fashion and its relationship to politics. "In Society the *habit habillé* is almost banished," he observed in 1787, "and they begin to go even to great supper in frock: the court and diplomatic corps however must always be excepted. They are too high to be reached by any improvement." Demonstrating his understanding of the mechanisms of court society, he added, "They are the last refuge from which etiquette, formality and folly will be driven. Take away these and they would be on a level with other people."[24] Whether or not the Anglophobic Jefferson was aware of the origins of the frock, his comment indicates his endorsement of its fashionable advance in France and the leveling process it signaled.

The coat that Jefferson wore for the Brown portrait appears to be a French version of the frock. A former curator of the Musée de la Mode et du Costume in Paris, Madeleine Delpierre, identified the French *frac* as a "men's coat in the English style, informal, loose-fitting, and without buttons or pockets."[25] Common to the English frock in the 1780s were flat, decorative metal buttons reaching below the waist and at the sleeve, either in a vertical row or edging the top of a small cuff, as in Brown's companion portrait of John Adams, completed in 1788 (Fig. 5). No buttons are visible on Jefferson's coat, and a survey of his accounting records does not indicate purchases of coats other than those from Parisian tailors.

Jefferson did set up an account with the London tailor Robert Cannon shortly after his arrival there. Extant invoices from Cannon and Jefferson's records of payment show purchases of waistcoats and breeches. In fact, it is possible that the elegant white-and-gold-striped waistcoat Jefferson wears in the Brown portrait was made by Cannon, as his invoice of March 14, 1786, three days after Jefferson's arrival in London, includes a charge for "making a waistcoat Silk Strip'd Compleat" along with two pair of breeches. The choice of stripes shows a fashion awareness, whether on the part of Jefferson or of his London tailor, as the curvilinear shapes of the rococo were giving way to the straight lines of the neoclassical. Jefferson continued to order waistcoats and breeches from Cannon during the remainder of his stay in London and even after his return to Paris, but the orders never included coats.[26] For Jefferson this major body garment remained French in both origin and style.

For Brown's portrait Jefferson's hair was dressed and heavily powdered in a style that reflected the formality of the French court. That Jefferson chose to have his own hair dressed with pomatum and then powdered rather than

Fig. 5. *John Adams (1735–1826)*, 1788, by Mather Brown, bequest of John Francis Parkman, 1908. (Boston Athenaeum)

wearing a wig was noted by Abigail Adams. Jefferson's "hair too is an other affliction which he is tempted to cut off," she reported to her American relatives. "He expects not to live above a dozen years & he shall loose one of those in hair dressing."[27] In addition, Jefferson's accounts show no purchases of wigs but rather a reimbursement to his *valet de chambre* for "apparatus for shaving & combing" and for pomatum.[28] Adrienne Petit, who would be promoted to *maitre d'hôtel* following their return to Paris, accompanied Jefferson to England and could have assisted with his hairdressing. Jefferson made one payment to a hairdresser while on his tour of the English countryside with Adams but none while in London. If indeed Petit was acting as his personal servant, it could account for Jefferson's hair being dressed somewhat higher and fuller in the Brown portrait, somewhat more in the French style than was Adams's in the companion portrait (see Figs. 1 and 5).

Because Jefferson's self-fashioning for the portrait created a very aristocratic image, it was left to the pose and props to add republican elements. Jefferson's hand rests upon a parchment, and though the document cannot be identified, such a prop was often used to indicate a scholar or statesman and in this case undoubtedly referred to Jefferson's contributions to American political and scientific thought.[29] An even more overt republican icon is the statue of the Goddess of Liberty that stands behind Jefferson. The statue is identifiable by her antique dress and staff supporting the pileus, or liberty cap. This symbol of *libertas* dates from the classical world and became a popular icon in Europe and the colonies after the German archaeologist Johann Joachim Winckelmann published his findings from Roman excavations in his *Versuch einer Allegorie* in 1766. In Roman rituals freeing slaves from bondage, the slave would be touched by the staff and then given the cap, a symbol of freedom. By the mid-eighteenth century the goddess with staff and cap, or just the cap and staff alone, began to appear on both sides of the Atlantic. In 1767 Charles Willson Peale used the icon in a commissioned portrait of the great British statesman and friend of America William Pitt. Paul Revere used the liberty cap on his Sons of Liberty bowl. When Franklin, Adams, and Jefferson considered designs for the Seal of the United States in July 1776, the Liberty Goddess with staff and cap was included in all their proposals. Although their designs were not adopted, the Liberty Goddess was incorporated into the Great Seal of Virginia, appearing on the reverse side. The symbol was well known to Jefferson, and its inclusion in his portrait underscored his association with the recent triumph of liberty in America.[30]

Jefferson had to wait two years to receive his portrait and the new portrait of Adams from Brown. As the Adams family prepared to return to the United States, Jefferson's correspondence with Adams's son-in-law, William Stephens Smith, became more anxious. "Remember Mr. Adam's picture," Jefferson wrote Smith, "When they shall be ready, I would wish to receive them with my own which Mr. Brown has." Shortly thereafter, Jefferson wrote again: "I must remind you also of Mr. Adams's picture, as I should be much mortified should I not get it done before he leaves Europe." In March

1788 Smith could at last report that Brown had begun Adams's portrait: "Brown is busy about the pictures. Mr. Adams is like. Yours I do not think so well of." In September 1788 Jefferson wrote that "the pictures are received in good condition."[31]

Brown's portrait of Adams may have been hurriedly done, but it was considered a good likeness (see Fig. 5). His matching coat and waistcoat, though subdued in color, were stylish by London standards, with fashionable metal buttons, the high collar of the frock coat, and the slimness of the sleeve with a vertical vent in the small cuff. The jabot on the front of Adams's shirt is far less elaborate than the double-fluted ruffle in Jefferson's portrait, but the ruffle at Adams's wrist appears to be of a very fine, lightweight linen edged with narrow lace that is obviously of high quality. His wig or hairdressing is formal, but in being dressed closer to the head and powdered only to a grey tone, it appears more conservative than Jefferson's in Mather Brown's portrait. In fact, these two companion portraits allow a comparison of the subtleties in men's clothing, accessories, and hairdressing that distinguished the French style from the English. It is possible that Jefferson appeared in London and at St. James's looking far too French and thus flaunting his preference in foreign relations. If so, it should not be surprising that he was snubbed by George III.

Like Jefferson, Adams is shown with a sheaf of papers and is seated in front of a deep red drape. There is a notable difference in props, however, as the Goddess of Liberty has been replaced with books. The title on the spine clearly visible reads *Jefferson's Hist. Of Virginia*. When the Adams family left France for their new post in London, Jefferson had presented them with a copy of his recently published *Notes on the State of Virginia*. Adams predicted that *Notes* would bring honor to both the author and his country. The obvious reference to the work in the Adams portrait was a tribute to the recipient of the portrait and a testimonial to viewers of Jefferson's collection of worthies at his Paris residence of Jefferson's own contribution to Enlightenment literature. As his initial sitting for Mather Brown took place the year before Adams began publication of his lengthy *Defence of the Constitutions of Government of the United States of America*, Jefferson could be excused for not reciprocating the gesture.

During the two years that Brown worked on the Jefferson-Adams commissions Jefferson's likeness was taken by John Trumbull. Jefferson had met Trumbull during his London trip and extended an invitation to visit him in Paris. It was at the Hôtel de Langeac that Trumbull developed the concept for his monumental *Declaration of Independence*, perhaps in response to suggestions from Jefferson. Trumbull later wrote, "I began the composition of the Declaration of Independence, with the assistance of [Jefferson's] infor-mation and advice."[32] Though it would be many years before this work was complete, Trumbull quickly produced three miniature portraits from his study of Jefferson that became gifts to three different women.

Two of the miniatures are quite similar and were painted at the request of women who were particular friends of Jefferson as well as close mutual friends, Maria Cosway and Angelica Church (see Figs. 2 and 3). Both min-iatures show Jefferson in a dark frock coat with an artistic bluish cast that is obviously in the English style, with large metal buttons, worn over a buff-colored waistcoat. His hair is formally dressed and powdered in a manner quite similar to that in the Mather Brown portrait.

The third miniature, painted for Jefferson's sixteen-year-old daughter, Martha, depicts Jefferson quite differently (see Fig. 4). Again Trumbull has him in a dark frock coat, English in style, with a buff waistcoat. This time, however, the hair is not formally dressed but given a definite red cast with only a hint of light powder. Though it is pulled back into the traditional queue, the sides are loose rather than formed into tight curls, and the crown is left low and smooth. The Jefferson created for Martha is much closer to the figure that would eventually stand in the center of Trumbull's painting celebrating the Declaration of Independence, and the formality given the miniatures painted for Cosway and Church, women who moved freely in the aristocratic circles of London and Paris, is missing.

It can be assumed that the clothing choices in these three miniatures were made by the artist, as all were painted in London, where Cosway and Church were living at the time. The miniature made for Jefferson's daugh-ter was sent to Paris as a surprise gift.[33] The only hint in the Cosway and Church miniatures of an American connection or Whig sensibility was Trumbull's dressing Jefferson in a blue coat with a buff waistcoat. This color combination, the buff and the blue, suggested support of the American cause, as it was used by General Washington and other revolutionaries in their uniforms and was adopted by friends of America in Parliament such as Charles James Fox.[34] Although Jefferson never stated a preference for this color combination, after his initial order all the waistcoats and breeches made for him by Robert Cannon were in buff.

More than the clothing, it is the hairstyle that distinguishes Jefferson as American in Martha's miniature. In his *Reminiscences,* Trumbull mentioned taking John Adams's likeness for his *Declaration* and shows his awareness of the difference in appearance appropriate for an American in his home country as opposed to Europe. Trumbull wrote, "In the course of the sum-mer of 1787, Mr. Adams took leave of the court of St. James, and preparatory to the voyage to America, had the powder combed out of his hair. Its color and natural curl were beautiful, and I took that opportunity to paint his portrait in the small Declaration of Independence."[35] Trumbull also managed to capture Jefferson without hair powder when he sketched him in Paris. "In the autumn of 1787," he later recalled, "I again visited Paris, where I painted the portrait of Mr. Jefferson in the original small Declaration of Independence."[36]

In the Revolutionary and post-Revolutionary years only one American had managed to be accepted in Paris in the rustic American provincial style, with hair unpowdered: Benjamin Franklin. Franklin's reputation as a man of science and a statesman had preceded him. Following his arrival in Paris late in 1776, the artist Elisabeth Vigée-Lebrun wrote in her description of Franklin that "no-one was more fashionable, more sought after in Paris than Doctor Franklin: the crowd chased after him in parks and public places; hats, canes and snuffboxes were designed in the Franklin style, and people thought themselves very lucky if they were invited to the same dinner party as this famous man." The first time she saw him, "he was dressed in grey and his unpowdered braided hair fell upon his shoulders; if it had not been for the nobility of his face, I would have taken him for a stocky farmer, such was the contrast he made with the other diplomats who were all powdered and dressed in their finest clothes, bedecked with gold and coloured sashes."[37]

Franklin must have relished the notoriety ignited by the image he had created for his return to Europe. He described himself with some glee as "very plainly dressed, wearing my thin, grey straight hair that peeps out under my only *coiffure*, a fine fur cap, which comes down my forehead almost to my spectacles. Think how this must appear among the powdered heads of Paris!"[38] It was Franklin in his fur cap and spectacles as sketched by the artist Charles Nicolas Cochin and engraved by Augustin de Saint-Aubin that caught Europe's attention (Fig. 6). The historian Charles Sellers explains that even though it was a good likeness, the print was never intended as a step toward a formal portrait; it was designed instead for publicity purposes. The print, as advertised in the *Journal de Paris* of June 1777, announced Franklin's arrival in his "sensational" costume and worked exceptionally well to create a strikingly effective image.[39]

Jefferson touted Franklin's abilities as a scientist and innovative thinker in his own *Notes on Virginia,* where he rebuffed the European charge that the New World was devoid of genius: "In physics we have produced a Franklin, than whom no one of the present age has made more important discoveries, nor has enriched philosophy with more, or more ingenious solutions of the phænomena of nature."[40] Upon his arrival in France, Jefferson relied on

BENJAMIN FRANKLIN.

Né à Bofton, dans la nouvelle Angleterre le 17 Janvier 1706.

Fig. 6. *Benjamin Franklin,* engraved by Augustin de Saint Aubin after a drawing by Charles Nicholas Cochin, 1777. (American Philosophical Society)

introductions from Franklin to gain access to fashionable salons. "I took a trip yesterday to Sannois and commenced an acquaintance with the old Countess d'Hocquetout," he reported happily in June 1785. "I received much pleasure from it and hope it has opened a door of admission for me to the circle of literati with which she is environed." At the salon of Madame Helvétius, widow of the famous philosophe and a close and particular friend of Franklin's, Jefferson met and established lasting relationships with members of the French literati such as the comte de Volney, Destutt de Tracy, and Pierre-Georges Cabanis.[41]

The formal portrait by Mather Brown and even the Trumbull miniatures for Cosway and Church give an impression of how Jefferson may have appeared socially in both Paris and London but do not definitively tell us how he presented himself at the French court. There is one written reference to Jefferson at Versailles in a letter from a young Philadelphian, Thomas Shippen, following his own presentation at court under Jefferson's patronage. According to Shippen, "I observed that although Mr. Jefferson was the plainest man in the room, and the most destitute of ribbands, crosses and other insignia of rank that he was most courted and most attended to (even by the Courtiers themselves) of the whole Diplomatic corps."[42]

The crosses and ribbons observed by Shippen are well illustrated in a portrait of the comte de Vaudreuil painted by Elisabeth Vigée-Lebrun in 1784 (Fig. 7). Vaudreuil held the Ordre du Saint-Esprit, the highest knightly order of France, as evidenced by the cross embroidered on the coat and the blue moiré ribbon (the cordon bleu) worn diagonally across the chest. From a buttonhole, suspended by a red ribbon, hangs the cross of the military order of St. Louis. Even young Nabby Adams learned to recognize the cordon bleu, observing of fellow dinner guests that "by their ribbons, I suppose [they] were great folks."[43]

Some Americans viewed knightly orders such as these with suspicion. Before leaving for Europe Jefferson wrote Washington to express his concerns about the Society of the Cincinnati, the American organization most comparable to a European military order. This hereditary society, formed by Revolutionary officers in 1783, took as its emblem an eagle suspended by a blue and white ribbon.[44] Jefferson's hostility to such "aristocratic" organizations may have accounted for his being "destitute" of such insignia.

In the absence of any image of Jefferson in court dress, some clues about his appearance may be drawn from a full-length formal portrait of his fellow diplomat John Adams by the Anglo-American artist John Singleton Copley (Fig. 8). When Adams sat for Copley, he had just arrived in London from signing the peace treaty in Paris and may have been wearing the same

Fig. 7. *The Comte de Vaudreuil,* 1784, by Elisabeth-Louise Vigée-Lebrun. (Virginia Museum of Fine Arts, Richmond; gift of Mrs. A. D. Williams. Photo: Katherine Wetzel; © Virginia Museum of Fine Arts)

Fig. 8. *John Adams (1735–1826)*, 1783, by John Singleton Copley. (Harvard Art Museum, Fogg Art Museum, Harvard University Portrait Collection; bequest of Ward Nicholas Boylston to Harvard College, 1828, H74. Photo: Imaging Department; © President and Fellows of Harvard College)

clothing he wore at Versailles. The painting, begun in the fall of 1783 and not completed until the following year, was contemporary with Vigée-Lebrun's portrait of the comte de Vaudreuil and so invites comparison. Adams posed in a full-dress coat with stiffened pleats in the skirt and wide cuffs. Copley's mimetic style tells us the coat was a rich velvet; however, in contrast to Vaudreuil's dress, Adams's only trim was the ornate buttons. The cut of the collar, much lower than Vaudreuil's, and the fullness in the skirt place Adams's coat far from the leading edge of fashion in the early 1780s. Adams adhered to the courtly tradition of lace at throat and wrists, wore a dress sword, and his hair (or wig) was powdered and formally dressed by pulling it back into a queue that was covered by a black silk bag and a large black bow. This style continued to be favored for court wear in both France and England.[45] Though in comparison to the comte de Vaudreuil's, Adams's look is understated, it was perhaps a bit too aristocratic by republican standards. Adams was somewhat embarrassed by the painting, referring to it as a "piece of vanity." When it was suggested as a frontispiece for a new edition of his *Defence of the Constitutions of Government of the United States,* he responded, "I should be much mortified to see such a Bijou affixed to those Republican Volumes."[46]

How closely Jefferson's appearance at court may have followed that of John Adams is unclear, but an anecdote repeated by Abigail Adams offers evidence that Jefferson respected court mandates regarding dress. Within a month of Jefferson's arrival in Paris a period of mourning was declared, which necessitated the purchase of a black suit. According to Abigail, "Mr. Jefferson had to hie away for a Tailor to get a whole black silk suit made up in two days, and at the end of Eleven days," the designated mourning period, "should an other death happen, he will be obliged to have a new Suit of mourning of Cloth, because that is the Season when Silk must be cast off. We may groan and scold but these are expences which cannot be avoided."[47] The date of her letter, September 5, and the designated mourning period of eleven days tells us that the season for silk ended about mid-September and that the appropriate fabric following that date would be wool broadcloth. Her comment that the expenses could not be avoided again speaks to the position of the American diplomats at court.

Before his assignment in Paris ended, Jefferson would complain about the cost of maintaining an appropriate appearance, as had his predecessors, Franklin and Adams. Jefferson wrote Foreign Secretary John Jay that "my furniture, carriage, apparel are all plain. Yet they have cost me more than a year's salary." The meaning of "plain" is subject to interpretation. Certainly his apparel was not as plain as Benjamin Franklin's untrimmed grey suit and straight, unpowdered hair, as described by Vigée-Lebrun. That option was not open to the relatively unknown Jefferson, who later remarked that "the succession to Dr. Franklin, at the court of France, was an excellent school of humility." To the question, "It is you, Sir, who replace Doctor Franklin?" Jefferson famously replied, "No one can replace him, Sir: I am only his successor."[48] Nor does Shippen's description of Jefferson as "the plainest man in the room" mean that he would have appeared at court in anything other than an appropriate dress coat with sword, lace, and *chapeau bras,* an *ancien régime* dress code that had not been relinquished among courtiers and diplomats even at a time when the less formal *frac* was gaining wider acceptance in pre-Revolutionary France.

Both visual and written references to Jefferson as an American diplomat suggest that he accepted the fashion expectations of the French court and the aristocratic salons of Paris. His concern for the reputation of the new American nation, both its government and its people, motivated him to conform to these expectations. It is undoubtedly true that his own aspirations to be accepted among the scientific and intellectual thinkers of Europe also guided his fashion behavior.

The formal portrait by Mather Brown and the miniatures by John Trumbull reflect a paradox similar to that expressed by Jefferson in his "My view of Europe" letter. In the Brown portrait his appearance is in keeping with the latest French style, yet he is surrounded with objects signaling his republican commitments. The Trumbull miniatures, when considered together, represent a similar dichotomy. The small portraits intended for women who were socially prominent in aristocratic European circles delineate a very European image, while the portrait for his daughter shows an American with unpowdered, informally dressed hair. These portraits reflect the Jefferson who criticized European despotism and corruption and extolled the virtue of the new American republic even while acknowledging his powerful attraction to the "vaunted scene of Europe."

NOTES

Some portions of the discussion of the Mather Brown portrait were previously published as "Fashioning an American Diplomat: The Mather Brown Portrait of Thomas Jefferson," by Gaye Wilson and Elizabeth V. Chew, in the annual journal of the Costume Society of America, *Dress,* 29 (2002): 19–24.

1. TJ to Charles Bellini, 30 Sept. 1785, *TJP,* 8:568–70.

2. TJ to John Page, 20 Jan. 1763, ibid., 1:7–9; TJ to Benjamin Franklin, 13 Aug. 1777, ibid., 2:27.

3. TJ to Bellini, 30 Sept. 1785, ibid., 8:569.

4. TJ to Baron Geismar, 6 Sept. 1785, ibid., 499–500; TJ, "Hints to Americans Travelling in Europe," ibid., 13:269–70; TJ to James Monroe, 11 Nov. 1784, ibid., 7:512.

5. Norbert Elias, *The Court Society,* trans. Edmund Jephcott (New York, 1983), 29, 64.

6. Franklin to JA, 26 Sept. 1778, *PJA,* 7:79; *Benjamin Franklin's Autobiographical Writings,* ed. Carl Van Doren (New York, 1945), 454.

7. *Diary and Autobiography of John Adams,* ed. L. H. Butterfield, 4 vols. (Cambridge, MA, 1961), 3:37.

8. Abigail Adams to Mary Smith Cranch, 5 Sept. 1784, *AFC,* 5:443; *Journal and Correspondence of Miss Adams, daughter of John Adams,* ed. her Daughter (New York, 1841), 14.

9. *Jefferson's Memorandum Books,* ed. James A. Bear Jr. and Lucia C. Stanton, 2 vols. (Princeton, NJ, 1997), 1:557–60 (hereafter *JMB*).

10. TJ to James Madison, 8 Dec. 1784, *TJP,* 7:559; TJ to Monroe, 10 Dec. 1784, ibid., 563.

11. *Diary and Autobiography of John Adams,* 3:182n2; TJ, *Autobiography, 1743–1790,* in *TJW,* 57; *JMB,* 1:613–23 (for Jefferson's purchases while in London); TJ, "Notes of a Tour of English Gardens," *TJP,* 9:369–75. For a summary of Jefferson's trip to London, see Dumas Malone, *Jefferson and His Time,* vol. 2, *Jefferson and the Rights of Man* (Boston, 1951), 50–63.

12. Dorinda Evans, *Mather Brown: Early American Artist in England* (Middletown, CT, 1982), 3, 14–16, 122–23.

13. Mather Brown, quoted in ibid., 42.

14. Evans, *Mather Brown,* 43–44, 53.

15. TJ to William Stephens Smith, 22 Oct. 1786, *TJP,* 10:479.

16. Brandon Brame Fortune, "Portraits of Virtue and Genius: Pantheons of Worthies and Public Portraiture in the Early American Republic, 1780–1820" (PhD diss., University of North Carolina at Chapel Hill, 1987), 1–14, 34; David Hackett Fischer, *Liberty and Freedom: A visual History of America's Founding Ideas* (Oxford, 2005), 178.

17. Susan R. Stein, *The Worlds of Thomas Jefferson at Monticello* (New York, 1993), 122; *JMB,* 1:550, entry of 28 May 1784, and n. 40; Patience Wright to Jefferson, 14 Aug. 1785, *TJP,* 8:380.

18. For Jefferson's commission of the Raleigh portrait, see TJ to Smith, 22 Oct. 1786, *TJP,* 10:478–79; for the commissions from the Uffizi Gallery, see TJ to Philip Mazzei, 17 Oct. 1787, ibid., 12:245, and TJ to John Trumbull, 12 Jan. 1789, ibid., 14:440; the two Jefferson quotations can be found in TJ to Joseph Delaplaine, 3 May 1814, L&B, 14:132–33; and for Jefferson's commission of the Newton, Bacon, and Locke portraits, see TJ to Trumbull, 15 Feb. 1788, *TJP,* 14:561, and Trumbull to TJ, 26 May 1789, ibid. 15:151–52. For a discussion of Jefferson's collection of worthies see Harold E. Dickson, "'TH.J.' Art Collector," published in *Jefferson and the Arts: An Extended View,* ed. William Howard Adams (Washington, DC, 1976), 114–16.

19. The various visitors to the American legation are discussed in Howard C. Rice Jr., *Thomas Jefferson's Paris* (Princeton, NJ, 1976), 53–54; and Marie Kimball, *Jefferson: The Scene of Europe 1784 to 1789* (New York, 1950), 93, 105.

20. For the origin of the term *frock,* see *Oxford English Dictionary,* 2nd ed.; and C. Willett and Phillis Cunnington, *Handbook of English Costume in the Eighteenth Century* (Boston, 1972). Two of the best sources for the development of the frock coat are ibid., 16–20, 193–203; and Nora Waugh, *The Cut of Men's Clothes* (London, 1964), 53–54.

21. Arthur Murphy, *The Grey's-Inn Journal,* 1752, quoted in both Waugh, *Cut of Men's Clothes,* 105, and Geoffrey Squire, *Dress and Society, 1560–1970* (New York, 1974), 125.

22. Waugh, *Cut of Men's Clothes,* 110; Squire, *Dress and Society,* 125.

23. A. J. P. de Ségur, *Memoirs,* 3 vols. (London, 1825–27), 1:21, quoted in Aileen Ribeiro, *Fashion in the French Revolution* (London, 1988), 39; *Journal and Correspondence of Miss Adams,* 63.

24. TJ to David Humphreys, 14 Aug. 1787, in *TJP,* 12:32.

25. Madeleine Delpierre, *Dress in France in the Eighteenth Century,* trans. Carolie Beamish (New Haven, CT, 1997), 165; see also Jacques Ruppert, *Le costume époques Louis XVI et Directoire* (Paris, 1990), 9: "Il y a des fracs sans boutons."

26. Robert Cannon invoices, 14 Mar., 1 and 24 Apr. 1786, Thomas Jefferson Papers, Special Collections, University of Virginia, Charlottesville; Jefferson's *Memorandum Books* show payments to three different Parisian tailors between the dates of his arrival in Paris, in August 1784, and his London visit, in March–April 1786. Most are not itemized, but one, a payment to "Lonpry, the tailor," lists payment for a coat at seventy-two francs. *JMB* 1:563–606.

27. Abigail Adams to Cotton Tufts, 8 Sept. 1784, in *AFC,* 5:458.

28. *JMB,* 1:560, 563.

29. How widely Jefferson was viewed as the principal author of the *Declaration of Independence* by the time he sat for Mather Brown in March–April 1786 is debatable; however, he had taken steps to have his *Statute for Religious Freedom for the State of Virginia* printed and circulated. He was able to report to James Madison in a letter of 16 December 1786 that "the Virginia act for religious freedom has been received with infinite approbation in Europe and propagated with enthusiasm.... It has been translated into French and Italian.... It is inserted in the new Encyclopedie, and is appearing in most of the publications respecting America." *TJP,* 10:603–4.

30. Fischer, *Liberty and Freedom,* 6, 41–42, 97–103; Yvonne Korshak, "The Liberty Cap as a Revolutionary Symbol in America and France," *Smithsonian Studies in American Art,* Fall 1987, 53–69; Jennifer Harris, "The Red Cap of Liberty: A Study of Dress Worn by French Revolutionary Partisans 1789–94," *Eighteenth Century Studies* 14, no. 3 (1981): 283–312.

31. TJ to Smith, 19 Feb. 1781 and 31 Dec. 1787, *TJP,* 11:169, 12:484; TJ to Trumbull, 10 Sept. 1788, ibid., 13:597.

32. *The Autobiography of Colonel John Trumbull, Patriot-Artist, 1756–1843,* ed. Theodore Sizer (New Haven, CT, 1953), 92–93.

33. Helen A. Cooper, *John Trumbull: The Hand and Spirit of a Painter* (New Haven, CT, 1982), 117.

34. Elisabeth McClellan, *Historic Dress in America, 1607–1870,* 2 vols. (1904–10; New York, 1977), 1:349, identifying Washington's uniform when he took command of

the Continental army as buff and blue; *The Historical and the Posthumous Memoirs of Sir Nathaniel William Wraxall, 1772–1784,* ed. Henry B. Wheatley, 4 vols. (London, 1884), 2:2–3. In 1806 Jefferson wrote of Fox, "In Mr. Fox, personally, I have more confidence than in any man in England." TJ to Monroe, 4 May 1806, Papers of Thomas Jefferson, LC.

35. John Trumbull, *Autobiography, Reminiscences and Letters of John Trumbull from 1756 to 1841* (New Haven, CT, 1841), 147.

36. Ibid., 150–51.

37. *Memoirs of Elisabeth Vigée-Lebrun,* trans. Siân Evans (Bloomington, IN, 1989), 318–19.

38. Franklin to Mrs. Emma Thompson, 8 Feb. 1777, reprinted in *Benjamin Franklin's Autobiographical Writings,* 427–28.

39. Charles Coleman Sellers, *Benjamin Franklin in Portraiture* (New Haven, CT, 1962), 228–29.

40. *Notes,* 64.

41. TJ to Abigail Adams, 21 June 1785, *TJP* 8:241; Rice, *Thomas Jefferson's Paris,* 94; Kimball, *Jefferson,* 78–107.

42. Thomas Lee Shippen to William Shippen, 24 Feb.–26 Mar. 1788, Shippen Family Papers, LC, quoted in *TJP,* 12:504.

43. These knightly orders are referenced in many clothing histories. A good illustration showing orders that correspond closely to those in the comte de Vaudreuil portrait can be found in Ribeiro, *Fashion in the French Revolution,* 40; *Journal and Correspondence of Miss Adams,* 30.

44. TJ to George Washington, 16 Apr. 1784, *TJP,* 7:105–8. The emblem of the Society of the Cincinnati is reproduced in Garry Wills, *Cincinnatus: George Washington and the Enlightenment* (New York, 1984), 143.

45. Aileen Ribeiro, *Dress in Eighteenth-Century Europe* (New Haven, CT, 2002), 29, 185.

46. JA to John Stockdale, 12 May 1793, quoted in Andrew Oliver, *Portraits of John and Abigail Adams* (Cambridge, MA, 1967), 25.

47. Abigail Adams to Cranch, 5 Sept. 1784.

48. TJ to Smith, 19 Feb. 1791, *TJP,* 19:113.

Negotiating Gifts
Jefferson's Diplomatic Presents

MARTHA ELENA ROJAS

In 1791 Thomas Jefferson accepted a gift from Louis XVI, a miniature portrait of the king set in "brilliants," marking the end of his tenure as the U.S. minister to France. What might seem a banal, even innocuous ceremonial gesture preoccupied Jefferson, who at first refused to accept the gift. His own distaste for this aspect of diplomatic culture was in step with a clause in the U.S. Constitution prohibiting representatives of the federal government from accepting "any present, Emolument, Office, or Title, of any kind whatever, from any King, Prince, or Foreign State."[1] Furthermore, Jefferson's service in France coincided with the first years of the French Revolution. In 1789 he had corresponded with the marquis de Lafayette about the drafting of the Declaration of the Rights of Man and he had hosted dinners for French republicans and philosophes during which the future roles of the king and that of the National Assembly were discussed and largely determined. Nonetheless, in 1791 Louis XVI still presided, however ceremoniously, over France, the nation that had stood as the crucial European ally of the United States during the American Revolution.

It quickly became evident that as a matter of form and protocol, gift exchange could not be avoided. Caught between the obligations of custom and the constitutional prohibition he had hoped would shield him from participation in gift exchange, Jefferson proceeded in a manner both calculated and tortured. In brief, once Thomas Jefferson, by this point secretary of state, resigned himself to the necessity of receiving and bestowing gifts, he requested that Louis XVI's present be delivered to William Short, his secretary, who had remained in Paris. Jefferson then instructed Short, in a letter written in cipher, to remove the diamonds, sell them, then rewrap the portrait and have it sent to him via a secure envoy. He required of Short the utmost secrecy, fearing above all that any detail of the affair would make its way into British newspapers. The money raised from the sale of the diamonds was used to pay for the presents Jefferson was in turn obliged to bestow upon two of the king's attendants at court in fulfillment of the diplomatic custom. Jefferson further specified that whatever sum remained be paid toward expenses incurred by the U.S. embassy in Paris during his tenure.[2]

The history of this miniature portrait is but one episode in a series of Jefferson's carefully considered yet awkward attempts to cope with the problem of the diplomatic present, as vexing for him as for the government of the new United States. Jefferson's insistence on secrecy, his determination to proceed without the scrutiny of Congress (the Constitution allowed for presents with the consent of Congress, an exception that curiously rendered them forbidden yet sometimes permissible objects), and his fear of being exposed by the British press suggest that Jefferson, in accepting, altering, and liquidating the bejeweled portrait, felt something like shame.

Capable of provoking secrecy, embarrassment, and concerns over reputation, gift exchange might best be conceived as a cultural practice with social as well as psychological effects within the political culture of the early republic. In this essay I explore this aspect of gift giving within the repertoire of the symbolic diplomacy of the new United States, as well as the anxiety occasioned by the need to determine objects that would serve as U.S. diplomatic gifts.

Because diplomatic presents often stood wholly in the place of language, these highly symbolic objects were subject to Jefferson's intense scrutiny and interpretation. Though gift giving was a conventional aspect of diplomatic protocol, Jefferson, as the first secretary of state, imagined that he might evade the practice, much as John Jay had done as secretary for foreign affairs before him.[3] In most cases, and like his predecessors, Jefferson ultimately followed customary practices, though not before requesting information, weighing options, deliberating about what a particular object would communicate about the nation and its people, and selecting a type of gift that made clear that the United States, while governed by fundamentally novel and distinct principles, belonged to the community of nations. The notable exception pertains to the management of affairs with North Africa. Jefferson's resentment about giving cash and other presents required in negotiations with Algiers, Tunis, Tripoli, and Morocco stands in stark contrast to his seeming comfort when it came to exchanging gifts with Native American nations.

In this essay I turn my attention to three objects of Jefferson's design—the Diplomatic Medal of 1790, the Indian Peace Medal, and the silver polygraph commissioned for the bey of Tunis. The three objects have in common a mechanical reproducibility that theoretically made possible an infinite number of copies. All three were honorific objects rendered precious by the novelty of their designs and the occasion of their presentation rather than by their putative uniqueness or the value of the materials used to make them. While the Diplomatic Medal of 1790 and the Indian peace medals had clear European (even Roman) antecedents with roles and histories in diplomatic, state, and courtly gift practices, the polygraph did not. Envisioned as prototypes that would yield reproductions, these gifts insist on a kind of universal model in which any "friend" of the United States might receive a specimen. Yet the very distinctiveness of the polygraph and the innovation it heralds, both in technology and as a kind of diplomatic gift, mark a departure in diplomatic practice and in Jefferson's conception of the United States in relation to North Africa. Despite his repeated efforts to design a standard gift, each diplomatic present reflected the relationship that Jefferson imagined (or wished) existed between the United States and the European, North African or Native American nation for which it was intended.

The task of selecting a suitable American diplomatic present repeatedly fell to Thomas Jefferson as U.S. minister, the first secretary of state, and then president. The problem of the U.S. diplomatic present began with gift exchange itself. The word *present* and the concept of the gift evoke a history of actual and ritualized hospitality, a latent expectation of munificence, and the increasingly abstract forms of symbolic representation preserved within the lexicon of diplomacy in particular and courtly etiquette more generally. Much of the diplomatic vocabulary consists of variations on the word *present:* as the verbs *to make a present to* and *to bring into the presence of;* as the noun connoting both a presence and a thing offered; and as the root of words like *presentation* and *representation*. Ministers, ambassadors, and other diplomats were incessantly being presented, presenting visitors, representing their counties, and giving presents. The early diplomatic correspondence of the United States invoked each of these senses and meanings of the word *present* at the time when the U.S. government was inventing the symbols of the nation, at the moment when the very existence of the United States (as measured by other nations recognizing it as a nation among nations) depended on the creation of representational forms.

Diplomatic and courtly rites of exchange presumed the existence of a head of state, of state power figured in the body of one person, *a* sovereign. The United States, a republic, possessed no such figure or structure. Silas Deane, Benjamin Franklin, and John Adams, all involved in securing

French aid for the American War of Independence, did not seriously question the protocols of the diplomatic corps and indeed often appeared preoccupied with comprehending those codes and fulfilling their requirements. Jefferson, however, sought to adjust courtly forms to practices he thought appropriate to a newly independent republican state. He struggled with two impulses at odds with each other, one that would resist and remake courtly diplomatic norms and one that sought to accommodate and meet those expectations. The process was particularly challenging when long-standing custom affronted Jefferson's conceptions of himself, the nation, and honorable comportment. He had explained to the marquis de Lafayette that he considered there to be "but one code of morality whether acting singly or collectively."[4] His refusal to distinguish between individuals and nations informed his attitude toward state gifts: his ambivalence toward customary presents is inextricable from the implications of gift exchange within an honor-bound culture, as vividly exemplified by his furor over the gifts and payment of tribute codified in European treaties with North African states and expected of the United States as it negotiated its own treaties.

Since the publication of Marcel Mauss's seminal 1925 study *The Gift: The Form and Reason for Exchange in Archaic Societies,* gifts have come to be understood as categorically complex social practices of exchange governed by particular norms, most often codes of honor. Scholars as diverse as Jacques Derrida and Natalie Zemon Davis have extended Mauss's central premises, that no thing can be freely given and that no gift is ever "free," to argue for the very impossibility of the coexistence of "the gift," on the one hand, and the "gift register" as a permanent feature of social relations over time, on the other. In other words, either there can never be a free gift and the category "gift" loses all meaning or the idea of the gift is so pervasive that it in fact structures all networks and associations. Bertram Wyatt-Brown has focused on the ways in which the honor of giver and receiver depend on the exchange: on what is given both initially and in return (since every gift must in some fashion be reciprocated, or in Jefferson's parlance, "countered") and on the manner in which presents are given and received. Furthermore, Kenneth S. Greenberg and Edmund Morgan have observed that the language of honor and the language of slavery have long been bound with notions of obligatory and voluntary giving, with the virtues of generosity and hospitality, and with the accompanying dishonor bestowed on the recipients of gifts meant to be left unreciprocated and on those either compelled to give or denied the opportunity of ever doing so.[5]

Within societies structured by the concept of honor, such as the circle of politicians and Virginia planters in the early republic, presents provoked ambivalence: an attitude of gratitude or condescension might expose or even generate inequities between giver and receiver.[6] The receiver might question whether the gift had been motivated by generosity or by calculation. A gift invited the receiver into a circle of exchange structured by reciprocity and governed by concerns over reputation. Or it acknowledged a hierarchical relationship and showcased not only the generosity of the giver but his power over the receiver.[7] The gifts that Jefferson regarded as "below suspicion" included pamphlets, books, and curiosities. However, the right kind of gift only partially determined the appropriateness of a gift exchange, which also depended on the social positions of the participants. For an exchange to be honorable, either the giver and the receiver had to be social equals or the giver had to stand in absolute mastery over the receiver.[8]

Greenberg has shown how southern slave owners, for instance, treated every single item necessary to sustain the lives and productivity of their slaves as gifts. To imply that the gift was part of a one-way transaction, that there was no expectation of a return gift, or, conversely, to demand a return gift could potentially be understood as an insult that might disgrace or degrade the other party. Gifts were evaluated for what they conveyed about reputation, character, and social standing, and they were intimately connected to the language of mastery and slavery. A gift to a southerner who fancied himself a man of honor was, as Greenberg points out, always at risk of being taken as an insult.[9] Jefferson's suspicion and defensiveness about gifts and the obligations they implied both tempted him to eschew diplomatic gift exchange altogether and led to his consequent meticulous attention to the matter of selecting state gifts.

Soon after Jefferson took office as secretary of state, Louis Guillaume Otto, the French chargé d'affaires in New York, sent him a confidential letter hinting that a "marque de souvenir et d'estime" to the departed French minister, the chevalier de la Luzerne, was appropriate, expected, and overdue.[10] Caught between personal embarrassment and annoyance at having to be prodded to act honorably in his official capacity, Jefferson proceeded swiftly and prudently, knowing that Otto, having suggested that the gift be a land grant, had cited the precedent of Georgia's territorial gift to Charles Hector, comte d'Estaing. Given the political turmoil in France and Luzerne's uncertain future under the Republican government, the request seems deeply pragmatic. Jefferson, though, did not entertain it. After his conversation with Otto, he quickly gathered information about the European protocols of gift exchange, the longer history of the practice, and more recent precedents involving U.S. representatives in order to determine how best to handle the exchanges required of him. Also, Jefferson realized that once the United

States gave a gift to Luzerne, the logic of reciprocity would oblige him to accept Louis XVI's miniature portrait.

The practice of giving royal portraits as diplomatic gifts circulated the image of the monarch beyond national boundaries. Popularized during the reign of Elizabeth I, miniatures—"counterfeit" likenesses first exchanged between royal lovers, family, and friends—and their bejeweled casings were hung around necks, pinned onto clothing, or kept close in lockets. The miniature portrait, like the snuffbox, was meant to be carried or worn on the body; thus the king's presents took intimate forms, not only commemorating service but also suggesting a close bond. These objects marked their possessors as belonging to the king's circle, at once corroborating the fiction that an official relation was necessarily also an affectionate one of kinship or friendship. The miniature vied for attention and value with the jewels that surrounded it; the entire object embodied the slippage between commodity and gift, possessing economic as well as sentimental value. Bought and sold, traded and pawned as well as collected, by the mid-eighteenth century miniatures were popular well beyond the royal court.

William Temple Franklin provided Jefferson with a description of the parting present given to his grandfather, Benjamin Franklin, by Louis XVI:

> The Present . . . was supposed to be worth fifteen hundred Louis d'ors, and consisted in a large Miniature of the King, set with four hundred and eight Diamonds, of a beautiful Water, forming a Wreath round the Picture and a Crown on the Top. This is the form of the Presents usually given to Ambassadors and Ministers Plenipotentiary, tho' of more or less value.—I had an Opportunity of seeing several given by the King of France, and some by other Princes, and they were generally in the form above mentioned. The Presents to our Commissioners Lee and Dean, consisted, if I am not mistaken, in a Gold Snuff-Box, curiously enamell'd, with a Miniature of the King or Queen, set round with Diamonds.[11]

Franklin surmised that bejeweled miniatures and enameled snuffboxes, with their long history of aristocratic and monarchical associations, might not be quite the right objects for the United States to give as diplomatic presents, "as we do not deal much in Jewels or Gold," and suggested instead that "a Tract of Land, or a present of valuable Furrs might answer the Purpose." Aware of the symbolic function of the diplomatic gift as a token that represented the nation, Franklin, in suggesting land or furs, implied that a sample of the nation's natural resources was both an appropriate emblem of the United States and readily available. He also acknowledged the limited financial resources of the United States. Elaborate jewels or gold tokens would have been prohibitively expensive. Yet, for Jefferson land and furs would not do. When choosing presents for European representatives, he resolutely avoided objects that alluded to the country's natural wealth and, by association, to its recent past as New World colonies. When he cataloged the presents received under the Confederation government by Benjamin Franklin, Silas Deane, Arthur Lee, John Jay, John Adams, and himself, he recorded the value and the substance of each gift, noting in particular each individual's rank and the length of his tenure in diplomatic service.[12] The items he enumerated included cash gifts, miniatures set in brilliants, gold snuffboxes, and the medal and gold chain given to Adams by the Dutch Republic.[13]

In the end, he modeled the U.S. present on the diplomatic medal given to John Adams by Holland. Turning to the example of a republic suggests that Jefferson aspired to a kind of gift that would register as distinct from, yet equivalent to, that of any court. Medals had their precedents in classical antiquity and like miniature portraits traced their formal roots to the profile portraits that had appeared on Roman coins. They also had a long history in North America, presented as gifts by the embassies of European empires to Indian nations. At the moment when Jefferson addressed Otto's complaint, he was also working on his report on coinage advocating the establishment of a U.S. mint. While there is no record of Jefferson's own deliberations on this topic, he had come to a decision little more than a week after receiving Otto's letter. Ancient, republican, customary, and having the possibility of eventual domestic production, medals emerged as eminently suitable.

In a letter to George Washington in which he enclosed drafts of letters to William Short and the marquis de la Luzerne, Jefferson drew the president's attention to the paragraphs respecting "devices for the Medal." Jefferson and Washington met to discuss the proposed arrangements for the diplomatic medal on the following day. Washington recorded their meeting in his diary and noted Jefferson's research on diplomatic presents. He described their conversation in this way:

> Fixed with the Secretary of State on the present which (according to the customs of other Nations) should be made to Diplomatic characters when they return from that employment in this Country—and this was a gold Medal, suspended to a gold Chain. . . . The reason why a Medal and Chain was fixed upon for the American present, is, that the die being once made the Medals could at any

time be struck at very little cost, and the chain made by our artisans, which (while the first should be retained as a memento) might be converted into Cash.[14]

Washington bluntly provided the reasoning behind the choice. By imagining the medal as a "memento," or a curiosity to be preserved for its commemorative value, and the chain as "cash," fungible and therefore purely of remunerative value, Jefferson's solution divided aspects of the gift that had previously been considered inextricable. His deliberations about the U.S. gift also coincided with his detailed instructions to William Short about converting the diamonds on the portrait he had received into cash. Locating the monetary value of the U.S. gift in a simple gold chain with no mark of provenance, Jefferson proceeded out of consideration for other diplomats who might find themselves embarrassingly short of funds.

Making the gift easy to replicate demystified it by turning a practice whose premise, however illusory, had been to bequeath a personal token of affirmation, if not outright affection, into a uniform, impersonal commemorative ritual. The choice of the diplomatic medal also permitted Jefferson to move away from the individually crafted artifacts circulated by monarchs, each unique despite their conventionality, toward one that might be mechanically and readily reproduced. He thus attempted to dissociate the state gift from a personal one, moving the diplomatic present away from the demands of gift exchange, though not quite rendering it a straightforward economic transaction (as payment for service). This desire seems to have been for a diplomatic present that would mark an end to a relationship between a foreign representative and the U.S. government rather than cultivate a continuing state-to-state relationship.

The United States presented Jefferson's Diplomatic Medal of 1790 only twice. Struck in gold for the gifts to Luzerne and De Moustier, the medals are the only materialization of Jefferson's ideal present. That Luzerne died before his medal made its way to France makes the failure of these objects to function successfully as gifts all the more poignant. William Temple Franklin's warning that there could be nothing "absolutely fixed" about diplomatic presents soon proved to be right. Jefferson's idea of a fixed, perpetual diplomatic present fell apart with the arrival of Edmund Genêt as the representative of the French Republic in 1793. Genêt's inappropriate disregard of the proclaimed U.S. neutrality in the war then raging between England and France resulted in President Washington's formally requesting his recall. Jefferson's medal did not fit this situation, making clear that gifts had to reflect the relationship that evolved between a "diplomatic character" and the United States, its people and its government.[15]

Though use of Jefferson's Diplomatic Medal of 1790 ceased, medals continued to serve as diplomatic gifts, as they long had, in negotiations with Native American nations. The process of striking, or minting, the diplomatic medal eroded the underlying tension between commodity and gift by undermining the distinction between literal and figurative forms of specie. In effect the U.S. Diplomatic Medal of 1790 was yet another currency, its monetary value simply displaced onto a chain deliberately made to be converted into money, suggesting deep cynicism about the nature of gifts. The ease with which the gold chain could be converted into cash drew the gift perilously close to the unacceptable: a bribe or remuneration. Indeed, Jefferson proceeded as if gifts were always either bribes, piling obligation on top of obligation, or payment for services already rendered.

Jefferson was most explicit about gifts and bribery, elaborating a strategy of achieving peace through compulsion, when he wrote about Indian policy to Charles Carroll in 1791:

> I hope we will give them a thorough drumming this summer, and then change our tomahawk into a golden chain of friendship. The most economical as well as most humane conduct toward them is to bribe them into peace, and to retain them in peace by eternal bribes. The expedition this year would have served for presents on the most liberal scale for one hundred years.[16]

In this instance Jefferson allows precious little distinction between the words *present* and *bribe*. His characterization of friendship as a "golden chain" that "retains" others is a far cry from the "free" commerce he imagined entering into with other (non-Indian) nations. However, it seems crucial that in this context Jefferson characterized friendship as a perpetually binding relationship with "eternal bribes" and gifts forecast "for one hundred years."[17] The purview of the Department of War, relations with Indian nations nominally fell outside Jefferson's jurisdiction, but the imperial interests of Britain and Spain made that bureaucratic distinction difficult to maintain.

For example, in 1793, while still serving as Washington's secretary of state, Jefferson provided William Short and William Carmichael (both serving in Spain) with a "short statement of facts" regarding what had ensued between the United States and "the Indian tribes within their neighborhood" during the course of the War of Independence. Written to counter a narrative circulated by Spanish ministers who charged that the United States had meddled in matters within Spanish territory, Jefferson's explanation offers a defense of government policy. When Spain complained of the United States "giving medals and marks of distinction to the Indian chiefs," Jefferson countered:

> This has been an antient Custom from time immemorial. The medals are considered as complimentary things, as marks of friendship to those who come to see us, or who do us good offices, conciliatory of their good will towards us, and not designed to produce a contrary disposition towards others. They confer no power, and seem to have taken their origin in the European practice of giving medals or other marks of friendship to the negotiators of treaties, and other diplomatic Characters, or visitors of distinction. The British government, while it prevailed here, practised the giving of Medals, Gorgets, and Bracelets to the Savages invariably. We have continued it, and we did imagine, without pretending to know, that Spain also did it.[18]

Even as he prevaricated, Jefferson wrote with indignation that this behavior, "an antient Custom" intended to be only "complimentary," could be construed as a grievance. But his account of the symbolic role of the medal was disingenuous, as he knew full well that the Indian peace medals marked not simply friendship but alliance. In fact, the medals were given to Indians in the expectation that if they had previously received French, British, or Spanish medals, they would exchange them. Accepting a medal signified allegiance. This was so much the case that when England gained control of Canada from France, British agents went about methodically attempting to replace French medals with British ones. Collected medals were often melted down and their metal refashioned. U.S. Indian agents followed that practice.[19]

During Jefferson's own presidency, the United States issued medals that bore his image and the date 1801, the year of his inauguration. Jefferson's design for the Indian peace medals closely resembled that of British medals; the United States would not simply continue British practices but would replace Great Britain in its relation to Indian nations and in its imperial aspirations on the North American continent. Moreover, during his administration Jefferson also instituted changes to the production of Indian peace medals that altered the manner of their distribution as well. Struck at the U.S. Mint, the medals bore his likeness in profile on the obverse, and on the reverse were the now familiar image of the clasped hands, the crossed tomahawk and peace pipe, and the inscription "Peace and Friendship."[20] Jefferson succeeded in standardizing the medals, so that thereafter they bore the same design on the reverse, and on the obverse the profile portrait of the president in office, a practice that continued until the end of Andrew Johnson's term. Using the U.S. Mint to strike medals lessened their cost and made striking large numbers on demand possible. The parallel between the coin and the medal could not have been made clearer, and it is a parallel that evokes Jefferson's earlier statement about the necessity of paying "eternal bribes" for peace with Indian nations. On occasion a U.S. silver dollar was improvised into a medal, though the relatively small size of coins made them less desirable as medals.[21] Mechanization resulted in a gift that was simple in design, economically reproduced, and fulfilled Jefferson's desire for a standard form with which to respond to the demands of gift exchange in a systematic fashion. For instance, Lewis and Clark were able to distribute eighty-seven Jefferson Indian peace medals during their expedition. However, giving mechanical copies of the same gift threatened to reduce the artifactual quality of a gift exchanged between two figures of power. In fact, some individual recipients resisted this very tendency, altering the medal by adding decorative feathers and thereby transforming it once again into a unique object.[22]

Indian peace medals, like miniature portraits, were worn on the body, and their use in establishing relations and negotiating peace with Indian nations played a role analogous to that of the miniature portrait in European diplomacy. Jefferson cited those precedents in the instructions to William Carmichael and William Short, who had to answer Spanish accusations of the misuse of medals. The power and effectiveness of the European Indian and diplomatic medals (with the exception of those of Holland) depended on the image of a single figure of absolute authority. Jefferson's Indian peace medal was in this way no different.

The "short statement of facts" about U.S. Indian affairs in the Southeast that Jefferson directed to Short and Carmichael also included a description of the comportment of Indian nations hostile to the United States during the Revolutionary War:

> They waged [war] in their usual cruel manner, murdering and scalping men, women and children indiscriminately, burning their houses, and desolating the country. They put us to vast expence, as well by the constant force we were obliged to keep up in that quarter, as by the expeditions of considerable magnitude which we were under the necessity of sending into their country from time to time.

Peace being at length concluded with England, we had it also to conclude with them. They had made war on us without the least provocation or pretence of injury. They had added greatly to the cost of that war; they had insulted our feelings by their savage cruelties, they were by our arms completely subdued and humbled.[23]

Jefferson continued to portray a situation in which the United States had the right to "demand substantial satisfaction," but the exercise of that right had been tempered because the government wished to encourage Indian nations to become "better neighbors." He closed his justification of the government's actions by noting that "we paid them a valuable consideration, and granted them annuities in money which have been regularly paid, and were equal to the prices for which they have usually sold their lands."

Jefferson strikingly transformed a report of the consequences of war into an account of injured feelings. Rhetorically this enabled him to dismiss any consideration of the previous alliances that might account for the involvement of Indian nations in the Revolutionary War or any discussion that might allow an account of the grievances Indian nations might have against the United States independent of those alliances. The rhetoric of injured feeling allowed him to portray Native American acts of war as incomprehensible, even irrational. With the shift to the register of feeling comes a shift to the logic of honor: for gestures of conciliation, such as the payment of "annuities in money," to be honorable, said Jefferson, the party giving money must have "subdued and humbled" its enemy. Defeat of a combatant transformed the regular payment of cash from tribute into charity. Furthermore, with the goal of producing "better neighbors" less likely to commit "savage cruelties," a strategy of buying peace and of fair and equitable treatment became muddled with the introduction of the "most useful arts," that is, with a paternalistic civilizing process.

"Eternal bribes" paid to Indian nations were one thing; paying tribute to the so-called Barbary Powers was quite another. Jefferson's outrage at paying tribute to North African nations might be said to have originated in a fundamental violation of the vocabulary and requirements of gift giving. In regard to the adaptation of older forms of the code of honor in the U.S. South, Bertram Wyatt-Brown has explained that in feudal societies warriors gave what were supposedly voluntary gifts to their lords as evidence of their loyalty and gratitude. The voluntary nature of these transactions may have been an evident fiction, yet if these "gifts" were treated too obviously as a right of the ruler, the vassal felt degraded. However expected or customary, gifts were honorable. Taxes and tribute were not; in fact, they were markers of slavery, signaling the abjection of the party compelled to give.[24]

In the cases of treaties with North Africa, without which U.S. sailors would be subject to seizure and literal enslavement, Jefferson found the figurative vassalage of the United States untenable. The language of the 1795 Treaty of Peace and Amity with Algiers makes explicit that undisturbed shipping depended on annual payment. The final clause of the treaty reads:

> The United States of North America agreed with Hassan Bashaw Dey of Algiers to keep the Articles Contained in this Treaty Sacred and inviolable which we the Dey & Divan Promise to Observe on Consideration of the United States Paying annually the Value of twelve thousand Algerine Sequins in Maritime Stores. . . . Any Vessel that may be Captured from the Date of this Treaty of Peace & Amity shall immediately be deliver'd upon her Arrival in Algiers.[25]

The inviolability of the treaty, and by extension the security of U.S. ships and their crews, was utterly conditional on the annual payment. Rather than signature and seal marking the agreement and the promise to adhere to the terms outlined, the treaty negotiated with Algiers substituted the presentation of the maritime stores as the marker of assent and authentication. Joel Barlow similarly negotiated the 1796 Treaty of Peace and Friendship with Tripoli to be sealed by a onetime transfer of goods, the substance of which is enumerated and included, in addition to naval stores, "forty thousand Spanish dollars, thirteen watches of gold, silver & pinsbach, five rings, of which three of diamonds, one of sapphire and one with a watch in it, one hundred & forty piques of cloth, and four caftans of brocade."[26] Both of these treaties were concluded and ratified while Jefferson was out of federal office, after his term as secretary of state and before he served as president.

From the onset of seizures of U.S. ships in the Mediterranean in 1785, whenever he discussed the ransom of U.S. captives or the negotiation of treaties with Morocco, Algiers, Tunis, and Tripoli, Jefferson invariably resorted to tropes of violated honor. In a 1785 letter written to John Page, a member of the Virginia House of Delegates and a longtime friend, soon after hearing news (still rumors) of the capture of U.S. sailors by Algiers, Jefferson explained that while he did not yet know what would be done about the situation in Algiers, prospects were excellent for a treaty with Morocco. That is, the emperor of Morocco was ready to receive the United States "into the number of his tributaries." He asked whether war or peace would be cheapest and then reframed his query: "But it is a question which should be addressed to our Honour as well as our Avarice? Nor does it respect us as to these pyrates only, but as to the nations of Europe. If we wish our commerce to be free and uninsulted, we must let these nations see that we have an energy which at present they disbelieve."[27]

On the subject of waging war in the Mediterranean, Jefferson wrote to John Jay:

> But how to prevent those produced by the wrongs of other nations? By putting ourselves in a condition to punish them. Weakness provokes insult and injury, while a condition to punish it often prevents it. This reasoning leads to the necessity of some naval force, that being the only weapon with which we can reach an enemy. I think it to our interest to punish the first insult: because an insult unpunished is the parent of many others. We are not at this moment in a condition to do it, but we should put ourselves into it as soon as possible.[28]

Jefferson's use of words like *insult, injury,* and *wrongs* illustrates how profoundly a code of honor structured the language that described and prescribed the behavior of nations as well as gentlemen. In this passage he speaks first of persons and then quickly switches to the pronouns *we* and *our,* which are meant to stand for the United States. The now-personified nation feels. It has interests. It is capable of being insulted. And therefore the nation must also police its honor. Like a gentleman who would aggressively seek an explanation when he feels that his honor has been intentionally violated, a nation should have a navy ready to act at "first insult." Otherwise nations could not be counted on to behave justly or, as is implied, civilly.

Treaty language conventionally designated the negotiated transfer of currency and goods as an annual "gift." When John Adams argued that paying "the necessary cost" was the most pragmatic course to follow in the Mediterranean, he wrote: "At present we are Sacrificing a Million annually to Save one Gift of two hundred Thousand Pounds. This is not good Oeconomy."[29] In his more candid writing, the gifts and presents enumerated in treaties became explicitly "tribute," and the nations that demanded its payment, no better than "banditti." Later in life Jefferson avoided using the euphemistic language of the gift altogether: "I was very unwilling that we should acquiesce in the European humiliation of paying a tribute to those lawless pirates, and endeavored to form an association of the powers subject to habitual depredations from them."[30] He rejected the attitude of the British and the Europeans, who treated aggressive maritime activity in the Mediterranean as lawful, state-sponsored privateering, and he argued that paying tribute to "pyrates" would publicly enact deference to nations for which he felt contempt. Jefferson bristled at the prospect of a never-ending obligation of the kind he considered disgraceful. He believed that the general opinion in Europe held that the United States did not possess sufficient "energy." Preoccupied with improving the international perception of the nation's character, he regarded the U.S. policy in North Africa as offering an opportunity to correct any impression that Europeans or North Africans might have of U.S. weakness.

For Jefferson, the expectation that the United States would acquiesce to the customary arrangement between Europe and North Africa was a "humiliation," regardless of whether this sort of agreement had a long history among European states. He found the unspoken obligations of gift exchange objectionable. *Contracted* gifts, straightforwardly specified, provided no useful fictions with which to paper over indignity. Treaties that required and codified compulsory one-way exchange contradicted any understanding of gifts as freely exchanged by national "friends." For instance, from the vantage of Algiers, the treaty process proceeded from the assumption that if there was no treaty, a state of war existed between nations. These treaties did not formalize a "friendship" out of an already friendly relation; they transformed enemies into friends.

Friendship also takes on hierarchical dimensions in Jefferson's writings about treaty relations with North African and Indian nations. Honor seemingly belonged to the nation that initiated negotiations for friendship and dictated its terms. The U.S. government could pay for peace with Indian nations and save the cost of interminable war presumably because the terms of that peace would be favorable to the United States. Though the continuing Indian Wars were a drain on national resources, Jefferson confidently presumed that the country would not ultimately suffer a military defeat. The position of the United States in the Mediterranean differed entirely. Before 1800, each time the United States entered into a treaty negotiation with a powerful European state, U.S. ministers and agents attempted to secure protection for U.S. ships in the Mediterranean. Lacking a navy, the United States could not defend itself. In the absence of its own peace treaties, U.S. trade diminished, since insurance rates became prohibitively expensive and merchants did not want to risk losses. One could say that Jefferson remained vigilant about possible "insults" precisely because the United States occupied a position of weakness that left its commerce, ships, and sailors perilously open to abuse. The question whether the United States should negotiate with the North African regencies or make plans to wage war in the region recurred repeatedly in the decades that followed U.S. independence. The decision did not rest with Jefferson until he became president, and it came in the form of the Tripolitan War of 1804–5.

Only after this show of force in the Mediterranean and the establishment of an aggressive naval presence in the region did Jefferson turn his attention once again to the question of diplomatic gifts. In his refusal to pay further tribute to Tripoli he had bucked long-standing conventions governing trade and commerce in the region. He had also "humiliated" Tripoli through naval defeat, showing that the United States had the means not only to defend its maritime commerce but also to retaliate effectively for any offenses against it. The balance of power had shifted in favor of the United States, and having broken with protocol, Jefferson went about fashioning an exchange of a different kind with the North African states.

For more than a decade U.S. ships were the most frequently requested type of gift by North African leaders. Innovations in U.S. shipbuilding technology had resulted in ships that were faster, more maneuverable, and better armed than those produced in the Mediterranean. Eschewing warships as well as naval stores, jewelry, or cash, the kinds of gifts that had become the norm in the Mediterranean, Jefferson countered with an altogether different kind of technology: the polygraph. In doing so, he also moved away from the register of the Indian peace medals that bore his likeness toward something more closely resembling what Silas Deane had requested about thirty years earlier. In 1776 Deane had written asking for American curiosities that he could distribute as gifts in Paris, where he labored as an agent for the not-yet-recognized new United States:

> I must mention some trifles. The queen is fond of parade, and I believe she wishes a war, and is our friend. She loves riding on horseback. Could you send me a narrowhegansett horse or two; the present might be money exceedingly well laid out. Rittenhouse's orrery, or Arnold's collection of insects, a phaeton of American make and a pair of bay horses, a few barrels of apples, of walnuts, of butternuts, etc., would be great curiosities here, where everything American is gazed at, and where the American contest engages the attention of all ages, ranks, and sexes.[31]

Deane, in his limited capacity as a U.S. agent in France, had quickly observed the importance of protocols of deference and the usefulness of presents to individuals in fomenting a greater attachment between states. His list enumerated natural curiosities, specimens of nature unique to the

North American continent. The orrery, the mechanical model of the solar system made by David Rittenhouse of Philadelphia, is the sole exception. A scientific instrument, the orrery also fascinated those who, like Queen Marie-Antoinette, had a genteel interest in astronomy. A tool used by natural philosophers, the orrery shared with the polygraph a capacity to showcase U.S. mechanical invention rather than natural bounty. Jefferson had received a polygraph, a writing machine that produced "two original copies," from Charles Willson Peale as a personal gift. He had greeted the duplicating machine with enthusiasm and a certain fascination.

On New Year's Day 1806 Jefferson wrote to Peale during the state visit of the Tunisian delegation to Washington, DC:

> We have to make up some presents for Tripoli & being desirous to compose it as much as we can of things rare, the produce of our own country, I propose to make the Polygraph an article. We want three of them, one for the Bey, one for his Secretary of State, and one for the Ambassador here, but they must be entirely mounted in silver; that is to say everything that is brass in your ordinary one must be of silver.[32]

To transform an "ordinary" polygraph into a "rare" one, and therefore into an object presentable as a diplomatic gift, Jefferson required adaptations to the materials of the polygraph's construction. Crucially, Jefferson chose the polygraph as an example of "the produce of our own country" and then set out to ensure that it would be recognized as being "rare" and valuable by rendering what was brass into silver. As a diplomatic gift the polygraph typified the ingenuity and pragmatism Jefferson wished to communicate as representative American traits to the North African recipients of his gift.

Jefferson had commissioned several polygraphs as gifts for friends such as James Madison and Constantin de Volney and as "counter-presents" for individuals upon whom he felt obliged to bestow an object of worth. But he also referred to the polygraph as "a handsome instrument of retribution," calling into question the associations of the gift, and the diplomatic gift in particular, with goodwill and with amicable and peaceful relations.[33] Jefferson had received a hogshead of Sicilian Marsala wine as a present from Edward Preble, who had commanded one of the squadrons sent to fight in the Tripolitan War but whom he did not know personally. He complained to Robert Smith, his secretary of the navy, about the gift: "It is really a painful & embarrassing thing. To reject it may be supposed to imply impure motives in the offer. To receive leads to horrid abuse." He informed Smith that he had determined on a "counter-present" and that it would be a polygraph, an invention "new, ingenious, useful and of equal cost with the hogshead of wine."[34]

In June 1805 Jefferson wrote to Peale with the commission: "Having determined never while in office to accept presents beyond a book or things of mere trifling value, I am sometimes placed in an embarrassing dilemma by persons whom a rejection would offend. In these cases I resort to counter-presents."[35] This letter, remarkable for its allusions to the language of dueling and affronts to honor, is all the more remarkable for its inclusion of instructions for the delivery of another polygraph, the gift meant for Volney, a man whom Jefferson readily called his friend. Moreover, Jefferson had already ordered the polygraphs for Madison and William Short. The contrast between what he took to be obligatory and voluntary giving corresponds to a distinction he drew between strangers ("certain characters") and friends.

Upon receipt, Preble praised the polygraph as "an additional specimen of the Mechanician and Inventive genius of our Country." Jefferson consistently hailed the polygraph as an object of "American" design, despite its European analogs. The copying machine was inordinately useful for those who wrote and required a record of their productions, but it also privileged qualities that Jefferson prized: efficiency, privacy, and standardization. An object that served both as present and counter-present, the polygraph stood as an emblem of aggression as well as conciliation. Jefferson, like many of his contemporaries, conceived of the North African states as largely operating outside the norms of civilized society: the act of giving a copying machine might as readily have been one of discipline as one of geniality. As a technology of writing, the polygraph seemed to require a certain relationship between a writer and his materials that saved an individual, or the individual's secretary, the labor of making multiple copies by hand. Given that at least one U.S. captive in Algiers served as the Christian secretary to the Algerian dey, might this gift of writing technology have been meant by Jefferson to discourage similar despotic aspects of Tunisian state culture by encouraging a degree of self-sufficiency?

The question raises the larger one of what becomes of an object once it is given: Does it reach its intended recipient? Is it welcome? Is it altered or even transformed? Does it lie untouched and unused? Had he lived, Lucerne might have resented a medal in lieu of a territorial gift that could become a refuge for himself and his family were he to feel it necessary to flee France. Indian recipients of Jefferson's peace medal repeatedly made it their own. Jefferson designed the chain of his diplomatic medal anticipating that it would be converted into cash. And let us not forget the diamonds on Louis XVI's miniature: Jefferson's directions to Short read as dissection notes, according to which the gift-object is to be dismembered, its parts cataloged and those of most value sold off. The whereabouts of the portrait itself remain unknown. The polygraph raises its own questions: Was it amenable to Arabic calligraphy? What was at stake in mechanizing writing, traditionally considered a sacred art form within Arab culture? Was the gift meant to encourage correspondence with the United States primarily, or even exclusively, in European languages? How did Sidi Soliman Melli Melli, the Tunisian ambassador who traveled to Washington and back with an extensive equipage, present the bey with such a mechanism?

Previously, American curiosities had generally been understood as natural ones, specimens of plants and animals particular to the United States. When William Temple Franklin suggested that land and furs might be appropriate U.S. diplomatic presents, he was thinking in a similar vein, imagining the most valuable of American natural resources that could be presented as gifts to an individual. In choosing a copying machine as his present to the Tunisian bey, Jefferson turned to technology, changing the definition of a typically American artifact from a natural specimen to a manufactured one, from a product of "nature" to one of American "Inventive genius," and in this way refashioning U.S. diplomatic practice and recasting what the United States had to offer as the pragmatic ingenuity of its citizens. In the process he raised the question of whether a manufactured luxury was in itself a rarity. Although it was the product of artisans, the polygraph belonged to the realm of machinery and not to that of the ornamental despite its being "entirely mounted in silver." Jefferson meant for the polygraph to be the most commodious and adaptable of presents. A useful rarity, a specimen that showcased the particular "Inventive genius" of the country, the polygraph was a present Jefferson could comfortably make to friends, personal and national, and deploy against those who were not quite his enemies.

NOTES

1. U.S. Constitution, art. 1, sec. 9, cl. 8. The full clause reads: "No Title of Nobility shall be granted by the United States: And no Person holding any Office of Profit or Trust under them, shall, without the Consent of the Congress, accept any present, Emolument, Office, or Title, of any kind whatever, from any King, Prince, or foreign State."

2. TJ to William Short, 24 Jan. 1791, *TJP,* 18:600–602. On this matter, see also Short to TJ, 30 Mar. 1791, ibid., 19:633.

3. John Jay had himself received a royal present for his diplomatic service and

was familiar with the well-established convention. See Julian Boyd, "Jefferson's Policy Concerning Presents to Foreign Diplomats," in ibid., 16:360.

4. TJ to the marquis de Lafayette, 2 Apr. 1790, ibid., 293.

5. Marcel Mauss, *The Gift: The Form and Reason for Exchange in Archaic Societies,* trans. W. D. Halls (New York, 1990); Jacques Derrida, *Given Time: 1. Counterfeit Money,* trans. Peggy Kamuf (Chicago, 1992); Natalie Zemon Davis, *The Gift in Sixteenth Century France* (Madison, WI, 2000). See also *The Question of the Gift: Essays across Disciplines,* ed. Mark Osteen (London, 2002); Bertram Wyatt-Brown, *Southern Honor: Ethics and Behavior in the Old South* (New York, 1982); Kenneth S. Greenberg, *Honor and Slavery* (Princeton, NJ, 1996); and Edmund Morgan, "The Price of Honor," in *The Genuine Article: A Historian Looks at Early America* (New York, 2004).

6. On the concept of honor and early American political culture, see Joanne B. Freeman, *Affairs of Honor: National Politics in the New Republic* (New Haven, CT, 2001).

7. Greenberg has constructively distinguished between reciprocal and one-way exchanges in *Honor and Slavery.*

8. Ibid., 65; Morgan, "Price of Honor," 128.

9. Greenberg, *Honor and Slavery,* 65–72.

10. Louis Guillaume Otto to TJ, 20 Apr. 1790, *TJP,* 16:354–56.

11. William Temple Franklin to TJ, 27 Apr. 1790, ibid., 364–66.

12. See Julian Boyd, "Notes of Presents Given to American Diplomats by Foreign Governments," in ibid., 366.

13. Ibid.

14. George Washington, 29 Apr. 1790, in *The Diaries of George Washington,* ed. Donald Jackson and Dorothy Twohig, 6 vols. (Charlottesville, VA, 1976), 6:70–71.

15. The diplomatic medal, though not struck after Genêt's term as French minister, survives in the form of the skippet attached to presentation copies of U.S. treaties throughout the nineteenth century.

16. TJ to Charles Carroll, 15 Apr. 1791, *TJP,* 20:214.

17. The inscription on the 1790 diplomatic medal, "Peace and Commerce," emphasizing trade relations and depersonalizing the relations between governments, stands in significant contrast to the inscription on the Indian peace medal, "Peace and Friendship."

18. TJ to William Carmichael and Short, 30 June 1793, *TJP,* 26:410.

19. Bauman L. Belden, *Indian Peace Medals Issued in the United States* (New Milford, CT, 1966), 8. See also Francis Paul Prucha, *Indian Peace Medals in American History* (Bluffton, SC, 1994); and Rita Laws, *Indian Peace Medals and Related Items* (Harrah, OK, 2003).

20. What appeared on the reverse of the Indian peace medal now appears on the reverse of the recent U.S. nickel, the 2004 "Jefferson Peace Medal Nickel." Belden, *Indian Peace Medals,* 24–26.

21. Laws, *Indian Peace Medals and Related Items,* 27.

22. The National Museum of the American Indian, in Washington, DC, displays an example of a modified Jefferson peace medal.

23. TJ to Carmichael and Short, 30 June 1793, *TJP,* 26:406.

24. Wyatt-Brown, *Southern Honor*, 70.

25. In 1795, twelve thousand Algerian sequins were equivalent to US $21,600. Hunter Miller, ed., *Treaties and Other International Acts of the United States of America*, vol. 2, *Documents 1–40, 1776–1818* (Washington, DC, 1931).

26. Ibid.

27. TJ to John Page, 20 Aug. 1785, *TJP*, 8:419.

28. TJ to John Jay, 23 Aug. 1785, ibid., 426–27.

29. JA to TJ, 3 July 1786, ibid., 10:86–87.

30. TJ, *Autobiography*, in *TJW*, 59.

31. Silas Deane to Jay, 3 Dec. 1776, in *The Revolutionary Diplomatic Correspondence of the United States*, ed. Francis Wharton, 6 vols. (Washington, DC, 1889), 2:214.

32. TJ to Charles Willson Peale, 1 Jan. 1806, in "Letters of Thomas Jefferson to Charles Willson Peale," *Pennsylvania Magazine of History and Biography* 28, no. 2 (1904): 305–6. The reference to Tripoli is a telling error suggesting that Jefferson considered the four Barbary Powers as to a degree interchangeable.

33. TJ to Peale, 13 Oct. and 7 Nov. 1804, in *Selected Papers of Charles Willson Peale*, ed. Lillian B. Miller, 5 vols. (New Haven, CT, 1983–2000), 2:151–52, 778–79. For a comprehensive treatment of Jefferson's interest in writing implements and copying machines, see Silvio A. Bedini, *Thomas Jefferson and His Copying Machines* (Charlottesville, VA, 1984).

34. TJ to Robert Smith, 31 May 1805, quoted in Bedini, *Thomas Jefferson and His Copying Machines*, 118.

35. TJ to Peale, 9 June 1805, in *Selected Papers of Charles Willson Peale*, 2:849. In 1806 Jefferson commissioned another polygraph, this one as a "counter-present" for James Bowdoin, who had given him the sculpture of Ariadne presently exhibited in the entrance hall of Monticello.

Better Tools for a New and Better World

Jefferson Perfects the Plow

LUCIA STANTON

In the spring of 1788 an elegant carriage bounced along the post roads of eastern France. The American minister to the court of Louis XVI, returning from a tour up the Rhine River, gazed from its window at a group of peasants working in a field. Traveling always stimulated Thomas Jefferson to engage in comparisons, and this sight of oxen, plows, and working women provoked a remarkable confluence of philosophical and mathematical reflections—on society and contrasting states of civilization, on soil preparation and Newtonian geometry. He entered his musings on the role of women into his travel journal, directly following his ideas for the best form for a critical part of a plow.

Jogging through Germany, Jefferson had confided to this journal: "The women do everything here. They dig the earth, plough, saw, cut, and split wood." And a week later, in the heart of the Lorraine, he encountered another scene that confounded his understanding of women's place in civilized society: "The women here, as in Germany do all sorts of work. . . . How valuable is that state of society which allots to them internal emploiments only, and external to the men. They are formed by nature for attentions and not for hard labour."[1] He later expanded this section of his journal to include the customs of Native Americans, among whom the men were wholly absorbed by war and hunting: "The civil part of the nation is reduced to women only. But this is a barbarous perversion of the natural destination of the two sexes."[2]

Thus, by extension, he lumped Europeans with American Indians in their uncivilized behavior and conveniently forgot the enslaved women hoeing and plowing back home at Monticello. Throughout his journey Jefferson had been measuring the effects of a greater or lesser degree of European despotism on the landscape, and here was a poverty that not only barbarously perverted the natural order on a human scale but also retarded the development of agricultural implements. The teams of oxen were pulling plows that struck Jefferson as crude and unwieldy ("barbarously heavy," as he later wrote).[3] He focused particularly on "the awkward figure of their mould board," which "leads one to consider what should be it's form."[4] (The main purpose of a moldboard is to raise the furrow slice and invert it.) That night in his inn at Nancy, as he pondered the consoling geometry that connected everything in his Newtonian universe, mathematics must have crowded even women out of his mind. He soon had an elegant solution to the problem posed by European awkwardness (Fig. 1).

This was only two months after he had written, in a playful letter to Angelica Church, that Europe had been the Creator's maiden effort, "a crude production," while his own nation had been "made on an improved plan."[5] By turning his attention to "the most useful of the instruments known to man," he could give these words a tangible effect. He would be improving a crude European object and linking the European world of Newtonian philosophy with a new world dedicated to the pursuit of happiness through the "first & most precious of all the arts," agriculture.[6] A new civilization, its emblem a perfected plow—at this time the accepted symbol of civilization's very beginnings—was rising across the Atlantic Ocean.

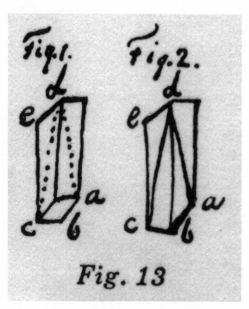

Fig. 1. Jefferson's first known sketch, in a 1788 travel journal, of his concept for a moldboard of least resistance. (Courtesy of the Massachusetts Historical Society)

In the famous debate between the Head and the Heart in Jefferson's letter of October 1786 to Maria Cosway, the Heart set out the parameters of the Head's dominion: "When the circle is to be squared, or the orbit of a comet to be traced; when the arch of greatest strength, or the solid of least resistance, is to be investigated, take up the problem; it is yours."[7] Jefferson had been investigating the wedge, also known as the inclined plane or solid of least resistance, at least since his college days, when he studied calculus in a popularization of the precepts in Newton's *Principia*, a "fountainhead" he periodically turned to in later life.[8] Jefferson's solution to the moldboard problem was based "on the principle of two wedges combined at right angles" and was thus, as Bernard Cohen has written, "a Newtonian exercise."[9]

Back in Paris, with the fate of the new American constitution still pending, Jefferson renewed his conversations with Thomas Paine and the marquis de Lafayette about the fundamental principles of society. It is clear that when Jefferson and Paine got together their discussion often veered off into the realms of science and technology. They seem to have spent many hours, both before and after Jefferson's German journey, exploring Newtonian principles and geometrical technicalities in connection with Paine's revolutionary iron bridge. Surely they also considered Jefferson's new concept for a mathematical moldboard. Yet plows vanish from Jefferson's records until his return to Virginia more than a year later.[10]

After returning to Monticello in 1789, Jefferson explained his idea to his son-in-law Thomas Mann Randolph, whose enthusiasm caused him to commission the first of dozens of moldboard models that he sent to friends and fellow philosophers for the next twenty years. But it was only in 1794, when he was retired to Monticello, that Jefferson began to conduct experiments to discover whether "it answers in practice to what it promises in theory."[11] He enlisted resident craftsmen, both enslaved and free, to turn out moldboard after moldboard for field tests while he refined his measurements and made countless modifications.[12] Since the field experiments went unrecorded, it is not known whether one particularly adept plowman was summoned to test each new version. The enslaved men appear only as "the ploughman," their skills outshone by the plow itself in Jefferson's memory twenty-five years later, when he recalled that in order to view the smooth sailing of his first plows, "I have made the ploughman let go the handle." Nor did Jefferson ever indicate in writing that he had consulted the opinions of his plowmen as his son-in-law did when developing his hillside plow. In 1825, at the first agricultural fair in Albemarle County (Jefferson seems not to have attended), the judges of the plowing match made a rare recognition of the contributions of African American laborers: "All the ploughmen performed remarkably well, but we award the premium to Mr. Geo. Gilmers man Richard, as having managed his plough and team with Superior Skill and gentleness."[13]

It was not until December 28 that Jefferson proudly announced his success, in a letter to a highly qualified judge, John Taylor, of Caroline County: "I have imagined and executed a mould-board which may be mathematically demonstrated to be perfect, as far as perfection depends on mathematical principles. And one great circumstance in it's favor is that it may be made by the most bungling carpenter, and cannot possibly vary a hair's breadth in it's form, but by gross negligence."[14] In this letter Jefferson conveys the principal aim of all moldboard designers at this time, to minimize friction, a proper goal for an Enlightenment seeker of efficiency. The greater the plow's resistance, the more animal power was required to pull it, the harder the plowman had to work, and the more difficult it was to plow a deep furrow.[15] At this time American publications were full of clarion calls for deeper plowing and denigrations of the mere stirring of the soil that was prevalent. A 1775 work on American husbandry reported on plowing styles "which rather scratch than turn the land."[16] Shallow cultivation was still decried as "that great error in American agriculture" decades later.[17]

The second major benefit mentioned by Jefferson was an artful method for exact replication. Hitherto most improvements in moldboards had died with the men who developed them because they had left no formula for reproducing them. Arthur Young wrote of an "ingenious blacksmith" in Suffolk whose renowned iron plow was impossible to duplicate after his death.[18] Jefferson had brought plow design out of the realm of empiricism and into the Newtonian world of mathematical principles. He was one of the first to approach a humble instrument of tillage as an Enlightenment philosopher, seeking a solution in the world of Newtonian mathematics and aiming for theoretical perfection by its laws.[19] Thus it is not surprising that when he finally unveiled his discovery, in an almost intentional act of American advertisement, it was not to a gathering of practical farmers but to a society of learned gentlemen. What is more arresting is that his chosen audience was British, not American.

He made that choice in 1798, almost four years after reporting to Taylor that his moldboard had received the "entire approbation" of men who saw it in action at Monticello.[20] Why, then, did he wait so long to broadcast it to the world? Much of that time he was retired at Monticello with leisure for such an enterprise, yet he mentioned his moldboard only once in his correspondence, in 1796, as "a little matter" he might "ere long" communicate to his fellows in the American Philosophical Society. This letter provides a clue to the long delay. While Jefferson had faith in the moldboard's mathematical principles and had admired its performance in his fields, he wished to demonstrate that his theory was "fully confirmed" by mechanical calculation: "I only wish for one of those instruments used in England for measuring the force exerted in the draught of different ploughs &c., that I might compare the resistance of my mould board with that of others."[21] He probably read about this device, which had been used to test the resistance of plows in England since the mid-1780s, in Arthur Young's *Annals of Agriculture*.[22] When William Strickland, a member of the British Board of Agriculture, visited Monticello in May 1795, Jefferson had asked him to enquire into the cost and availability of such a "machine for ascertaining the resistance of Plows." Yet, although Jefferson received purchasing details from Strickland in the fall of 1796, he apparently made no attempt to acquire the device at that time.[23]

In the spring of 1797 Jefferson, the newly elected president of the American Philosophical Society, chose to assume the mantle of the late David Rittenhouse accompanied by the bones of an extinct sloth rather than a nine-inch model of a plow part. So it was not until the following spring, and without benefit of mathematical measurement, that he finally unveiled his creation, first to the world's most eminent agricultural institution and only second to the most eminent American scientific institution. On March 23, 1798, Jefferson drew up a minutely detailed description of the moldboard and the method of making it and sent it off to London, along with a set of interlocking models, addressed to Sir John Sinclair, president of the British Board of Agriculture.

Did recent political events have anything to do with Jefferson's decision to draft a letter of ten closely-written pages about agricultural implements? He did this just a few days after John Adams's "insane message" to Congress announcing the failure of the American mission to France, a preliminary to the full revelation of the XYZ debacle.[24] A moldboard was now more than just "a little matter." It could be the physical expression of Jefferson's commitment to the long-standing practice among the "votaries of science" of ignoring national boundaries, of acting as "one family."[25] With the scales of war and peace in a perilous "equilibrio," Jefferson the philosopher chose to reach out to a foreign country that as a politician he hoped the French would invade and "republicanize."[26]

Still unaware of the extent to which "philosophy" would be under siege in the next months, Jefferson decided to set a conspicuous example of the "coolness of philosophers," a virtue that a decade earlier he had attributed to Americans confronted by political emergencies, "while every other nation on earth must have recourse to arms."[27] His letter to Sinclair concluded with one of his longest and most impassioned condemnations of the horrors of war and its inhibiting effects on internal improvements and the spread of the "comforts of society." He then singled out Sinclair and his creation, the British Board of Agriculture, as "an evidence that we are advancing towards a better state of things." Sinclair's labors tended "eminently to ameliorate the condition of man." Since Jefferson's letter had opened with reference to his own "zeal for improving the condition of human life by an interchange of it's comforts & of the information which may increase them," he thus bound himself and Sinclair together as part of a fraternity of enlightened philosophers bent on benefiting mankind.[28]

Jefferson's own account of the destination of his letter characteristically raises more questions than it answers. As he told the Philadelphia mathematician Robert Patterson, he had first contemplated publicizing his moldboard through the American Philosophical Society but "doubted whether it was worth their notice, and supposed it not exactly in the line of their ordinary publications." Philosophical Society members were notably indifferent to agriculture, but that was hardly a strong reason to bypass the country's leading scientific institution, and one whose president Jefferson had been for more than a year. Next he had contemplated sharing the news with some American agricultural societies, when, as he said, he received a request from the British Board of Agriculture for a description and model of his invention.[29] No such request, however, has been found in Jefferson's correspondence with Sinclair, whose periodic letters in 1796 asked for "important" communications on agriculture, without being specific, and hinted that membership would follow on their receipt. In March 1797 Jefferson finally wrote that he would soon be sending "some farming implements of our invention."[30] That fall he received from London a letter, a resolution, and a diploma, all welcoming him as a "Foreign Honorary Member" of the board and reminding him of an obligation, namely, his "promise" to send a "Specimen of the Agricultural Implements of America on an improved construction."[31]

Jefferson's friendly feelings for two of the board members also probably influenced his decision. As Sir John Sinclair recalled in later life, Jefferson told him that on his visit to England in 1786 "there was no other individual in London who had paid him any particular attention, which rendered my civilities to him peculiarly gratifying."[32] And Strickland seems to have completely won his host's heart on his visit to Monticello in 1795. He was a kindred spirit, a guest whose bread-and-butter letter included the statement, "Where the improvement of the agriculture of a country can go hand in hand, with the improvement of the morals of a people, and the increase of their happiness, there it must stand in its most exalted state." Jefferson and Strickland were also of one mind in believing that agriculture was a legitimate object of study for a philosopher. Regarding the current lack of understanding of soil chemistry, Strickland wrote, "Philosophy has not yet sufficiently accompanied agriculture to have ascertained how the earth regains the properties of which it has been deprived."[33] Jefferson's entire moldboard enterprise was similarly founded on the combination of European enlightenment ideas and American agrarian ideals.

Virginia plowmen were, after all, slaves, hardly the "chosen people of God" of Jefferson's famous paean to "those who labour in the earth."[34] Better, then, to put some distance between himself and the soil that was cultivated by a harsh labor system, to plow heaven rather than earth. Thus, even when dealing with a practical implement of husbandry, Jefferson functioned in an idealized world, where Virgil's *agricola* met his American equivalent, the industrious, virtuous, and independent farmer. Spreading the news of his moldboard was carried out on a similar plane.

Jefferson adopted gentlemanly methods of dispersing information about the moldboard that were entirely appropriate for an Enlightenment philosopher. He was not about to try to manufacture and market his invention, a route taken by others that rapidly led to improved plowing after the War of 1812. Had he had his moldboard cast in iron, as he once intended, it might have been more speedily dispersed. He did not do this until 1814, taking to heart the advice of Richard Peters, his main mentor in farming matters, that cast iron was too fragile.[35] Even to patent the moldboard was out of the question. In 1815 he wrote to Charles Willson Peale, "You will be at perfect liberty to use the form of the mould-board, as all the world is, having never thought of monopolising by patent any useful idea which happens to offer itself to me."[36] Thomas Paine also eschewed the patent process for his bridge (except in England, where a patent was essential to getting a sample built), and his letters suggest that when he and Jefferson discussed their respective technology projects in Paris in 1788, they agreed that they should spread the benefits of their ideas as widely and "freely" as possible.[37]

Jefferson did not entirely neglect the American audience. A month after sending his letter to Sinclair, he presided at a meeting of the American Philosophical Society in which his description of the moldboard was read to the assembled members. Two weeks later the society resolved to publish the description in its annual *Transactions*, which became one of the major means of circulating information about Jefferson's improvement in the United States. Another was James Mease's American edition of the *Domestic Encyclopaedia* (Fig. 2).[38] Through these two publications and some of the models Jefferson distributed, the moldboard reached professional men such as Dr. Samuel Brown, Judge Harry Innes, and even his nemesis, Timothy Pickering, who encountered a model in John Beale Bordley's parlor and was instantly sure he had a better and simpler solution.[39] But did full-time farmers ever hear about Jefferson's moldboard? Even among his own acquaintances Jefferson seems to have been slow to impose his idea on practical farmers. In 1805 he sent a set of models and the relevant volume of the *Domestic Encyclopaedia* to his farming friend John Strode, of Culpeper County, "venturing to submit it to your judgment." This communication was made ten years after perfection of the moldboard, years in which Jefferson spent the night at Strode's house on all his journeys between Monticello and the seat of government.[40]

There were political as well as philosophical aims implicit in Jefferson's choice of England, and later France, to receive an official account of his moldboard.[41] By this means American ingenuity, tied to the agrarian ideal, would have an international audience. A perfected moldboard could be a token of the benefits of republican government, in which the dreams and aspirations of its citizens were unfettered by the inequities of autocratic regimes. A note of nationalism was part of Jefferson's subsequent plow ventures as well as those of other Americans interested in agricultural reform.

Jefferson sent more than twenty wooden models of his invention to farming friends, learned gentlemen, and European and American institutions. Of all those miniature moldboards only two are known to survive, both in Paris.[42] Jefferson must have been delighted to receive his greatest acclaim from Paris, then the acknowledged center of scientific advancement. A leading physicist, the Abbé Haüy, declared that Jefferson's moldboard was "mathematically exact, and incapable of further improvement." And in April 1805 the gentlemen of the Société d'Agriculture du Département de la Seine awarded President Jefferson a prize with the following citation: "One cannot see without interest the first Magistrate of such a great Republic linking his name and his glory to the improvement of an instrument of tillage. This is a characteristic remarkable in the history of our century and in that of the New World."[43]

This tribute was followed in November 1806 by the arrival of a gold medal that was carefully preserved in the family and may have been displayed in the President's House along with a model of the moldboard itself, which Jefferson was keen to show to visitors.[44] What is not well known is

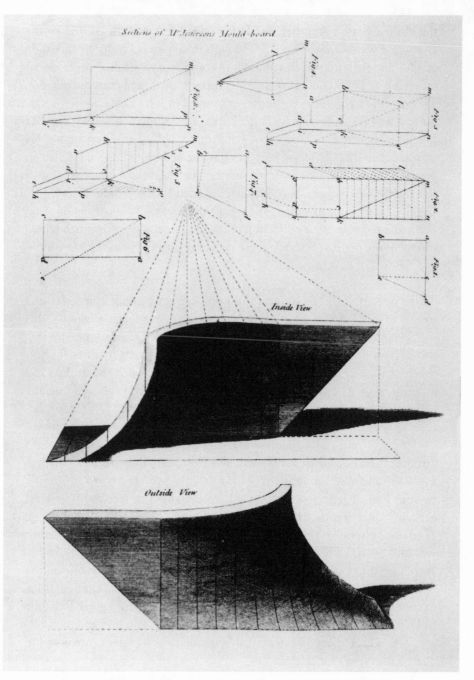

Fig. 2. Plate accompanying description of Jefferson's moldboard in
A. F. M. Willich's *The Domestic Encyclopaedia* (1803).

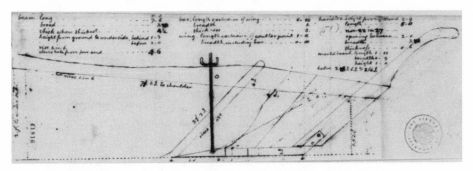

Fig. 3. Jefferson's drawing of a barshare plow with his moldboard, the basis for Monticello's full-scale reproduction. (Library of Congress)

that Jefferson's gold medal was a second-place prize. The Paris agricultural society had awarded first place to Charles Guillaume for a wheel plow that required only "half the force to draw it necessary for what had till then been deemed the best plough in France." The judges were eager to compare the two improvements and asked Jefferson to ship a full-scale plow with his moldboard to France for a head-to-head contest in the field.[45]

Jefferson was galvanized by the prospects of this competition—"It was my wish while [responding to their request], to make a plough which might compete with theirs, and I am confident, excel it"—and was relieved on the arrival of the French plow in 1808 to see that its only advantage was that it was "lightly made," unlike the massive plows usual in Europe. "I shall now not be afraid of sending to the society one of our best ploughs, according to their request, with my mouldboard to it."[46] He reluctantly postponed this project until he had retired to Monticello. Late in 1809 the enslaved woodworker John Hemmings began construction of what Jefferson dubbed "the finest plough which has ever been constructed in America" (Figs. 3 and 4).[47] Before he shipped it off, however, he was eager to put the French and American plows to a mathematical test. In order to use the same standard of measurement as the Parisian judges, he imported the recently invented *dynamomètre* of Edme Regnier. He was soon mourning the loss of this instrument—"the only one in America"—which was stolen by an enslaved James River boatman named Ned. Jefferson considered Ned's theft a hanging offense.[48]

Eventually Jefferson was able to borrow a dynamometer from Robert Fulton, and the "experiment" duly took place, probably sometime in 1810.[49] But of this international plowing contest or its results not a word has been found in Jefferson's papers. Nor, apparently, did he ever send the "finest plough" in America to France. This silence inevitably suggests that Jefferson's plow went down to defeat.

Plowing matches did not become a regular feature of the American rural scene until the 1820s, when county agricultural societies and their attendant agricultural fairs began to flourish. In the meantime several Americans eagerly engaged in transatlantic competition. The Philadelphian James Mease, one of the most enthusiastic advocates of Jefferson's moldboard, reported that a friend, after a summer visit to England in 1803, "reprobates the various ploughs which he saw working.—He describes them as heavy unwieldy implements, which are drawn by several horses or oxen, making irregular furroughs; and declares that a common American plough is far preferable." In his American edition of the *Domestic Encyclopaedia* Mease featured Jefferson's improvement and included an illustration of the Beverstone plow, considered by the English "the ultimatum of perfection in ploughs," "on purpose that the Citizens of this Country might contrast it with the simple and powerful Jefferson plough."[50]

In 1816 Richard Peters wrote of his own efforts to best the British: "I long ago told some of my english Correspondents, that our Ploughs were more simple & better than theirs. But they laughed at my Nationality. One of them was, however, daring enough to venture at a comparative Experiment."

Fig. 4. Full-scale reproduction of Jefferson's plow and moldboard by Robert Self; irons made by Peter Ross and the Colonial Williamsburg Blacksmith Shop. (Photo courtesy of Robert Self)

Peters sent three American plows (no mention of the Jeffersonian mold-board here) to Robert Barclay, in Middlesex, where they were pitted against the best local plows. A leading English agricultural journal published an eyewitness account of these "Trials" that raised Peters's competitive spirit another notch:

> They eulogize the American Plough, for its Simplicity & Neatness of Work; & allow it to be equal to the best english Plough. But they say it will not do in stony & heavy Soils, as well as the english Plough. I am sure they are mistaken; & will have it put to the Test.... It is a great Point, that they allow an Equality in Work with their *crack* plough; & they agree that it is superior in Simplicity, & Facility of Management. If *they* talk of a drawn Battle, it looks like a Defeat.[51]

There was an international plow competition on paper as well as on the ground. Enter one William Amos, a minor English agricultural writer who, in his "Essays on Agricultural Machines" (1810), reviewed the development in Britain of what was called variously the Rotherham, the Dutch, or the "patent" plow:

> At length the Americans having obtained a knowledge of those principles either from Britain or Holland, claimed the priority of the invention; in consequence of which, Mr. Jefferson, President of the United States, presented the principles for the construction of a mould-board, first to the Institute of France, and next to the Board of Agriculture in England, as a wonderful discovery in mathematics.[52]

Jefferson may never have seen this account, but one of his first biographers did. Henry S. Randall rose up to defend his hero from these aspersions. Randall, an active farmer and agricultural author himself, took aim at the "misstatements, suppressions and inconsistencies of this singularly bungling yet self-complacent writer" in an article on Jefferson's plow in the New York Agricultural Society's *Transactions* for 1862. He declared the absurdity of Amos's statement, saying that Jefferson "believed himself the first discoverer of that particular mathematical formula (or of its application to such an object,) on which his mold-board was constructed. If there is any documentary or other contemporaneous evidence to the contrary, let it be produced." In tracing British plow development, wrote Randall, "Mr. Amos leaps with one bound from the Rotherham plow to himself!" Thus Amos completely ignored the most successful and popular plow in the land, one developed by the Scotsman James Small, which had a moldboard that most observers found strikingly similar to Jefferson's. Randall called on various authorities, including Sir John Sinclair, to show that Small had perfected his plow gradually, through repeated experiments, without a guiding mathematical principle. He therefore resoundingly concluded that Jefferson "still retains intact the sole credit of the 'discovery in mathematics'" that Amos had so disparaged.[53] It must be noted that Small provided the world with a complete description of his plow and moldboard in a 1784 publication.[54] While Jefferson may not have seen a copy, he certainly had read the words of his favorite Lord Kames, who "boldly" recommended Small's plow over all others in his *Gentleman Farmer* (1776).[55]

Five years after Randall's defense, an anonymous author wrote a history of American plows,[56] drawing on Randall for much of what he said about Jefferson's moldboard and seconding Randall's view of Jefferson's priority: "There can be no doubt whatever that Mr. Jefferson is solely entitled to the honor of inventing the first mould-board made on mathematical principles." Moreover, "the discovery of Mr. Jefferson, by which mould-boards could be made by any one with the absolute certainty of having them all exactly alike, was an era in agriculture, and the root of all real progress in the manufacture of this all-important implement."[57]

One set of ingenious Americans took note of Jefferson's improvement and were inspired by the attention of such an eminent statesman to the affairs of the field. These were the mechanics and plow developers of rural America, men who needed the patent process, who were not afraid to experiment with iron, who licensed their creations to manufacturers and merchants or marketed them themselves. With the rise of annual "exhibitions," or fairs, in the 1820s, they pitted their designs against one another's in plowing matches and used the columns of agricultural periodicals to advertise their prizewinning designs. A grateful experimenter, William Hendrick of New York, used Jefferson's specifications to make a moldboard to compare to his own and wrote to the president: "It is with the Greatest Pleasure I have heard of the Cheif Magistrate of a Great Nation lending his assistance in the forming the Instruments of Husbandry, & raises in Mind an Idea of your true Greatness, that your [*sic*] are far above the silly vulgar prejudice of thinking it beneath your dignity to be aiding in producing food for mankind."[58]

From a hotbed of plow developers in Cayuga County, New York, Jethro Wood in 1816 sent his first patent plow to Jefferson "as a respectfull tribute to thy Ingenuity in improving that important Instrument." The moldboard of Wood's plow, the most successful in the nation until the arrival of Joel

Nourse's Eagle plows, was usually described as based largely on Jefferson's principle.[59] Wood also wished to give a plow to the largest grain-producing country in the world. Jefferson's friend Samuel Latham Mitchill, always eager to display American genius, assisted Wood in sending this plow, "superior to any instrument of the kind that has ever been invented," as a "Georgical offering" to the czar of Russia.[60]

The virtues of Wood's plow and its imitators and successors were almost universally described as simplicity and strength.[61] These quintessentially American virtues were often noted as characteristics of the technological improvements that grew from a trickle to a flood after the War of 1812.[62] James Mease omitted a novel English harrow design from his *Domestic Encyclopaedia* as too complicated for Americans, who he said needed "simple, strong, and cheap utensils."[63] For Richard Peters and other American observers, scarcity of labor drove the American quest for labor-saving machinery, and dispersed settlement honed mechanical skills. As Jefferson wrote in 1787, "Remote from all other aid, we are obliged to invent and to execute; to find means within ourselves, and not to lean on others."[64] Peters, who used the words *simple* and *simplicity* a total of three times in one paragraph in the letter quoted earlier, wrote in an article on American plows that "in England, the complexity of their ploughs is much out of date; and they find the advantage of simplicity of construction." Like the "barbarously heavy" plows Jefferson had seen in France, even the plows of England were inefficiently ponderous, requiring long strings of draft animals and "unnecessary drivers, or the incumbrances of wheels, &c."[65]

What a contrast there was between these European implements and "the simple and powerful Jefferson plough" praised by Mease and Thomas Paine's iron bridge, which was described by the committee that examined it for the Académie des Sciences in Paris as "the simplest, strongest, and lightest."[66] James Fenimore Cooper later read the American character in plows: "I have seen more graceful, and convenient ploughs in positive use here than are probably to be found in the whole of Europe united. In this single fact may be traced the history of the character of the people and the germ of their future greatness."[67]

Jefferson and Paine gave American simplicity a good name. This was not rude simplicity but one based on mathematical perfection, both efficient and beautiful. Jefferson and others responded to the "elegance and beauty" of Paine's geometrical bridge, and Lord Sheffield, of the Board of Agriculture, praised the "beautiful simplicity" of Jefferson's method of replicating his moldboard.[68] While he was living in the midst of "European luxury and dissipation," Jefferson intensified his celebration of the "honest simplicity" of his own nation. Once back in America, he was the vocal advocate of a "simple & economical mode of government" as well as simple and economical agricultural tools. A youthful New York editor in 1791 saw virtues in Jefferson that paralleled what others observed in his moldboard: "republican firmness and democratic simplicity."[69] By 1820 the connection had become almost a formula of Jeffersonian values. In the words of a Virginia farmer, "Machines, like governments, are generally useful in proportion to their simplicity."[70]

In his eagerness to reach an international audience for his moldboard, Jefferson let his dove of peace wing its way almost out of the consciousness of his own countrymen. It is particularly interesting that the New York author of the 1868 plow history chose to describe Jefferson's improvement—in almost fifteen pages—in the section on European plows, because, as he said, Jefferson's method "was first published in Europe." He went on to declare that "the existence of his method was hardly known in this country until within quite a recent period, although it was well known and much talked of in Europe."[71] While this statement was in error (the first actual publication was in Philadelphia), it reflected a perception that must have been almost universal, making the moldboard almost a European creation. To cap all, it was to a European source—the *Edinburgh Encyclopaedia*—that the author turned when reproducing Jefferson's letter to Sinclair in full, complete with diagrams.[72]

This version of Jefferson's letter is strangely different in its details from his original. The author prefaced his quotation by stating that he had replaced the "antiquated names" Jefferson used with nouns more suitable for his readers. Some of the nouns are very quaint indeed, particularly *plough-ear* in place of *moldboard*. This word, along with an accompanying illustration cited as from the Muséum d'Histoire Naturelle, betrayed the author's source and revealed the original description's long and circuitous journey. *Plough-ear* is a literal translation of *oreille de charrue*, the French term for *moldboard*. The Scottish encyclopedia's source was almost certainly a French translation of Jefferson's original that his old friend André Thouin, head of the natural history museum in Paris, made and published in its *Annales* in 1802 and as a separate pamphlet a few years later.[73] Thus, Jefferson's 1798 account passed through the hands of two translators and an editor, made two transatlantic voyages and a Channel crossing, and appeared seventy years later in the first history of American plows, garbled but well traveled.

This same author, while lauding Jefferson for applying rule to the construction of a plow, admitted that the actual moldboard design exhibited "very great defects," principally an overhang insufficient to fully invert the furrow slice: "We cannot find, and we have never seen or heard of, a single plow having been made on the principle laid down by Mr. Jefferson in his day, except those made by himself.[74] While the Jeffersonian moldboard definitely had its greatest success at Monticello, it was reproduced by a number of Americans both philosophical and practical in bent, including, after Jefferson's death, the most successful plow designer of the mid-nineteenth century, Joel Nourse.[75] Still, an account of plows and farming in Albemarle County from 1800 to 1830 by John H. Craven, a tenant of Jefferson's at Tufton for nine years, makes no mention at all of Jefferson's improvement.[76] The most amusing negative judgment comes, unsurprisingly, from John Randolph, who summoned up the maker of moldboards in his objection to the abolition of county courts at the Virginia constitutional convention of 1829–30:

> We are not to be struck down by the authority of Mr. Jefferson. Sir, if there be any point in which the authority of Mr. Jefferson might be considered as valid, it is in the mechanism of a plough. He once mathematically and geometrically demonstrated the form of a mould-board which should present the least resistance. His mould-board was sent to Paris, to the *Savants*—it was exhibited to all the visitors at the Garden of Plants. The *Savants* all declared *una voce* that this was the best mould-board that had ever been devised. They did not decree to Mr. Jefferson the honours of Hermes Trismegistus, but they cast his mould-board in plaster; and there it remains, an eternal proof that this form of mould-board presents less resistance than any other on the face of the earth. Some time after, an adversary brought into Virginia the Carey plough; but it was such an awkward, ill-looking thing, that it would not sell. At length, some one tried it, and though its mould-board was not that of least resistance, it beat Mr. Jefferson's plough as much as common sense will always beat theory and reveries. Now there is not in Virginia, I believe, one plough with the *mould-board of least resistance*. I have had some experience in its use, and find it the handsomest plough to draw I ever saw. So much for authority![77]

Jefferson's reveries did show that mathematical principles could be successfully applied to an agricultural tool and that agriculture, which, according to Lord Kames, had "the signal pre-eminence of combining philosophy with useful practice," was a legitimate aspect of natural philosophy.[78] By demonstrating that making effective moldboards no longer had to be accidental, Jefferson brought to the disorganized landscape of tillage the American goals of economy and simplicity as well as the Enlightenment ideals of efficiency and order. In his moldboard enterprise he tried out his own method of mixing European knowledge and American genius. He must have particularly appreciated the comment of the Parisian intellectuals who bestowed a gold medal on his idea: "America received the plow from Europe; how beautiful it would be if America sent back to Europe its gift perfected."[79]

NOTES

1. TJ, "Notes of a Tour through Holland and the Rhine Valley," 11 and 19 Apr. 1788, *TJP,* 13:18, 27.

2. Ibid., 36. Jefferson expanded this section when making a fair copy of his travel journal from his rough notes after his return to Paris.

3. TJ to John Taylor, 20 Aug. 1808, in *Thomas Jefferson's Garden Book,* ed. Edwin M. Betts (Philadelphia, 1944), 376.

4. TJ, "Notes of a Tour," *TJP,* 13:27.

5. TJ to Angelica Church, 17 Feb. 1788, ibid., 12:601.

6. TJ to Sir John Sinclair, 23 Mar. 1798, ibid., 30:205; TJ to Robert R. Livingston, 30 Apr. 1800, ibid., 31:549.

7. TJ to Maria Cosway, 12 Oct. 1786, ibid., 10:450.

8. TJ to Robert Patterson, 30 Mar. 1798, ibid., 30:234; TJ to David Rittenhouse, 20 June 1790, ibid., 16:542. Jefferson's college text was William Emerson's *Doctrine of Fluxions* (London, 1757).

9. TJ to Taylor, 29 Dec. 1794, *TJP,* 28:234; I. Bernard Cohen, *Science and the Founding Fathers* (New York, 1995), 101–2, 293–95, quotation from 102. Music may also have played a part in the concept, as Jefferson explained (in the letter to Taylor) the principle of his moldboard by comparing it to a sticcado, a musical instrument Benjamin Franklin had carried home in his luggage when he left France in 1785.

10. See Thomas Paine to TJ, undated and May 1788, *TJP,* 13:4–8, 222–28, and correspondence later in 1788 and 1789. Some geometrical doodles Jefferson made on the back of a scrap of paper used for recording travel expenses by his manservant, Espagnol, have been illustrated as preliminary sketches for the moldboard (ibid., xxv–xxvii). Mathematicians and geometers I have consulted can find no link between these sketches and Jefferson's moldboard design. I am especially grateful to John R. Faulkner and Rachel Fletcher for their wisdom on issues of mathematics and geometry.

11. TJ to Sinclair, 23 Mar. 1798, ibid., 30:201.

12. No particular workmen are mentioned in this context, but probably the makers were the free woodworker David Watson and the enslaved men John Hemmings and David Hern. Lucia Stanton, "'A Little Matter': Jefferson's Moldboard of Least

Resistance," *Chronicle of the Early American Industries Association* 58, no. 1 (2005): 3–11, 36, provides a full account of the evolution and distribution of Jefferson's moldboard. Hemmings, who was literate, spelled his name with two *m*'s.

13. TJ to Charles Willson Peale, 22 Apr. 1820, in *Thomas Jefferson's Farm Book*, ed. Edwin M. Betts (Princeton, NJ, 1953), 64; Rodney H. True, ed., *Minute Book of the Albemarle (Virginia) Agricultural Society* (Washington, DC, 1920), 314. Thomas Mann Randolph wrote that "the neighbours, my overseer and the black people all say that for a Hill-side plough it must answer" (Randolph to TJ, 14 Oct. 1808, Edgehill-Randolph Papers, University of Virginia Library, Charlottesville).

14. TJ to Taylor, 28 Dec. 1794, *TJP,* 28:233–34.

15. I am considerably indebted to Peter D. McClelland, *Sowing Modernity: America's First Agricultural Revolution* (Ithaca, NY, 1997), a masterful account of agricultural technology in the early nineteenth century; on plow function and form, see pp. 18–29, essential to understanding the context for Jefferson's design goals.

16. *American Husbandry* (London, 1775), 1:81, quoted in Leo Rogin, *The Introduction of Farm Machinery in its Relation to the Productivity of Labor in the Agriculture of the United States during the Nineteenth Century* (Berkeley, CA, 1931), 11.

17. Thomas Moore, "Deep Ploughing," *Agricultural Museum* 2, no. 8 (1812): 221. Among the countless other critiques of shallow planting in agricultural publications was James Madison's address to the Agricultural Society of Albemarle on 12 May 1819, in *American Farmer,* 27 Aug. 1819, 170.

18. Quoted in *Report on the Trial of Plows, Held at Utica, by the N. Y. State Agricultural Society* (Albany, 1868), 22.

19. Mathematicians today do not agree with Jefferson on the mathematical perfection of his design. "It is not 'mathematically perfect' in the sense of being the surface of least resistance, even by Jefferson's own standards. Jefferson based his analysis on the principle that the optimal method to raise a load is to use a wedge. . . . He then constructed a surface which is 'doubly ruled,' so there are two families of straight lines embedded in the surface. If the wedge principle were correct and if the soil moved along the straight lines, the surface would be indeed 'perfect.' . . . However, if one considers the path that soil would move along his surface, one can see that it does not follow the straight lines embedded in the surface, but rather follows a curved path. Thus, the surface is not perfect even using his own principle." John R. Faulkner, University of Virginia, e-mail message to author, 6 Sept. 2005.

20. TJ to Taylor, 4 June 1798, *TJP,* 30:388.

21. TJ to Jonathan Williams, 3 July 1796, ibid., 29:140. This letter contains Jefferson's first known use of the title his invention would bear, "Mouldboard *of least resistance.*"

22. In 1784 the London Society of Arts conducted experiments to determine the force needed to draw various plows. "Experiments to Ascertain the Force Necessary to Draw Various Ploughs," *Annals of Agriculture and Other Useful Arts* 1 (1790): 113–19. Twenty different plows were tested with "a machine for measuring the force exerted by horses in drawing" invented by Samuel More: "It is a spring, coiled within a cylindrical case, having a dial-plate marked with numbers like that of a clock, and so

contrived that a hand moves with the motion of the spring, and points to the numbers in proportion as the force is exerted."

23. William Strickland to TJ, 20 and 28 May 1796, *TJP,* 29:105, 115–16; TJ received the latter letter on 14 October and the former not until 1797. The measuring device was made and sold for five guineas by the "Engine maker" William Winlaw, of Cavendish Square, London, and acted "by means of a spring fixed on the swinging-tree," which "shews by means of an index the number of lbs: weight (and consequently proportion of strength) required to draw the plough, or any other body, to which it may be applied."

24. TJ to James Madison, 21 Mar. 1798, ibid., 30:189.

25. TJ to Casper Wistar, 16 Dec. 1800, ibid., 32:311.

26. TJ to Edmund Pendleton, 2 Apr. 1798, ibid., 30:241; TJ to Thomas Mann Randolph, 11 Jan. 1798, ibid., 25.

27. TJ to C. W. F. Dumas, 10 Sept. 1787, ibid., 12:113. For comments on the "hue and cry against the sacred name of philosophy," see TJ to Thomas Mann Randolph, 3 May 1798, ibid., 30:326; and TJ to Elbridge Gerry, 26 Jan. 1799, ibid., 646.

28. TJ to Sinclair, 23 Mar. 1798, ibid., 30:206, 198. Jefferson's fullest statement of his belief that men of science knew no boundaries is in a letter of 1809 in which he cites his 1798 exchange with Sinclair and refers to "societies instituted for the benevolent purpose of communicating to all parts of the world whatever useful is discovered by any one of them. These societies are always in peace, however their nations may be at war." TJ to John Hollins, 19 Feb. 1809, in Betts, *Garden Book,* 408.

29. TJ to Patterson, 27 Mar. 1798, *TJP,* 30:224.

30. Sinclair to TJ, 28 May and 10 Sept. 1796, ibid., 29:114, 183; TJ to Sinclair, 12 Mar. 1797, ibid., 318.

31. Sinclair to TJ, 21 June 1797, ibid., 449–50; Rufus King to TJ, 22 Aug. 1797, ibid., 514.

32. *The Correspondence of the Right Honourable Sir John Sinclair,* 2 vols. (London, 1831), 2:39–40.

33. Strickland to TJ, 20 May 1796, *TJP,* 29:103–4.

34. *Notes,* 164–65.

35. TJ to James Mease, 19 Aug. 1803, Jefferson Papers, LC.

36. TJ to Peale, 13 June 1815, in Betts, *Garden Book,* 545–46.

37. Thomas Paine, "The Construction of Iron Bridges," 13 June 1803, in *Collected Writings,* ed. Eric Foner (New York, 1995), 422; Paine to TJ, 6 Sept. 1788, *TJP,* 13:588; Edward G. Gray, "Tom Paine's Bridge: Or, Building a Better World with Iron," *Common-Place* 5 (July 2005), http://www.common-place.org/vol-05/no-04/. The famous iron bridge at Coalbrookdale, of which Jefferson had a print, was made without plans that would allow the construction of similar structures. Paine's bridge, like Jefferson's moldboard, was the result of a tested principle, suitable for limitless and easy replication. Gray's article stimulated me to think about the bridge and moldboard in unison.

38. *Proceedings of the American Philosophical Society* 22, no. 119 (1885): 270–71; *Transactions of the American Philosophical Society* 4 (1799): 313–22; A. F. M. Willich, *The Domestic Encyclopaedia; or, A Dictionary of Facts, and Useful Knowledge,* 5 vols.

(Philadelphia, 1803–4). There were further full reprintings of Jefferson's moldboard description (e.g., in *American Farmer*, 8 Sept. 1820, 186–87), as well as more abbreviated accounts.

39. See Stanton, "A Little Matter," 5–6.

40. TJ to John Strode, 11 Mar. 1805, in Betts, *Farm Book*, facsimile p. 54; *Jefferson's Memorandum Books: Accounts, with Legal Records and Miscellany, 1767–1826*, ed. James A. Bear Jr. and Lucia C. Stanton (Princeton, NJ, 1997), 834–1232 passim.

41. Jefferson's 1798 account of the moldboard was published in Paris in 1802. See below.

42. Stanton, "A Little Matter," 5.

43. Société d'Agriculture du Département de la Seine, *Mémoires d'Agriculture, d'Economie rurale et domestique* 7 (28 Apr. 1805), author's translation from the original French.

44. Stanton, "A Little Matter," 6.

45. TJ to Taylor, 23 June 1808, in Betts, *Garden Book*, 372; Société d'Agriculture du Département de la Seine, *Mémoires d'Agriculture*. Jefferson first learned of the society's request in December 1807, when he received letters from A. F. Silvestre and David Baillie Warden. Silvestre to TJ, 19 Sept. 1807, Jefferson Papers, LC; Warden to TJ, 21 Oct. 1807, in Betts, *Farm Book*, 57.

46. TJ to Joel Barlow, 31 Dec. 1809, in *The Papers of Thomas Jefferson: Retirement Series*, ed. J. Jefferson Looney et al., 5 vols. to date (Princeton, NJ, 2004–), 2:111; TJ to Taylor, 20 Aug. 1808.

47. TJ to Robert Fulton, 16 Apr. 1810, in *Papers of Thomas Jefferson: Retirement Series*, 2:333. Although there are no references to Hemmings as the maker of this plow, it is virtually certain that he was. Hired free workmen had left Monticello by this time, and Hemmings was the usual maker of plow frames. TJ to Joel Yancey, 17 Jan. 1819, Jefferson Papers, Massachusetts Historical Society, Boston.

48. TJ to George Jefferson, 18 May 1809, *Papers of Thomas Jefferson: Retirement Series*, 1:204; TJ to John Barnes, 3 Aug. 1809, ibid., 408; Stanton, "A Little Matter," 3, 6–7.

49. TJ to Fulton, 16 Apr. 1810, *Papers of Thomas Jefferson: Retirement Series*, 2:333; TJ to Fulton, 8 Mar. 1813, Jefferson Papers, LC.

50. Mease to TJ, 28 Mar. 1804, in Betts, *Farm Book*, 53; Willich, *Domestic Encyclopaedia*, 4:288–92.

51. Richard Peters to TJ, 25 Mar. 1816, Jefferson Papers, LC; *Evans & Ruffy's Farmers' Journal and Agricultural Advertizer*, 20 Nov. 1815, which included the following: "The whole of the ploughing was witnessed by those present with feelings of pleasure and satisfaction, and the result of their opinion was, that one, especially, of the American ploughs was, for free and mellow soils, a most valuable implement, of easy draught and effective operation, equal to any, and superior to many in present use; but that in foul grounds it could not fully clear itself, and was not sufficiently powerful for very heavy soils."

52. William Amos, "Essays on Agricultural Machines," in *Communications to the Board of Agriculture; on Subjects Relative to the Husbandry, and Internal Improvement of the Country* (London, 1810), 437–38.

53. Henry S. Randall, "President Jefferson's Plow," in *Transactions of the New York State Agricultural Society,* vol. 22, *1862* (Albany, 1863), 66–73. After proclaiming Jefferson's false priority, Amos went on in his account to describe his own method for duplicating moldboards, developed after having learned of Jefferson's method through "an accidental circumstance" and found it "very defective." Very strange to say, Amos's method was virtually identical to Jefferson's in dimensions, scribed lines, removal of the "pyramid," and even language ("breadth of a hair"). Amos, "Essays on Agricultural Machines," 438–45. On whether Small's plow was based on mathematical principles, see McClelland, *Sowing Modernity,* 38–39, 245.

54. James Small, *Treatise of Ploughs and Wheel Carriages* (Edinburgh, 1784).

55. Henry Home, Lord Kames, *Gentleman Farmer* (Edinburgh, 1776), 4.

56. *Report on the Trial of Plows,* 3–134.

57. Ibid., 35, 23.

58. William Hendrick to TJ, 7 July 1806, Jefferson Papers, LC, printed, with some transcription errors, in Betts, *Farm Book,* 56.

59. Jethro Wood to TJ, 1 Oct. 1816, in Betts, *Farm Book,* 561; TJ to Wood, 23 Mar. 1817, ibid., 569 ("I have examined it with care, and think it promises well in all it's parts; and shall exhibit it with pleasure to the notice of our practical, as well as our theoretical farmers"); Frank Gilbert, *Jethro Wood, Inventor of the Modern Plow* (1882; Ovid, NY, 1989), 9–20; *Report on the Trial of Plows,* 98; Rogin, *Introduction of Farm Machinery,* 29. Moldboards of other plow designers after the War of 1812 were also noted as similar to, and thus possibly inspired by, Jefferson's. See William Noland to George W. Jeffreys, 1 Mar. 1819, in *American Farmer,* 19 May 1820, 61, stating that the Peacock, Chenoweth, and "Freeborn" (i.e., Wood) plows were "much upon the principle of the Jefferson mouldboard."

60. Samuel L. Mitchill to Czar Alexander, 22 June 1818, in *American Farmer,* 4 June 1819, 80; Mitchill to George Washington Campbell, 22 June 1818, Campbell Papers, LC (my thanks to C. M. Harris for providing this letter); Gilbert, *Jethro Wood,* 22–23. Emperor Alexander responded with a diamond ring for the inventor. Mitchill, who failed to pass it on to Wood, was blamed by Wood's supporters for keeping it for his own benefit. Mitchill himself is said to have explained that he had donated it to the Greek cause against the Turks.

61. See, e.g., *Plough Boy,* 16 Sept. 1820, 123, describing the virtues of Wood's plow as "simplicity, strength, and durability"; and *Richmond Enquirer,* 24 Dec. 1825, describing the virtues of Stephen McCormick's plow as "simplicity, durability, and excellent performance."

62. See McClelland, *Sowing Modernity,* on this technological explosion.

63. Willich, *Domestic Encyclopaedia,* 252, quoted in McClelland, *Sowing Modernity,* 97.

64. TJ to Martha Jefferson, 28 Mar. 1787, *TJP,* 11:251.

65. Richard Peters, "American Ploughs," *Memoirs of the Philadelphia Agricultural Society* 4 (1818): 163–64.

66. Jean-Baptiste Le Roy to Benjamin Franklin, 21 June [1787], typescript in Franklin Papers, American Philosophical Society, Philadelphia, quoted in David Freeman Hawke, *Paine* (New York, 1974), 179.

67. James Fenimore Cooper, *Notions of the Americans* (Philadelphia, 1828), quoted in Hawke, *Paine,* 7.

68. TJ to Paine, 23 Dec. 1788, *TJP,* 14:373; Paine to TJ, 16 Feb. 1789, ibid., 564 (quoting a Mr. Foljambe); Lord Sheffield to TJ, 24 Mar. 1806, in Betts, *Garden Book,* 317. Although Jefferson apparently did not use *simple* or *simplicity* in descriptions of his moldboard, he did speak of the "easy" rule by which it was made. TJ to Philip Tabb, 1 June 1809, *Papers of Thomas Jefferson: Retirement Series,* 1:252.

69. TJ, "Hints for Traveling," *TJP,* 13:270; TJ to John Banister, 15 Oct. 1785, ibid., 8:636; TJ to Gideon Granger, 13 Aug. 1800, ibid., 32:96. See also TJ to J. L. de Unger, 16 Feb. 1788, ibid., 12:599. Samuel Harrison Smith described Jefferson—and ignited a major controversy—in his 1791 edition of Paine's *Rights of Man. TJP,* 20:272.

70. Augustus M. Hicks, of Matthews, VA, 27 May 1820, in *American Farmer,* 30 June 1820, 110. Hicks was complaining about overly complicated threshing machines.

71. *Report on the Trial of Plows,* 35, 65.

72. See *Edinburgh Encyclopaedia,* 1st American ed., 18 vols. (Philadelphia, 1832), 1:242–44. Robert Brown, the author of the section on agriculture, published it separately in 1811 as *Treatise on Rural Affairs; being the substance of the article Agriculture, originally published in the Edinburgh Encyclopaedia. With improvements and additions* (Edinburgh, 1811).

73. *Annales du Muséum* 1 (1802); *Description d'une Oreille de Charrue* (Paris, n.d.). The materials gathered in Paris half a century ago by Howard C. Rice have been essential to my understanding of the French connection. Howard C. Rice Collection, Jefferson Library, Monticello. It seems that Thouin should get the credit for preserving the only known Jeffersonian moldboard models in existence. As he wrote at the end of the *Description,* "It is to fulfill [Jefferson's] liberal intentions that his Memoir is printed here, and that the model of his moldboard for plows has been deposited in the gallery of agricultural implements to be used in the course on agriculture given each year at the Muséum." (Howard C. Rice translation).

74. *Report on the Trial of Plows,* 32–33, 65.

75. Harry Innes, Benjamin H. Latrobe, James Mease, and Charles Willson Peale had moldboards made, as did several professional plow improvers. Stanton, "A Little Matter," 5–8. I have as yet found no other Jefferson contemporaries who did so.

76. John H. Craven to Mr. Smith, 12 June 1833, *Farmer's Register* 1, no. 3 (1833): 150–52.

77. John Randolph, quoted in Russell Kirk, *John Randolph of Roanoke* (1951; Indianapolis, 1978), 540–41. I am grateful to Douglas Bradburn for bringing this gem to my attention. See *American Farmer,* 6 Dec. 1822, 291, for James M. Garnett's account of Virginia farmers' reluctance to try Cary plows, which lay in a tavern stable yard for two years, "the objects of doubt and cunning suspicion, to all the knowing ones, each fearing to meddle with them, lest he should render himself a mark of ridicule to the rest, for putting any faith in so ill-looking a tool. And there probably they would have continued for years, if an enterprising Yankee, then a resident here, had not boldly resolved, at every risk, to achieve the perilous adventure of making the first trial."

78. TJ to Banister, 15 Oct. 1785; Lord Kames quoted, in William C. Lehmann,

Henry Home, Lord Kames, and the Scottish Enlightenment: A Study in National Character and in the History of Ideas (The Hague, 1971), 93.

79. Société d'Agriculture du Département de la Seine, *Mémoires d'Agriculture.* See Mease to TJ, 27 July 1814, Jefferson Papers, LC, where Mease speaks of a newly invented loom: "We may say with respect to the loom what the French Soc: of Agric. said of your plough—America received the loom from Europe, and returned it perfected."

The End of a Beautiful Friendship
Americans in Paris and Public Diplomacy during the War Scare of 1798–1799

PHILIPP ZIESCHE

Even by the standards of the early twenty-first century the year 1798 marked a low point in Franco-American relations. Diplomatic negotiations between the two republics broke down completely amidst mutual recriminations and were replaced by undeclared warfare on the high seas. Since the ratification of Jay's Treaty and the recall of American minister to France James Monroe in 1796, hundreds of American ships had been captured by French privateers in the Caribbean or confiscated in French ports. The French executive body, the five-man Directory, had refused to receive Monroe's successor, Charles Cotesworth Pinckney.

At the same time, there were more Americans in Paris than ever before. In 1791 the American chargé d'affaires, William Short, had celebrated the Fourth of July with fewer than twenty Americans. The outbreak of war in Europe in 1792 had drawn increasing numbers of merchants, speculators, and adventurers to the French capital. In 1795 close to a hundred Americans attended an elaborate Independence Day fête hosted by James Monroe. By the end of 1797 the number of Americans had grown to more than 250. Most were merchants from New England who sought to take advantage of the food shortages in France and Saint-Domingue, demand redress for ships and cargoes impounded in French harbors or seized by French privateers, sell American lands, speculate in French currency, or buy real estate.[1]

While war among Europeans was good for American business, open conflict between the United States and France was not. Therefore, Americans in Paris witnessed the deterioration of Franco-American relations with great concern. There was hope for improvement in 1797, when the new president, John Adams, sent three commissioners to Paris to restore amicable relations while preserving American neutrality.

The envoys, John Marshall, Elbridge Gerry, and Pinckney, arrived in Paris in October 1797, on the heels of a political upheaval. After the coup

d'état of September 4, 1797 (18 Fructidor on the French revolutionary cal-
endar), the Directory was even more committed to an aggressive foreign
policy and even more dependent on the army to stay in power than before.
Preoccupied with plans for an invasion of Britain, the French government
was also in desperate need of money. Consequently, the agents of French
Foreign Minister Charles Maurice de Talleyrand-Périgord informed the
American envoys that a number of preconditions had to be met before any
official negotiations could begin. The agents, Jean Hottinguer, Pierre Bel-
lamy, and Lucien Hauteval, demanded that the U.S. government assume
all private American claims against the French Republic, grant a loan of
32 million Dutch florins, offer an apology for President Adams's belliger-
ent speech to Congress of May 16, 1797, and pay a bribe of fifty thousand
pounds to Talleyrand. The American envoys refused, not because they were
outraged at the demand for bribes but because it was far from certain that
they would receive anything in return.

In March 1798 Marshall and Pinckney, who had fallen out with Gerry
over how to proceed in the absence of official negotiations, left France. On
April 3 Secretary of State Timothy Pickering presented Marshall's dispatches from Paris to Congress, substituting the letters *X, Y,* and *Z* for the
names of the French agents. Soon the full texts of the reports were available
in pamphlets and newspapers to readers all across the United States.[2]

Even before the enormous publicity generated by the XYZ dispatches,
a number of Americans in Paris had decided to intervene and reverse the
decline of Franco-American friendship. After trying unsuccessfully to mediate between the American envoys and the French Foreign Ministry, they
turned their attention to the political scene in America. In letters to friends
and allies in the United States, spokesmen of the American community in
Paris, such as the author Joel Barlow and Consul General Fulwar Skipwith,
explained that France wanted to avoid war and was eager to renew diplomatic negotiations. At the same time, the prominent Jeffersonian George
Logan traveled to Paris on his own initiative to persuade the Directory that
reconciliation with America was possible and in France's best interest.

Historians have dismissed Americans in Paris as "a gang of hustlers"
who, owing to their commercial interests, had "a selfish stake in peace." I
argue here that the reactions in America and France to the peace initiatives
by Americans in Paris shed new light on early American diplomacy and on
Franco-American relations at the end of the 1790s.[3]

Since the American Revolution, in the absence of a well-established diplomatic corps, private Americans abroad sometimes had been called upon to
informally represent American interests or had assumed this task on their

own initiative. Moreover, the letters written by Americans in Paris were similar to previous efforts by official American representatives in Europe to influence public opinion at home and abroad. These private interventions reflected the deep American investment in the French Revolution. Since 1789, Americans in Paris had shared their experiences with correspondents in the United States. Like many Americans, they believed that the outcome of the French Revolution would shape the future of their own republic. Therefore, some Americans in Paris understood their political activism in Paris as an extension of their patriotic duties at home.[4]

By 1798, however, this cosmopolitan patriotism had become highly contentious in the United States. The mediation attempts of Americans in Paris helped fuel a heated debate about the boundaries of the national community and the limits of private political activism in foreign countries. Contrary to standard accounts of a universal surge in popular patriotic fervor after the XYZ affair, the controversy surrounding Americans in Paris highlights the difficulties that Federalists encountered in manufacturing a nationalist consensus.

Federalist newspapers and politicians derided the Americans in Paris as meddlers or denounced them as traitors, in collusion with Jacobin agents and the "French party" in the United States. Ironically, however, by attacking the Americans in Paris in print, the Federalists gave unprecedented publicity to their activities and thereby inadvertently elevated their importance in Franco-American relations. The Directory adroitly played on this dynamic and used the American mediators to seek rapprochement with the Adams administration while allowing the Republican opposition to take credit for the peaceful resolution of the crisis.

When Marshall, Pinckney, and Gerry arrived in Paris, many longtime American residents of the city felt that they knew more about the French government's procedures and personnel than the envoys, and they freely offered their advice. For example, Barlow and Skipwith cautioned the new arrivals that they would need to be patient, as the Directory was preoccupied with affairs in Europe and likely to prolong negotiations as much as possible. James Mountflorence, who worked for the American consulate in Paris, offered his services as intermediary between the envoys and the Foreign Ministry, as he had good relations with Baron d'Osmond, one of Talleyrand's private secretaries, and was also a trusted source of information for Pinckney.[5]

Such private interventions were not without precedent. During the colonial era the British government, in formulating its American policy, frequently consulted with private individuals from the colonies who were staying in London. Americans in London with access to government ministers acted independently from the official colonial agents and without formal authority. As Julie Flavell has shown, when the colonial agencies became defunct in late 1774, these Americans became the only remaining channel of communication between Britain and her North American colonies. Private colonists such as William Lee, Stephen Sayre, Josiah Quincy Jr., and Ralph Izard by default assumed the tasks of representing the Patriot position to members of the North administration and opposition politicians, sending intelligence to Patriot leaders in the colonies, and putting the case for colonial resistance before the British public through newspaper articles and pamphlets. In the eyes of Americans in Paris, Talleyrand's refusal to officially receive the envoys made similar kinds of private intervention both necessary and legitimate.[6]

The French penchant for informal negotiations in private conversations and at dinner parties irritated Marshall and Pinckney but provided an opportunity for private Americans to become involved. The merchant Nathaniel Cutting boasted, "I have frequently had *unofficial* communications with some individuals connected in the French government; now and then I have had the honor to converse with the American Envoys." The artist John Trumbull was invited to meet Talleyrand at a dinner party at Mme de Staël's and later visited the minister at his office to discuss the state of negotiations.[7]

Marshall and Pinckney were deeply suspicious of these "French Americans." Pinckney thought the Americans in Paris were conspiring with the French to aggravate the divisions between Gerry and the other envoys. He noted that the "American Jacobins here pay him [Gerry] a great court" and that "every art is used by Talleyrand and French Americans here to detach Mr. Gerry from his colleagues." Similarly, after a visit by Edward Church, of Boston, who had extensive property interests in Paris, Marshall described him sarcastically as "an American I believe *by birth*, who had been consul of France."[8]

Unsuccessful in their attempts to mediate between the envoys and the French Foreign Ministry, Barlow and Skipwith turned to influential friends in America for help. Again, they were following common practice. During and after the American Revolution, official American representatives had engaged in what today would be called "public diplomacy": the attempt to influence opinion in other countries through well-placed letters, pamphlets, or newspaper articles. Diplomatic historians have traced the origins of public diplomacy to the efforts of the restored European monarchies to control public opinion after the French Revolution, but American representatives were practicing public diplomacy even before the fall of the Bastille. Having observed the power of public opinion in their own country, American diplomats hoped that information management might compensate somewhat for the United States' glaring lack of economic and political influence in Europe.[9]

Benjamin Franklin was the first master of public diplomacy. During his stay in France from 1776 to 1785 Franklin worked tirelessly to bring French and European opinion onto the side of the American struggle for independence by funneling information to sympathetic publications such as the *Affaires de l'Angleterre et de l'Amérique* and by encouraging the translation and distribution of American state constitutions. Similarly, Franklin's successor, Thomas Jefferson, provided the *Gazette de Leyde* with pro-American news items throughout his tenure as minister to France. In 1795 minister James Monroe sought to influence American public opinion by asking political allies at home to publish his optimistic and therefore "more correct" reports on the French Revolution. In 1797 Charles Pinckney printed a pamphlet in Amsterdam (where he and his family had moved after their expulsion from France) based on a report on Franco-American relations by Timothy Pickering and sent a copy to every member of the French legislature. French newspapers protested that the High Federalist Pinckney's appeal to a foreign legislature to challenge its executive was no different from the activities of the Federalist bête noire Edmund Genet.[10]

As in Monroe's case, the target of Barlow and Skipwith was opinion in the United States, which they feared had been poisoned by British and Federalist misinformation and propaganda. They did not see themselves as spokesmen for the French Republic, but as American patriots who were trying to save their country from the misguided policies of its own government.

Barlow wrote a letter to his brother-in-law Senator Abraham Baldwin, of Georgia, to set the record straight on the true origins of Franco-American estrangement. In case Congress adjourned before the letter could reach Baldwin, Barlow also sent a copy to Vice President Jefferson, "trusting in your prudence to make such use of it only as may do the most good to the cause of truth, & the least mischief to me." This indicates that the letter was of a "public-minded" nature but intended to be circulated only among political allies. Skipwith likewise addressed a letter on the subject to Jefferson, and both he and Barlow entrusted their messages to William Lee, an American merchant in Paris who was returning to America.[11]

Barlow's and Skipwith's letters highlighted the central role that

Americans in Paris had played in Franco-American relations. Barlow depicted the falling out between the United States and France as the product not of geopolitical calculations but of a great, unrequited love. The main characters in this tragic tale were the Americans on the ground in Paris, who represented the United States to its French devotees.

The French revolutionaries of 1789, Barlow wrote, had looked up to America for having solved "the frightful problem of representative democracy" and had regarded America with "the most extravagant affections." If American policymakers had "properly nourished" these affections, the result would have been "confidence without bounds." Instead, "slighted or answered with indifference," these feelings had turned into "a jealousy uncontrolled by the rules of justice & blind to the light of truth."

Gouverneur Morris, who had served as minister to France from 1792 to 1794, had been "personally detested by all the leaders in the revolution" and had destroyed the goodwill that Jefferson's presence had generated earlier. Monroe and other "Americans in Paris, of characters far more respectable than that of Morris"—Barlow likely had Thomas Paine and perhaps himself in mind—had tried to repair the damage. However, after Monroe's recall, "for the apparent crime of preventing a war," and the election of Adams, the French had concluded that American hostility toward them had been "nationalized." Deeply wounded, they were "determined to fleece you of your property to a sufficient degree to bring you to your feeling in the only point in which it was presumed your sensibility lay, which was your pecuniary interest."[12]

Barlow and Skipwith insisted on the bond between the American and French republics, based on the shared principles of their revolutions, and on America's continued obligation to France for its support during the War of Independence. The recent negotiations had failed, they argued, because the hostility of Marshall and Pinckney toward the French Revolution made them unfit to represent the United States. The only policy that could save the American republic from a French invasion, Skipwith advised, was to "confess some of our errors, to lay their sins heavily upon the shoulders of a few persons who have perpetrated them, to modify or break the English treaty with Jay, and to lend France as much money, should she ask it, as she lent us in the hour of distress." For good measure, Barlow added that Congress should have sent President Adams to the "Mad-house" for his anti-French rants.[13]

Both letters were blatantly one-sided, denouncing American insensitivity while excusing French attacks on U.S. commerce. But they accurately reflected the attitudes of other Americans in Paris. Mary Pinckney found that many of her compatriots "are amazingly fearful of hurting the feelings of this government, but are ready to find fault with their own—if an indecent paragraph against this government appears in our papers, where the press is free, they snort with anger and fear, but they can read violent tirades against us in the french papers without any emotion."[14]

This partiality stemmed in some cases from previous experience of the French Revolution. Despite the Directory's lack of popular legitimacy and its dependence on the army, many Americans in Paris regarded it as the only bulwark against a return of either the Terror or the monarchy. Especially those who had lived through the Terror were willing to give the Directory the benefit of the doubt when it claimed that it was curtailing civil liberties and canceling election results for the sake of law and order.

For example, Thomas Paine publicly justified the coup d'état of Fructidor as dictated by "the supreme law of absolute necessity" to save the republic from a royalist conspiracy. Paine insisted that the coup could even be seen as following the blueprint of the American Revolution: "At one time congress invested general Washington with dictatorial powers. At another time the government of Pennsylvania suspended itself and declared martial law." The Directory gratefully received copies of his pamphlet from Paine and immediately authorized a French translation.[15]

Moreover, Paine, Barlow, and Skipwith were not the only Americans for whom loyalty to the French Revolution was an expression of American patriotism. As Matthew Hale, Seth Cotlar, Marie Rossignol, and other scholars have argued, American patriotism contained a powerful cosmopolitan strain. For many Americans, allegiance to the United States coexisted with deeply felt attachment to the French Republic and to the universal principles of republicanism and popular sovereignty. In fact, many Americans argued that being a true American patriot entailed supporting the French Revolution. Newspapers catered to the public's passionate interest in news from abroad, which was hotly debated in streets and taverns and celebrated in civic festivals.[16]

By the time Barlow's and Skipwith's letters reached the United States, this cosmopolitan patriotism had come under severe attack in the wake of the XYZ affair. Historians have used the natural metaphors of a "great explosion of national feeling" or a "wave of patriotism" to describe the public reaction to the publication of Marshall's dispatches. According to the standard account, Americans everywhere united behind the Adams administration and against French belligerence. Francophiles publicly repudiated their former positions. Congress formally abrogated the Franco-American Alliance of 1778, imposed an embargo on trade with France, and authorized the construction of warships as well as the creation of a Navy Department. American nationalism took on new characteristics, such as nativism, xenophobia, and the exaltation of American moral superiority, which culminated in the Naturalization and Alien Acts of 1798.[17]

Conversely, Seth Cotlar has argued that this "explosion of national feeling" was far from a natural phenomenon, being instead the product of a carefully orchestrated "cultural offensive" by the Federalist Party. Rather than tapping into a preexisting well of widespread anti-Jacobinism, Federalists worked hard to manufacture a nationalist consensus through the press, pamphlets, rallies, and mass petitions. The xenophobic, deferential, and explicitly anti-revolutionary vision of American politics that Federalists disseminated for the first time on a grand scale in 1798 succeeded in putting their Republican opponents on the defensive.[18]

Still, although Federalists enjoyed electoral gains in the South and doubled their margin in the House in the congressional elections of 1798–99, they lost the governorship of Pennsylvania and representation in the key states of Pennsylvania, New Jersey, and Maryland. Federalists continued to bemoan the American people's insufficient sense of nationalism. Joseph Hopkinson, author of the song "Hail Columbia," reported to Secretary of the Treasury Oliver Wolcott from New York: "It is a mortifying fact, my dear sir, that the federal spirit of this city is not worth a farthing." George Cabot noticed the same lack of outrage in other parts of the country. "It is impossible," he lamented, "to make the people feel or see distinctly that we have much more to fear from peace than [from] war." He was convinced that "war, open and declared, would not only deprive our external enemy of his best hopes, but would also extinguish the hopes of internal foes."[19]

Cosmopolitanism was a particular target of the Federalists' "cultural offensive" because it was said to undermine the ties of nationhood that preserved social order. Federalist authors and speakers urged their fellow citizens to see themselves as part of a historically grown community with strong ties of customs, values, and blood. While the Alien and Sedition Acts of 1798 resulted in few actual persecutions, their real significance lay in codifying this new exclusive language of nationhood. Barlow's and Skipwith's letters were a direct challenge to this new nationalist consensus.[20]

Skipwith's letter never reached its destination. At the same time that he and Barlow gave their letters to William Lee in Paris, Talleyrand sent to the United States an open letter to the American envoys for publication in American newspapers. Trying to shift responsibility for the crisis from himself and the Directory to the Adams administration, Talleyrand restated French grievances against the United States and suggested that he would be willing to negotiate with more conciliatory envoys. Marshall and Pinckney immediately composed a rejoinder and made sure that copies made their way to America as quickly as possible. Negotiations between France and the United States were now conducted as much in the American public sphere as in Parisian government chambers and salons.[21]

The Federalist press had long been eager to prove that the Republican editor Benjamin Franklin Bache was in direct correspondence with the French government. When Bache's *Aurora* published Talleyrand's message on June 16, 1798, Federalists charged that Bache had received it directly from the French minister and that he and his paper were part of a network of French agents in the United States. A few days later, the *Gazette of the United States* and other papers claimed to have found additional evidence in a packet bearing the official seal of the French Foreign Ministry and addressed to Bache that William Lee had carried across the Atlantic.

When questioned by Oliver Wolcott about the mail he had brought over from France, Lee turned over several letters, including the one from Skipwith, but not Barlow's. To allay suspicions that he was an agent of Talleyrand, Lee also issued a public statement disclaiming any knowledge of the contents of the letters he had received in France. The interception of the mail became the subject of a bitter newspaper battle between Bache and his opponents, and Bache's published comments during the controversy led the government to charge him with seditious libel even prior to the passage of the Sedition Act.[22]

Barlow's letter did reach its addressee but then fell into the hands of the wrong public. Soon after Senator Baldwin began to discreetly circulate the letter among other Republicans, it was stolen. Earlier, Baldwin had allowed Congressman Matthew Lyon to make a copy of the letter, provided that he would not publish it. Lyon proceeded to regularly read the letter aloud on the campaign trail in western Vermont, where, according to the testimony of two young Federalists, it elicited violent reactions from the audience. Then the letter appeared as a pamphlet whose author was described only as "an American Diplomatic Character in France" but was quickly identified as Barlow in the *Connecticut Courant.* Lyon claimed that his wife had given his copy of the letter to another printer in his absence and that he had tried to prevent its publication. In fact, Lyon was eager to test the recently passed Sedition Act, and publication of Barlow's letter constituted part of his indictment. His case was the first under the new law, and he was sentenced to four months in prison and a fine of one thousand dollars. As he had intended, Lyon became a martyr for freedom of the press and from his cell successfully ran for reelection to Congress.[23]

Meanwhile, Barlow's letter was widely reprinted and vigorously denounced in Federalist newspapers. The Boston *Columbian Centinel* declared that it undoubtedly had been written in Talleyrand's office while the French foreign minister, "arch apostate, sat at the elbow of the duped American and dictated every word. A greater quantum of folly, arrogance, egotism, and falsehood could not be condensed within equal limits." The letter constituted a betrayal "compared with which that of *Judas Iscariot* is but a foible."[24]

Accusations of atheism and blasphemy were standard in anti-Jacobin propaganda but had particular resonance in Barlow's case owing to his involvement in the publication of Paine's *Age of Reason* (1794). Many of Barlow's old friends in Connecticut, now prominent Federalists, homed in on this connection. Richard Alsop combined Barlow's alleged atheism with the image of the rootless cosmopolitan in the kind of doggerel for which Barlow and the Connecticut Wits had been renowned a decade earlier:

> This 'Jack-at-all-trades, good *at one*'
> This ever-changing, Proteus mind
> In all his turns, thro' every wind
> From telling sinners where they go
> To speculations in Scioto
> From morals pure, and manners plain
> To herding with Munroe and Paine
> From feeding on his country's bread
> To aping X, and Y, and Z
> From preaching Christ, to Age of Reason
> From writing psalms, to writing treason.[25]

In an open letter to Barlow published in the *Commercial Advertiser* Noah Webster explicitly denied that the United States owed anything to France. On the contrary, the Franco-American Alliance of 1778 had in fact unnecessarily prolonged the war with Britain. Closing on a personal note, Webster publicly ended his decades-long friendship with Barlow: "One more word, Sir, from an old friend who once loved and respected you. The contemptuous manner in which you speak of the President and the Senate of America is a striking proof of the effect of atheism and licentious examples on the civility and good manners of a well-bred man."[26]

Another old friend, Senator James Watson of New York, responded to a private letter from Barlow, who had argued that a war between the republics would "disgrace the principles of both their revolutions," by declaring that he was happy to see Americans recover from "our preposterous predilection for France." In fact, it was "indispensable to our national existence that we should be cured of that idolatry to France of which we were guilty in the early stages of our revolution." Barlow had reappeared as an embarrassing reminder of those "early stages," and judging by the intensity of the attacks on him, many Federalists feared that their countrymen had not fully outgrown them.[27]

Such attacks were not limited to Barlow. In the *Philadelphia Gazette* Samuel Hopkins declared that Americans in Paris were, with a few exceptions, "the fugitives of America, and the dregs and out-laws of Europe. I need not observe, that they and their connections here have been the most active despoilers of our commerce—the most inveterate calumniators of our country and our government—nor that they have continually contradicted and embarrassed all our public missionaries, except Mr. Monroe."[28]

Watson likewise accused the Americans in Paris of putting their own financial interests above the interests of their native country: "It has been said that some Americans in Paris have shown by calculation, that to pay the gratuity of fifty thousand sterling and the loan of thirty millions of florins would be cheaper than a war." This "renegade arithmetic" proved how much French influence had corrupted their morals, as it was "something worse than is used when a man sets a price upon his integrity or a virgin upon her chastity." Alongside treason and atheism, this was the most common charge against Americans in Paris. Mrs. Pinckney, like her husband and John Marshall, believed that beneath the flowery rhetoric it was greed that inspired the "French Americans'" overzealous defense of French policy: "In short they would have their own government and its ministers to consider what may affect their fortunes in France and act accordingly." The dismissal of the cosmopolitan ideals professed by Barlow and other Americans in Paris as a cover for selfish ambition followed logically from the new Federalist dogma that only national allegiances could count as authentic motives.[29]

Ironically, by denouncing Barlow and others as traitors to a narrowly defined American nation, Federalist politicians and newspapers gave their activities broader publicity than ever before. This inadvertently created the impression among some readers that these Americans were indeed important players in the transatlantic relationship.

Federalists always had a conflicted relationship with the popular politics that seemed to be turning their way in 1798. As David Waldstreicher and others have pointed out, the new forms of mass mobilization that the Federalists used to launch their "cultural offensive" against Jacobinism and the Republican opposition were at odds with their ideal of a deferential, politically passive citizenry. Federalists were aware of this contradiction and worried that trying to beat the Republicans at their own game of print warfare might demean their party and the federal government. Still, national security seemed to require that Federalists dirty their hands with the Jacobin tool of character assassination. Barlow's friend-turned-nemesis Noah Webster declared that "the friends of govt must be active & vigilant—they must lay aside that delicacy about characters which men of honor observe in ordinary cases—they must expose the *real characters public & private,* of the leaders of opposition." But while exposing their nefarious character and designs, the denunciation of American Francophiles also exposed a greater audience to their views and activities.[30]

When George Washington received a letter from Joel Barlow imploring the former president to use his influence for a peaceful resolution of the conflict with France, he immediately contacted his successor, John Adams. Washington was unsure whether and how to respond. He did not know Barlow personally, but recently there had been much in the press about his exploits and close ties with the Directory, so perhaps he could be an important mediator. Adams was incensed at this suggestion. He responded that he had just resolved to reopen negotiations but vehemently denied that Barlow's advice, or that of any other American in Paris, had influenced his decision in any way whatsoever. Barlow was certainly not worthy of a response: "The wretch has destroyed his own character to such a degree, that I think it would be derogatory of yours to give any answer at all to his letter. Tom Paine is not a more worthless fellow."[31]

Federalists' repeated highlighting of the close links between the French government, Americans in Paris, and French-loving Republicans in America also played into the hands of the Directory. The occasion was the spectacular peace mission of the Philadelphia merchant-farmer George Logan. A member of one of the oldest Quaker families in Pennsylvania, Logan was a friend and supporter of Jefferson's, had published newspaper articles and pamphlets against the Hamiltonian economic program, and in 1785 had been elected to the Pennsylvania Assembly. He had served on the Committee of Correspondence of the newly formed Democratic Society in Philadelphia in 1793. Disturbed by the Federalist agitation around the XYZ affair, Logan traveled to Europe in June 1798 to head off a war with France.[32]

The Federalist press immediately seized upon the departure of the prominent Republican as evidence of a treasonable plot. "There cannot be the least question," declared the *Philadelphia Gazette*, "but the Doctor, from his *inordinate* love of *French liberty*, and hatred of the *sacred constitution* of the United States, has gone to the French directory, fraught with intelligence of the *most dangerous tendency to this country*." Logan's "infernal design" had to be "the introduction of a French army, to *teach us the genuine value of true and essential liberty* by re-organizing our government, through the brutal operation of the bayonet and the guillotine." On the floor of Congress, Robert Goodloe Harper of South Carolina announced that an event had taken place that "would lead to the discovery of a treasonable correspondence, carried on by persons in this country with France, of the most criminal nature." Moreover, Logan's departure coincided with Bache's publication of Talleyrand's letter, which lent additional credibility and urgency to these allegations.[33]

Once in Paris, Logan found that Gerry, the last remaining envoy, had already left France. After consulting with Skipwith and Barlow, Logan decided to stay on and try to persuade the French authorities to lift a recently imposed embargo on American trade and release a number of American sailors who had been imprisoned as Englishmen. Not all Americans in Paris welcomed Logan's unauthorized intervention. Two days after Logan's arrival, James Mountflorence sent a letter to Talleyrand warning the minister against "criminal and unaccredited negotiations" with an agent of "the party of the opposition."[34]

Logan's mission could not have come at a worse moment for Talleyrand. By mid-May 1798 published copies of Marshall's dispatches had reached Britain, where they were reprinted for distribution throughout Europe. The reports accused Talleyrand of personal corruption, a charge that came as no surprise to most readers but had never before been so widely publicized. Fearful for his position, Talleyrand denounced X, Y, and Z as renegade agents who at no point had acted in his name. In an elaborate defense submitted to the Directory, the minister blamed the episode on the American envoys, whom he described as "picky men, shy and stubborn," who lacked any understanding of the workings of diplomacy and its fluid boundaries of public and private conversations. How could he be expected to deal with "negotiators who, angered at not being received officially, neglected the opportunity of meetings in society and nowhere presented themselves to the minister"?[35] At the same time, Talleyrand discussed his readiness to receive new American envoys with Richard Codman, an American merchant with

Federalist leanings, and Skipwith, no doubt hoping that they would convey the reformed French attitude to their correspondents in the United States.[36]

Talleyrand feared that Logan's arrival in Paris might jeopardize his covert efforts to reopen negotiations with the United States through William Vans Murray, the staunchly Federalist American minister at The Hague, and went out of his way to reassure Murray that the Directory would not treat with an unaccredited agent.[37] However, Logan managed to secure audiences with all three directors, who enthusiastically welcomed his mission. At a dinner party Director Merlin de Douai and Logan shared a toast to the United States and the "speedy restoration of amity between them and France."

According to his own account, published in the *Aurora,* Logan told the directors that he attributed the falling out between the two republics to the intrigues of William Pitt. Pro-British propagandists in America were using earlier "atrocities" of the French Revolution and the recent attacks by French privateers to stigmatize "every friend to France and republican principles" as an enemy of the United States. He also appealed to French economic self-interest to respect American neutrality and thereby increase trade in French harbors.[38]

Shortly after meeting with Logan, the Directory announced the lifting of all restrictions on American commerce and a ban on privateering. This decision to avoid war with the United States had already been made before Logan's arrival, for a variety of geopolitical reasons, including the specter of an official Anglo-American alliance, the fear of losing French colonies in the West Indies, the failure of a French-sponsored insurrection in Ireland, Nelson's annihilation of the French fleet off the coast of Egypt, and the economic damage that war would cause for France's satellite republic in the Netherlands. Nonetheless, the Parisian press, from the republican *Le Bien informé* to the conservative *Publiciste,* credited "le brave L . . . n" with bringing about the end of the embargo. Within a few days, the same report appeared in the *Gazette de Leyde,* now titled *Nouvelles Politiques publiées a Leyde,* one of the most widely read and most respected newspapers in Europe.[39]

Without informing Talleyrand, whom they had treated with undisguised contempt since the XYZ scandal, the directors took Logan's much-publicized mission as an opportunity to make a gesture of goodwill to the Adams administration and at the same time allow the Republican opposition to claim that one of their own had facilitated this rapprochement. Federalist observers in Europe saw through this maneuver and in their indignation tacitly acknowledged its effectiveness. Thomas Boylston Adams, the president's youngest son, wrote from Berlin to the merchant Joseph Pitcairn, in Paris, on the raising of the embargo:

> Wonderful act of justice & generosity! Why, all the ships embargo'd in their ports don't amount I dare say to *a dozen.* ... But an *Embargo raised* as a proof of pacific intentions, reads just as well in a news-paper, when only one ship or even a fishing schooner is released by it, as if all the British navy were the prize renounced. You must know too, that for the raising of this embargo the merit is claimed by *several* pretenders, neither of which, probably brought it about.[40]

In order to prevent Murray from breaking off negotiations over the Logan mission, Talleyrand and his agent Louis-André Pichon had to devise the contorted argument that the reports of Logan's success emanated from an "anarchical" newspaper in Paris (meaning *Le Bien informé,* edited by Paine's close friend Nicolas de Bonneville) and had been supplied by "the *Americans* at Paris." However, trying at the same time to absolve the prominent Republican Logan, Talleyrand claimed that the source of the false rumor that the Directory had negotiated with Logan was Thomas Paine, with whom Logan himself had supposedly disavowed any connection. Murray remained unconvinced by these denials and surmised that the Directory had allowed the reports about Logan to be published in order to court Republican opinion in the United States.[41]

Republicans in America were indeed only too happy to credit Logan with bringing about the peaceful resolution of the crisis. The *Aurora* published a slew of letters from anonymous Americans in Paris written during Logan's stay in the city, all calling for peace and praising Logan as a "true patriot" and "friend to humanity." Jefferson declared, "Logan's enthusiastic enterprize was fortunate, as it prevented the effect which our actual hostilities on their vessels would have produced."[42]

When George Logan returned to the United States in November 1798, his official reception was hostile. Timothy Pickering, George Washington, and John Adams all censured his mission. By receiving Logan after the rejection of the official envoys, the Directory had rubbed salt into American wounded pride. Washington noted bitterly to Logan that it was "very singular" that "he who could be viewed as a private character; unarmed with proper powers; and presumably unknown in France; should suppose he could effect what these gentlemen [the envoys] of the first respectability in our Country, specially charged under the authority of the Government, were unable to do." In his address to Congress on December 12, Adams declared with obvious reference to Logan and other Americans in Paris: "Although the officious interference of individuals without official character or authority, is not entitled to any credit, yet it deserves to be considered whether the temerity and impertinence of individuals affecting to interfere in public affairs between France and the United States should not be inquired into and corrected."[43]

Within days, a committee formed within the House of Representatives to follow up on the president's suggestion and consider an amendment to the Sedition Act that would have made it illegal for any citizen to "usurp the Executive authority of this Government by commencing or carrying on any correspondence with the government of any foreign prince or state relative to controversies or disputes between such prince or state and the United States." However, Republican representatives put up unexpected resistance to the new law, also known as the Logan Act, and the ensuing debate lasted for three weeks.[44]

In the course of the debate, Robert Harper, one of the chief proponents of the law, produced an anonymous letter to Talleyrand that he claimed was written by Logan. However, the Republican Albert Gallatin of Pennsylvania persuasively countered that the author was in fact the Federalist merchant Richard Codman. The author of the letter described himself as "a firm friend to the principles of the French Revolution." He warned the French foreign minister not to walk into a trap laid by "the enemies of France and America," who sought to persuade the French that if they launched an attack on the United States, they could count on the active support of the Republicans. In fact, "the very idea strikes all true Americans with horror." Rather than playing into the hands of Britain, France should "by a great and magnanimous conduct . . . draw back those wandering affections which Intrigue and misunderstandings have estranged for a moment and leave the true American character to blaze forth in the approaching elections." Clearly, the "true American character" included both patriotic unity in case of an outside attack and cosmopolitan solidarity with other nations founded on similar political principles. As Gallatin gleefully noted, "The clamour which gentlemen have thought proper to raise about this paper, when the public knows the fact, may recoil on themselves."[45]

Moreover, Harper inadvertently revealed the thin line between friendly advice and intervention in official foreign policy. Responding to arguments that the law would criminalize any harmless social interaction with foreigners, Harper declared that if he were in France even after the law had been enacted and if Talleyrand invited him to dinner and asked for his opinion on the relations between the two countries, he would not hesitate a second to speak his mind.[46]

Republicans were quick to pounce on this statement. Gallatin responded that what Federalists seemed to object to was not Americans' offering their advice to Frenchmen but rather the nature of their advice: "What does this amount to, connected with what has been said about the existence of a dangerous combination of men—a French party in this country, and other expressions of the same import? Does it not mean that the law is to attach to a certain description of men, and not to others? . . . If a man is a federalist, he will be innocent, but if he is an anti-federalist he will be guilty."[47]

Targeting the paradox of Federalist anti-French publicity, Gallatin argued that it was the Federalists who endangered the United States by constantly assuring the French in the press and in Congress that a "French party" that would welcome them with open arms really existed. By contrast, Logan and others had merely tried to act as mediators, combining love of their country with knowledge and appreciation of other nations in their desire to preserve peace.

Despite this spirited defense of the cosmopolitan ideal, the House passed the Logan Act on January 17, 1799, by a vote of 58 to 36. The law barred citizens from all contact with agents of foreign governments without official authorization, thereby rendering illegal a decade of American participation in the French Revolution. The law also put an end to private individuals informally representing American interests abroad. This colonial tradition had become an embarrassment to a national government trying to win the respect of the European powers.[48]

Only nine days after Adams denounced his "officious interference," Logan was elected to the Pennsylvania Assembly with a resounding majority. The *Aurora* exulted, "The election of Dr. Logan is the best reply which could have been given by the *people* to the President." James Monroe predicted that the Federalist persecution of Logan would ultimately backfire, to the benefit of the Republicans: "The enterprise of Logan with its consequences will not hurt any in his political sentiments, while the attempt to make it instrumental to that end will have its advantages. The ill humour shewn by the head and all the members of the opposit party, at an interference forbidden by no law, prompted by benevolent motives, & wh. was useful to the publick, is a circumstance wh. will tend to shew the views of that party."[49]

Barely two weeks after signing the Logan Act into law, Adams announced his nomination of William Vans Murray as minister to negotiate with the French government. Like the Directory, Adams had many reasons to seek an accommodation that had little to do with the interventions of any American in Paris. War with France would further increase the already considerable influence of Alexander Hamilton over Adams's cabinet and the growing U.S. army. In his letter about Barlow, Washington had noted that peace was "the ardent desire of all the friends of this rising Empire," which signaled to Adams that the former president would not oppose the reopening of negotiations. Finally, Adams had received reliable information from many different sources in Europe—including his sons John Quincy and Thomas Boylston, Murray, and Gerry, as well as Richard Codman and George Logan—that the French government was genuinely seeking a peaceful resolution and was willing to make amends for the disrespectful treatment of the envoys.[50]

Adams's unexpected turnabout shocked and dismayed the Federalists. Theodore Sedgwick lamented, "Had the foulest heart & the ablest head in the world, been permitted to select the most embarrassing and ruinous measure, perhaps, it would have been precisely the one which had been adopted." Adams's and Hamilton's respective followers quickly turned on each other with the same severity that had previously been reserved for Jacobins. Still, it was the party as a whole that had become a victim of its own publicity. After months of alarmist rhetoric about an imminent French attack and the subversive activities of American Jacobins, the Federalists had boxed themselves in an all-or-nothing, war-or-surrender foreign policy. The government already faced a popular backlash against the Alien and Seditions Acts, the new taxes required for the expansion of the military, and the creation of a standing army. But Sedgwick was correct that nothing could have damaged Federalist credibility more than to suddenly reverse policy toward France, especially along the lines suggested by prominent Republicans like Logan.[51]

The published documents, speeches, pamphlets, newspaper articles, and letters to the editor that made up the public diplomacy of the XYZ affair proved to be a double-edged sword for both the French and the American government. The publicity of the XYZ affair embarrassed French officials and made American popular support for the Adams administration appear more unified than it actually was. But public diplomacy also allowed the Directory to play the two American parties off against each other and to hand a public-relations success to the Republican opposition.

Do the Americans in Paris deserve any credit for averting a war between the two republics? Barlow certainly thought so. In a public letter "to His Fellow Citizens" Barlow denounced the Logan Act and refused to accept "that it is a crime in a private citizen to serve his country." While he and "a few other men, not commissioned for the purpose, have hitherto prevented a war," the Adams administration had done "little for America but increase her debt, and nothing for Europe but imitate her follies."[52] Americans in Paris did not shape the decisions of either the Directory or John Adams, but they struggled hard to keep communications between the two sides open. Even though neither French nor American officials entirely trusted what these Americans had to say, their letters and newspaper articles kept the history of Franco-American friendship and alternatives to war in the public sphere. Once Talleyrand and the Directory decided that the time for serious accommodation with the United States had come, Americans in Paris were available and ready to serve as go-betweens.

Still, even as cosmopolitan ideal embodied by the Americans in Paris appeared vindicated, the controversy over their interventions demonstrated to their Republican allies what a burden the party's ideological attachment to France had become. In a final ironic twist, it was the success of Adams's new envoys in negotiating an end to the Franco-American Alliance that enabled Jefferson to declare in his inaugural address that his administration would pursue "peace, commerce, and honest friendship with all nations, entangling alliances with none."[53]

NOTES

1. William Short to John Cutting, 28 June 1791, William Short Papers, LC; James Monroe, *The Autobiography of James Monroe,* ed. Stuart Gerry Brown (Syracuse, NY, 1959), 102–3; Thomas Perkins, Journal, 4 July 1795, Thomas H. Perkins Papers, Massachusetts Historical Society, Boston; William C. Stinchcombe, *The XYZ Affair* (Westport, CT, 1980), 81.

2. The names of the French agents were withheld because the American envoys had promised never to make them public and to ensure the envoy's safety. There was a fourth French agent involved in the negotiations, Nicholas Hubbard (W); however, since he appeared only a few times in the printed accounts of the negotiations, the episode became known as the XYZ Affair, the most complete account of which is Stinchcombe, *XYZ Affair.*

3. For critical assessments of Americans in Paris during this period, see Stanley Elkins and Eric McKitrick, *The Age of Federalism* (New York, 1993), 609–10; Alexander DeConde, *The Quasi-War: The Politics and Diplomacy of the Undeclared War with France, 1797–1801* (New York, 1966), 157; and Stinchcombe, *XYZ Affair,* ch. 5.

4. Philipp Ziesche, *Cosmopolitan Patriots: Americans in Paris in the Age of Revolution* (Charlottesville, VA, 2010).

5. Joel Barlow to James Cathalan, 14 June 1799, Joel Barlow Papers, Houghton Library, Harvard University; Fulwar Skipwith to James Monroe, 20 Oct. 1797, James Monroe Papers, LC. On Mountflorence, see John Marshall, "Paris Journal," 14 Oct.,

6 and 7 Nov. 1797, in *The Papers of John Marshall*, ed. Herbert A. Johnson et al., 6 vols. (Chapel Hill, NC, 1974–90), 3:162, 185–86; Marvin R. Zahniser, *Charles Cotesworth Pinckney: Founding Father* (Chapel Hill, NC, 1967), 155n54, 211; and Gerald Clarfield, *Timothy Pickering and American Diplomacy* (Columbia, MS, 1969), 112.

6. Julie M. Flavell, "American Patriots in London and the Quest for Talks, 1774–1775," *Journal of Imperial and Commonwealth History* 20, no. 3 (1992): 335–69.

7. Nathaniel Cutting to Pierce Butler, 13 Mar. 1798, Nathaniel Cutting Papers, Massachusetts Historical Society, emphasis in original; John Trumbull, *The Autobiography of Colonel John Trumbull, Patriot-Artist, 1756–1843*, ed. Theodore Sizer (New Haven, CT, 1953), 220–23.

8. Charles Pinckney to Rufus King, 14 Dec. 1797, Rufus King Papers, LC; Charles Pinckney to Thomas Pinckney, 22 Feb. 1798, Timothy Pickering Papers, Massachusetts Historical Society; Marshall, "Paris Journal," 11 Oct. 1797, in *Papers of John Marshall*, 3:160, emphasis in original. Church had been the American consul at Lisbon.

9. Keith Hamilton and Richard Langhorne, *The Practice of Diplomacy: Its Evolution, Theory and Administration* (London, 1995), 124–28.

10. "'Lettre du Comte de Chanmburg [Schaumberg]': a Satire Attributed to Franklin," [before 13 Mar. 1777], and Duc de La Rochefoucauld to Franklin and Silas Deane, 20 Jan. [1777], in *The Papers of Benjamin Franklin*, ed. Leonard W. Labaree et al., 39 vols. to date (New Haven, CT, 1959–), 23:214, 480–82. TJ to Charles F. Dumas, 31 July 1788, in *TJP*, 13:438–39; see also TJ to Dumas, 15 May 1788, ibid., 160, and TJ to Dumas, 30 July 1788, ibid., 436. Monroe to TJ, 27 June 1795, ibid., 28:390–97. Timothy Pickering to Charles Pinckney, 16 Jan. 1797, in *American State Papers: Foreign Relations*, ed. Walter Lowrie and Matthew St. Clair Clarke, 38 vols. (Washington, DC, 1832–61), 1:559–76. See also Zahniser, *Pinckney*, 156; Clarfield, *Timothy Pickering*, 112; and Albert H. Bowman, The *Struggle for Neutrality: Franco-American Diplomacy during the Federalist Era* (Knoxville, TN, 1974), 300–305.

11. Barlow to Abraham Baldwin, 4 Mar. 1798, reprinted in John Dos Passos, *The Ground We Stand On* (New York, 1941), 346–58; Barlow to TJ, 12 Mar. 1798, in *TJP*, 30:174. On "public-minded" letters, see Joanne B. Freeman, *Affairs of Honor: National Politics in the New Republic* (New Haven, CT, 2001), 114–15.

12. Barlow to Baldwin, 4 Mar. 1798, in Dos Passos, *Ground We Stand On*, 348–49, 351, 352.

13. Skipwith to TJ, 17 Mar. 1798, in *TJP*, 30:184–85; Barlow to Baldwin, 4 Mar. 1798, in Dos Passos, *Ground We Stand On*, 353.

14. Mary Pinckney to Margaret Manigault, 6 Dec. 1797, quoted in Stinchcombe, *XYZ Affair*, 80.

15. Thomas Paine, *Letter to the People of France, and the French Armies, on the Event of the 18th Fructidor—Sep. 4—and its Consequences* (New York, 1798), 17–18. For the grateful response of the Directory, see François de Neufchâteau to Thomas Paine, 13 Nov. 1797, AF III/478/2955, Archives Nationales, Paris.

16. Matthew Rainbow Hale, "'Many Who Wandered in Darkness': The Contest over American National Identity, 1795–1798," *Early American Studies* 1 (Spring 2003): 127–75; Marie-Jeanne Rossignol, *The Nationalist Ferment: The Origins of U.S. Foreign*

Policy, 1789–1812, trans. Lillian A. Parrott (Columbus, OH, 2004), 60–63, 99–105; Seth Cotlar, "In Paine's Absence: The Trans-Atlantic Dynamics of American Popular Political Thought, 1789–1804" (PhD diss., Northwestern University, 2000); David Waldstreicher, *In the Midst of Perpetual Fetes: The Making of American Nationalism, 1776–1820* (Chapel Hill, NC, 1997), 112–40; Simon P. Newman, *Parades, Festivals, and the Politics of the Street: Popular Political Culture in the Early American Republic* (Philadelphia, 1997), ch. 5; David Brion Davis, *Revolutions: Reflections on American Equality and Foreign Liberations* (Cambridge, MA, 1990), ch. 2; Ruth Bloch, *Visionary Republic: Millennial Themes in American Thought, 1756–1800* (New York, 1985), 150–86.

17. Elkins and McKitrick, *Age of Federalism,* 550; Rossignol, *Nationalist Ferment,* 105. See also Thomas M. Ray, "'Not One Cent for Tribute': The Public Addresses and American Popular Reaction to the XYZ Affair, 1798–1799," *JER* 3 (Winter 1983): 389–412.

18. Seth Cotlar, "The Federalists' Transatlantic Cultural Offensive of 1798 and the Moderation of American Democratic Discourse," in *Beyond the Founders: New Approaches to the Political History of the Early American Republic,* ed. Jeffrey L. Pasley, Andrew W. Robertson, and David Waldstreicher (Chapel Hill, NC, 2004), 274–99.

19. Joseph Hopkinson to Oliver Wolcott, 17 May 1798, in *Memoirs of the Administrations of Washington and John Adams, Edited from the Papers of Oliver Wolcott,* ed. George Gibbs, 2 vols. (New York, 1846), 2:49; George Cabot to Wolcott, 25 Oct. 1798, in ibid., 2:109. On Federalist electoral gains, see James Roger Sharp, *American Politics in the Early Republic: The New Nation in Crisis* (New Haven, CT, 1993), 223. But see also John C. Miller, *The Federalist Era, 1789–1801* (New York, 1963), 255; and Noble E. Cunningham Jr., *The Jeffersonian Republicans: The Formation of Party Organization, 1789–1801* (Chapel Hill, NC, 1957), 133–35.

20. Cotlar, "Federalists' Transatlantic Cultural Offensive," 276, 278, 281–82, 293–94. See also Rogers M. Smith, "Constructing American National Identity: Strategies of the Federalists," in *Federalists Reconsidered,* ed. Doron Ben-Atar and Barbara B. Oberg (Charlottesville, VA, 1998), 19–40.

21. Talleyrand to American envoys, 18 Mar. 1798, in *Papers of John Marshall,* 3: 413–22; American envoys to Talleyrand, 3 Apr. 1798, ibid., 426–59; Stinchcombe, *XYZ Affair,* 111.

22. James Morton Smith, *Freedom's Fetters: The Alien and Sedition Laws and American Civil Liberties* (Ithaca, NY, 1956), 194–200; James Tagg, *Benjamin Franklin Bache and the Philadelphia "Aurora"* (Philadelphia, 1991), 378–88.

23. Joel Barlow, *Copy of a Letter from an American Diplomatic Character in France to a Member of Congress in Philadelphia* ([Fairhaven, VT?], 1798); *Connecticut Courant* (Hartford), 12 Nov. 1798; Baldwin to Barlow, 14 Feb. and 30 Mar. 1799, Monroe Wakeman Holman Collection, Beinecke Library, Yale University; Aleine Austin, *Matthew Lyon, "New Man" of the Democratic Revolution, 1749–1822* (University Park, PA, 1981), 109–10, 114; James Morton Smith, *Freedom's Fetters,* 226–27.

24. *Columbian Centinel* (Boston), 22 Dec. 1798. Barlow later claimed that the *Centinel* had "mutilated and distorted" his letter to Baldwin until there was "not a paragraph without some omissions, additions or changes." At the same time, however,

Barlow defiantly declared that he found nothing in the allegedly mangled letter to retract or correct. *Joel Barlow to His Fellow Citizens, of the United States of America. Letter I. On the system of policy hitherto pursued by their Government. Paris 4 March 1799* ([Paris], [1799]), 2.

25. Richard Alsop, *The Political Green-House, for the Year 1798, Addressed to the Readers of the Connecticut Courant, January 1st, 1799* (Hartford, CT, [1799]). A kind of capsule biography of Barlow, the poem alludes to his various occupations as a chaplain in the Continental Army, a real-estate agent in France for the Scioto Company, author of *The Hasty Pudding,* and author of a revised edition of Watts's Psalms.

26. Noah Webster to Barlow, 16 Nov. 1798, in *Letters of Noah Webster,* ed. Harry Warfel (New York, 1953), 187–94. The letter appeared in the *Commercial Advertiser* (New York), 16 Nov. 1798.

27. Barlow to James Watson, 26 July 1798, and Watson to Barlow, 26 Oct. 1798, in Gibbs, *Memoirs of the Administrations,* 2:111–15.

28. *Philadelphia Gazette,* 6 July 1798. See also Skipwith's response in *Aurora* (Philadelphia), 26 Jan. 1799.

29. Watson to Barlow, 26 Oct. 1798, in Gibbs, *Memoirs of the Administrations,* 2:113; Mary Pinckney to Manigault, 6 Dec. 1797, quoted in Stinchcombe, *XYZ Affair,* 80.

30. Waldstreicher, *In the Midst of Perpetual Fetes,* 113–14; see also Todd Estes, "Shaping the Politics of Public Opinion: Federalists and the Jay Treaty Debate," *Journal of the Early Republic* 20, no. 3 (2000): 393–422. Webster to Wolcott, 23 June 1800, quoted in Joanne B. Freeman, "Explaining the Unexplainable: The Cultural Context of the Sedition Act," in *The Democratic Experiment: New Directions in American Political History,* ed. Meg Jacobs, William J. Novak, and Julian E. Zelizer (Princeton, NJ, 2003), 27–30, emphasis in original.

31. Barlow to George Washington, 2 Oct. 1798, in *Joel Barlow to His Fellow Citizens, of the United States of America. Letter I,* 41–49; Washington to JA, 1 Feb. 1799, in *The Writings of George Washington,* ed. John C. Fitzpatrick, 39 vols. (Washington, DC, 1931–44), 37:119–20; JA to Washington, 19 Feb. 1799, in *The Works of JA,* ed. Charles Francis Adams, 10 vols. (Boston, 1856), 8:624–26.

32. Frederick B. Tolles, *George Logan of Philadelphia* (New York, 1953), esp. 153–204.

33. *Philadelphia Gazette,* quoted in Deborah N. Logan, *Memoir of Dr. George Logan of Stenton,* ed. Frances A. Logan (Philadelphia, 1899), 59–60, emphases in original; see also *Porcupine's Gazette* (Philadelphia), 18 June 1798, and *Gazette of the United States* (Philadelphia), 18 and 23 June 1798. *The Debates and Proceedings in the Congress of the United States,* 18 vols. (Washington, DC, 1834–56), 5th Cong., 2nd sess., 8:1972 (hereafter *Annals of Congress*); see also James Morton Smith, *Freedom's Fetters,* 101–6. The correspondence in question was nothing more sinister than letters of introduction from the French minister Philippe de Létombe and certificates of citizenship from Thomas McKean, the Pennsylvania chief justice, and Jefferson.

34. James Mountflorence to Talleyrand, 22 Thermidor an VI [9 Aug. 1798], Correspondance Politique: États-Unis, 50:159, Archives du Ministère des Affaires Étrangères, Paris.

35. Talleyrand, Report to the Executive Directory, 12 Prairial an VI [31 May 1798],

Correspondance Politique: États-Unis, 49:393–404, quoted in DeConde, *Quasi-War,* 145. Because of the public nature of this diplomatic crisis, Talleyrand also considered it necessary to issue a defense pamphlet, which was quickly translated into English under the title *Talleyrand's Defence* (London, 1798).

36. Skipwith to Elbridge Gerry, 6 Aug. 1798, Elbridge Gerry Papers, Pierpont Morgan Library, New York. Codman described his meeting with Talleyrand in a letter to the Federalist congressman Harrison Gray Otis and advocated the appointment of a new commission. Codman to Otis, 26 Aug. 1798, in *The Life and Letters of Harrison Gray Otis,* ed. Samuel E. Morrison, 2 vols. (Boston, 1913), 1:168–70.

37. Talleyrand to Louis-André Pichon, 29 Thermidor an VI [16 Aug. 1798], Correspondance Politique: États-Unis, 50:169. On Talleyrand's overtures to Murray, see Bowman, *Struggle for Neutrality,* 350–59; and DeConde, *Quasi-War,* 147–54.

38. George Logan, "To the Citizens of the United States," *Aurora* (Philadelphia), 3 Jan. 1799.

39. *Le Bien informé* (Paris), 7 Fructidor an VI [24 Aug. 1798]; *Le Publiciste* (Paris), 8 Fructidor an VI [25 Aug. 1798]; *Nouvelles Politiques publiées a Leyde,* 31 Aug. 1798, suppl.

40. Thomas Boylston Adams to Joseph Pitcairn, 7 Sept. 1798, in "Letters of Thomas Boylston Adams to Joseph Pitcairn," *Quarterly Publication of the Historical and Philosophical Society of Ohio* 12 (Jan.–Mar. 1917): 20, emphases in original.

41. Talleyrand to Pichon, 11 Fructidor an VI [28 Aug. 1798], Correspondance Politique: États-Unis, 50:202; William Vans Murray to Pickering, 1 Sept. 1798, in "Letters of William Vans Murray," ed. W. C. Ford, *Annual Report of the American Historical Association,* 1912, 463; Murray to Pickering, 19 Sept. 1798, Timothy Pickering Papers, Massachusetts Historical Society.

42. *Aurora* (Philadelphia), 16, 22, and 30 Nov. 1798, 9 Jan. and 1 Feb. 1799; Nathaniel Cutting to TJ, 27 Aug. 1798, in *TJP,* 30:499–500; Short to TJ, 24 Aug. 1798, ibid., 489–90; TJ to John Wayles Eppes, 21 Jan. 1799, ibid., 631.

43. Deborah N. Logan, *Memoir of Dr. George Logan,* 86–87; "Memorandum of an Interview," 13 Nov. 1798, in *Writings of George Washington,* 37:18–20; *Journal of the Senate of the United States,* 5 vols. (Washington, DC, 1820–21), 2:562–63.

44. *Annals of Congress,* 5th Cong., 3rd sess., 9:2493.

45. Ibid., 2619–26, 2637–45, 2694, 2703–4, 2708–9. The authorship of this letter is not entirely certain. Joseph Woodward brought an unsigned copy to the United States, and in a letter to Harrison Gray Otis he identified George Logan and Joel Barlow as its authors. Woodward to Otis, 25 Jan. 1799, in *Life and Letters of Harrison Gray Otis,* 1:170–71. Logan vehemently denied this and claimed to have been shown a draft by Richard Codman, who he said had asked him to present it to Talleyrand; Logan said that he had refused to do so because it would have had "too much the appearance of an official act." *Aurora* (Philadelphia), 14 and 15 Jan. 1799. There is no copy in the Archives du Ministère des Affaires Étrangères, which suggests that it never reached Talleyrand. Codman's praise for Logan in his letter to Otis of 26 August indicates that he approved of the content of the letter, whether he wrote it or not. Codman also argued that it was the display of American national unity that had convinced the Directory to revise its position, but he said that this new national spirit

should not prevent the reconciliation between the two republics, "which ought to be desired by all true friends to both countries." Codman to Otis, 26 Aug. 1798, in *Life and Letters of Harrison Gray Otis*, 1:169.

46. *Annals of Congress*, 5th Cong., 3rd sess., 9:2618.

47. Ibid., 2629.

48. Ibid., 3795. The law is still in effect, although there has been only one indictment under it in two centuries. In 1803 Francis Flournoy was prosecuted for publishing a newspaper article advocating the secession of Kentucky and its French annexation. Tolles, *George Logan*, 238–39. In 1947 the House Un-American Activities Committee (HUAC) considered using the law to prosecute Henry Wallace for criticizing American foreign policy toward the Soviet Union while traveling abroad. John C. Culver and John Hyde, *American Dreamer: The Life and Times of Henry A. Wallace* (New York, 2000), 441. See also Detlev F. Vagts, "The Logan Act: Paper Tiger or Sleeping Giant?" *American Journal of International Law* 60, no. 2 (1966): 268–302.

49. *Aurora* (Philadelphia), 24 Dec. 1798, emphasis in original; Monroe to TJ, 26 Jan. 1799, in *TJP*, 30:658.

50. On the considerations behind and long gestation of Adams's decision to send a new minister to France, see Elkins and McKitrick, *Age of Federalism*, 614–20; and DeConde, *Quasi-War*, 112, 165–68, 172–76, 178–80.

51. Theodore Sedgwick to Alexander Hamilton, 17 Feb. 1799, in *The Papers of Alexander Hamilton*, ed. Harold C. Syrett et al., 27 vols. (New York, 1961–81), 22:488.

52. *Joel Barlow to His Fellow Citizens, of the United States of America. Letter I*, 37–38, 39.

53. TJ, first inaugural address, 4 Mar. 1801, in *TJP*, 33:150.

Elizabeth Patterson Bonaparte
A Woman between Two Worlds

CHARLENE BOYER LEWIS

The decades after 1800 were a period of uncertainty and anxiety. "*Four* memorable evils" still threatened the "unexampled *freedom*" of the republic, warned Thomas Ritchie, the editor of the Richmond *Enquirer,* in 1806: "war," "party spirit," disunion, and "luxury."[1] Each of these "evils" appeared at one time or another in the first two decades of the nineteenth century. Scholars have fully examined the divisions of the first party system and the diplomatic challenges that culminated in the War of 1812. And they have recently turned more serious attention to the fears of disunion.[2] But they have had very little to say about the widespread concerns about luxury and Americans' complex ideas regarding this particular evil.

Unlike their colonial and Revolutionary ancestors, early nineteenth-century Americans were no longer ambivalent about refinement.[3] For most men and women, refinement was acceptable, even necessary, for the new republic. It gave polish—and legitimacy—to republican society and those ladies and gentlemen who led it. But luxury corrupted. Luxury threatened the republican experiment, since it could, in Ritchie's words, "unnerve the zeal that would watch over the public welfare."[4] By 1800 Americans had made a distinction between refined manners and ideas, which were suitable for the republic, and corrupting behaviors and thoughts, which threatened to bring on the evils of luxury. Though their colonial forebears had drawn directly upon the English gentry for their ideas about refinement, early nineteenth-century Americans explicitly linked luxury with aristocratic behavior, ideas, and objects and regarded aristocratic luxury as the opposite of a desirable republican simplicity. By the early 1800s Americans had combined their definitions of refinement with feelings of nationalism. While refined manners and minds may have drawn upon courtly antecedents, good republicans would no longer celebrate them as such. It seems that elite Americans had agreed to reject aristocratic luxury and laud republican simplicity as the focus of refinement. Indeed, they would create an *American* version of refinement. Courtly ways would still have a place, but it would be a limited one. Americans concurred that refinement should and would work to celebrate the nation, not the European court.

As Americans of the early nineteenth century struggled to decide just what constituted "American" character and culture, they necessarily did so in a transatlantic context. In spite of their political independence, the image of "Europe," not specifically London, still stood as the center of culture and fashion for Americans. While they constructed their culture and their national identity, and even while they traveled in Europe, Americans sought to redefine the old, colonial division of American provincial and European metropolitan. Europe remained the yardstick by which Americans measured their cultural attainments—and they often suffered feelings of inferiority when they did so. But for Americans, Europe also represented corrupting luxury. When they thought about the nature of American character and culture, many Americans feared the corrupting influence of European individuals, manners, and ideas; many dreaded that American culture might replicate that of monarchical Europe.

Given Americans' deep concerns over the dangers of luxury to the new nation, women, who had long been linked to fashion and luxury, seemed especially worrisome. They could mislead men through their public roles as conveyors of refinement or, even worse, reward aristocratic fops instead of virtuous republican suitors by agreeing to marry them.[5] Yet, scholars have paid little attention to women's influence on American culture in this era. Judith Sargent Murray, Susanna Rowson, and a few others from the 1780s and 1790s who contributed to the ideals of republican motherhood have received some attention. And women who influenced the culture of the nation's capital, whether in New York, Philadelphia, or Washington, have been addressed thoroughly and creatively.[6] In a broader sense, however, women have been relatively absent from the historiography of the creation of a national culture in the new republic. Before and especially after 1800, women, at least elite women, fully participated in these cultural debates and greatly influenced the formation of a national identity. Culture, even political culture, as many historians have persuasively argued, is a public realm shared by men *and* women. In drawing rooms, dining rooms, ballrooms, and even the halls of government power, American men and women engaged in strident debates over the place of aristocratic ways in the new nation's culture.

During the early decades of the nineteenth century one woman in particular served as a lightning rod for those who feared that aristocratic excess threatened republican culture. Elizabeth Patterson Bonaparte not only contributed to the debates over the correct forms for American society and culture but also became a subject of these debates. She was a threat on multiple levels. Her marriage to Napoleon Bonaparte's youngest brother, Jerome, in 1803 gave her strong connections to the most powerful man in Europe. Furthermore, their child, Jerome Napoleon Bonaparte, was potentially in line for a European throne. Divorced from Jerome by Napoleon in 1806, Elizabeth became a "manless woman" who nevertheless remained a very public character. She wore dresses that not only proclaimed her preference for European fashions but also scandalized polite American society. And her European experiences and sensibilities led her to find fault with many aspects of her native land and society, which she openly criticized in elite circles both at home and abroad. She believed that a monarchy was superior to a republic. She despised the increasing democratization of America and longed for the strict social hierarchies of Europe. Compared with the excitement and elegance of European circles, she found American society insipid and stagnant, lacking in "imagination, feeling, taste, [and] intelligence."[7] Because of her aristocratic ways and ties, Elizabeth was not content—nor fit, according to her detractors—to play the role of republican wife. Indeed, the French imperial image that she cultivated, even as her country labored to shape a new republican culture, and her French connections, particularly her potentially imperial son, led family members, society matrons, and congressmen to seek ways to neutralize her power—even to the point of a constitutional amendment.

Elizabeth was a true celebrity, one of the first female celebrities in the United States. She captured and cultivated public attention with her ultra-fashionable clothes and glamorous Bonaparte connections. As a woman with a public persona, she became the controversial subject of debates over the meanings of respectable refinement and aristocratic luxury. She existed, even flourished, at the boundaries of acceptable behavior for her class, thereby helping Americans define their national culture and character. She avidly played the role of the cosmopolite for Americans who were struggling to overcome their cultural provincialism as their nation gained political status in the transatlantic world. Since she unashamedly represented the metropolis of Europe for them, Elizabeth gained both social power and condemnation. She personified not only everything that Americans admired and envied but also everything they feared and denigrated about Europe. Many, therefore, adored her, but many also found her a threat to the republic, and some even sought to subdue her. Elizabeth's movements between countries and cultures as she actively sought to construct a transatlantic life that blended what she thought was the best of both American and European ways created sharp contradictions in her life. But her personal choices became political ones as Americans analyzed and judged her in this era of fierce cultural debate.

In 1803 Elizabeth Patterson, the eldest daughter of one of Baltimore's wealthiest merchants, met and married Jerome Bonaparte, Napoleon's youngest brother and a lieutenant in the French navy. Eighteen months later they had a son. Elizabeth envisioned a beautiful and brilliant future for herself and Jerome at Napoleon's grand court or even in their own kingdom, but Napoleon dashed her dreams. She quickly found her marriage repudiated by Napoleon, whose dynastic visions for his brother only increased after he crowned himself emperor in December 1804. When Jerome and a pregnant Elizabeth arrived in Lisbon in April 1805, the emperor refused to see Jerome's "little girl," as he called her, even though she carried a possible imperial heir.[8]

After spending a few days in Lisbon with Elizabeth and reassuring her of his undying love and fidelity, Jerome left, under an armed escort, to plead their case with Napoleon. She would not see him again for decades. In August she delivered their son alone in England. By September she had given up any hope that Jerome would send for her and returned to the United States. She had gambled on a happy and exciting future in imperial France and lost. In 1806 Napoleon formally annulled the marriage so that Jerome could marry the Princess of Wurttemberg and become king of Westphalia. Elizabeth never became a queen, but she insisted on using the name Bonaparte for the rest of her life. She never remarried, refusing to let go of this prestigious French connection.

At the end of 1805 a dejected Madame Bonaparte returned to her father's house in Baltimore with her young son, but she would never feel truly American. She found herself caught between two worlds, living in the one she hated and excluded from the one she desired. She would have to negotiate as satisfactory a place as possible for herself and her son. Her low opinion of republican government and society ensured that she would always remain an outsider, though a celebrated one. Elizabeth adored Dolley Madison, the highest female representation of republican society at the time, and visited her often at the Executive Mansion. The two shared a love of courtly ways and fashion. But Madison sought to give distinction to the presidency and the republic, while Elizabeth simply preferred European over American modes, choosing clothes, jewelry, furniture, and even a husband in the Continental style.[9] Both Madison and Elizabeth would construct female public roles, but they did so in very different ways. Elizabeth eschewed anything American, considering the place and its ways too provincial, and embraced the metropolis of Europe. She turned her back on her American upbringing and reinvented herself as a cosmopolitan. Whether in the capital or at home in Baltimore (and later in Continental circles), Elizabeth boldly flaunted her French connections, modeled herself after European aristocrats, and maintained her place as one of the most fashionable and influential women in the new nation, even after her infamous divorce.

In spite of the scandal that she caused, Elizabeth continued to attract attention and, more importantly, to construct her social and political identity as a cosmopolitan by wearing the French fashions she so admired. She returned from Europe in 1805 with an enormous wardrobe of morning dresses, evening gowns, hats, jewelry, and more. In the early nineteenth century, clothing was one of the most visible markers not only of gender and class but also of the wearer's acceptance of, or divergence from, the new nation's ideals. Elizabeth perfectly understood the symbolic power of fashion, and she used it skillfully in creating her "self-narrative," the way in which society was to understand her.[10]

For Elizabeth, early nineteenth-century French fashions perfectly symbolized the freedoms that European women enjoyed. The simple, columnar dress in the Grecian style, with its "empire waist," fell straight from under the breasts and required no tight corset or metal hoops or layers of heavy petticoats (or, on occasion, even underwear). In these dresses women literally enjoyed more freedom to move than they had earlier or would later. Given the real freedom these French dresses allowed and the behavioral freedom they symbolized, it was no surprise that many Americans considered them immoral. In November 1811 Catharine Mitchill reported on the sensation that Elizabeth caused at a presidential dinner, wearing a dress that "exposed so much of her bosom" and "laid bare" her back "nearly half way down to the bottom of her waist." "The state of nudity in which she appeared," Mitchill informed her sister, "attracted the attention of the Gentlemen, for I saw several of them take a look at her bubbies when they were conversing with her."[11]

Elizabeth's clothing made clear how she thought of herself and her place in American society. No one could have misunderstood the message: Elizabeth obviously regarded herself as a member not only of the finest French circles but also of the imperial family into which she had married. The style of her clothing—as well as her decorated coach with liveried footmen—publicly signaled that she had chosen France over the United States, an empire over a republic. These French clothes empowered her, and she wore them with pride, confident that she represented the height of European fashion and nobility. And since she continued wearing them to public functions, she was clearly unconcerned that provincial Americans considered her too daring and immodest. She cultivated an ardently European image, forgoing the republican modesty prescribed for women by many American writers. Though nicknamed "Madame Eve" and cautioned that she "must promise to have more clothes on" or she would not receive social invitations, Elizabeth ignored the warnings, certain that the social and political force of her French connections, including her clothes, would always give her easy admittance into any refined gathering.[12]

While her anti-republican sentiments may not have been followed, her fashions were, even in this period of intermittent Francophobia. Americans simply could not resist the powerful lure of European styles; indeed, despite the paeans to republican simplicity, stylish aristocratic clothing still retained its high status, and Elizabeth wore it so well. In 1813, the year that Elizabeth received an official divorce by legislative decree in Maryland, Sarah Gales Seaton, the wife of the editor of the *National Intelligencer,* declared that "Madame Bonaparte is a model of fashion, and many of our belles strive to imitate her ... but without equal *éclat,* as Madame Bonaparte has certainly the most transcendently beautiful back and shoulders that ever were seen."[13] Elizabeth brazenly led a fashion trend among younger women that many commentators found to be at the very least disturbing, if not threatening to the virtue of the republic. Obviously, not every woman who wore French dresses wanted to signal that she preferred an empire over a republic, but that was the conclusion critical observers reached.

Americans worried about the fragility of the republic and found fashionable French (as well as British) dress and manners threatening, doubly so in the case of women. One newspaper editor pleaded with "the ladies of this country" to reject "the destroying evil" of French fashions and return to "a fashion of dress which should be truly American, healthful and decorous."[14] As Elizabeth well understood, social commentators feared what the dress and behavior represented more than the clothing itself. Nevertheless, her beauty, name, son, clothes, conversation, and, in time, repeated trips to Europe reinforced her cosmopolitan status in the United States and protected her high place in fashionable society.

Paradoxically, however, those very attributes that gained her status and popularity, namely, her French connections, caused others to perceive her as a threat to the entire republican experiment. Elizabeth was affiliated with a European empire—a fact that attracted many and worried others—and had willingly chosen it. Americans may have admired her beauty, style, and courage, but they still found her unsettling; she was just too European in her manners and views, too much the cosmopolitan. In a letter to his wife, Huldah, Waller Holladay gushed over "the charms" and "perfections calculated to captivate the brother of the first Consul," including Elizabeth's "beautiful, well-turned Ancle" and "the more gorgeous display of a breast, luxuriantly rising under the hand of nature." He then conceded, however, that if he were her husband, "I should like to see her contented with a more modest exhibition of her beauties."[15] In response to her husband's flattering—and quite sexual—portrait of Elizabeth, Huldah responded that Madame Bonaparte's celebrated charms were "better calculated to encite momentary admiration, than lasting respect and admiration," since she was "deficient in modesty & female delicacy." And couching her comments in terms of American simplicity versus European debauchery, Huldah further concluded that Elizabeth was "no doubt *charming* in the eyes of a *French*man" but would be better off in Paris, "where the manners & customs of people would be quite congenial to her taste."[16]

Some Americans came to see Elizabeth's dramatic life as one that might tempt other young women. Across the nation, even deep into the interior, young women could read about her romantic exploits with Jerome and her rocky relationship with Napoleon.[17] Worried Americans publicly regarded Elizabeth as an unacceptable model for the republic in terms of both gender and citizenship. Poems that simultaneously praised her beauty and questioned her republicanism (and modesty) quietly circulated among the elite; some even appeared in newspapers. After one party at which she wore a very sheer French-styled dress that "threw all the company into confusion," Thomas Law wrote a poem proclaiming that Elizabeth's "lustful looks" and "bosom bare" made her "ill suitted for the life / Of a Columbians modest wife."[18] Another ode admired the "charms which deck thy form" and "the graces of thy soul" but then linked her with a "despotic empire."[19] Echoing the ambivalence of others, newspaper articles celebrated her beauty, acknowledged the importance of her European connections, and even came to her defense on occasion. Boston's *Columbian Centinel,* for example, took great affront at Napoleon's rejection of a woman who was "of superior rank and virtue" to most of the "little low Corsican-born we know not of whom" Bonapartes.[20] But at other times editors attacked her vanity and questioned her appropriateness for a republic.[21] Like elites in the capital and elsewhere, these editors responded to her with a mix of admiration and disdain as they judged her impact on American society, revealing as well their persistent provincialism and their struggles to overcome it.

Just a few years after her return to America, Elizabeth became the center

Fig. 1. *Elizabeth Patterson Bonaparte*, 1823, by Firmin Massot. (Courtesy of Maryland Historical Society)

of a serious debate not in genteel drawing rooms but in Congress. By the summer of 1809 rumors swirled in Washington, Baltimore, Philadelphia, and other parts of the United States that Napoleon intended to make his brother's former wife a duchess. Napoleon had handed out dozens of titles after crowning himself emperor, turning commoners into nobles, so the granting of a title itself was not surprising. But letters, newspapers, and parlors were abuzz for months as everyone wondered whether the emperor would actually bestow such a title on an *American* woman living in their midst. Since the summer of 1808 Elizabeth and Napoleon had corresponded through Louis Marie Turreau, the French minister to the United States, about her son Jerome, the possibility of an annuity for his education and other expenses, and a title befitting her station. By mid-1809 Napoleon, impressed with her confidence and savvy, had ordered Turreau to arrange an annual pension of 60,000 francs (about $12,000 dollars) for Elizabeth and her son until they could return to Europe.[22] No promises were made regarding a title, but at some point Napoleon or Turreau mentioned the possibility of her becoming the Duchess of Oldenburg.

Throughout the fall of 1809 and early 1810, as more and more people discovered that Elizabeth Patterson Bonaparte had contacted the emperor and would indeed accept an annuity and title if they were offered to her, the rumors reached a crescendo. Even abroad, Americans demanded news about the possible Duchess of Baltimore. From Stockholm, John Spear Smith wondered whether the rumors were true. Sally McKean Yrujo, wife of the former Spanish minister, informed Dolley Madison that there was gossip about the tantalizing story even in Rio de Janeiro.[23] The arrival of Colonel M. Toussard from France, under orders from Napoleon to attend both Elizabeth and her son "in their official characters," as one newspaper reported in mid-November 1809, made the matter seem a fait accompli.[24] A member of the French nobility had been established in Baltimore, which was to be "the *Imperial and Royal residence* for the present."[25] "No doubt [was] entertained" any longer of "the Creation of the Dutchess and Prince, by the Emperor Napoleon," an article noted as it announced a trip of the "Dutchess of Baltimore (Mrs Jerome Bonaparte)" and "the young Prince" to "honour" Philadelphia "with their August presence."[26] A visitor to Philadelphia notified another newspaper that while he had initially thought the paper's "publication of the New Nobility" "nothing but a joke," he was "now certain it is true."[27]

After much public and private gossiping, curiosity began to develop into real concern. Gossips passed the rumors along as truth, and concern over Napoleon's plans for this new nobility flourished. By conferring on "Madame Jerome the title of Duchess of the House of Napoleon and her son Prince of the French Empire" as well as "an annuity of forty thousand crowns," the "Emperor Napoleon" afforded Philadelphia not only a "great field for conversation" but also "*much apprehension of french influence.*"[28] The newspapers echoed these concerns. Federalist newspaper editors, long convinced of French influence over the Republicans, leapt at the opportunity to detail the dire consequences of these *American* members of Napoleon's court. One prophesied that not only would Napoleon regain Louisiana but "the little limb of French royalty at Baltimore" would reign as "The Emperor of the West." Another predicted that "*all of America* would fall to monarchical tyranny." Republican editors fought back, calling Federalist claims "nonsense" and drolly asking, "What court officers would 'the puissant little baby' require? A Master of the Rocking Horse?" They insisted that administration officials could not be held responsible "for a [marital] connection which they neither sought nor promoted," for, as everyone knew, "women will bestow their hearts and their hands where they please."[29]

While Republican editors tried to downplay Federalist fears and present the potential American duchess and her child prince as harmless, they could not ignore a geopolitical context that made the prospect of a titled nobility tied to Napoleon living in the United States a real concern. The tremendous anxiety many policymakers felt over the future of Spanish America intensified the problem of the American Bonapartes. Napoleon's decision to place his brother Joseph on the Spanish throne in 1808 had ignited American fears. If Spain's colonies remained loyal to the new king, Napoleon would gain a powerful foothold in the New World, one that extended to the uncertain southern and western borders of the United States.[30] Elizabeth and her son, therefore, could easily have seemed part of a larger Bonapartist incursion into the Western Hemisphere.

Even though Elizabeth had confided to a few friends that "tho' Napoleon supports them now," "neither she or her son ... has a title yet,"[31] the fear of Napoleon's influence through the two soon spread beyond snippets in newspapers, letters, and drawing rooms to Congress itself, engaging some of the preeminent statesmen of the era. On January 18, 1810, the Republican senator Philip Reed of Maryland introduced a resolution calling for an amendment to the Constitution that became known as the "Titles of Nobility Amendment." The proposal that emerged from the committee for Senate consideration in late January stated that either the acceptance of a title or marriage "with any descendant of any emperor, king or prince, or with any person of the blood royal" would cost a person "the rights and immunities of a free citizen of the U.S."[32] The committee had targeted two of Elizabeth's betrayals of the republic. By mid-February a revision to the proposed amendment had added her third: no citizen could accept a present, office, or *pension* from "any emperor, king, prince or foreign state."[33] Clearly, this amendment meant to neutralize the domestic and diplomatic threat presented by Elizabeth and her son.

Legal historians have long debated the motivation for the proposed Titles of Nobility Amendment. Most agree that "no particular event precipitated the introduction of the amendment." Instead, "the general animosity to foreigners" on the eve of the War of 1812 produced overwhelming support for the proposed amendment in both parties.[34] A few have suggested some link between the amendment and Elizabeth, Jerome, and their son by noting, erroneously, that Jerome himself was in the United States at that time or, correctly, that he had married "a Maryland lady" or, as one scholar called her, "a prostitute."[35] But even these scholars have been quick to dismiss Elizabeth and her son as direct causes, returning to the "animosity toward foreigners" theory as the "more logical explanation."[36] They have drawn this conclusion despite acknowledging the paucity of sources concerning the proposal. Neither the *Annals of Congress* nor contemporary newspapers reported the debates. But a careful examination of the private letters and papers—and one published circular letter—of congressmen make it perfectly clear that the Titles of Nobility Amendment resolution grew out of the fear of Elizabeth, her possibly imperial son, and their potential impact upon the new nation.

Reactions to Elizabeth and her son as powerful symbols of the debate over European luxury and monarchy crossed party lines. Federalists attacked her and so did Republicans. Congressmen in both parties supported the amendment, though for differing reasons. Some regarded Elizabeth as an annoyance causing undue concern. Others grew suspicious of the connections between Elizabeth's uncles Samuel and Robert Smith, a Maryland senator and Madison's secretary of state, respectively, and Napoleon. Still others genuinely believed that the presence of the Duchess of Baltimore and her son meant the downfall of the republic. These people worried that the example of her luxurious, aristocratic lifestyle would corrupt republican citizens. The Republican congressman Richard M. Johnson of Kentucky admitted that "some people" in Washington "effect to be frightened at this infant being allied to Napoleon," since the emperor had no children and his brother Louis's only son was "sickly & not very promising." Johnson proclaimed that he himself feared "neither Napoleon, nor King George nor their power," because Americans' liberties "depend on no such despots, nor their Creatures." But he did seem relieved that the Senate had the "very proper amendment before them ... disfranchising a Citizen who shall accept letters of nobility from Foreign Potentates."[37] In early February 1810 Samuel Taggart, a Federalist congressman from Massachusetts, characterized the visit of "the newly made Dutchess" and her son to Washington as a trip "to familiarize the citizens of America with the view of their future sovreign." Taggart saw a worrisome significance in the willingness of "the heads of department and other gentlemen" of Congress to call on Elizabeth "to pay their respects." He also fretted that the adoration paid her related directly to the "various reports" he had heard "about a projected alliance with

France" of which "some members of Congress . . . [spoke] openly in favour." Taggart wished, as others surely did, that "both she and her offspring were safe in Westphalia" instead of threatening the republic in its capital.[38]

Others were much more alarmed and saw, as General William Eaton had even before the resolution, "political annihilation and voluntary transmigration into reptiles" in Napoleon's plan to make "his well beloved nephew DON JEROME PATTERSON NAPOLEON" into the "*King of these States.*" Only if Americans "put on our armor" and "resist the lure and fraud of a blood stained son of rapine" could they "be loosed from the shackles which depress the nation."[39] Under the pseudonym Mutius the Republican curmudgeon John Randolph of Roanoke published a letter to President James Madison outlining the history of the "beautiful American woman" who had married "the brother of the emperor of France" and seemed "destined again to become (with the unoffending fruit of her womb) the sport of avarice and ambition." As Taggart had hinted, Randolph feared her politically powerful relatives more than he did Elizabeth herself, "the disconsolate mother." Randolph linked Elizabeth's uncles, his hated enemies Samuel and Robert Smith, not only with James Wilkinson and Aaron Burr's plot to sever the West but also with Napoleon's plan "to make use of [Elizabeth's relatives] through his nephew" to "obtain possession of the government of the United States." All the evidence Randolph needed could be found in the fact that just after "Madame Bonaparte" had been "created a duchess, and her son a prince of the empire," "the councils of the United States after a momentary fluctuation accommodate themselves, at once, to the views of France!" "The inference," according to Randolph, "is irresistible."[40]

Senator Timothy Pickering, the staunch Federalist from Massachusetts, never doubted that Elizabeth and her son were directly responsible for the proposed amendment. "Every one's eye is doubtless turned to the case of Mrs. Bonaparte and her son," began his notes for a speech in support of the amendment. According to Pickering, many believed that little Jerome was "undoubtedly" "destined by his imperial uncle to a throne," perhaps even to become "the imperial successor." Since "neither [Elizabeth's] ambition nor her maternal affection [would] permit her son to be torn from her & carried to France," the two were expected to remain in the United States or go to France together. Pickering and other senators feared that "a lady of this character" and her "so connected" son could not "with safety be allowed to reside within the United States" and desired that the amendment be expanded to prohibit persons "of imperial or royal blood" from residing in the United States. In his musings over possible objections to the resolution, he asked: "What danger can arise in a republic from the residence of a solitary woman & her child?" His answer was, "Much every way." Pickering may not have been speaking for all who supported the resolution, but he clearly believed that "this member of the imperial family & his mother" posed a threat to "Republican Government." The first step toward disaster had come when Elizabeth received "the homage of the officers & representatives of this nation." The next step in Napoleon's diabolical plan, according to Pickering, was "the establishment of a Court, which in splendour, [would] outshine, & in expences & attentions, surpass, the palace of the first magistrate of our nation." Then, Pickering argued logically, "our eyes are to be introduced to the gorgeous scenes of royalty . . . till at length, seduced & corrupted by the charms . . . & the promises of royalty, the citizens of these republican states are to be prepared to receive a king." Elizabeth and her son would be the beginning of the end of a republican United States. He "entertain[ed]" no doubt that Napoleon had "already contemplated the erection of a throne in Washington on which his nephew is to be placed." "Such expectations," Pickering concluded, "should receive no countenance from our forbearance."[41] For Pickering, the republic would not fall to an aristocracy of power if the Constitution was enforced to protect Americans against examples of aristocratic lifestyles.

In its final form the proposed amendment read: "If any citizen of the United States shall accept, claim, receive, or retain any title of nobility or honour, or shall without the consent of Congress, accept and retain any present, pension, office or emolument of any kind whatever, from any EMPEROR, KING, PRINCE or foreign POWER, such person shall cease to be a citizen of the United States and shall be incapable of holding any office of trust or profit under them, or either of them."[42] It easily passed the Senate on April 26 and the House of Representatives on May 1, 1810.

Even after the amendment passed Congress and was sent to the states for ratification, Elizabeth did not curtail her aristocratic behavior (though she still did not have her title). At parties in Washington she acted the part of the duchess at court, wearing "the most superb dress" Robert Bayly had "ever beheld" and "a crown on her head sent by the emperor of France, which . . . cost $15000." In such regal attire she reminded Bayly "very much of Burke's description of the Queen of France."[43] "*The pretty little Duchess of Baltimore*" outshone "all the Ladies here for the splendour and elegance of her dress," Catharine Mitchill believed, "even Mrs. M[adison] cannot sport Dimonds and pearls in such profusion."[44] Is it any wonder that so many saw her as capable of seducing American citizens into becoming subjects with such "gorgeous scenes of royalty"? Her public conversation matched her appearance. Far from assuming a retiring pose during the firestorm of debate, Elizabeth flaunted her connections to imperial blood as well as her cosmopolitan clout. In November 1811 Samuel Smith reported to his daughter that her cousin "Madame B." "laughs and talks, defends the Emperor and hopes he will destroy all his enemies."[45] Instead of feeling cowed or embarrassed by the proposed amendment, Elizabeth considered it "injurious to my future prospects and vexatious in every point of view." Though she had thought about "seeking to avert its future pernicious consequences," "after mature consideration," she decided "to see it pass into effect."[46] And although Elizabeth and her French connections had instilled fear in many and terror in some, Delaware's George B. Milligan noted the effect that she still had in Washington in 1812: "Sover[eigns] seem to send their ambassadors here less to negotiate with the Government than to pay their adoration to her," while "the wise legislators of the nation (Senator & representatives) seem to have forgotten their errand to the capitol & their wives at home to pour forth their admiration to her beauty."[47] Her aristocratic credentials and pretensions had gotten her into trouble with Congress and staid matrons, but they still made her powerful in polite circles. Her behavior may have been condemned by some and regarded as threatening by others, but ultimately her role as a cosmopolitan—the personification of European culture and fashion—proved to be more powerful. Americans continued to admire her, not shun her, as they continued to admire European aristocratic culture and not shun it. Elizabeth hovered at the boundaries of acceptable refined behavior, but neither her divorce, her scanty clothing, nor even a movement in Congress directed at her personally for wanting to be an aristocrat could bring down the woman so many admired.

Luckily for Elizabeth, the amendment failed. From late 1810 to early 1811 six states rushed to ratify the amendment, and six more had done so by the end of 1812. Then the momentum dwindled just two states short of ratification.[48] The War of 1812, Napoleon's downfall, and Elizabeth's departure for Europe at war's end dissipated the initial support for the amendment, though for decades many assumed that it had become the thirteenth amendment.

After Elizabeth left the United States in 1815, when Napoleon's final defeat allowed her to travel to Europe with little fear of imperial reprisal, her name appeared less frequently in newspapers, and people gossiped less frequently about the Duchess of Baltimore and her French connections. But during her lengthy stay in Europe, Elizabeth's conversation and writings about Americans and their society took on an intensity they had not had previously.

Before 1815, Americans had made her the subject of much scrutiny and judgment; after 1815, she scrutinized and judged Americans.

Among elite Americans, it was not uncommon for women to make one or two trips to Europe. Elizabeth ultimately crossed the Atlantic eight times. Her 1805 trip with Jerome provided her first glimpse of the Continent. While she never enjoyed the desired audience with Napoleon, what she experienced on that six-month trip confirmed her belief that women with her qualities belonged in the glittering and convivial salons of Europe, not the insipid and simple parlors of America. Her desperate need to be at the center of fashionable aristocratic life, not the furor over the amendment, had propelled her to the Continent in 1815. As she prepared for an exclusive ball in England during her second trip in 1815, she assured her father: "I get on extremely well, and I assure you that altho' you have always taken me for a fool, it is not my character here. In America I appeared more simple than I am, because I was completely out of my element. It was my misfortune, not my fault, that I was born in a country which was not congenial to my desires. Here I am completely in my sphere . . . and in contact with modes of life for which nature intended me."[49]

In the nineteen years from the summer of 1815 to the summer of 1834, when she returned to Baltimore to meet her three-year-old grandson, Elizabeth spent just three years in the United States. Her antipathy toward American society, politics, and culture colored her letters throughout these years. But those from 1815 and 1816 offer especially eloquent testimony to her thinking about her relationship with the American republic and her fellow countrymen and to the still open question whether a republic without aristocratic elements was desirable. Her social successes in the most brilliant European circles never astonished Elizabeth. Knowing that she was destined for such environments, she expected to move within them easily. Her expert cultivation of her cosmopolitan image in the United States served her well on the Continent. Drawing on her talents, Elizabeth became a transatlantic celebrity after 1815. In France, England, Switzerland, and Italy aristocrats, artists, writers, socialites of all kinds, and even members of the exiled Bonaparte family sought her company, admired her, and appreciated her qualities. An American who returned from Paris in 1816 described Elizabeth's "doors as surrounded[,] Stairs thronged with Dukes, Counts, Marquis, [her]self as a little Queen, giving & receiving the most supreme happiness."[50] The fashionable French, including Madame Récamier and Voltaire's protégé the Marchioness de Villette, embraced her as one of their own and hoped to assuage some of the pains that their former ruler had caused her. Though normally cautious with regard to American visitors, they opened their doors to her and befriended her. Elizabeth was finally in her proper element.

Returning to Europe after 1815 allowed Elizabeth to take advantage of a new Europe, where the old lines of wealth and aristocratic prestige had been scrambled. The Atlantic world of the early 1800s had been transformed, first by revolution and then by Napoleon. When Elizabeth finally made her long-awaited trip to France, social hierarchies had been redrawn, though not in completely new ways. Aristocrats who possessed grand estates still dominated society, but the definition of who constituted an aristocrat had been rewritten. Long-lined aristocrats now mingled, intermarried, and shared social and economic power with aristocrats of much more recent vintage. That it was a new aristocratic world mattered little to Elizabeth. She cared little if the aristocrats with whom she socialized were not of the old guard, with little or no lineage, and had been plucked by Napoleon out of obscurity and put into the aristocracy. In fact, this new order made her entrée and claims to status even easier. The welcoming reception that she received there reinforced the privileged views she held of herself and her idea of Europe, as well as her negative views of America as hopelessly provincial.

Traveling to Europe offered elite American women a unique opportunity to contribute directly to the debate over the nature of American culture in the early republic. Though devoted to their own country, some of these traveling women attempted to use their ties to and experiences with European aristocratic ways to influence or improve the new nation's character. In the 1790s the renowned American salonnière Anne Bingham, for example, recreated French modes of entertaining at her Philadelphia mansion in an attempt to impart a certain cultivated style to the ruling class of the new republic.[51] Indeed, many genteel American women, especially those who had seen Europe, chose this public role as their special province, controlling "polite society" in the early republic. "Polite society" was public in the sense that it inhabited a realm outside of the household and the family. While not overtly political, it was not domestic and private. Therefore, women's involvement in and, indeed, control over this social arena made them public figures in their own right. Men granted them control, regarding refinement as a natural characteristic of women and crediting women with leading mankind's progression from a rude to a civilized state.[52] Ironically, then, women's long-standing association with luxury gave them power in the public cultural arena of polite society. Their gender and their class supported these women's concerns with fashion and manners and encouraged their cultural "borrowing" from Europe. First Ladies Elizabeth Monroe and Louisa Catherine Adams, each of whom had spent several years at various Continental courts, saw the adoption of some European ways at the Executive Mansion as a means of giving grandeur and authority to the nation's capital, of bringing refinement—in a European sense—to the rude capital.[53] This was what good republican women were supposed to do in the late eighteenth and early nineteenth centuries. They were expected to prefer the United States and its forms of government and society to any other country's and to work, both at home and in society, to improve the republic and its citizens. For American women who had traveled abroad, their efforts at improvement often included adapting European aristocratic forms of refinement to an American milieu.

Like other elite American women travelers, Elizabeth "participated actively and creatively in [the] debate about national character and destiny."[54] But she stood on the opposite side from most of them. Elizabeth never used her European experiences to help mold republican culture; instead, they formed the basis upon which she denigrated it. Her anti-Americanism intensified with every trip abroad. On her travels she saw only the positive aspects of aristocratic European culture and the negative ones of republican American culture. Unlike Anne Bingham or Elizabeth Monroe, Elizabeth never tried to bring the metropolis to the provinces, to recreate a Parisian salon in her American dining room or parlor, though she possessed all the requisite "aristocratic" attributes of beauty, wealth, ease, "droll maxims, uncommon eloquence, and an admirable fund of new things to say."[55] The American situation, in her opinion, was simply too hopeless. Americans knew nothing of the art of living. "The waste of life which takes place with us shut up in our melancholy Country Houses where we vegetate for months alone is happily not endured here [in Paris]," she informed her cousin in 1816. "Those long, wearisome winter Evenings varied only by the entrance of the Tea Equipage, mending the Fire & handing round apples & nuts do not form any part of the 12 months in happy, wise France. No Family ever spends an evening without society."[56] A cosmopolitan salon of refinement, grace, and intelligence was an impossibility in the land of "apples & nuts," she believed. Living lives on the periphery, American men and women lacked the required elegance and wit. The men were too focused on their business affairs and the women on their children to discuss genteel subjects. Moreover, she professed, in what was probably an allusion to her father's household, that "all people living in the same house with each other" could never "be society for each other." After a while, "they exhaust their topics, their curiosity, their activity of intercourse, and nothing but ennui and contention remains."[57] Instead of trying to recreate her European experiences in America, she drew upon them flatly and openly to condemn the republican experiment. When at home in Baltimore or even in Washington, Elizabeth was as much in exile as any of the Bonapartes.

In Europe, especially in Paris, Elizabeth found the social and political life superior in almost every way to that of her homeland. She criticized not only the lack of true refinement in American culture but also the direction in which the United States, its society, and, above all, its gender roles and expectations were headed in its early decades. Like some other American travelers, including James Fenimore Cooper on occasion, Elizabeth disparaged American society for being too democratic and disorderly. She saw little merit in a republican government or society based upon ideas of equality, liberty, and popular participation and never hesitated to share her views with friends and family. She found it entirely impossible, she informed her father, "to be contented in a country where there exists no nobility."[58] Refined republicans were not enough. Her admiration for Napoleon's empire never waned, not even when he shunned her and deprived her of a husband, and her son of a father. Her only criticism was that he had "hurled me back on what I most hated on earth—my Baltimore obscurity."[59] Even then, she fully understood that Napoleon had acted for his empire. It was Jerome she hated, intensely and until she died, for not fighting for her and finding some way for her too to be made a part of the grand imperial court. When Napoleon's empire crumbled, she took solace in the restoration of the Bourbon monarchy; when her beloved France threw off its king and became a republic again in 1848, she despaired. To a friend who assumed that she would be delighted that the French people had elected her nephew, the future Napoleon III, as president of the new republic, she replied that it would have been more to their credit to have elected him emperor (which he became in 1852, to Elizabeth's great joy).[60]

Not surprisingly, Elizabeth's criticisms frequently targeted the situation of women in the United States. Having witnessed her mother's submissiveness and read Mary Wollstonecraft's and Germaine de Staël's views about women's rights, the equality of the sexes, and companionate marriage surely influenced her as a young woman and earned her a reputation for being "modern."[61] Her choice of a husband and many of the subsequent decisions she made about her life made it clear that she did not want to live within the gender expectations of the new nation. She rejoiced, for example, in having only one child, "never having envied any one the honor of being a mother of a family, which is generally a thankless position."[62] Like some other women of her class, she could not abide the increasingly circumscribed role assigned to women as republican mothers.[63] And she recoiled from the idea, which became increasingly popular as the century progressed, that women's modesty, morality, and piety made them uniquely suited to the domestic realm instead of the public world. Babies, in her opinion, only ruined a woman's appearance and rendered mothers thoroughly uninteresting. Salons, balls, and dinners—not firesides and nurseries—were, she strongly believed, the appropriate arenas for a woman with her cosmopolitan qualities. "I can never be satisfied in America. It was always my misfortune to be unfitted for the modes of existence there, nor can I return to them without a sacrifice of all I value on earth."[64] Though she took a different course, Elizabeth, like Anne Bingham or Louisa Catherine Adams, desired and actively pursued broader "cultural horizons" (though not political ones) than American society allowed most wives and mothers in this era.[65]

Elizabeth's travels to Europe exposed her to a different set of women's roles, as well as to alternative beliefs about women. European women could think and act (and dress) in ways outside of the social prescriptions for American women in the early 1800s. In France, Elizabeth believed, women knew how to be women—attractive, intelligent, interesting, and entertaining—and not simply wives and mothers. In spite of the legal and political restrictions placed on them by the Napoleonic Code, elite French women were allowed a great deal of independence in thought and action. The gender roles and expectations of European aristocrats, Elizabeth believed, encouraged women to express not just their opinions but their real selves. For Elizabeth, the true role for women, at least those with her background, was to promote sociability, and the European circles in which she moved seemed to assign women that role instead of a mostly domestic one. As a socialite or hostess, a refined woman brought together and eased the distinctions between the public and private worlds in her drawing room, dining room, and ballroom. As a few of her female American counterparts discovered, these women exerted cultural, if not political, power and garnered a good deal more social independence than most American women.[66] The French fashions that Elizabeth preferred simply reinforced these views of women's social freedom. Her exposure to European views of women allowed her to conceive of a life very different from that expected of most elite American women, but it was her legal status as a divorcée that gave her the uncommon luxury of actually living that different life. With no man holding legal control over her and with sufficient wealth, she truly was an independent woman, though she never felt so. Ultimately, her strong hatred of the United States probably derived mainly from its gender limitations and principally in cultural, not political or legal, terms. In Europe she saw these limitations weakened, and she thus chose to embrace the European version of womanhood. After her second trip to Europe, she formulated a definition of "happiness for a woman": "to be handsome, to be a wit, to have a fortune, to live in Paris, and to have the freedom of the houses of the best circles there."[67]

Whether her preference for European modes of gender roles and relations reflected a larger criticism of women's place in American society or whether she simply appreciated the freedoms elite women like herself found there is difficult to discern from her extant writings. Her class and gender intertwined in her reactions to American and European society. Her dissatisfaction with the United States, however, seems to have come more from her personal frustration with the social limitations placed on women with her qualities than from a larger sense of gender injustice. Her writings do not reveal a woman dedicated to any general notion of women's rights but rather a woman who firmly believed in her personal right to decide her own course of life and then follow it. Her pleasure with Europe came from the individual freedoms that she found there, but she also clearly acknowledged the benefits of European gender norms, as she understood them, for women's place in general. Her comments about motherhood, marriage, and women's key roles in refinement reflect a clear and coherent analysis of the limitations of American definitions of womanhood. Furthermore, the European women that she most admired, and with whom she formed friendships, were famous writers and thinkers, such as the Irish novelist Lady Sidney Morgan, the Marquise de Villette, and Madame de Staël, women who had stepped beyond even the bounds of European womanhood. As Elizabeth grew older, she thought more about the place of women in American as opposed to European, especially French, society and about the nature of marriage, but she continued to criticize the United States and praise Europe. Her dashed dreams only made her more pessimistic over the years.

By never remarrying and living in Europe for years at a time, Elizabeth managed, at least to some degree, to remove herself from American gender expectations. Unlike the vast majority of women in the United States (or in Europe), she was a wealthy woman in charge of her own financial affairs, had full control over her son, and could live how and where she wished. Given this extraordinary independence, the virulence with which she denounced the United States and its prescribed gender roles seems surprising. Few women—or even men—expressed such bitter anti-Americanism and such scathing commentary on gender relations and the republic. Her strident views made her highly unusual for this era, placing her far outside the majority of American women and even distinguishing her from those few who did criticize women's roles, such as Judith Sargent Murray and Mercy Otis

Warren.[68] These critics may have disliked the place of women in American society, but they did not hate their country. Perhaps Elizabeth's virulence reflected a struggle within herself about rejecting the accustomed paths for American women of republican wife and mother. She had been raised as a republican woman in a strongly patriotic Baltimore household and had chosen to become French and aristocratic. Her comments reveal her antipathy not only to the idea of republican motherhood but also, and more importantly, the social pressures on elite women to conform to American notions of womanhood. Most women accepted these notions, however much they privately resented them. Elizabeth, in contrast, chose to break from this expected conformity. She did not have a husband for whom she could play the dutiful wife, and her hostile relationship with her father foreclosed the role of dutiful daughter. She took motherhood seriously but had no desire to be a "republican mother." She expended all of her energies—and a great deal of her money—on raising her son in such a way as to make him suitable for a monarchy or empire, not a republic. Jerome spoke French fluently, became a Catholic, and received part of his education at a private school in Geneva. Perhaps Elizabeth's harsh condemnations were a form of defense. Women simply were not supposed to act or feel as she did. At the very least, their actions or criticisms were not supposed to be so public. Though she never wrote anything for publication or even circulation, she never shied from voicing her views in letters to family or friends, both in the United States and in Europe, or at dinner parties on the Continent or in Baltimore, New York, or even Washington. Her anti-American sentiments were well known among many of the nation's wealthy and powerful.

As a woman fully in control of her own life and not content to play the role of the modest lady, Elizabeth represented a very threatening form of new woman at a time when men were growing "anxious about out-of-control women."[69] Unlike other elite women who eschewed republican motherhood, Elizabeth had also forgone the role of wife. She was a "manless" woman, a rarity in early nineteenth-century America. And that, combined with her own steady income, gave her a great deal of independence compared with other women of her class. The unconventional choices she had made during her life certainly flew in the face of the growing nationalism of the era and the growing domestication of ideal womanhood. Consequently, she found herself regularly attacked by family members, especially her father, and neighbors for violating gender norms and embracing aristocratic French ways. Furthermore, her complete dissatisfaction with the United States was shocking to her contemporaries, men and women who enthusiastically supported and firmly believed in republican ideals and the promising future of their new nation. Her old friend Eliza Godefroy, wife of the architect Maximilian Godefroy, scolded Elizabeth in 1817 for being "so impolite as to abuse your own country as you do." Though each woman knew "Love of Country" was "a fashionable cant" of the era, Elizabeth's comments had been regarded as "nothing less than treason." "All the Americans come back" from Europe "furious against you," Godefroy reported. "Be witty as you will," she warned, "but for God's sake chuse some other subject or I am afraid if you ever come back you will share the fate of Ovid amongst the Goths."[70] But Elizabeth had found a society that valued her particular ideas about women and admired the qualities that she possessed, qualities unsuitable for a republic and its notions of proper womanhood.

While Elizabeth occasionally "deplore[d] the absence of American friends [who could] witness the estimation in which I am held," she socialized with only a select few of the Americans who did visit in Europe, including John Jacob Astor and the Gallatins.[71] "My object is French Society," she wrote to her cousin in 1816. She stayed as far away as possible from her provincial "compatriots," who tended to congregate together rather than visit "in either French or English Houses," as she did.[72] She quickly comprehended that American travelers often sought to use her to gain admittance to select gatherings. But not wanting to be linked with boorish Americans, she refused to play this role. American visitors had looked to Elizabeth, their own cosmopolitan role model, to serve as the gatekeeper to the exclusive circles of European aristocrats. She found it offensive, however, that visiting Americans considered her "business in Paris to be Introductrice des Americains." "Not being paid by the United States for so troublesome a place," she noted, "I declined the honour & ceremonies of the Office & left my fellow travelers to present themselves in the societies of Paris." This infuriated a number of Americans, who, upon returning home, spread the word about how "very ungrateful & unamiable" Elizabeth Patterson Bonaparte had become. She little heeded the criticisms of her fellow Americans, however. She had been granted access to the centers of culture and fashion, and once she entered, she had jettisoned her own provincial ties. But her achievement would have been threatened if she had regularly played the role of "introductrice" and let more than a handful of worthy Americans into that circle.

Furthermore, she knew the real reason why visitors wanted to enter aristocratic circles. Elite Americans traveled for the cachet a trip to Europe would gain them at home, and they knew that socializing with a few aristocrats would gain them even more cultural capital upon their return. That is why so many of them desperately wanted Elizabeth to get them access to aristocratic circles. But by the second and third decades of the nineteenth century American travelers were also using a trip to Europe to develop or deepen their sense of nationalism while traveling abroad, to assuage their feelings of provincial inferiority while at the metropolitan center by comparing their country's republican simplicity with Europe's aristocratic luxury.[73] As Elizabeth explained to her cousin, Americans "sought to know" European high society "for the virtuous purpose of being disgusted with vice and confirmed in [their] primitive simplicity & republican opinions."[74] As American men and women traveled through Europe, they assessed its society and politics, often convincing themselves of the superiority of their homeland. Elizabeth completely understood the cultural work that a trip to Europe performed for Americans, whom she recognized as "offended & complaining Moralists," in the early decades of the nineteenth century. She "found their whinings so uninteresting [about] the corruption of European morals," and she tired of their hypocritical "growling at my selfishness for engrossing these corrupt people to myself."[75] She knew, perhaps better than the tourists themselves, that Americans visited Europe to condemn it and, in turn, fuel their growing sense of native pride and overcome their feelings of inferiority, but all the while they secretly adored it. Elizabeth was fully acquainted with the language of moralistic nationalism, of American virtue and simplicity versus European vice and corruption, that Americans regularly utilized in their comparisons. She also recognized their feelings of inferiority when confronted with the luxurious culture of aristocratic Europe.

Elizabeth's subsequent travels only confirmed her admiration for Europe, especially France, and her disgust with the United States. When she returned to Baltimore in the summer of 1834, after spending sixteen of the previous nineteen years abroad, she was depressed and saw little chance for future happiness. Her son had not married into the Bonapartes or any other noble European family. Instead, to her mortification and dismay, he had married a Baltimore heiress. Defying her even more, he had become as ardent a patriot as his grandfather and decided to live in Baltimore and engage in mercantile and other commercial ventures. Unlike his mother, he chose a republic over an empire. It was only because of her efforts that Napoleon III later recognized her son as a legal member of the family, though one who could never be in line for the succession. She spent the rest of her life and part of her fortune encouraging her grandson to embrace her imperial aspirations. He served admirably in the French army and was a personal protector of Empress Eugenie, but that was as much as he achieved. Elizabeth made at least three more trips to Europe, but none lasted longer than a year or so.

By 1845 she had resigned herself to her "Baltimore obscurity." In fact, during her "vegetation in this Baltimore," she gave up "all correspondence with my friends in Europe." "There is nothing here worth attention or interest," she wrote to Lady Sidney Morgan, "save the money market." Her sentiments about the state of American society had not changed in more than forty-five years. In her opinion, "society, conversation, friendship, belong to older countries, and are not yet cultivated in any part of the United States." "You ought to thank your stars for your European birth," she assured her friend.[76]

In the early 1800s Elizabeth Patterson Bonaparte cultivated an image of herself, but not necessarily one that would be instructive to other women. She was a celebrity, not a role model, and probably vastly preferred the former identity to the latter. Her image, literally and figuratively, embodied Europe as the cosmopolitan center; far from celebrating American refinement, she rejected it. She paraded her stylish French fashions and exploited her glamorous connection to the Bonapartes. Given the new, more fluid definitions of aristocracy, her French connections and aristocratic sentiments gained her public fame and social power in American as well as European social circles. But her adoption of European in preference to American notions of fashion, womanhood, and citizenship also earned her criticism and condemnation. Americans recognized all the signs of a woman who chose to act more like a luxurious aristocrat than a refined republican, and they feared what this kind of woman could do to their republic. The proposed Titles of Nobility Amendment clearly encapsulated the threat Americans saw in Elizabeth and her son. She recognized that in her native land, a new country actively working at nation-building and creating an American culture, "they consider me an apostate from the Republic, an impudent & successful imitator of high Life, which they [profess] to dispise[;] in short[,] a bad Citizen."[77] But she had never wanted to be an admired member of that republic or a good citizen; nor had she ever desired to play the role of a "Columbians modest wife." She had wanted attention and acclaim—and to live in Europe. Despite her rejection of the prescriptions of republican society, Elizabeth enjoyed celebrity and extraordinary social success during the first decade of the new century, garnering social and cultural power because of her cosmopolitan status, including even her scandalous clothes. Yet her behavior, ideas, and imperial connections simultaneously offended and worried Americans.

More importantly, the words and actions of Elizabeth Patterson Bonaparte and the reactions of others to her remind us of the contingency of the republican experiment and of the active role of women in the debates over American society and culture. Society's reaction to her was as ambivalent as refined republicans' attitudes about European aristocratic culture. As Americans assessed her, they assessed themselves and their cultural beliefs. Reflecting their indecision about the corrupting influence of aristocratic culture on their republic, many criticized Elizabeth for moving beyond the acceptable bounds of refinement, but they could never bring themselves to exclude her from polite circles. They found her too captivating. They may have regarded her as unsuitable for a woman of the republic, but because of her cosmopolitan character they often granted her the lead in fashionable society. After all, she embodied their ideal of it. Elizabeth was a visible reminder of early nineteenth-century Americans' persistent love of court life. They knew that republican simplicity, even one that included some degree of refinement, should be part of their national character and culture, but many of them still longed for aristocratic glitter, which Elizabeth Patterson Bonaparte actively and unabashedly pursued on both sides of the Atlantic.

NOTES

Portions of this essay have been published in another form in "Elizabeth Patterson Bonaparte: 'Ill Suitted for the Life of a Columbians Modest Wife,'" *Journal of Women's History* 18, no. 2 (June 2006): 38, 40-47, 50-54. © Journal of Women's History. I am indebted to Peter Onuf and James E. Lewis Jr. for their invaluable suggestions for revising this essay.

1. *Enquirer* (Richmond), 4 Nov. 1806. Unless otherwise noted, emphasis is in the original.

2. For new work on disunion, see, e.g., Peter S. Onuf, *Jefferson's Empire: The Language of American Nationhood* (Charlottesville, VA, 2000), and two works by James E. Lewis Jr., *The American Union and the Problem of Neighborhood: The United States and the Collapse of the Spanish Empire, 1783-1829* (Chapel Hill, NC, 1998) and *The Louisiana Purchase: Jefferson's Noble Bargain?* (Chapel Hill, NC, 2003).

3. On refinement, see Richard Bushman, *The Refinement of America: Persons, Houses, Cities* (New York, 1993).

4. *Enquirer* (Richmond), 4 Nov. 1806.

5. On the latter point, see Jan E. Lewis, "The Republican Wife: Virtue and Seduction in the Early Republic," *WMQ* 44 (1987): 689-721.

6. See Catherine Allgor, *Parlor Politics: In Which the Ladies of Washington Help Build a City and a Government* (Charlottesville, VA, 2000); Susan Branson, *These Fiery Frenchified Dames: Women and Political Culture in Early National Philadelphia* (Philadelphia, 2001); and Ethel Rasmusson, "Democratic Environment—Aristocratic Aspiration," *Pennsylvania Magazine of History and Biography* 90 (1966): 155-82.

7. Elizabeth Patterson Bonaparte (hereafter EPB) to John Spear Smith, 22 Aug. 1816, Elizabeth Patterson Bonaparte Papers, MS 142 (hereafter EPB Papers), box 3, Maryland Historical Society, Baltimore (hereafter MdHS).

8. Captain Bentalou to Robert Patterson, 17 Oct. 1805, in *The Bonaparte-Patterson Marriage in 1803, and the Secret Correspondence on the Subject,* by W. T. R. Saffell (Philadelphia, 1873), 218. Napoleon also implied that he considered Elizabeth nothing more than Jerome's mistress.

9. See Allgor, *Parlor Politics,* ch. 2.

10. For the importance of fashion in constructing a "self-narrative," see Diane Crane, *Fashion and Its Social Agendas: Class, Gender, and Identity in Clothing* (Chicago, 2000), quotation on 10. See also Fred Davis, *Fashion, Culture, and Identity* (Chicago, 1992). For the link between politics and French fashion in the United States, see Branson, *These Fiery Frenchified Dames,* 71. For the importance of male fashion and political identity in the early republic, see David Waldstreicher, "Why Thomas Jefferson and African Americans Wore Their Politics on Their Sleeves: Dress and Mobilization between American Revolutions," in *Beyond the Founders: New Approaches to the Political History of the Early American Republic,* ed. Jeffrey L. Pasley, Andrew W. Robertson, and David Waldstreicher (Chapel Hill, NC, 2004), 79-103.

11. Catharine Mitchill to Margaret Akerly Miller, 21 Nov. 1811, in Carolyn Hoover Sung, "Catharine Mitchill's Letters from Washington, 1806-1812," *Quarterly Journal of the Library of Congress,* 1977, 184.

12. Mary Caton Smith to EPB, quoted in Alice Curtis Desmond, *Bewitching Betsy Bonaparte* (New York, 1958), 243.

13. Sarah Gales Seaton, letter of 2 Jan. 1813, quoted in Elisabeth McClellan, *Historic Dress in America, 1607-1870,* 2 vols. (New York, 1904-10), 2:103.

14. *Alexandria (VA) Daily Advertiser,* 9 Sept. 1807. For a few examples, see editorials and letters in the *Western Spy* (Cincinnati), 9 Dec. 1806; the *Enquirer* (Richmond), 3 Feb. 1807; and the *People's Friend* (New York), 15 May 1807.

15. Waller Holladay to Huldah Holladay, 9 Apr. 1804, Holladay Family Papers, Virginia Historical Society, Richmond.

16. Huldah Holladay to Waller Holladay, 22 Apr. 1804, ibid. For a similar response by a society matron, see Catherine Carroll Harper to Robert Goodloe Harper, 30 Jan. [1804], Robert Goodloe Harper Papers (microfilm ed.), MdHS.

17. See, e.g., *Scioto Gazette* (Chillicothe, OH), 29 July 1805; *Pittsburgh Gazette,* 12 Aug. 1806; and *Impartial Review and Cumberland Repository* (Nashville), 6 Sept. 1806.

18. Margaret Bayard Smith to Mrs. Kirkpatrick, 23 Jan. 1804, in *First Forty Years of Washington Society,* ed. Gaillard Hunt (New York, 1906), 46-47; Thomas Law, poem enclosed in Rosalie Stier Calvert to Madame H. J. Stier, 2 Mar. 1804, in *Mistress of Riversdale: The Plantation Letters of Rosalie Stier Calvert, 1795-1821,* ed. Margaret Law Callcott (Baltimore, 1991), 78-79.

19. *American and Commercial Daily Advertiser* (Baltimore), 24 Aug. 1804.

20. *Columbian Centinel* (Boston), 3 Apr. 1805.

21. See *American and Commercial Daily Advertiser* (Baltimore), 30 July 1804.

22. Elizabeth continued to receive her 60,000 francs annually from Napoleon at least until March 1815, almost a year after his first abdication, in April 1814.

23. John Spear Smith to Samuel Smith, 9 Jan. 1810, Samuel Smith Papers, LC; and Sally McKean Yrujo to Dolley Madison, 20 June 1812, in *Selected Letters of Dolley Payne Madison,* ed. David B. Mattern and Holly C. Shulman (Charlottesville, VA, 2003), 167.

24. Newspaper clipping, 20 Nov. 1809, Clippings Booklet, EPB Papers, box 15, MdHS.

25. Newspaper clipping, 10 Nov. 1809, ibid.

26. Newspaper clipping, 20 Nov. 1809, ibid.

27. Clipping, *Statesman* (Newburyport, MA), 28 Dec. 1809, ibid.

28. Deborah Onderdonk to Henry U. Onderdonk, 20 Nov. 1809, Society Collection, Historical Society of Pennsylvania, Philadelphia, emphasis added. Onderdonk must have read this fact in some newspaper, for her language is almost exactly that of a contemporary newspaper clipping in Elizabeth Bonaparte's clippings booklet at the MdHS.

29. Quoted in W. H. Earle, in "The Phantom Amendment and the Duchess of Baltimore," *American History Illustrated* 22 (1987): 37.

30. See Lewis, *American Union and the Problem of Neighborhood,* 32–40.

31. Lydia E. Hollingsworth to Ruth Tobin, 10 Jan. 1810, Hollingsworth Papers, MdHS.

32. *National Intelligencer* (Washington, DC), 31 Jan. 1810.

33. Ibid., 16 Feb. 1810.

34. Curt E. Conklin, "The Case of the Phantom Thirteenth Amendment: A Historical and Bibliographic Nightmare," *Law Library Journal* 88 (1996): 124; Joel A. Silversmith, "The 'Missing Thirteenth Amendment': Constitutional Nonsense and Titles of Nobility," *Southern California Interdisciplinary Law Journal* 8 (1999): 583. See also David E. Kyvig, *Explicit and Authentic Acts: Amending the U.S. Constitution, 1776–1995* (Lawrence: University Press of Kansas, 1996), 117.

35. Richard B. Bernstein, in his *Amending America: If We Love the Constitution So Much, Why Do We Keep Trying to Change It?* (New York, 1993), acknowledges that Jerome Bonaparte's "liaison with a Baltimore prostitute named Betsy Patterson, whom he made pregnant," was a partial impetus for the amendment (178). That a legal historian described her as a prostitute attests to Elizabeth's troubled historical legacy.

36. Conklin, "Case of the Phantom Amendment," 124. See also Tom Pendergast, Sara Pendergast, and John Sousanis, eds., *Constitutional Amendments: From Freedom of Speech to Flag Burning,* vol. 3 (Detroit, 2001); and John R. Vile, *Encyclopedia of Constitutional Amendments, Proposed Amendments, and Amending Issues, 1789–2002* (Santa Barbara, CA, 2003), 454-55. Only W. H. Earle, in "The Phantom Amendment and the Duchess of Baltimore," 33, solidly identifies the cause of the amendment as "the lovely, witty, tragic, vain, ambitious, calculating 'Duchess of Baltimore.'"

37. Richard M. Johnson to Joseph Hamilton Daveiss, 20 Feb. 1810, Joseph Hamilton Daveiss Papers, Filson Club Historical Society, Louisville, KY.

38. Samuel Taggart to Rev. John W. Taylor, 12 Feb. 1810, in "Letters of Samuel Taggart, 1803-1814," *Proceedings of the American Antiquarian Society* 33 (1923): 345.

39. William Eaton, address at Brimfield, MA, town meeting, 29 Aug. 1808, in *The Life of the Late Gen. William Eaton,* ed. Charles Prentiss (Brookfield, MA, 1813), 415.

40. [John Randolph], *The Letters of Mutius, Addressed to the President of the United States* (Washington, DC, 1810), 10-11.

41. Timothy Pickering, Notes on "Amendment of Constitution[;] Mr. Reid resolution—with an *Addition,*" 1810, Timothy Pickering Papers (microfilm ed., reel 54), Massachusetts Historical Society, Boston.

42. *Annals of Congress,* 11th Cong., 2nd sess., 20:671, 21:2050.

43. Robert Bayly to John Payne, 14 Dec. 1811, John Payne Papers, LC.

44. Mitchill to Miller, 21 Nov. 1811, TS, Catharine Mitchill Papers, LC.

45. Samuel Smith to Mary B. Mansfield, 6 Nov. 1811, TS, Carter-Smith Family Papers, University of Virginia, Charlottesville.

46. EPB to Lescallier, 10 Oct. 1811, EPB Papers, box 2, MdHS.

47. George B. Milligan to aunt, 16 Feb. [1812], Milligan-McLane Papers, folder 7, Delaware Historical Society, Wilmington. See also Samuel Smith to Mansfield, 6 Nov. 1811, Carter-Smith Family Papers, University of Virginia.

48. Silversmith, "Missing Thirteenth Amendment," 585.

49. EPB to William Patterson, 2 Sept. 1815, in Eugene L. Didier, *The Life and Letters of Madame Bonaparte* (New York, 1879), 44.

50. [Nancy] Ann Spear to EPB, 30 May 1816, EPB Papers, box 3, MdHS.

51. Branson, *These Fiery Frenchified Dames,* 133-36; Wendy Anne Nicholson, "Making the Private Public: Anne Willing Bingham's Role as a Leader of Philadelphia's Social Elite in the Late Eighteenth Century" (MA thesis, University of Delaware, 1988).

52. For an excellent discussion of Enlightenment thought that credited and popularized the idea of women's historic role in the progress of mankind, see Mary Catherine Moran, "From Rudeness to Refinement: Gender, Genre and Scottish Enlightenment Discourse" (PhD diss., Johns Hopkins University, 1999).

53. Allgor, *Parlor Politics,* ch. 4.

54. Daniel Kilbride, "Avoiding a 'Little, Mean [and] Despicable' Republic: Privileged Women and the Cultural Work of the Grand Tour in the Post-revolutionary Era" (paper presented at the annual meeting of the Society of the Historians of the Early American Republic, Buffalo, NY, July 2000).

55. Horace Holley to Mary Austin Holley, 3 Apr. 1818, Holley Papers, University of Michigan (hereafter MiU).

56. EPB to John Spear Smith, 22 Aug. 1816, EPB Papers, MdHS.

57. Horace Holley Journal, 19 Mar. 1818, Horace Holley Papers, MiU. In this entry, Holley was recording a dinner conversation he had had with Elizabeth.

58. EPB to William Patterson, 4 Dec. 1829, in Didier, *Life and Letters,* 218.

59. EPB to Lady Sidney Morgan, 14 Mar. 1849, ibid., 253.

60. Ibid.

61. Calvert to Stier, Nov. 1803, in Callcott, *Mistress of Riversdale,* 62.

62. EPB to William Patterson, 10 Apr. 1820, in Didier, *Life and Letters,* 56-57.

63. On the increasing limitations on women's activities in the civic arena after 1800 and the turn toward women's influencing the public sphere mainly as wives and mothers, see Branson, *These Fiery Frenchified Dames;* and Rosemarie Zagarri, "Gender and the First Party System," in *Federalists Reconsidered,* ed. Doron Ben-Atar and Barbara B. Oberg (Charlottesville, VA, 1998), 118-34.

64. EPB to William Patterson, 22 Feb. 1816, in Didier, *Life and Letters,* 52-53.

65. Amanda Vickery describes the "cultural horizons" in which gentlewomen of eighteenth-century England participated. See her *The Gentleman's Daughter: Women's Lives in Georgian England* (New Haven, CT, 1998), quotation on 9.

66. European women's historians support Elizabeth's conclusions. See, e.g., Dena Goodman, *The Republic of Letters: A Cultural History of the French Enlightenment* (Ithaca, NY, 1994); Amanda Foreman, *Georgiana: Duchess of Devonshire* (New York, 1998); and Vickery, *Gentleman's Daughter.* For an examination of elite women's cultural authority in the social arenas of Washington, DC, see Allgor, *Parlor Politics.*

67. Horace Holley to Mary Austin Holley, 20 Mar. 1818, Holley Papers, MiU.

68. See Sheila Skemp, *Judith Sargent Murray: A Brief Biography with Documents* (Boston, 1998); and Rosemarie Zagarri, *A Woman's Dilemma: Mercy Otis Warren and the American Revolution* (Wheeling, IL, 1995).

69. Christopher L. Doyle, "The Randolph Scandal in Early National Virginia, 1792-1815: New Voices in the 'Court of Honor,'" *JSH* 69 (2003): 283-318. Doyle examines the response to Nancy Randolph Morris, another woman who apparently had too much control over her own life and went beyond the acceptable bounds of womanhood in the new nation, but in a vastly different manner than Elizabeth Patterson Bonaparte.

70. Eliza Godefroy to EPB, 10 May 1817, EPB Papers, box 3, MdHS. See also Robert Goodloe Harper to Emily Caton, 12 Mar. 1816, Robert Goodloe Harper Papers (microfilm ed.), MdHS.

71. EPB to William Patterson, 2 Sept. 1815 in Didier, *Life and Letters,* 43.

72. EPB to John Spear Smith, 22 Aug. 1816.

73. Daniel Kilbride, "Travel, Ritual, and National Identity: Planters on the European Tour, 1820-1860," *JSH* 69 (2003): 549-84. See also Harvey Levenstein, *Seductive Journey: American Tourists in France from Jefferson to the Jazz Age* (Chicago, 1998); and William W. Stowe, *Going Abroad: European Travel in Nineteenth-Century American Culture* (Princeton, NJ, 1994).

74. EPB to John Spear Smith, 22 Aug. 1816.

75. Ibid.

76. EPB to Morgan, 14 Mar. 1849.

77. EPB to John Spear Smith, 22 Aug. 1816.

Contributors

JULIE FLAVELL is an independent scholar working in the United Kingdom. Her essays have appeared in numerous journals, including the *William and Mary Quarterly*, the *Journal of Imperial and Commonwealth History*, and the *Journal of Interdisciplinary History*. She is the coeditor (with Stephen Conway) of *Britain and America Go to War: The Impact of War and Warfare in Anglo-America, 1754–1815* (2004).

CHARLENE BOYER LEWIS is associate professor of history at Kalamazoo College in Kalamazoo, Michigan, and a past Batten Fellow at the Robert H. Smith International Center for Jefferson Studies at Monticello. She is the author of *Ladies and Gentlemen on Display: Planter Society at the Virginia Springs, 1790–1860* (2001).

PETER NICOLAISEN is professor emeritus of English at the University of Flensburg in Flensburg, Germany. A fellow at the Robert H. Smith International Center at Monticello, he is the author of several German-language books on various topics in American history and culture, including Thomas Jefferson, William Faulkner, and Ernest Hemingway. His essays have appeared in scholarly journals on both sides of the Atlantic, including the *Journal of American Studies, Amerikastudien-American Studies*, the *Mississippi Quarterly*, and the *Southern Quarterly*.

PETER S. ONUF is Thomas Jefferson Foundation Professor of History at the University of Virginia, Charlottesville. He is the author, most recently, of *The Mind of Thomas Jefferson* (2007), (with Nicholas Onuf) *Nations, Markets, and War: Modern History and the American Civil War* (2006), and *Jefferson's Empire: The Language of American Nationhood* (2000).

ANDREW J. O'SHAUGHNESSY is Saunders Director of the Robert H. Smith International Center for Jefferson Studies at Monticello. He is a fellow of the Royal Historical Society and a past Barra Senior Fellow at the McNeil Center for Early American Studies at the University of Pennsylvania

(2002). His essays and reviews have appeared in numerous journals, and he is the author of *An Empire Divided: The American Revolution and the British Caribbean* (2000).

SARAH M. S. PEARSALL is lecturer in history at Oxford Brookes University. She was a Mellon Foundation/National Endowment for the Humanities Fellow at the Newberry Library, Chicago, 2004–5, and has been published in the *William and Mary Quarterly* and in several essay collections. She is the author of *Atlantic Families: Lives and Letters in the Later Eighteenth Century* (2008).

MARTHA ELENA ROJAS is assistant professor of English at the University of Rhode Island, Kingston. She is a past fellow at the McNeil Center for Early American Studies at the University of Pennsylvania and held the Honors Post-Doctoral Fellowship at Sweet Briar College, 2004–5. She has been published in *Early American Studies* and is currently revising her dissertation for publication as *Diplomatic Letters: The Conduct and Culture of Foreign Affairs in the Early Republic*.

RICHARD A. RYERSON is academic director of the David Library of the American Revolution in Washington Crossing, Pennsylvania. He is a past editor in chief of the *Papers of John Adams* and is the author, most recently, of (with Gregory Fremont-Barnes) *The Encyclopedia of the American Revolutionary War* (2006) and *John Adams and the Founding of the Republic* (2001).

LEONARD J. SADOSKY is assistant professor of history at Iowa State University. He was the Patrick Henry Fellow at Johns Hopkins University, 2006–7, and is a past Glider Lehrman Fellow at the Robert H. Smith International Center for Jefferson Studies at Monticello. He is the author (with Peter Onuf) of *Jeffersonian America* (2002) and of *Revolutionary Negotiations: Indians, Empires, and Diplomats in the Founding of America* (2009).

LUCIA STANTON is Shannon Senior Historian at the Robert H. Smith International Center for Jefferson Studies at Monticello. She is the author of several books, including *Slavery at Monticello* (2002) and *Free Some Day: The African-American Families of Monticello* (2002), and the coeditor (with Douglas Wilson) of *Thomas Jefferson Abroad* (1999) and (with Jame A. Bear Jr.) of *Thomas Jefferson's Memorandum Books* (1997).

GAYE WILSON is research historian at the Robert H. Smith International Center for Jefferson Studies at Monticello. She has taught the history of dress and was curator of the historic clothing collection for the Department of Theatre at the University of Texas. She has several publications and conference presentations to her credit, including an essay (with Elizabeth Chew) published in *Dress: the Journal of the Costume Society of America.*

GORDON S. WOOD is Alva O. Way University Professor and professor of history at Brown University. He is the author, most recently, of *Revolutionary Characters: What Made the Founders Different* (2006), *The Americanization of Benjamin Franklin* (2004), and *The American Revolution: A History* (2002). He won the Pulitzer Prize in 1993 for *The Radicalism of the American Revolution.*

PHILIPP ZIESCHE is assistant editor of the *Papers of Benjamin Franklin* at Yale University. He was the Gilder Lehrman Research Fellow at the Robert H. Smith International Center for Jefferson Studies at Monticello, 2005–6. His book *Cosmopolitan Patriots: Americans in Paris in the Age of Revolution* is forthcoming.

Index

Jeffersonian America

Jan Ellen Lewis and Peter S. Onuf, editors
Sally Hemings and Thomas Jefferson: History, Memory, and Civic Culture

Peter S. Onuf
Jefferson's Empire: The Language of American Nationhood

Catherine Allgor
*Parlor Politics: In Which the Ladies of Washington Help Build a City
and a Government*

Jeffrey L. Pasley
"The Tyranny of Printers": Newspaper Politics in the Early American Republic

Herbert E. Sloan
Principle and Interest: Thomas Jefferson and the Problem of Debt (reprint)

James Horn, Jan Ellen Lewis, and Peter S. Onuf, editors
The Revolution of 1800: Democracy, Race, and the New Republic

Phillip Hamilton
*The Making and Unmaking of a Revolutionary Family: The Tuckers of
Virginia, 1752–1830*

Robert M. S. McDonald, editor
Thomas Jefferson's Military Academy: Founding West Point

Martha Tomhave Blauvelt
The Work of the Heart: Young Women and Emotion, 1780–1830

Francis D. Cogliano
Thomas Jefferson: Reputation and Legacy

Albrecht Koschnik
*"Let a Common Interest Bind Us Together": Associations, Partisanship, and
Culture in Philadelphia, 1775–1840*

John Craig Hammond
Slavery, Freedom, and Expansion in the Early American West, 1787–1820

David Andrew Nichols
*Red Gentlemen and White Savages: Indians, Federalists, and the Search for
Order on the American Frontier*

Douglas Bradburn
*The Citizenship Revolution: Politics and the Creation of the
American Union, 1774–1804*